QUALITY BOOKS OF INTEREST FROM ST. LUCIE PRESS

The 90-Day ISO 9000 Manual and Implementation Guide

Deming: The Way We Knew Him

The Executive Guide to Implementing Quality Systems

Focused Quality: Managing for Results

Improving Service Quality: Achieving High Performance in the Public and Private Sectors

Introduction to Modern Statistical Quality Control and Management

ISO 9000: Implementation Guide for Small to Mid-Sized Businesses

Organization Teams: Continuous Quality Improvement

Organization Teams: Facilitator's Guide

Principles of Total Quality

Quality Improvement Handbook: Team Guide to Tools and Techniques

The Textbook of Total Quality in Healthcare

Total Quality in Organizational Development

Total Quality in Higher Education

Total Quality in Managing Human Resources

Total Quality in Marketing

Total Quality in Purchasing and Supplier Management

Total Quality in Radiology: A Guide to Implementation

Total Quality in Research and Development

Total Quality Management for Custodial Operations

Total Quality Management: Text, Cases, and Readings, 2nd Edition

Total Quality Service: Principles, Practices, and Implementation

For more information about these titles
simply call, fax or write St. Lucie Press.

St. Lucie Press
100 E. Linton Blvd., Suite 403B
Delray Beach, FL 33483
TEL (407) 274-9906
FAX (407) 274-9927

Total Quality in
MANAGING
HUMAN
RESOURCES

The St. Lucie Press
Total Quality Series™

BOOKS IN THE SERIES:

Total Quality in HIGHER EDUCATION

Total Quality in PURCHASING and SUPPLIER MANAGEMENT

Total Quality in INFORMATION SYSTEMS

Total Quality in RESEARCH and DEVELOPMENT

Total Quality in MANAGING HUMAN RESOURCES

Total Quality in ORGANIZATIONAL DEVELOPMENT

Total Quality in MARKETING

MACROLOGISTICS STRATEGY MANAGEMENT

For more information about these books call St. Lucie Press at (407) 274-9906

Series Editor • Frank Voehl
Series Development Editor • Sandy Pearlman

Total Quality in

MANAGING HUMAN RESOURCES

By
Joseph A. Petrick,
Ph.D., M.B.A., S.P.H.R., R.O.D.P.
Associate Professor of Management
Wright State University
Dayton, Ohio
CEO, Performance Leadership Associates
Founding Partner, Organizational Ethics Associates

Diana S. Furr
Chief Executive Officer
Business Performance Group, Inc.
Tampa, Florida

S^t_L

St. Lucie Press
Delray Beach, Florida

HF
5549
P4553
1995

Printed and bound in the U.S.A. Printed on acid-free paper.
10 9 8 7 6 5 4 3 2 1

Library of Congress Cataloging-in-Publication Data
Petrick, Joseph A., 1946–
    Total quality in managing human resources / by Joseph A. Petrick,
Diana S. Furr.
      p.   cm.
    Includes index.
    ISBN 1-884015-24-7
    1. Personnel management. 2. Total quality management. I. Furr,
Diana S. II. Title.
HF5549.P4553 1995   94-46630
658.3—dc20   CIP

Phone: (407) 274-9906
Fax: (407) 274-9927

Published by

S$_L^t$

St. Lucie Press
Delray Beach, Florida

Co-sponsored by
Anna Maria College

TOTAL QUALITY
The Master's Degree

Educational Series on Quality
Robert James Gee, Ph.D., Director

DEDICATION

With gratitude for the loving support
of family and friends;
with respect for those current and past victims
of institutionalized mediocrity,
who always knew there was a better way;
and with hope for improving work
and the quality of life
for future generations.

Joe

To J.C.
With gratitude and love,
for finding me when I was lost
and for lighting the way back home.

Diana

CONTENTS

Foreword   xi

Series Preface   xiii

Authors' Preface   xv

1   Why Total Quality in Managing Human Resources? 1
Driving Forces Reshaping the Human Resource Environment   2
A Brief History of U.S. Human Resource Management   7
The House of Total Quality: The Challenging Opportunity
    for Human Resources   16
Ethical Work Culture and Expanded Human
    Resource Roles   26
Human Resource Management and the Total Quality
    Difference   36
Barriers and Responses to Total Quality Human Resource
    Management Implementation   43
Review/Discussion Questions   46
Endnotes   48
Appendix   56

2   Customer Satisfaction: Strategy Dimensions 59
The Total Quality Business Strategy   59
Total Quality Business Strategy Planning   62
Total Quality Business Strategy Management   81
The Total Quality Human Resource Strategy   86
Total Quality Human Resource Strategy Planning   88
Total Quality Human Resource Strategy Management   96
Review/Discussion Questions   102
Endnotes   104
Practitioner Assessment Instruments   114

3   Continuous Improvement: Process Dimensions 119
The Total Quality Business Processes   119
Total Quality Business Process Planning   124

Total Quality Business Process Management   133
Total Quality Human Resource Processes   139
Total Quality Human Resource Process Planning   142
Total Quality Human Resource Process Management   150
Review/Discussion Questions   157
Endnotes   158
Practitioner Assessment Instruments   165

4   **Speaking with Facts: Project Dimensions** 175
The Total Quality Business Projects   175
Total Quality Business Project Planning   178
Total Quality Business Project Management   190
Total Quality Human Resource Projects   197
Total Quality Human Resource Project Planning   200
Total Quality Human Resource Project Management   208
Review/Discussion Questions   215
Endnotes   216
Practitioner Assessment Instruments   220

5   **Respect for People: Performance Dimensions** 233
The Total Quality Business Individual Performance   233
Total Quality Business Performance Planning   237
Total Quality Business Performance Management   242
Total Quality Human Resource Performance   246
Total Quality Human Resource Performance Planning   251
Total Quality Human Resource Performance Management   258
Review/Discussion Questions   261
Endnotes   262
Practitioner Assessment Instruments   274

6   **Implementing Total Quality Human Resource
Management** 289
Total Quality Integrated Implementation Plan for Managing
   Human Resources   291
The MichCon Case: A Snapshot of Successful Total Quality
   Human Resource Management   306
International Implementation of Total Quality Human
   Resource Practices   335
Review/Discussion Questions   343
Endnotes   345

Minicases 349

Index 363

FOREWORD

As the principles and practice of total quality management become pervasive in the private sector, a required core competency for practitioners, and a necessary part of contemporary education in management, there is increasing need for texts that focus on distinct applications of quality management. This emerging need for texts that specialize in areas of management is a tribute to the growing sophistication of those who use quality principles in their daily work, in their training, and in their classrooms. Whereas it was sufficient as recently as the early 1990s to encourage simple "awareness" of quality in an employee, a corporate trainee, or a student, the higher level of awareness among those who come to learn about quality requires a similarly enhanced knowledge among those who teach or practice it. Consequently, *Total Quality in Managing Human Resources* is particularly useful for both the experienced human resource practitioner and the educator who require advanced applications of quality in human resource management.

Knowledgeable students of management would agree that the pivotal event in the successful application of quality was the Japanese insistence that quality principles be applied as an integrated system. Up to that point, quality principles, although worthy, were sporadically effective when applied as isolated problem-solving techniques. For example, while attempts to form quality circles or to instill inspection-driven quality assurance were progressive, they were undercut by their lack of connection to other organization-wide improvement efforts. The layout of *Total Quality in Managing Human Resources* purposefully addresses the need to apply quality principles in a systematic way; Chapter 1 provides a review of the knowledge base for practitioners and students alike and examines the context in which the principles and practices of quality have gradually emerged. The authors speak directly to the practitioner when they trace the history of human resource management and note the accelerating integration of quality practices into general human resource practice. The brief review of "Barriers and Responses to Total Quality Human Resource Management Implementation" will give practitioners a thumbnail sketch of troubleshooting solutions and assist educators in placing before their students minicases to be drawn out in class discussion.

As management practice has matured from the command-and-control to the team-driven approach, there has been a concomitant realization that neither quality management nor the human resource function can be an afterthought of organizational strategy. Chapters 2 through 6 of the text provide a consistent and easily understandable framework for ensuring that both quality principles and human resource management are integrated into strategy through four pillars: customer satisfaction, continuous improvement, speaking with facts, and respect for people. In addition, the text quite rightly emphasizes that the challenge of expanded roles for the human resource practitioner cannot be met by the traditional reliance on regulations and compliance which mirrored earlier hierarchical management styles; thus, the text presents real-life examples of how the shift to quality management may be made by including plentiful management matrices and practitioner assessment instruments at the end of each chapter on the four pillars. In testing with corporate trainees and advanced students, these proved especially helpful in initiating discussion and healthy controversy.

Testimonial to the importance of human resource development and management is given by its inclusion as one of the seven categories in the Malcolm Baldrige National Quality Award criteria. The criteria also require that human resource practices be actively deployed and that they achieve tangible results. To the authors' credit, they have focused on tactical strategies which can help both practitioners and educators to reach these achievements.

Robert James Gee, Ph.D.

SERIES PREFACE

The St. Lucie Press Series on Total Quality originated in 1993 when some of us realized that the rapidly expanding field of quality management was neither well defined nor well focused. This realization, coupled with America's hunger for specific, how-to examples, led to the formulation of a plan to publish a series of subject-specific books on total quality, a new direction for books in the field to follow.

The essence of this series consists of a core nucleus of seven new direction books, around which the remaining books in the series will revolve over a three-year period:

- Education Transformation: *Total Quality in Higher Education*
- Respect for People: *Total Quality in Managing Human Resources*
- Speak with Facts: *Total Quality in Information Systems*
- Customer Satisfaction: *Total Quality in Marketing and Sales*
- Continuous Improvement: *Total Quality in R&D*
- Supplier Partnerships: *Total Quality in Purchasing and Supplier Management*
- Cost-Effective, Value-Added Services: *Total Quality and Measurement*

We at St. Lucie Press have been privileged to contribute to the convergence of philosophy and underlying principles of total quality, leading to a common set of assumptions. One of the most important deals with the challenges facing the transformation of the human resource area for the 21st century. This is a particularly exciting and turbulent time in the human resource field, both domestically and globally, and change may be viewed as either an opportunity or a threat. As an opportunity, the principles and practices of total quality can aid in this transformation.

As the authors of this text explain, the total quality orientation to managing human resources redefines line managerial roles and identifies new responsibilities for the traditional human resource management function. The human resource practitioner's role now includes strategic input and continual development of the human resource system to increase customer satisfaction both now and in the future. The full meaning of these changes is explored in light of the driving forces reshaping the human resource environment.

As Series Editor, I am pleased with the manner in which the series is coming together. Its premise is that excellence can be achieved through a singular focus on customers and their interests as a number one priority. However, no book or series can tell an organization how to achieve total quality; only the customers and stakeholders can tell you when you have it and when you do not.

We trust that you will find this book both usable and beneficial and wish you maximum success on the quality journey. If it in some way makes a contribution, then we can say, as Dr. Deming often did at the end of his seminars, "I have done my best."

Frank Voehl
Series Editor

AUTHORS' PREFACE

It is during turbulent times at sea that those on watch at the lighthouse must project a clear, reliable guiding light to ships struggling against crashing waves, treacherous tides, and the ever-present danger of running aground. We believe many organizations, groups, and individuals are in just this type of situation at work today; they have been battered by rightsizing, reengineering, downsizing, and an array of cost-cutting measures brought on by increasingly stormy global economic seas and are in urgent need of revitalized commitment to collaborative performance. In a bittersweet way, today people sense that "we are in this together, and we will survive or perish together." But they are also saying, "Since we are in this ship together in rough waters, why not run it as effectively, efficiently, and cooperatively as possible to more likely ensure success?"

This is why we wrote *Total Quality in Managing Human Resources*. We wanted to add value to current approaches to managing human resources and better prepare organizations, work groups, and individuals for future sustainable survival and development in an increasingly competitive global environment.

This book is targeted toward those individuals who are in a position of influence: educators who are supporting the learning of future leaders, students who are preparing themselves to assume tomorrow's leadership responsibilities, and business executives, middle managers, and human resource professionals who are making decisions every day that influence both the quality of work results and the quality of work life for millions of employees.

The business imperative for a focus on quality in managing human resources has emerged for a number of reasons. First, the ever-increasing complexity of the challenges facing organizations and the pace of change both signal the escalating pressure that will be brought to bear on human resource professionals to either play proactive, strategic partnership roles or be left behind as marginal contributors.

Second, the challenge to develop a world-class work culture that integrates human resource quality and strategic concerns is imminent. Organizations that cannot or will not develop the coordinated integration of strategic management, total quality, and human resource management will, in the long run or in the short run, become ineffective global competitors.

A third reason for a focus on quality in managing human resources involves changing customer satisfaction standards. Employees, as internal customers, are attracted, retained, and developed in part by the reputation and actual practices that companies engage in to nurture customer satisfaction inside the organization. External customers expect rapid customization of products and services and genuine responsiveness to their changing needs in order to sustain their purchasing commitment.

Fourth, the breaking of the psychological contract that used to exist between employer and employee has accelerated as international competition has promoted restructuring, downsizing, and rightsizing. This has led to a considerable amount of economic uncertainty, lack of security, and a regression to employee self-interest rather than organizational well-being. Total quality offers one way to address the issue of the ruptured psychological contract by providing incentives and practical ways to align individual and organizational interests, heal the wounds of downsizing survivors, and revitalize performance commitment without developing organizational codependence.

Fifth, total quality is one way for human resource departments to provide input into the strategic options of an organization. Human resource professionals are often criticized for focusing on narrow administrative responsibilities that implement strategy without providing direct strategic input into options that would enhance the prospects of a business in the marketplace. Total quality offers the human resource function an opportunity to take a more proactive partnership role with senior management in all of its subfunctions, including quality recruitment, selection, socialization, training and development, compensation and benefits, and health, safety, and security of the organization.

Finally, in an era of limited growth both globally and domestically, organizations and human resource departments are being forced to do more with less. One effective way to respond to that challenge is for human resource professionals to become more familiar with total quality management and to review their policies and practices to ensure that the highest quality of services is being rendered and continuously improved to their external and internal customers.

In sum, human resource professionals must begin *today* to address the challenges they will face in the coming century. This book has some distinctive strengths: (1) a state-of-the-art conceptual integration of the fields of total quality and human resource management, supported by their related disciplines; (2) an introduction of new dimensions of concepts, such as ethical work culture, empowerment readiness, and cross-unit competitiveness, as they relate to total quality human resource management; (3) the scholarly quality of the referenced chapters, combined with concrete case studies, minicases, and examples for ease of understanding; (4) a total quality integrated implementation plan with detailed recommendations for practical actions in order to institutionalize total quality human resource management; and (5) practitioner assessment instruments and total quality tools that apply concepts in the text to improve real work situations.

The material is organized into six chapters. Chapter 1 elaborates on the question "Why Total Quality in Managing Human Resources?" and includes some possible barriers to implementing the principles of total quality in managing human resources. It introduces the framework of the House of Total Quality and the role of the ethical work culture in developing and sustaining total quality.

Chapters 2 to 5 focus on the four pillars of the House of Total Quality—customer satisfaction, continuous improvement, speaking with facts, and respect for people—as they apply to both the organization as a whole and human resource activities in particular. The cornerstone and foundation of each pillar (first pillar: strategy planning and management; second pillar: process planning and management; third pillar: project planning and management; and fourth pillar: individual performance planning and management) provide the internal organizational structure of each chapter.

Finally, Chapter 6 provides an integrated implementation plan for managing human resources along total quality lines, a detailed case study of a company that successfully implemented total quality human resource management, and a brief treatment of international implementation of total quality human resource practices.

In addition, four minicases further exemplify the management of human resources using the House of Total Quality pillars.

We trust you will find this book beneficial and usable. We wish those readers who attempt to implement total quality improvement efforts in managing human resources maximum success and minimal constraints. We encourage you to contact us to share your successes and your concerns and to provide feedback on ways to improve this book.

We would like to acknowledge the series editor, Frank Voehl; the publisher, Dennis Buda; and the reviewers who provided excellent feedback for improvement on earlier drafts of this book. In addition, we wish to express our deep appreciation to our support staffs: Joy Fletcher, Judy Copeland, and Rose Ramos at Business Performance Group; Donna Stirnkorb at Performance Leadership Associates; and Marjorie Hodson and Long Wu at Wright State University. Their support services strengthened our results through many weeks of hard work. Furthermore, we acknowledge the invaluable contributions of colleagues: Barbara Ann Blue at Business Performance Group, John F. Quinn at Organizational Ethics Associates, and the entire Management Department and the College of Business and Administration at Wright State University.

Finally, we wish to offer a special tribute to our respective spouses, Warwick (Bud) Furr and Kimberly Petrick, whose patience, understanding, encouragement, and personal sacrifice supported our efforts and sustained our spirits during the writing of this book.

Joseph A. Petrick
Diana S. Furr

CHAPTER 1

WHY TOTAL QUALITY IN MANAGING HUMAN RESOURCES?

Why read a book about total quality in managing human resources? There are at least four possible answers to this question. First, it may be a matter of intellectual curiosity. The terms *total quality management, continuous quality improvement, and managerial and corporate reengineering* are currently very popular. Why not find out what they are about and how they may apply to managing human resources? Second, someone may be involved with the subspecialties of human resource management (HRM) concerned with recruitment, selection, placement, training and development, compensation and benefits, or labor relations and safety and want to know how total quality impacts each area. Third, someone may be concerned about the conditions and changes in the organizational environment surrounding the human resource (HR) functions. In fact, one may be motivated to read this book because such changes are viewed as threats to HR professionals. Finally, this book may be read in the search for a better way to help create a more effective and efficient work culture for the future.[1]

Whatever the reason for reading this book, one of its goals is to help establish that a need exists to transform HRM for the 21st century. This is a particularly exciting and turbulent time in the HR field, both domestically and globally.[2] Nevertheless, change may be viewed as an opportunity rather than a threat, and the principles and practices of total quality can aid in this transformation.

The focus of this book is on five targeted groups: (1) educators and students who address HRM, strategic management, total quality and organizational development areas; (2) practicing senior-level and line business managers involved in HR decision making; (3) practicing HR professionals integrating quality into their repertoire of skills; (4) practicing administrators/managers involved in HR decisions in public, nonprofit, and professional contexts; and (5) prospective business and HR professionals undergoing formal in-service training to assume future work responsibilities. Each group of stakeholders can benefit from the material contained in this text.

The domain of the book is the area of managing human resources. The traditional nature and scope of responsibility for most HR professionals has been that of staff support geared to administrative compliance procedures. The total quality orientation to managing human resources redefines line managerial and employee roles and accords new responsibilities to the traditional HRM function. The latter's new role includes strategic input and continual development of the HR system to increase customer satisfaction now and in the future. The full meaning of these role changes will become apparent in light of the driving forces that are reshaping the HR environment, as discussed in the next section.

The outcome of this book for the individual reader is an increased understanding of the impact of total quality on managing human resources and practical guidance on meeting the new HR challenges in today's work environment.

DRIVING FORCES RESHAPING
THE HUMAN RESOURCE ENVIRONMENT

The need to focus on total quality and managing human resources is indicated by the following six trends.

1. Successful international competitors have challenged U.S. HRM practices. It is possible to look at all businesses as having three principal resources: capital, natural, and human resources. Many economic competitors of the United States, such as Japan, Korea, Taiwan, and Singapore, have few natural resources but they use the same basic technologies as the United States. They have been forced to develop their competitive international advantage primarily through their cultivation of human resources. The human resource is the only one that competitors cannot copy and is the only one that can synergize; that is, produce output whose value is greater than the sum of its parts.[3] Konosuke Matsushita, a leading Japanese industrialist, reinforced the critical importance of the HR emphasis in a speech before a group of U.S. executives in 1988:[4]

> We will win and you will lose. You cannot do anything about it because your failure is an internal disease. You firmly believe that good management means executives on one side and workers on the other. On one side men who think and on the other side men who can only work. For you, management is the art of smoothly transferring the executives' ideas to the workers' hands.
>
> We have passed [that stage]. For us, management is the entire work force's intellectual commitment to the service of the company, without self-imposed functional or class barriers. Only the commitment of the minds of all its employees can permit a company to live with the ups and downs and requirements of its new environment. Yes, we will win and you will lose. For you are not able to rid your minds of the obsolete [human resources practices] that we never had.

This Japanese prediction has begun to be realized in the multi-billion-dollar U.S. trade deficit with Japan, the wholesale takeover of industries that were once dominated by U.S. firms, the absence of Japanese union strikes to disrupt production, and the level of coordinated technical expertise brought to bear on producing high-quality, low-cost products.[5] While Japanese firms have utilized an array of different resources to achieve their stunning victories, superior HRM policies and practices have been a contributing factor to their success and a challenge to U.S. HR professionals.[6] Japan grafted highly scientific and rational work processes onto the minds of the work force, allowing them to be exceedingly data-driven and rigorously scientific in researching and improving work processes—without engendering burnout.

2. Successful organizations accord high priority to proactively and systematically understanding and responding to current and future external customer needs. The evident economic success of Japanese firms and the preeminence they accord anticipating, meeting, and exceeding customer expectations through interviews, focus groups, and surveys has been an important lesson for U.S. managers and HR professionals.[7] U.S. corporations typically place highest priority on investor returns and focus on increasing short-term and long-term financial payoffs for stockholders. In contrast, corporations in Japan accord lower priority to short-term business profitability and higher priority to market share through increased customer satisfaction and work process improvements.[8] Better financial results such as cost reduction and higher profits can be viewed as the outcomes of process improvements based on increased customer sensitivity. Therefore, the objectives of these corporations include a systematic attunement to and strategic alignment with customer satisfaction.[9]

Customer satisfaction has, in fact, become an umbrella phrase for a range of additional conceptual refinements made in successful organizations. Distinctions have been made between **customers** (purchasers of products and services) and **consumers** (the end users of products and services), both of whom need to be satisfied but are sometimes the same and at other times different. Distinctions have also been made among **dissatisfiers** (unstated customer expectations that are taken for granted and if absent result in customer dissatisfaction), **satisfiers** (stated customer expectations which, if fulfilled, lead to satisfaction), and **exciters/delighters** (unstated and unexpected consumer desires which, if met, lead to high perceptions of quality and likely purchase). Over time, exciters/delighters become satisfiers as customers become used to them, and eventually satisfiers become dissatisfiers, thereby requiring ongoing innovation and customer research to ensure customer satisfaction.

The examples of successful international and domestic companies that place a priority on customer satisfaction provide important signals to mainstream U.S. businesses to indicate that meeting and exceeding customer expectations is an area that has been deemphasized too long.[10] The challenge for HR professionals is to move beyond their technical subspecialties to provide improvements to the HR dimension of organizational systems focused on increasing customer satisfaction.[11] Those HR professionals who cannot or will not contribute to and support the new alignment expectations of HR policies with strategic priorities are likely to play only marginal roles.

3. Successful organizations proactively and systematically understand and respond to current and future internal customer needs. The ultimate competitive advantage is an organization and a culture that develops the creative energies of all employees better than the competition through formal processes that anticipate, meet, and exceed employee expectations. The reality today in the United States is that employee needs are often ignored and unmet in a frenzy of restructuring and downsizing to cut costs and enhance profit margins. Granted that recent periods of slow growth have caused even some Japanese employers to dismiss employees for financial reasons, the balance of impersonal financial factors and personal HR needs always accords the latter a significant weight in Japan.

Because domestic and international firms in this information age require high-level technical, analytical, and problem-solving skills to compete, knowledge workers are at a premium.[12] Their sustained and committed contributions to organizational survival and prosperity were previously secured through an implicit and/or explicit psychological contract.[13] The psychological contract of reciprocal commitments between employer and employee that once existed has, however, been broken by significant downsizing in every sector of the knowledge economy, resulting in sagging morale and loyalty. Some specific examples of this trend include:[14]

- The parking lot of GE's appliance factory was built in 1953 to hold 25,000 cars; today's work force is only 10,000.

- In 1985, 406,000 people worked for IBM, which made profits of $6.6 billion. Today, a third of the people and all of the profits are gone.

- Automaker Volkswagen says it needs just two-thirds of its present work force.

- Procter & Gamble, with sales rising, has dismissed 12% of its employees.

- Cigna Reinsurance, an arm of the Philadelphia giant, has trimmed its work force 25% since 1990.

HR professionals are learning that in order to attract and retain committed, sophisticated knowledge workers, they must first provide a satisfying, and preferably delightful, work culture for them. Rosenbluth Travel, a domestic firm, experienced a 7500% growth in revenue within a 15-year span, building revenue from $20 million dollars to $1.5 billion while maintaining profitability above industry standards. CEO Hal Rosenbluth attributes the success of his company to the high HR commitment to employee satisfaction in word and deed: "For our people, the clients are priority number one. Our company has built a solid reputation in the field of customer service (in fact, our client retention rate is 96%), but we have actually done it by focusing inside on our own people."[15]

While the knowledge skills of committed, competent employees are an asset that grows more valuable with use, many U.S. firms have come to regard human resources as expenses to be controlled or eliminated as opposed to assets to be enhanced in order to achieve exceptional results. Benefit and retirement packages have been cut back by companies, and knowledge workers have taken their skills with them out the door, depriving the organization of competitive advantage.[16] Total quality provides a way for HR managers to rebuild and restore balance to the psychological contract by apportioning increased responsibility to employees for continued learning and increased responsibility to employers for providing support for the sustained employability of full-time employees. By investing in human capital to ensure employability security, managers form an economic partnership with employees and the norm of the internal customer as partner is reinstated on a more realistic basis.

4. Work force diversity and mobility are creating new employee needs and expectations about the work culture of the future. Simultaneous with the wave of downsizing is another key trend in the changing work force of the United States. The work force is becoming more diverse; it is aging, more women are entering the work force than ever before, the ethnic and racial mix in the work force is being altered, the educational profile of the new work force members is changing (with a widening gap in education among workers), and workers with disabilities are emerging as an untapped resource.[17] These work force changes have led to heightened expectations that traditional HR managers have not previously encountered, including the need for diversity to be viewed as a strategic advantage, the need for rapid inclusion in work settings, the need for schedule flexibility, the need for a wide range of employee services, and the need for ongoing personal and professional development. In addition, nations with slow growth in the work force but rapid growth in service jobs (Japan, the United States, Germany) have become magnets for immigrants. Even U.S. workers are relocating with greater frequency.[18]

Not only are new psychological needs and expectations being brought into the workplace by the changing work force, but there has been a flurry of new regulatory guidelines and legislation to shape compliance standards for managing this changing work force.[19] Examples include the Americans with Disabilities Act of 1990, which prohibits employers from discriminating against the disabled; the explosion of sexual harassment suits against employers, which require managers to develop work climates devoid of sexual harassment; and accent discrimination cases against employers, which challenge managers to alter accent discrimination practices against competent immigrant workers.

Those companies that are able to design work cultures to effectively capitalize on work force diversity and mobility trends will be the companies best able to attract and retain the intellectual capital necessary for future success. Those HR professionals who can effectively respond to this company need will be regarded as invaluable business partners.

5. The information technology revolution is reshaping the core competencies needed in a knowledge economy. In 1991, business investment in computers and telecommunication equipment tools of the new economy—tools that create, sort, store, and ship knowledge—for the first time exceeded capital spending for industrial, construction, and other "old economy" equipment.[20] The figures, while impressive, understate investment in knowledge machines because they do not show the growing intellectual ability of industrial gear. For example, more than half of machine tool spending in the United States is for equipment with built-in computer numerical controls.[21]

The revolution in information technology has impacts on many levels for

HR professionals. First, it intensifies the need to develop and update computer literacy skills on an ongoing basis. Second, the distribution of technical and decision-making abilities throughout the organization by means of computer networking creates a redistribution of power. This redistribution of core competency power expands the retention and redeployment responsibilities of HR professionals. Third, the speed and immediacy of information exchange, both within the work organization at all levels and between organizations and key external stakeholders (suppliers and customers), has the potential to redefine business relationships from the ordering of products and services to the sharing of feedback on performance and satisfaction. Fourth, employee expectations for sophisticated human resource information systems to generate and/or support company-wide skills inventories, computer-assisted career tracking and feedback, and leadership succession planning will only increase.

6. Organizational and HR leaders are being challenged to become effective strategic partners in the creation of world-class work cultures. Within the HR profession, there has been a growing movement away from the staff support functional role to the strategic partner role.[22] HR professionals are being encouraged to strengthen the linkage between business strategies and HR practices such as planning, staffing, appraising, compensating, and training and development.[23] In addition, senior managers need the input of HR professionals on organizational structures that promote empowered, high-performing, learning organizations for strategic success.[24] Numerous organizational redesign approaches such as virtual organizations,[25] organizational federalism,[26] reengineering,[27] and organizational architecture theory[28] present competing and confusing options for aligning business strategy and corporate structure. For example, process reengineering is requiring more cross-functional cooperation and information sharing, which demands more HR involvement in terms of group facilitation, privacy protection, and project support. To effectively address the preceding five driving forces, the successful integration of strategy, quality, organization, and HR concerns requires the forging of new strong partnerships between senior managers and HR professionals.

A BRIEF HISTORY OF U.S. HUMAN RESOURCE MANAGEMENT

A brief history of U.S. HRM provides hope for meeting the challenges posed by the current driving forces for change. The increased recognition of the importance of HR activities in fact contributed to the emergence in the 1970s of the term *human resource management*. Earlier references to the discipline included titles such as personnel management, personnel administration, and industrial relations. While most U.S. corporations have not accorded HR professionals full strategic partnership, senior managers are gradually acknowledging the impact of HR professionals on organizational effectiveness.

During the early periods of U.S. history, there was no systematic, uniform HR policy in the private or public sector. The predominantly Christian European demographic profile of U.S. immigrant workers supported the belief in hard work and pride in sound craftsmanship.[29] Early associations of artisans and craftspeople paralleled European medieval guilds that were the recipients of feudal protection. Early U.S. craftspeople (e.g., New England shipbuilders, colonial Williamsburg artisans, New York garment makers) brought with them detailed knowledge of materials, skills in developing processes and using tools to work on the materials, and attitudes toward work and its prime beneficiary—customers—that provided the bedrock upon which the major changes of the Industrial Revolution built in the late 19th century.

HR professionals today are struggling with retrieving the U.S. worker commitment to quality craftsmanship in a world that does not offer employees feudal protections. They have relied on balancing the competing theories and practices of a wide range of experts to cope with massive HR changes in the last century. The conflicting advice offered at different times by HR professionals has caused many managers to regard the field as "mostly good intentions and whistling in the dark or averting unionization."[30] Also, the absence of emotion transmission paths across the organization has blocked the deepening of worker commitment. One of the most basic dynamics at work is "how you treat your employees is how they will treat customers."

Nevertheless, it is possible to interpret the history of U.S. HRM as a series of attempts to address internal and external issues that required different emphases on HR flexibility and control as situations warranted. This interpretation is depicted in the grid of organizational HRM approaches in Figure 1.1.

The grid consists of four organizational quadrants (internal control, internal flexibility, external control, and external flexibility), with individual approaches categorized and alphabetically labeled to indicate the historical sequence of occurrence. The grid presupposes a continual tension among competing human resource approaches; some approaches are implemented at one time, place, or context, while others are deemphasized. When efficient use of resources in a stable external environment becomes paramount, internal control approaches are emphasized; when effective use of resources in a rapidly changing external environment is paramount, external flexibility approaches predominate. As HRM has evolved in the United States, different approaches have demanded different competencies of HR professionals, e.g., the skills required to devise and enforce Equal Employ-

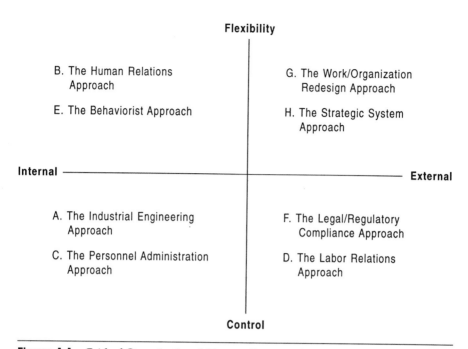

Figure 1.1 Grid of Organizational Human Resource Management Approaches.

ment Opportunity compliance policies are different than those needed to build self-managing teams. Today, the demands for both external flexibility and internal control are stretching HR professionals to address total quality concerns.

A. The Industrial Engineering Approach

The influx of large numbers of workers in manufacturing environments in the late 1800s and early 1900s caused employers to consider new methods to increase internal control and reduce waste. Frederick Taylor's Scientific Management approach to human resources responded by making industrial engineering improvements in the workplace. Taylor was one of the first theorists to consider work as a system. For Taylor, acquiring efficiency required that tasks be systematically and uniformly analyzed and measured, using time and motion studies as the principal means of investigation. His findings provide the basis of some current HR policies, including the systematic and uniform collection of task information to produce a detailed list of task instructions, the recruitment and selection of the best person to perform a job, and pay for worker performance.[31]

B. The Human Relations Approach

In contrast to the internal control emphasis of Taylor's engineering improvements, the human relations approach emphasizes the need for internal flexibility to increase productivity due to different motivation needs of employees. Employees resented being treated as cogs in a machine, continually prodded to work harder and faster by efficiency engineers. In the 1920s, at the Western Electric Company Hawthorne Works plant in Chicago, researchers led by Elton Mayo demonstrated that the attitudes which workers had toward management and their work groups were directly related to their productivity.[32] From these findings, the famous Hawthorne Effect was established, according to which productivity is a direct result of management involvement with workers; HR professionals could no longer ignore human motivation as a key factor in productivity.

Six theorists later provided the content and process motivational models to undergird the human relations approach: Abraham Maslow, Frederick Herzberg, Douglas McGregor, Victor Vroom, Lyman Porter, and Edward Lawler.[33] Content theories specify what sort of events, needs, or outcomes motivate behavior, while process theories specify how different kinds of events, conditions, or outcomes motivate behavior.

Maslow argued for the existence of five innate, genetically determined needs: physiological, safety, belonging, esteem, and self-actualization. Behavior is driven by the urge to fulfill these five fundamental needs in a prepotent manner, i.e., higher order needs (esteem and self-actualization) could only influence motivation if lower order needs (physiological, safety, and belonging) were largely satisfied. For HR professionals, this meant that additional job recognition would not motivate a hungry employee, since the latter is a prepotent need requiring a different level of fulfillment.

Herzberg argued for a motivation-maintenance model that separated motivational factors (the work itself, achievement, possibility for growth, responsibility, advancement, and recognition) from maintenance or hygiene factors (status, job security, interpersonal relations, salary, working conditions). Only the former, according to Herzberg, positively motivated behavior, while the latter, if absent, could be demotivators and would never act as motivators. Herzberg applied his model to work contexts and promoted job enrichment by increasing the areas of responsibility of workers in order to increase motivation, rather than relying on salary increases. Job enrichment has been utilized by HR professionals to support employee involvement programs and self-managed work teams, as well as motivational work through work redesign programs. HR professionals, therefore, are to be sensitive to true motivators and internally flexible in order to respond on an ongoing basis to the relative attraction of need satisfiers for different employees at different times.

McGregor provided a model of managerial leadership assumptions: Theory X and Theory Y. Theory X assumes that employees dislike work, need to be coerced to perform, and will avoid responsibility whenever possible. Theory Y assumes that employees do *not* dislike work, can become committed to meet organizational objectives without coercive pressures, and will learn not only to accept but also to seek responsibility. Under Theory X, HR professionals focused on incentives and penalties along with close supervision and inspection to guarantee productivity. Under Theory Y, HR professionals focused on system improvements that required participation, delegation of responsibility, and appropriate resources for competent, trustworthy people to be productive. McGregor was one of the first to codify the win–win vs. lose–lose concept of behavior.

Vroom's expectancy theory, extended by Porter and Lawler, proposed a dynamic process model of motivation to supplement the prior static content models.[34] The model is based on three major concepts: valence (perceived value of reward), instrumentality (subjective belief about effort–reward probability), and expectancy (perceived link between effort–performance and performance–outcome). The first letters of these concepts are used to form the acronym VIE to identify the model. The combination of initial employee valence (incorporating the Maslow and Herzberg theories) and employee belief about effort–reward probability will determine the initial work effort exerted. Effort, in turn, leads to performance, which is affected by abilities and traits as well as accurate role perceptions. In the dynamic flowchart of motivation, performance influences actual intrinsic and extrinsic rewards and the perceived equity of rewards determines future employee work effort expended. If rewards are perceived as equitable, then satisfaction occurs and accelerates a cycle of renewed motivation to produce. The goal of HR professionals for Vroom is to optimize motivated performance by focusing on people and work processes and increasing employee valence, instrumentality, and expectancy.

C. The Personnel Administration Approach

In the Depression years of the early 1930s, firms made drastic cost reductions in order to survive. Organizational programs based on human relations approaches were cut back, and personnel employees focused more on operational efficiency in administering such normal subfunctions as recruitment, selection, placement, socialization, training, development, compensation, benefits, employee and labor relations, and health, safety, and security concerns. For example, during construction of the Hoover Dam in the Southwest during the 1930s, the supply of workers was so vast and the demand for work so intense that personnel officers did not focus on motivating workers but simply on recruiting enough eager "hands" to meet daily construction schedules. In the 1990s, in which restructuring and downsizing are daily occurrences, the Depression mindset has affected some HR departments in the form of being told by senior management to make 10% across-the-board cuts in personnel within tight timelines.

D. The Labor Relations Approach

As a direct result of the Depression, Roosevelt's New Deal policies increased government involvement in labor relations and two laws were passed in the United States which expanded the role of HR professionals. The Norris-LaGuardia Act of 1932 limited the use of covert injunctions and outlawed "yellow dog" contracts (i.e., contracts that stated, as a condition of employment, that a worker would not join a union). The Wagner Act of 1935 guaranteed workers the right to organize and bargain collectively, which provided unions with the impetus needed to mount massive organizing efforts. The result was a drastic increase in the total number of unionized workers in the labor force and an influx of unions into previously non-unionized occupations.

The increase in unionization created new external pressures for HRM. Companies created HR departments to handle union negotiations and bargaining. HR departments that had previously existed solely for the purpose of administering personnel benefit programs were now totally immersed in labor–management negotiations. This shifted the emphasis of HR professionals, and the external industrial relations era of HRM evolved from these 1930s developments.

The impact of labor unions carried on into the 1940s. Labor unions were heavily involved in efforts to organize the work force, and adversarial relations with management intensified. These organizing efforts often had unsettling effects on the work force, as rival unions vied for external representation rights. Realizing that the country could ill afford work stoppages and other disrupting influences on productivity during wartime, the government created the National War Labor Board to avert labor disputes.

Wage and salary control programs initiated by the War and the Labor Board have had a lasting impact on present-day HR programs. With the ability to exercise authority over any employer with nine or more employees, the National War Labor Board handed down formulas for establishing limits on the amount of salary increases, as well as other benefits, employers were permitted to provide. As a direct result of these actions, unions began to demand and employers provided compensation in the form of fringe benefits. In addition, since employers did not have to obtain government approval in order to provide raises under a progressive wage increase system, these programs began to develop in large numbers. Present-day compensation programs which include benefit packages and cost-of-living adjustments are direct descendants of these early wage plans.[35]

E. The Behaviorist Approach

The influence of behavioral science became widespread in the 1950s due to the work of B.F. Skinner.[36] Behaviorism was a scientifically based learning theory which maintained that human behavior could be controlled through a variety of classical and operant conditioning procedures and properly applied reinforcements. The behaviorists believed that people and animals were motivated to engage in or avoid certain behaviors because of past rewards and punishments associated with those behaviors. Behaviorism assumed that learning was not a cognitive process but simply a process of associating rewards received with behavior performed, thereby denying key principles of the human relations approach (i.e., freedom, cognition, dignity, and justice).[37]

The influence of behavioral sciences pervaded the 1950s and provided a variety of scientific tools to understand, influence, and control human behavior in work settings. These tools were utilized by both managers and HR professionals in order to improve overall productivity. Variations on the behavioral theme exist today in the widely popular *The One-Minute Manager*.[38] HR professional competencies began to include scientific techniques for behaviorally modifying and rewarding worker performance.

F. The Legal/Regulatory Compliance Approach

HR managers during the past three decades have been strongly impacted by the flow of government legislation imposed on businesses and the need to exert some control over these rapid political/legal/regulatory changes. Beginning with the Equal Pay Act of 1963 and Title VII of the Civil Rights Act of 1964 and extending through the present day, the past three decades have witnessed unprecedented amounts of employment legislation and litigation. The rights of individual employees have become of paramount importance in the legal and legislative arenas. Probably more than any other single factor, the seemingly unending and complex stream of government legislation has caused many organizations to reevaluate the importance of the HRM function. Today, HR professional activities, which were once thought of as unnecessary and frivolous, are being recognized as necessary to reduce legal risks and possible financial losses. Simply keeping up with the stream of legal standards and regulatory guidelines has challenged HR professionals. Legal analysis and regulatory relations skills have been added to the core competencies list for today's HR professional.

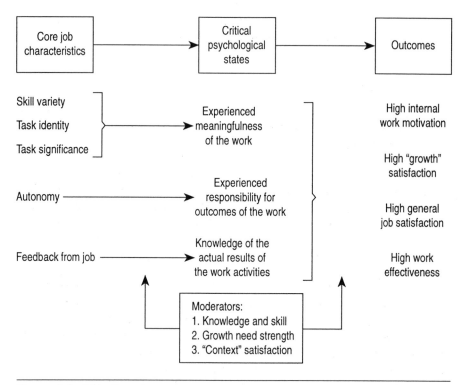

Figure 1.2 The Complete Job Characteristics Model of Hackman and Oldham. (Source: Hackman, J. Richard and Oldham, Greg R. (1980). *Work Redesign*. Reading, Mass.: Addison-Wesley, p. 95.)

G. The Work/Organization Redesign Approach

The work/organization redesign approach includes individual task, team configuration, and organization transformation skills to motivate flexible responses to external forces. The Hackman and Oldham job characteristics model in Figure 1.2 identifies core job characteristics, critical psychological states, and work outcomes to improve individual productivity and increase motivation.[39] For HR professionals, the model generates responsibilities to analyze job design, measure the motivational potential score of jobs, and maximize the five core job characteristics. The degree to which an employee recognizes the importance of his or her job, perceives the task from start to finish, uses a variety of skills and talents, can exercise personal control over the work, and receives clear, timely feedback on performance will determine how effectively he or she will meet external work challenges in a motivated manner.

The quality approach to managing human resources is deeply indebted to the work of Hackman and Oldham. Quality is related in a primary or secondary sense to all five of the core job characteristics of their model. Quality of a product or service undoubtedly is benefited by a worker's dedicated application of skills, as enhanced by *task identity* and a feeling of *task significance*. More directly, quality of work is enhanced by a task design that incorporates *autonomy* and *feedback* relating to quality characteristics. The key outcomes of high general job satisfaction and high work effectiveness can then be seen as results that propel continuous improvement at work.[40]

In addition to individual job design, group work redesign based on sociotechnical principles and team dynamics indicates that employees benefit from working in groups that allow them to talk with each other about their work as they do it.[41] It is important in managing human resources to recognize, especially in light of information technology networks, that employees need the opportunity to give and receive help as well as have their work recognized by others in the workplace.[42]

Team development as a HR responsibility has been emerging since teams have been identified as one of the best ways to integrate across structural organizational boundaries and to both design and energize core work processes. In fact, in many high-performing organizations, teams are surpassing individuals as the primary performance unit in the company.[43]

Finally, linking individual, team, and work organization design changes has become essential as the pace of infrastructure changes to meet external competition has accelerated.[44] Managing human resources entails familiarity with organizational change and development processes and the design of competitive organizational architecture arrangements to enhance competitive capability.[45]

H. The Strategic System Approach

The HR professional also has been challenged to assume full strategic partnership with senior management to flexibly adapt to external forces.[46] This includes familiarity with domestic and global business strategies,[47] open systems models,[48] contingency approaches to leadership,[49] strategic benchmarking,[50] and strategic organizational learning development processes[51] to align HR professionals with the strategic thrust of a firm.

These diverse HR system challenges to meet organizational external adaptation and internal integration needs while playing an active role in mergers, acquisitions, and rightsizing decisions have stretched HR professionals during these turbulent times.

Yet it is precisely during these rapidly changing times that HR professionals have the opportunity for high impact. The traditional definition of the discipline of *human resource management as a specialty field that attempts to develop programs, policies, and activities to promote the satisfaction of both individual and organizational needs, goals, and objectives* is taking on new dimensions.[52] The prospect of substantially contributing to organizational, national, and global economic leadership is both daunting and appealing.

THE HOUSE OF TOTAL QUALITY: THE CHALLENGING OPPORTUNITY FOR HUMAN RESOURCES

If the preceding analysis of environmental changes and HRM history is accurate, then there is no questioning the conclusion that HR professionals are facing imminent challenges. The question to be asked is whether these challenges will be viewed as threats or opportunities. HR professionals who define their world in terms of a threat may engage in defensive actions and focus on preserving the past or retreating into narrow technical specialties. In contrast, HR professionals can define their world in terms of an opportunity by focusing on the future and carrying forward the best of the past. As HR professionals become familiar with and understand the promise of total quality, the urgency of seizing the opportunity will become evident.

To begin that process of understanding, one definition of total quality recently endorsed by the Total Quality Forum is:

> ...a people-focused management system that aims at continual increase in customer satisfaction at continually lower cost. TQ is a total system approach (not a separate area or program), and an integral part of high-level strategy. It works horizontally across functions and departments, involving all employees, top to bottom, and extends backwards and forwards to include the supply chain and the customer chain.[53]

This definition is expanded and diagrammed in the appendix at the end of this chapter, but it is clear that HR professionals who adopt total quality will become strategic partners in system analysis and improvement that will empower employees to control their own work across traditional organizational barriers in order to achieve world-class performance. In fact, the principles and practices associated with total quality impact all the traditional HRM approaches and will require role changes for all key organizational stakeholders, including HR professionals.

The House of Total Quality, as depicted in Figure 1.3, provides a conceptual framework for understanding the interdependent components of a total quality system.[54] It is the model around which this book is built. It offers HR

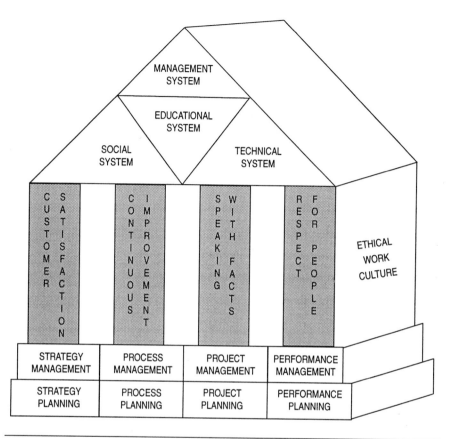

Figure 1.3 The House of Total Quality. (Source: Voehl, Frank (1992). *The House of Total Quality*. Coral Springs, Fla.: Strategy Associates, p. 17. Modified by the authors.)

professionals the integrated overview to facilitate a transition from past traditional HR responsibilities to the future challenging opportunities afforded total quality HR professionals.

The House of Total Quality consists of six components, as depicted in Figure 1.3: (1) the roof or superstructure of four **organizational subsystems** within which the actual work of any organization takes place: the management, social, technical, and educational subsystems; (2) the four **pillars of quality**: customer satisfaction, continuous improvement, speaking with facts, and respect for people; (3) the four **foundations**: strategy management, process management, project management, and performance management; (4) the four **cornerstones**: strategic planning, process planning, project planning, and performance planning; (5) the **mortar** of deployment between the joints of the roof, the pillars, the foundations and the cornerstones; and (6) the **ethical work culture**. The first five components of the House of Total Quality are treated here, and the ethical work culture is treated in the next section of this chapter. See the diagram in the appendix at the end of this chapter for a contemporary rendition of the scope of total quality.

This integrated view of an organization requires more than mastering the traditional HR subspecialties. It requires, in addition, an expanded emphasis on the external flexibility quadrant of HR approaches (e.g., increased strategic thinking competencies and increased work/organization redesign competencies). In fact, the House of Total Quality explored in this book is a comprehensive organization design and human relations system, as opposed to the scope and meaning of the House of Quality, a more limited concept, which is only a technical means of quality function deployment in *hoshin* planning.[55]

The roof or superstructure of the House of Total Quality includes a system composed of four subsystems: social, technical, educational, and managerial. Their interdependencies are depicted in the three interlocking circles of the ballantine, as shown in Figure 1.4. Successful implementation of total quality and continuous improvement efforts requires the redefinition of HRM to recognize the importance of systems. Deming states: "The people work in a system. The job of the manager is to work on the system, to improve it continuously, with their help." Within the House of Total Quality, the HR manager must work on the four subsystems.

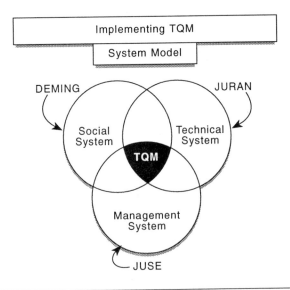

Figure 1.4 The Subsystem Roof of the House of Total Quality.

The social system advocated by Deming includes factors associated with the formal and informal characteristics of the "personality" of the organization: (1) organizational norms, role responsibilities, and sociopsychological relationship expectations; (2) status and power relationships between individual members and among groups; and (3) the extent to which the work organization is a work community. It is the social system that has the greatest impact on such factors as competition, cooperation, motivation, creativity, innovative behavior, and teamwork. HR managers have a major responsibility for the nature and "personality" of the organization. To achieve total quality, a social system must be developed in which constituent or customer satisfaction, continuous improvement, speaking with facts, and genuine respect for people are accepted social practices in managing human resources.

The technical system advocated by Juran is concerned with the flow of work through the organization. It includes all the tools and machinery, the practice of quality, and the quantitative aspects of quality.[56] If you can measure it, you can probably describe and perhaps improve it using the technical systems approach. In most organizations, the technical system contains the following core elements:

- Accumulation of technology
- Pursuit of standardization
- Work flow, materials, and specifications
- Job definitions and responsibility
- Machine/person interface
- Number and type of work steps
- Availability and use of information
- Decision-making processes
- Problem-solving tools and processes
- Physical arrangements of equipment, tools, and people

The expected benefits from analyzing and improving the technical system(s) are to:

- Reduce (eliminate) waste and rework
- Reduce (eliminate) negative variation
- Reduce (eliminate) interruptions and idle time
- Save time and money

- Increase employee control over the work process
- Reduce bottlenecks and frustration
- Improve safety and quality of work life
- Increase speed and responsiveness
- Improve customer satisfaction

The educational system is focused on creating and developing a global learning organization dedicated to continuously expanding the knowledge horizons of its stakeholders to gain competitive advantage. Honda, Xerox, Motorola, and GE are examples of organizations that put a premium on developing their quality educational systems. The educational system not only requires HR professionals to enhance their internal training and development efforts, but also demands that learning partnerships with other public and private institutions be forged to continuously network and upgrade the knowledge of all employees.

The managerial system advocated by the Union of Japanese Scientists and Engineers includes factors associated with (1) the organizational structure (formal design, policies, patterns of authority, and budgetary controls); (2) the mission, vision, and goals of the institution; and (3) administrative activities (planning, organizing, directing, coordinating, and controlling organizational activities). Management provides the leadership and framework for the policies, procedures, and practices of the organization. The management system is deployed at four levels: strategy, process, project, and personal performance management. These comprise the foundations and cornerstones of the House of Total Quality and are briefly discussed at this point.

The roof and four pillars of the House of Total Quality rest upon the four cornerstones of planning and the four foundations of management that relate to strategies, processes, projects, and performance. While the roof (subsystems) is the most theoretical part of the House of Total Quality, with the pillars (outcomes) providing direction for actualizing the system, they still do not ground the edifice in reality. It remains for the planning and managerial operations to be put into action in order to actualize the quality improvement process.

The cornerstone of the first pillar of customer satisfaction is **strategy planning**. *Strategy planning is the process of environmental analysis and strategy formulation to determine an organization's future directional stability.* It is most effectively conducted as an iterative, participative, focus design process that enhances the adequacy, increases the accuracy, and generates the commitment of organizational stakeholders' adaptation to and transformation of the environment.

The foundation of the first pillar is **strategy management**. *Strategy management is the process of strategic plan implementation, evaluation, and control to develop competitive advantage and to ensure a favorable organizational future.* It is most effectively conducted as an active, iterative, feedback process to determine the long-run performance of an organization.

The cornerstone of the second pillar of continuous improvement is **process planning**. *Process planning is the step which assures that all key processes work in harmony with the mission and meet the needs and expectations of the constituents or customers by maximizing operational effectiveness.* Its key agenda is to design operations to hear and respond rapidly to the changing voices of the customer.

The foundation of the second pillar is **process management**. *Process management is the coordination and implementation of measured, streamlined, and controlled processes to continually improve operations.* Efforts at this managerial stage are often cross-functional, since many functions cross departmental boundaries. This requires interdepartmental collaboration, with process and indicator functions appropriately assigned. The outcomes are a common language for documenting activities and shared rationales for decisions to eliminate waste, redundancy, and bottlenecks. To enhance HR professional performance in process management, seven major process management tools and six supplemental process management tools are treated in Chapter 3. The seven major process management tools are the affinity diagram/KJ method, interrelationship digraph, tree diagram, matrix diagram, arrow diagram, process decision program chart, and matrix data analysis. The six supplemental process management tools are competitive benchmarking, flowcharts, nominal group technique, structured surveys, trend charts, and Excelerator.

The cornerstone of the third pillar of speaking with facts is **project planning**. *Project planning is the establishment of a system to effectively plan, organize, implement, and control all activities needed for successful completion of project initiatives.* It is at this stage that teams are formed to solve and carry out both process- and policy-related initiatives. Team activities are linked to operational objectives and improvement targets. They develop the critical success factors: control systems, schedules, tracking mechanisms, performance indicators, and skill analysis.

The foundation of the third pillar is **project management**. *Project management is the implementation and control of a single, nonrecurring event that activates organizational change through structured phases and specified outcomes and requires teamwork for successful completion.* Sound project management links organizational objectives and processes, implements a work plan with designated milestones, establishes a communication process for documenting key decisions and improvements, resolves project problems, and results in a project completed on time and within budget. To enhance HR professional performance in project management, seven major project management tools and six supplemental project management tools are treated in Chapter 4. The seven major project management tools are cause-and-effect diagrams, check sheets, display graphs, histograms, Pareto charts, scatter diagrams, and control charts. The six supplemental project management tools are force-field analysis, prioritization matrix, run charts, block diagrams, customer/supplier relations checklist, and quality mapping.

The cornerstone of the fourth pillar of respect for people is **performance planning.** *Personal performance planning is the process that provides all employees with the means to implement continuous improvement of the preceding processes and systems through completion of individual tasks and activities.* Each individual is guided through the development of a personal mission and an analysis of how his or her work performance contributes to the rest of the organization's success and sense of community.

The foundation of the fourth pillar is **performance management.** *Performance management is the implementation and control of respectful regard for oneself and others in line with total quality strategies, processes, and projects.* Key objectives, with quality indicators and personal controls, are developed. The result of personal performance management is a committed organizational vision; people empowered to make decisions and solve problems; a greater sense of job satisfaction and work community; improved communication, respect, and trust; and better integrated work systems.

The outcomes of the cornerstones and foundations of the House of Total Quality are its four pillars: customer satisfaction, continuous improvement, speaking with facts, and respect for people. *The first pillar,* **customer satisfaction,** *is the successful fulfillment of customer expectations over time, which provides strategic direction, organizational identity, and prioritized objectives for the total quality firm.* Sustaining customer satisfaction and producing "associate delight," which increases market share and ultimately profitability, provides directional stability for organizations during turbulent times.

The second pillar, **continuous improvement,** *is both a commitment and a process to design and implement an operational system that responds to the voices of internal and external customers.* Continuous improvement is the outcome of solid process planning and management. Continuous improvement for HR professionals entails learning new processes, tools, and skills and applying them to the traditional HR specializations. Continuous improvement focuses on increasing system effectiveness and efficiency in order to gain competitive advantages in meeting changing customer expectations.

The third pillar, **speaking with facts,** *is the result of an organization's providing resources and methods to determine what is factually true and structuring itself to ensure that its members can safely give voice to the truth.* It is the outcome of comprehensive project planning and management and requires extensive teamwork contributions. Speaking with facts requires the disciplined command of and regular team application of total quality tools to obtain timely, reliable information for decision making. HR professionals require dual competencies in technical project management tools and group dynamics to build self-directed work teams. HR professionals need to interact with teams to share information and endorse group projects that are likely to achieve organizational objectives.

The fourth pillar, **respect for people,** *is the positive regard for others and oneself that enables and sustains personal commitment to total quality.* It is the outcome of systematic personal performance planning and management. Performance includes technical task completion and considerate relationship development in order to create and sustain a work community in which respect for people is the norm. Personal responsibility for contributing to organizational objectives, system processes, and team projects is a characteristic HR professionals screen for, recognize, and reward on a timely basis.

Finally, the glue of **deployment** bonds the roof, pillars, foundations, and cornerstones of the House of Total Quality. *Deployment is the interactive process of participation and feedback that builds a sense of ownership and commitment to the expansion of the House of Total Quality, both domestically and internationally.*

A comparison of the components of the House of Total Quality with Baldrige categories and Deming principles is presented in Table 1.1. The second column in Table 1.1 presents the seven categories and core values and concepts of the Malcolm Baldrige National Quality Award. The Baldrige criteria are included in this book for three reasons. First, the seven criteria are sound and provide a reliable basis for organizational self-assessment. Second, the award and its criteria are well known in the U.S. manufacturing, service, and small business sectors. Third, knowledge and use of the criteria enhance communication between these sectors and the academy.

An abridged listing of the principles and concepts developed by W. Edwards Deming is presented in the third column in Table 1.1. Deming's beliefs are included for two reasons. First, Deming was an early practitioner of total quality, and much of the work in the field is directly or indirectly influenced by his ideas. Second, his ideas are provocative; Deming's Fourteen Principles stimulate exploration of their implications for individual institutions.

The House of Total Quality model incorporates the quality principles of Deming and the Baldrige criteria. Its comprehensiveness provides an excellent structure to explore the relations between total quality and HRM.

Table 1.1 Comparison of the House of Total Quality with the Baldrige Categories and Deming Principles

House of Total Quality[a]	Baldrige categories[b]	Deming principles[c]
THE ROOF		
Management System		
1. Systems, processes	2. Leadership	1. Create constancy of purpose
2. Leadership	3. Strategic quality planning	2. Adopt the new philosophy
3. Strategy	• Long-range planning	7. Institute leadership
4. Mission, vision, values		
Social System		
1. Structure	• Employee development	• Hierarchic style of management must change
2. Social norms	• Partnership development	• Transformation can only be accomplished by people, not hardware
3. Teams	• Cross-functional teams	
4. Organizational personality		
Technical System		
1. Work processes	5. Management of process quality	9. Break down departmental barriers
2. Job descriptions	• Reduce cycle time	• Statistical measurement
3. Problem-solving tools	• Design quality	
4. Decision making		
6. Measurement tools		
Educational system		
1. Lifelong learning	4. Human resource development and management	• Continual learning
2. Retraining	• Employee participation and development	6. Institute training on the job

THE PILLARS

Customer satisfaction	7. Customer focus and satisfaction	• Aim quality at the needs of the customer, present and future
Continuous improvement	2. Information and analysis 5. Management of process quality 6. Quality and operational results	3. Cease dependence on mass inspection
Speak with facts	2. Information and analysis • Management by fact	• In God we trust; all others bring facts • Statistical measurement
Respect for people	4. Human resource development and management • Employee participation and development	14. Involve everyone in the transformational process 10. Eliminate slogans and targets 11. Eliminate numerical quotas 12. Remove barriers to worker's pride

ETHICAL WORK CULTURE

Ethical work culture	1. Leadership 4. Human resource development and management • Manage for organization integrity	8. Drive out fear • Create and maintain system integrity

a Voehl, Frank (1992). *The House of Total Quality.* Coral Springs, Fla.: Strategy Associates.
b 1993 Award Criteria, Malcolm Baldrige National Quality Award, Milwaukee: American Society for Quality Control.
c Walton, Mary (1986). *The Deming Management Method.* New York: G.P. Putnam and Sons.

ETHICAL WORK CULTURE AND
EXPANDED HUMAN RESOURCE ROLES

While the House of Total Quality provides the structural facade for total quality, the organizational ethical work culture provides its depth and determines what it "feels like" to internal and external stakeholders who dwell there.[57] The ethical work culture of an organization determines whether the house becomes a home—a place where respect, cooperation, trust, caring, justice, and high-performance standards prevail. Organizations with highly developed ethical work cultures demonstrate **integrity**. Organizational integrity is the alignment of moral awareness, judgment, intention, and action that results in a supportive context. Managing for organization integrity develops habitual patterns of decision making, policy formation, and procedures implementation that form **organizational character**. Organizational character is what a firm stands for; it is the set of principles, values, and practices to which it holds itself and others accountable. Organizational character is different from organizational personality; the former accords principled caring relationships a higher priority than rapid socioeconomic adaptability. Total quality organizations are organizations that stand for certain principles and caring relationships, which HR practitioners are expected to respect and endorse.

Culture has been defined as:

> a pattern of basic assumptions—invented, discovered, or developed by a given group as it learns to cope with its problems of external adaptation and internal integration—that has worked well enough to be considered valid and, therefore, to be taught to new members as the correct way to perceive, think, and feel in relation to those problems.[58]

The word *culture* can be applied to a social unit of any size, from civilizations, countries, ethnic groups, occupations, and communities to organizations or groups. Culture can be viewed in terms of three levels: artifacts and creations (technology, art, visible and audible behavior patterns), values (espoused normative claims testable either in the physical environment or by social consensus), and assumptions (logically fundamental, preconscious beliefs about the nature of reality, human beings, human activity, and human relationship to the environment).[59] Organizational cultures can be categorized by a variety of typologies as indicated in Table 1.2.

Ethical work cultures can also be changed by deliberate interventions that focus on key leverage points.[60] The greater the fluidity of the current organizational ethical values, the greater the availability of alternative ethical work culture stages of development; the lower the commitment of the mem-

Table 1.2 Examples of Typologies of Organizational Cultures

Types of organizational cultures	Dominant ideologies	Authors
Type A	Hierarchical control, high specialization, short-term employment, individual responsibility, individual decision making	Ouchi and Jaeger, 1978; Ouchi, 1981
Type J	Clan control, low specialization, lifetime employment, collective responsibility, collective decision making	
Type Z	Clan control, moderate specialization, long-term employment, individual responsibility, consensual decision making	
Process	Low risk, "cover your ass" mentality, tight hierarchy	Deal and Kennedy, 1982
Tough-guy–macho	High risk, quick feedback, fluctuating structure	
Word-hard–play-hard	Moderately low risk, race to the quick, flexible structure	
Bet-your-company	Very high risk, slow feedback, clear-cut hierarchy	
Sensation–thinking	Impersonal, abstract, certainty, specifically authoritarian	Mitroff and Kilmann, 1975
Intuition–thinking	Flexible, adaptive, global notions, goal-driven	
Intuition–feeling	Caring, decentralized, flexible, no explicit rules or regulations	
Sensation–feeling	Personal, home-like, relationship-driven, nonbureaucratic	
Apathetic	Demoralizing and cynical orientation	Sethia and Von Glinow, 1985
Caring	High concerns for employees, no high-performance expectations	
Exacting	Performance and success really count	
Integrative	High concern for employees with high concern for performance	

Table 1.2 Examples of Typologies of Organizational Cultures (continued)

Types of organizational cultures	Dominant ideologies	Authors
Paranoid	Fear, distrust, suspicion	Kets de Vries and Miller, 1984
Avoidant	Lack of self-confidence, powerless, inaction	
Charismatic	Drama, power, success, abject followership	
Bureaucratic	Compulsive, detailed, depersonalized, rigid	
Schizoid	Politicized, social isolation	
Instrumental	Maximizing self-interest of the individual	Victor and Cullen, 1988
Caring	Maximization of joint interests on all levels	
Independence	Use of personal ethical principles	
Rules	Use of organizational ethical principles	
Law and code	Use of ethical principles from outside the organization	
Constructive norms	Achievement, self-actualizing, humanistic–encouraging, affirmative	Cooke and Szumal, 1993
Passive–defensive norms	Approval, conventional, dependent, and avoidance	
Aggressive–defensive norms	Oppositional, power, competitive, and perfectionistic	

Source: Adapted and modified from Trice, Harrison M. and Beyer, Janice M. (1993). *The Cultures of Work Organizations.* Englewood Cliffs, N.J.: Prentice-Hall, p. 17.

bers to the status quo, the easier it will be to effect organizational ethical work culture and subculture change.[61]

Because organizational work cultures and subcultures differ but can be morally developed by appropriately introducing the next maturity stage of ethical work culture, it is important for HR professionals to be able to identify and support those cultures that provide the moral maturity required in the

House of Total Quality. Organizational ethical work cultures provide the depth of principled commitment to the House of Total Quality; ethical work cultures provide continuity of commitment to principles and practices that survive leadership transitions. A strong ethical work culture holds leaders and all employees accountable for their adherence to standards of integrity. Organizations without well-developed ethical work cultures do not have the staying power to implement total quality and are rightly regarded as lacking character or being shallow. To assist the responsible management of human resources, the authors have adapted the work of Kohlberg[62] and Gilligan[63] on moral development to organizational ethical culture stages; a six-stage road map of ethical work culture stages and the work environments they sustain is provided in Table 1.3.[64]

Stages 1 and 2: The House of Manipulation. The House of Manipulation is the work environment that is created and sustained by stages 1 and 2 of organization ethical work culture: Social Darwinism and Machiavellianism. Although it is possible to formulate an amoral stage of organizational existence, the organizational moral jungle—the lowest or first stage of organizational ethical work culture formation—can be described as a form of survival of the fittest. At this stage, the most powerful individual, coalition, or network determines what is right or wrong and punishes those who deviate from accepted behavior. The lion or lion prides are appropriate metaphors for forceful ruling individuals or cliques that devise and monitor organizational policies and procedures.

At the next level of ethical work culture development is Machiavellianism, which entails routine acceptance of dishonesty for organizational advantage. Unlike the forceful lion, the Machiavellian fox is more likely to resort to backstabbing, cunning, and treachery to maximize organizational gain. Organizations operating at the second stage of ethical work culture development are above the blood baths of the first stage, but when every employee seeks to get ahead by stepping on others, an atmosphere of distrust is created, which precludes collaborative activity.

Organizations that operate at the first two stages are mired in a moral jungle, and their predatory rewards are meager compared to the benefits that await them at higher levels.

Stages 3 and 4: The House of Compliance. At the third and fourth stages of ethical work culture development, Popular Conformity and Allegiance to Authority are the two leading strategies. At the third stage, an organization adopts conventional procedures to which it expects members to adhere if they are to remain employed. While lions and foxes are not tolerated at this stage, public bureaucracies and family businesses often become inordinately attached to familiar operating procedures, and their resistance to change can lead to institutionalized mediocrity.

Table 1.3 Model of Organizational Ethical Work Culture Stages
and the Work Environments They Sustain

Organizational ethical work culture stages	Work environment
Stage 1: Social Darwinism Dread of extinction and the urgency of financial survival dictate moral conduct. The direct use of force is the accepted norm. An atmosphere of fear pervades. **Stage 2: Machiavellianism** Organization's gain guides actions. Successfully attaining goals justifies the use of any effective means, including dishonesty. An atmosphere of distrust pervades.	House of Manipulation
Stage 3: Popular Conformity There is a tradition of standard operating procedures. Peer pressure to adhere to social norms dictates what is right or wrong conduct. **Stage 4: Allegiance to Authority** Directions from legitimate authority, inside and outside the firm, determine organizational moral standards. Right and wrong are based on the decisions of those with legal and hierarchical power to legitimately optimize investor wealth.	House of Compliance
Stage 5: Democratic Participation Egalitarian participation in decision making and reliance on majority rule become organizational moral standards and shape investor financial expectations. **Stage 6: Principled Integrity** Justice, utility, caring, dignity, freedom, service, and accountability become guiding principles and serve as the basis for creating multiple stakeholder relationships. Sustained enhancement of these relationships forms organization character. Conscious, daily integration of the guiding principles in all systems and processes overrides other ethical work culture stages and creates an atmosphere of trust and commitment.	House of Total Quality

At the fourth stage, organizational ethical work culture is based not on a need for peer approval, but rather on respect for legitimate authority needs within and outside the organization. The work climate is one in which employees do not think or act for themselves, but always check out the position of legal officers and/or senior managers before uttering an opinion.

Compliance with authority is the behavioral norm in this process of hierarchical socialization. Whether it entails indoctrination processes, detailed by William Whyte in the 1950s, or powerful socialization pressures in organizational cultures, delineated by Terrence Deal and Allan Kennedy for the 1990s, the absence of individual moral autonomy severely limits organizational ethical work culture development. The group-centered mentality of stage 3 can blind the organization to external, environmental challenges, and uncritical subservience to organizational authority and legal guidelines characteristic of stage 4 can institutionalize a reactive posture to external change. Both of these conditions can adversely affect an organization's survival and growth in a globally competitive environment.

Nevertheless, recent moral development research on American business professionals and business school graduate students indicates that a preponderance of business practitioners seem to be reasoning at a level that will sustain the House of Compliance. Given this reality, it is important for HR professionals who are committed to participative quality processes to realize that the key motivators for moral conduct in many private and public sector organizations today may well be conformity to existing organizational procedures, seeking recognition from others, and maintaining the existing socioeconomic system. Resistance to expanding the roles of the HR professional is to be expected, given the demanding task of keeping up with ever-changing operating procedures and legal/regulatory guidelines. However, *human resource professionals need to stretch in order to move from the House of Compliance to the House of Total Quality.*

Stages 5 and 6: The House of Total Quality. At the fifth and sixth stages of organizational ethical work culture development, Democratic Participation and Principled Integrity are the dominant stages. Employees who work in organizations operating at the fifth stage are not guided by the need for social approval or respect for legitimate authority typical of the House of Compliance. Instead, the majority vote of individual members, or their representatives, ultimately determines policy and procedure.

Surveying majority trends is an important basis for organizational decision making at this stage. An obvious defect in this stage is that just as a lion, fox, peer groups, or heavy-handed authority figures can abuse power to the detriment of the organization, so can the tyranny of the majority. The majority can override the creative few and prematurely silence excellent minority contributors, thereby depriving the organization of vital inputs and potential innovations.

Nevertheless, the roots of participative management and quality circles are located in egalitarian, democratic ideals. A stage 5 ethical work culture, therefore, is most conducive to the growth of participative quality processes. Less developed ethical work cultures will normally resist the full implementation of participative quality processes. Therefore, it is important for HR professionals to be aware of an organization's ethical work culture level to prevent premature introduction of the quality technical subsystem into a culture that is resistant to democratic participation.

The sixth and final stage of organizational ethical work culture development requires respect for justice and the minority rights of productive and creative individuals, as well as searching for consensus relationships and community-building voices rather than relying on a majority vote. Designing effective, efficient, caring, and just systems that protect key organizational contributors from unwarranted blame become abiding features for employees working at the summit of organizational ethical work culture development. The organization thrives by nurturing consensus rather than censoring creativity, thereby gaining the valuable insights of innovative individuals and groups that dare to go beyond the prevailing majority view.

Employees who work in organizations at the sixth stage of ethical work culture development cannot rest on their laurels. They are continually developing their intellectual virtues (knowledge, understanding, and wisdom), their moral virtues (justice, honesty, courage, moderation, and prudence), and their social-emotional virtues (caring, assertiveness, sincerity, modesty, openness, and cooperativeness). To sustain this virtuous character development and nurture commitment to a learning organization that makes them better people, they must continually improve the relationships created with multiple stakeholders. Daily integration of principles such as justice, utility, caring, dignity, freedom, service, and accountability into all systems, processes, practices, and relationships develops a reputation for excellence and builds momentum to sustain the learning organization. It is the dynamic habit of "walking the talk" with multiple stakeholders that constitutes the ethical work culture that supports the House of Total Quality.

Because competent, committed employees will naturally expect a learning organization with the ethical work culture of the House of Total Quality, HR professionals need the concepts, practices, and tools to bring it about.[65] Recruitment, retention, and development of the best talent now demands that expanded HR competency. HR professionals are expected to know how to assess and develop the ethical work culture of an organization so that the House of Total Quality can become an inviting "work home" for the best available talent. Otherwise, the best talent will migrate to those competitors that can create that "home away from home" work climate.

In addition to the ethical stages of development, an organizational ethical work culture consists of key economic and primary stakeholder assumptions. Key assumptions about the types of capitalism essential to economic success, the primary stakeholders of organizational activity, and rationales for and behavioral priorities in organizations are identified in Table 1.4 and related to different stories in the House of Total Quality.

Table 1.4 Key Organizational Economic and Stakeholder Assumptions
and Different Stories in the House of Total Quality

Types of capitalism essential to economic success	Primary stakeholder of organizational activity	Rationale for and behavioral priorities in organizations	Different stories in the House of Total Quality
Managerial capitalism	Managers	Getting ahead; building careers	Doing things right
Financial capitalism	Investors	Getting financial results; building wealth	Doing things right and doing the right things
Stakeholder capitalism	Customers Employees Investors Managers Suppliers Community Society Natural environment	Adding value: building reputation for satisfied customers, productive employees, loyal investors, managerial leaders, responsive suppliers, and responsible citizenship	Doing things right, doing the right things, and doing things with and for the right stakeholder

The first column in Table 1.4 shows the types of Western capitalism that have evolved over the last century. From the managerial capitalism of impulsive entrepreneurs and robber barons who imposed their strategic managerial and moral views on society to the adherents of financial capitalism, the history records multiple struggles over priorities accorded productive resources. The abuses of incompetent managers (agents), who neglected their fiduciary obligations to stockholders (principals), made way for financial capitalists, who in turn reasserted the primacy of investor returns. The financial capitalist advocates thrived in the deregulated economic environment of the 1980s in the United States, which provided incentives for mergers, acquisitions, hostile takeovers, and other sophisticated financial maneuvers to absorb debt, break up companies, and sell off parts for better financial returns.

The abuses of financial capitalism, however, led to severe adverse impacts for a wide range of stakeholders in the 1990s (consumers, communities, governments, employees, and environmentalists). The advocates of stakeholder capitalism reasserted the need for multiple stakeholder enfranchisement to ensure satisfied customers and respectful treatment of employees while improving organizational efficiency and financial returns to stockholders.[66]

The second column in Table 1.4 addresses the primary beneficiaries of organizational activity with different types of capitalism. With managerial capitalism, managers accept the agency contract to optimize the efficiency of a firm.[67] The managers become contractually bound to act as the agents of the principal (i.e., owners/investors) by efficiently transforming resources into profitable, marketable goods and/or services. Often, however, resources are devoted solely for managerial career success or lavish perks, thereby breaching the terms of the agency contract. Abuse of managerial prerogatives invites the reassertion of the priority of fiduciary interests in the form of proxy battles, hostile takeovers, and other leveraged techniques to ensure that investor obligations are honored by a new management team. Managerial capitalism is overridden by financial capitalism.

With financial capitalism, the primary beneficiary is the investor. The new management team accepts the terms of the fiduciary contract that specifies the scope, priority, and depth of investor obligations.[68] Management promises an adequate return on investment and legal compliance that will sustain and prioritize the principal–agent relationships; managers, in effect, become partisan advocates of fiduciary interests. At this stage, new managers are hired hands of the stockholders, legally bound to advance and accord priority to stockholder interests within the limits of the law. Strategic decisions that conform to financial, economic, and legal standards of propriety are regarded as final determinants of strategic choices and HR policies.

The abuses of financial capitalism become apparent, however, when obsessively profit-driven managers act as if they are morally immune from the basic nonfiduciary obligations that would apply to any human being who exists in a moral community. Rampant financial capitalism can destroy productive companies, saddle other companies with unmanageable debt burdens, and create an economic atmosphere that is defensive, risk averse, oriented to short-term financial returns, and indifferent to customer satisfaction or employee morale. To ensure that nonfiduciary obligations to a wide range of stakeholders are not ignored, multiple stakeholder social contracts can be formed. Diverse social contracts can be formed at different stakeholder levels (national, cross-cultural, and universal) and require prioritization of customer, employee, investor, managerial, supplier, and community claims. Sometimes these contracts enforce fair and/or just outcomes[69] and sometimes they enforce the value of caring relationships[70] in both intra-organizational and extra-organizational contexts.[71] Nevertheless, acknowledging and responding to these stakeholder nonfiduciary claims for affordable product quality, organizational justice, and community-building workplaces is the basis for correcting both managerial and financial abuses. It is these very nonfiduciary obligations (e.g., not to harm, coerce, lie, cheat, or steal) that are cited in regulatory, legislative, special interest, and judicial arguments for constraining efficiency-driven management teams and exclusively profit-driven business activities.

The third and fourth columns in Table 1.4 provide the rationales for and behavioral priorities in different types of capitalism, as well as the stories of the House of Total Quality they construct. With managerial capitalism, the rationale for organizations and the behavioral priorities are geared to "getting ahead" through building careers. In the first story of the House of Total Quality, this amounts to organizational policies that focus on doing things right in order to avoid career mistakes. With financial capitalism, the rationales and priorities include getting financial results in order to build wealth. In the second story of the House of Total Quality, this amounts to organizational policies that focus not only on doing things right to avoid managerial career mistakes, but also doing the right things to build wealth for investors. Finally, with stakeholder capitalism, the rationales and priorities expand to include adding value by building a corporate reputation for satisfied customers, productive employees, loyal investors, managerial leaders, responsive suppliers, and responsible citizenship. In the third story of the House of Total Quality, this amounts to doing things right, doing the right things, and doing things with and for the right stakeholders.

In effect, monitoring and developing the organizational ethical work culture and key cultural assumptions will become critical if total quality implementation is to succeed. While the roof, the pillars, the foundations, and the cornerstones provide the height and breadth of the House of Quality, its ethical work culture determines its depth. An organization with a weak, underdeveloped ethical work culture will not have the character for sustained implementation of total quality.

It is important for general and HR managers to realize that the ethical work culture is part of the system of total quality that requires regular assessment, monitoring, and development. Expecting sustained world-class ethical behavior without a supportive organizational context that has an institutionalized ethics program places both employees and the company at ethical risk.

Ten items demonstrate concrete commitment to sustaining a total quality ethical work culture: (1) organizational leaders who are personally committed, credible, visible, and willing to take action on the ethical values of the work culture; (2) a statement of prioritized core values, guiding principles, and a code of ethics to provide broad and specific guidance for employees; (3) an ethics council or central coordinating group to establish and update policies, ultimately resolve ethical disputes, and provide a top-level conduit for internal and external customer ethical voice; (4) routine ethical work culture assessments with results shared and problems addressed; (5) consideration of organizational ethical impacts in HR selection, socialization, performance appraisal, promotion, and dismissal decisions, as well as organizational design and structure; (6) ongoing ethics training at all levels to ensure both compliance to standards and enhanced moral decision-making skills that enable responsible conduct on a daily basis; (7) a formal mechanism for reporting unethical and/or illegal practices to an individual and/or office with the authority to take action (e.g., a policy of whistleblower protection for person(s) reporting unethical practices to an organizational ethics officer); (8) a mechanism and/or process for the resolution and enforcement of ethical standards, with timely, fair, and just decisions rendered to the person(s) and/or systems involved; (9) formal and informal communication channels that reinforce the importance of continually improving the ethical work culture; and (10) regular recognition and/or commendation rituals for individuals and/or groups that exhibit exemplary ethical contributions.

Neglecting the ethical work culture of an organization can lead not only to productivity losses, but to major financial costs as well, as the escalating size of corporate fines under the 1991 U.S. Federal Sentencing Guidelines attests.[72] The preceding ten features of a total quality ethics program are feasible, and if organizations do not have the requisite skills in house, a judicious selection of qualified organizational ethics consultants is warranted.[73]

The House of Total Quality, therefore, graphically represents the tripartite impact that total quality is having on expanding the responsibilities of HR managers: (1) developing the full vertical implementation of each pillar of the facade of the House of Quality, (2) developing the full horizontal alignment of each aspect of the facade of the house with each of the others, and (3) developing the full depth of the house through assessing and developing the ethical work culture.

HUMAN RESOURCE MANAGEMENT AND THE TOTAL QUALITY DIFFERENCE

The total quality approach is changing the role of HR managers by changing the expectations of stakeholders, within and outside the profession, with regard to HRM responsibilities. Thus, while HR professionals reflect the organizational culture within which they are working, they also are expected to influence and shape it. A preview of these changing expectations and the difference total quality makes is indicated in Table 1.5, in which a comparison of traditional and total quality HRM approaches is provided.

In the traditional HRM approach, the business objectives are productivity and profit, while the quality objective is often restricted to meet minimum required standards of federal regulations. Information is only shared if it is needed, and the primary constituencies in the organization are managers and stockholders; customers and employees are accorded a much lower priority

Table 1.5 Comparison of Traditional and Total Quality Human Resource Management Approaches

	Traditional HRM approach	Total quality HRM approach
Philosophy	A fair day's work for a fair day's pay	Shared responsibility, commitment, rewards
Business objectives	Increased productivity, profitability; quality is secondary; focus on labor	Increased quality, productivity, customer satisfaction, employee satisfaction, and loyalty
Quality objectives	Adequate quality to remain in business; staff-driven approaches to quality improvement	Total quality management and continuous improvement at and across every level
Business information sharing	Limited to information on an as-needed basis for job performance	Open books, share broad information on profits, productivity, quality, costs, capital spending plans
Major constituencies	Managers, stockholders, customers, employees	Customers, all employees, stockholders
Employee involvement	Programs: suggestions, plans, individual employee awards; usually no formal system	Extensive within and between levels and functions; "way of life"
Education and training	On-the-job training, feedback on job performance	Quality and economic education, multiple skill training, problem solving and group process
Reward structure	Management designed and administered	Designed and adjusted by management–employee committee; formal, early union involvement
Job security	Labor as a variable cost; layoffs common during business downturns	Formal commitment a key consideration in all decisions

Source: Adapted from O'Dell, Carla, "Sharing the Productivity Payoff," reprinted from Production Brief 24 with permission of the American Productivity and Quality Center, Houston, in Werther, William B. et al. (1980). *Productivity through People.* St. Paul, Minn.: West Publishing, p. 336.

in the organization. Employee involvement programs, if they exist at all, are primarily suggestion plan approaches. Education and training are strictly job related rather than broadening the overall capacities of employees. Finally, rewards are management designed and driven by productivity requirements. Regular layoffs and plant shutdowns occur without retraining, thereby undermining job security for the average employee.

In contrast, the business objectives of the total quality HRM approach are to increase customer satisfaction and market share through improved quality and to develop a more cooperative, flexible, loyal, and innovative work environment. It is based on according preeminence to human resources in meeting customer needs with a focus on sharing information, responsibility, and rewards. Employee involvement within and between levels and functions becomes a way of life, with ongoing education and multiple skill training. Training and development resources are available to all employees. The reward structure is designed and adjusted through management and employee input, and involvement in the formation of HR policies and practices is built into the infrastructure of the organization. Job security and job transitioning become partially an organizational responsibility that HRM leaders routinely address.

Another way to perceive the total quality difference in HRM is to examine the relevant HRM areas identified by the Baldrige Award criteria to determine similarities and differences between traditional and total quality HRM approaches, as exhibited in Table 1.6.

With regard to the first HRM-related Baldrige Award criterion, both traditional and total quality approaches treat the alignment of HR planning and management with company strategy.[74] Employee selection for organization and job fit reflects the emphasis of total quality on situation or system, more than person, as a determinant of employee effectiveness.[75] As a situational approach, total quality usually stresses training, recognition, rewards, and socialization practices as context variables that override the influence of individual differences.[76] However, increasing numbers of total-quality–oriented firms are developing more selective hiring practices to determine the "whole" person/organizational fit and are considering ethical work culture compatibility.

With regard to the second HRM-related Baldrige Award criterion, certain traditional and all total quality HRM approaches indicate the importance of employee involvement and empowerment.[77] However, while the total quality approach assumes the universal applicability of involvement and empowerment, the traditional HRM approach assumes their contingency on individual growth needs, business strategy, nature of relationship with customers, technology, organizational structure and size, and organizational life cycle stage.[78]

In fact, the co-authors of this text are arguing for another contingency variable set to the use of employee empowerment, e.g., the stage of individual moral development and organizational ethical work culture development. In this respect, total quality advocates may have something to learn from traditional HRM approaches because forced participation from employees unable or unwilling to assume responsibility for cooperatively contributing to collective efforts can become counterproductive. Those individuals screened for teamwork potential in organizations with a supportive ethical work culture will benefit from involvement and empowerment activities.

On the other hand, mandatory team participation has been interpreted by some theorists as forcing employees to engage in their own exploitation, since teams can become a source of tighter, more aggressive control than hierarchy.[79] The individual, group, and organizational moral readiness to assume constructive involvement and responsible empowerment roles appears to the authors to be an important, and often overlooked, contingency variable for total quality researchers and practitioners to assess and develop.

With regard to the third HRM-related Baldrige Award criterion, both traditional and total quality approaches endorse systematic and ongoing employee education and training, as well as horizontal career development. The rationale for horizontal career development in total quality is the acquisition of a system perspective, whereas the traditional HRM rationale is expediency in the face of cohort size and widespread career plateauing.[80] Employee attitudes toward horizontal career development in the former are likely to include acceptance and anticipation; in the latter context, employees are more likely to feel disappointment and resentment.

With regard to the fourth HRM-related Baldrige Award criterion, employee performance and recognition, the traditional HRM approach has been primarily psychological in nature, with an emphasis on the meaningfulness of individual differences. The total quality approach is predicated on statistical concepts of variation and its proponents analyze performance issues by targeting system-based causes of variation.[81] *This emphasis on system rather than person is a significant difference between the two approaches in addressing work performance.*

Work performance can be viewed as the resulting outcome from the influence of four factors: (1) systematic system, (2) random system, (3) person, and (4) person/system interactions.[82] A **system** *can be defined as a network of interacting units and processes intended to realize some purpose.*[83] Systematic system factors (e.g., employees on an assembly line who use the same automated process) represent the first category, equally influence all parties, and, therefore, cannot explain variations in individual performance. Random system factors (e.g., a sales representative who is fortunate enough to be assigned to a rapidly expanding sales territory or a person who has to contend with substandard variations in raw materials

Table 1.6 Comparison of Traditional and Total Quality Human Resource Management Approaches Using Baldrige Award Criteria

HRM-related Baldrige Award criteria	Traditional HRM approach	Total quality HRM approach
1. Human resource planning and management	• Alignment with company strategy	• Alignment with company strategy
	• Employee selection for job fit	• Employee selection for organization and job fit
	• Hiring for individual knowledge, skills, and/or abilities match	• Hiring for "whole person" match
2. Employee participation	• Involvement and empowerment within a contingency framework	• Involvement and empowerment as a universalistic prescription
3. Employee development	• Endorsement of systematic, ongoing education and training	• Endorsement of systematic ongoing education and training
	• Horizontal career development as an expedient response to vertical blockage	• Horizontal career development as desirable for acquiring a total system orientation

4. Employee performance and recognition	• Assumes that person factors are the primary influence on performance • Assessment of individual differences in performance is always meaningful • Limited attention to recognition rewards • Reliance on individual-based incentive pay systems that reinforce short-term, quantity-oriented achievement of personal objectives	• Assumes that system factors are the primary influence on performance • Assessment of individual differences in performance is rarely meaningful • Heavy emphasis on recognition rewards • Reliance on team and individual pay systems that reinforce long-term, quality-oriented achievement of organizational objectives
5. Employee fulfillment	• Focus on employee work performance, rather than satisfaction, as contributing to organizational effectiveness • Assume, at best, a modest relationship between job satisfaction and work performance	• Emphasize employee satisfaction as necessary to support continuous improvement and organizational effectiveness • Assume strong correlations among job satisfaction, work performance, and organizational citizenship behavior

Source: Adapted from Dean, James W. Jr. and Bowen, David E. (1994). "Management Theory and Total Quality: Improving Research and Practice through Theory Development." *Academy of Management Review.* Vol. 19, No. 3, pp. 399–403.

in a specific department) represent the random category, affect employees differentially, and can account for variations in individual performance. Employees who are either given credit or assigned blame for performance variations due to random system causes are being mismanaged, according to the total quality perspective. In a system that is under control, the majority of workers should be delivering average, uniform performance and should be rewarded accordingly. *The responsibility of the manager is to stabilize the system and not overcontrol the person.* Person factors (e.g., personal knowledge, skills, abilities, and other characteristics) affect individual performance and are the preeminent concern of traditional HRM approaches.[84] Personal performance appraisal, person/job match, and stratified compensation policies are the traditional HRM recommendations. Total quality proponents argue that reliance on individual-based appraisal and incentive pay systems reinforces short-term, quantity-oriented achievement of personal objectives, to the detriment of organizational effectiveness. In fact, leading-edge traditional HRM researchers are insisting that effective HRM programs need to focus more on organizational rather than job analysis.[85] Finally, person/system interaction factors (e.g., some persons perform better in routine processes with autocratic management, others respond better to teamwork with participatory management, and still others prefer to use their autonomy and hierarchy status to change systems) may cause personal performance differences, even if the system itself is invariant.[86]

One result of this work performance analysis is to highlight and pinpoint a significant difference between traditional HRM and total quality approaches. The organizational system emphasis is being carried through in the selection and retention of employees at total quality management firms. Personal characteristics such as flexibility, reliability, persistence, conscientious attention to detail, the desire to learn and solve problems, team orientation, and collectivist values typify individuals who successfully adjust to total quality management organizations; others are turnover candidates.[87] Personal congruence with the values, norms, and moral behavior expected of the total quality ethical work culture is becoming a selection and retention factor in total quality firms. Celebrating total quality team successes with recognition rituals reinforces organizational solidarity more than in a traditional HRM work environment.

With regard to the fifth HRM-related Baldrige Award criterion, traditional HRM approaches focus on employee work performance and assume, at best, that only a modest relationship, if any, exists between job satisfaction and work performance.[88] **Work performance** can be defined as behavior associated with the accomplishment of expected, specified, or formal role requirements on the part of individual organizational members.[89] Work performance is normally distinguished from **organizational citizenship**

behavior (OCB), which is viewed as discretionary behavior not formally recognized by organizational reward systems and more geared toward enhancing group commitment and organizational effectiveness.[90] In the total quality context, however, work performance and OCB (e.g., taking on improvement initiatives above and beyond the call of duty and sustained teamwork collaboration) are both expected of employees in order to promote continuous improvement of teams and the organization. This supererogatory effort can only be sustained if employee fulfillment and job satisfaction are accorded a high priority.

A more detailed treatment of the difference total quality makes for HR professionals is provided in Chapters 2 to 5. It is important to recognize, however, that "changes in corporate culture come slowly, and even managers who have adopted the TQM philosophy do not necessarily have the power to move their organization and its systems overnight."[91] HR professionals, therefore, need to be aware of the barriers to total quality HRM.

BARRIERS AND RESPONSES TO TOTAL QUALITY HUMAN RESOURCE MANAGEMENT IMPLEMENTATION

It is important for HR professionals to realize that pitfalls to total quality practices exist but can be overcome. Successful total quality efforts recognize cultural change as a continuous, long-term process, with initial concentrations of support investments required for at least three to five years. Some factors may make it difficult to successfully carry out these efforts in organizations, but the total quality subsystems (management, social, technical, and educational) can address each barrier.

1. Strategic Barrier #1 and the Management System Response. Differences over strategic priorities is often a major corporate barrier. If managers risk losing power and perks or investors risk losing financial returns in the short run, expect direct opposition to quality strategic priorities for customer satisfaction and increased market share. The intense North American emphasis on short-term financial returns is probably the most potent deterrent to long-term total quality progress. The former strategic priorities can be absorbed by HR departments, and quality resistance can be solidified at the functional level as well. The management system addresses this issue by adequate strategic planning, as discussed in Chapter 2.

2. Strategic Barrier #2 and the Educational System Response. Resistance to the HRM/senior management strategic partnership from either side can become a barrier to effective implementation of total quality. Active involvement of senior leadership and the strategic co-partnership of HR professionals will be necessary to change the House of Compliance into the

House of Total Quality. To this end, it is imperative that HR professionals strengthen and expand their core business acumen. Building some practical line experience with bottom-line accountability into their career paths will help HR professionals close the credibility gap they suffer in the eyes of many business executives. The educational system addresses this issue by adequate strategic and operations planning for senior and functional-level managers, as alluded to in Chapters 2 and 3.

3. Cultural Barrier #1 and the Social System Response. An underdeveloped organizational ethical work culture that supports either the House of Manipulation or the House of Compliance will criticize the House of Total Quality as being too idealistic, overly optimistic, or naive at face value and question the motives for initiating the change. The path toward ethical work culture maturity is a long one but worth the effort of HR professionals. The social system addresses this issue by adequate ethical work culture assessment and development, as alluded to in Chapters 2 to 5.

4. Cultural Barrier #2 and the Social System Response. Unrealistic social expectations can be created by trying too much improvement at once and feeling frustrated when these unrealistic expectations are unmet. The social system addresses this issue by realistic strategy planning as discussed in Chapter 2, incremental process improvement as discussed in Chapter 3, and participative incremental project planning as discussed in Chapter 4.

5. Specialization Barrier #1 and the Educational System Response. HR specialists who focus on staffing, compensation and benefits, training and development, or other specialties may resist the expansion of role responsibilities beyond these narrow technical areas. Specialization accords professional status to many individuals in the HR field, and relinquishing some of these duties to line managers and employees and learning new skills is psychologically uncomfortable. In some firms, however, HR professionals need to change or be marginalized. The educational system addresses this issue by providing training and development for HR professionals to prepare them for confidently assuming new responsibilities, as discussed in Chapter 5.

6. Specialization Barrier #2 and the Social System Response. Some HR specialists will claim that continuous improvement and participation already exist, so there is no need to change. Granted there are ongoing professional development, collegial relations, and professional codes to sustain specialization improvement, but organization-wide, cross-functional system improvement rarely exists. Functional myopia can be cured with total quality management of human resources. The social system addresses this issue through broadened role expectations and reward systems, as treated in Chapter 3.

7. Structural Barrier #1 and the Management System Response. Intensive divisionalization encourages identification with groups, departments, or subdivisions rather than the total institution. Total quality emphasizes inter-departmental, interdisciplinary, and system-wide collaboration on problem solving and project completion. HR professionals face the same resistance to matrix structures. The management system addresses this issue of cross-functional integration, as discussed in the operations planning section of Chapter 3.

8. Structural Barrier #2 and the Management System Response. Hierarchy inertia is likely to exercise benign or not-so-benign neglect to total quality since it advocates a pancake-style rather than a pyramid-style structure. Persons who have hierarchical power are likely to resist total quality initiatives because they will likely entail loss of power and authority. HR professionals who support quality, however, cannot prevent the inevitable drift toward flatter organizations that are technically linked. The management system addresses this issue of facilitating horizontal structures and process, as discussed in the operations planning section of Chapter 3.

9. Structural Barrier #3 and the Management System Response. The compensation system in most organizations is geared toward individual performance, and the lack of widespread gainsharing, profit sharing, and group rewards provides a convenient excuse for HR professionals not to adopt an advocacy role in changing the system to build a quality work culture. The management system addresses this issue by restructuring the reward system to include a wide range of group reward policies, as treated in Chapter 3.

10. Linguistic Barrier #1 and the Educational System Response. By encouraging standardization and minimizing variation, the language of statistical process control generates aversion from individuals geared toward innovation and creativity. It seems to require limits on individual freedom. In total quality improvement, however, positive variations within desired outcomes are encouraged so that creativity is not squelched but unacceptable variation is controlled. The educational system addresses this issue on creativity and self-discipline, as covered in Chapter 5.

11. Linguistic Barrier #2 and the Educational System Response. Managing quality control often generates linguistic opposition because it seems to imply intrusive limits on personal work style. In total quality improvement, however, the emphasis is on identifying and doing whatever is necessary to achieve what the members want the organization to do rather than what top management orders them to do. The educational system addresses this issue by increasing awareness of the expanded freedom that proper quality processes provide, as discussed in Chapter 5.

12. Operational Barriers and the Technical System Response. HR professionals can claim that there is insufficient time to do their jobs and work on job improvement, but that is the total quality operational challenge—to simultaneously do the job and improve the way the job is done. Once HR managers learn the technical skills in thinking statistically, however, they save time because they stop treating all variation as if it were due to special causes and therefore stop overreacting. By focusing on the vital few improvements possible in an organization, the technical system can address this issue, as covered in Chapter 4.

13. Attitudinal Barriers and the Educational System Response. Employees may regard total quality as a passing fad which won't work and which focuses attention on internal processes rather than external results.[92] The educational system addresses this issue by pointing to specific benefits of total quality implementation, as discussed in Chapter 6: labor–management partnerships are enhanced, operating procedures improved, customer satisfaction increased, and financial performance strengthened.

In short, the potential for change exists, and the degree of change required is dependent upon the balance of forces that drive and resist the principles of total quality improvement. The resistant forces may be so severe that a radical transformation may be required. The intent of this book is to help sensitize all managers of human resources and specifically HR professionals to these issues in order to realistically and constructively develop world-class competitive work cultures.

REVIEW QUESTIONS

1.1. What are the six driving forces that are reshaping the human resource environment of the future?

1.2. What are eight distinct approaches to human resource management that have emerged in the United States since the late 1800s?

1.3. What is the House of Total Quality? How might it be a useful model for human resource practitioners?

1.4. What are the six essential components of the House of Total Quality? Why is each one important to the strength and solidity of the overall structure?

1.5. How would you characterize each of the six stages of ethical work culture development and their relationship to the realization of a total quality environment?

1.6. What are the ten components of a total quality ethical work culture?

1.7. What are eight differences between the traditional and total quality approaches to human resource management?

1.8. What are six strategic barriers to successful implementation of total quality? How can the total quality subsystems effectively address each one?

DISCUSSION QUESTIONS

1.1. Do you agree with Konosuke Matsushita's assertion that Japan will win the economic "war" against the U.S. because of its differing view of good management and human resource practices? Why or why not?

1.2. What challenges or opportunities has the changing nature and diversity of the work force presented to you personally? How have you addressed those challenges or opportunities and what insights have you gained from your experience?

1.3. Compare and contrast managerial, financial, and stakeholder capitalism. Identify actual examples of each in U.S. or international business.

1.4. Elaborate on your experiences if you have worked in an ethical work culture that supports the House of Manipulation, the House of Compliance, and/or the House of Total Quality.

1.5. Why do you agree or disagree with the claim that the total quality approach to human resource management is another form of worker exploitation?

ENDNOTES

1. Lewis, Ralph G. and Smith, Douglas H. (1994). *Total Quality in Higher Education.* Delray Beach, Fla.: St. Lucie Press; Champy, James (1995). *Reengineering Management: The Mandate for New Leadership.* New York: Harper Business.

2. Johnston, William (1991). "Global Workforce 2000: The New World Labor Market." *Harvard Business Review.* March–April, pp. 115–127.

3. Evans, James R. and Lindsay, William M. (1995). *The Management and Control of Quality.* 3rd edition, Minneapolis: West Publishing, p. 281; Bounds, Gregory M., Dobbins, Gregory H., and Fowler, Oscar (1995). *Management: A Total Quality Perspective.* Cincinnati: South-Western, pp. 308–345.

4. Cited in Shores, A. Richard (1990). *A TQM Approach to Achieving Manufacturing Excellence.* Milwaukee: ASQC Quality Press, p. 270.

5. Prestowitz, C.V. (1990). *Trading Places: How We Allowed Japan to Take the Lead.* New York: Harper Collins; Thurow, Lester (1992). *Head to Head: The Coming Economic Battle Among Japan, Europe and America.* New York: William Morrow and Company.

6. Fingleton, E. (1995). *Blindside: Why Japan Is Still on Track to Overtake the U.S. by the Year 2000.* Boston: Houghton Mifflin; Stewart, Thomas A. (1991). "Brainpower." *Fortune.* June 3, pp. 44–60.

7. Stahl, M.J. and Bounds, G.M., Eds. (1991). *Competing Globally through Customer Value: The Management of Strategic Suprasystems.* Westport, Conn.: Quorum Books; Whiteley, R.C. (1991). *The Customer-Driven Company: Moving from Talk to Action.* New York: Addison-Wesley; Lele, M.M. and Sheth, J.N. (1987). *The Customer Is Key: Gaining an Unbeatable Advantage through Customer Satisfaction.* New York: John Wiley & Sons; Greene, Richard Tabor (1993). *Global Quality: A Synthesis of the World's Best Management Methods.* Greenwich, Conn.: Quorum Books.

8. Yoshida, Kosaku (1992). "New Economic Principles in America—Competition and Cooperation: A Comparative Study of the U.S. and Japan." *Columbia Journal of World Business.* Vol. 26, No. 4, pp. 2–15; Ishihara, S. (1991). *The Japan That Can Say No: Why Japan Will Be First Among Equals.* New York: Simon & Schuster, pp. 95–105.

9. Ishikawa, K. and Lu, D. (1985). *What Is Total Quality Control?* Englewood Cliffs, N.J.: Prentice-Hall, pp. 45–46.

10. Spechler, J.W. (1988). *When America Does It Right: Case Studies in Service Quality.* Norcross, Ga.: Industrial Engineering and Management Press.

11. Bounds, G.M. and Pace, L.A. (1991). "Human Resource Management for Competitive Capability." In M.J. Stahl and G.M. Bounds, Eds. *Competing Globally through Customer Value: The Management of Strategic Suprasystems.* New York: Quorum Books, pp. 95–112.

12. Reich, Robert B. (1991). *The Work of Nations: Preparing Ourselves for 21st Century Capitalism.* New York: Vintage Books, pp. 171–242.

13. Keeley, Michael (1988). *A Social Contract Theory of Organizations*. Notre Dame, Ind.: University of Notre Dame Press, pp. 15–45.

14. Stewart, Thomas A. (1993). "Welcome to the Revolution." *Fortune*. December 13, pp. 68–70.

15. Rosenbluth, Hal F. and Peters, D.M. (1992). *The Customer Comes Second: And Other Secrets of Exceptional Service*. New York: William Morrow, pp. 14–15.

16. Cascio, Wayne F. (1987). *Costing Human Resources: The Financial Impact of Behavior in Organizations*. Boston: PWS-Kent, pp. 2–10; McCaffery, Robert M. (1988). *Employee Benefit Programs: A Total Compensation Perspective*. Boston: PWS-Kent, pp. 6–12.

17. Jamieson, David and O'Mara, Julie (1991). *Managing Workforce 2000: Gaining the Diversity Advantage*. San Francisco: Jossey-Bass; Fernandez, John (1991). *Managing a Diverse Workforce*. New York: Free Press, pp. 15–90; Fernandez, J. and Bass, M. (1993). *The Diversity Advantage*. Lexington, Mass.: Heath and Company, pp. 10–70.

18. Marquardt, Michael and Reynolds, Angus (1994). *The Global Learning Organization*. Burr Ridge, Ill.: Irwin, pp. 16–18.

19. Jamieson, David and O'Mara, Julie (1991). *Managing Workforce 2000: Gaining the Diversity Advantage*. San Francisco: Jossey-Bass, pp. 160–170.

20. Wriston, Walter (1992). *The Twilight of Sovereignty: How the Information Revolution Is Transforming the World*. New York: Charles Scribner & Sons, pp. 50–70.

21. Wriston, Walter (1992). *The Twilight of Sovereignty: How the Information Revolution Is Transforming the World*. New York: Charles Scribner & Sons, p. 75.

22. Lengnick-Hall, Cynthia A. and Lengnick-Hall, Mark L. (1988). "Strategic Human Resources Management: A Review of the Literature and a Proposed Typology." *Academy of Management Review*. Vol. 13, No. 3, pp. 454–470.

23. Schuler, Randall S. and Harris, Drew L. (1992). *Managing Quality*. Reading, Mass,: Macmillan, pp. 25–53; Schuler, R.S. (1990). "Repositioning the Human Resource Function: Transformation or Demise?" *Academy of Management Executive*. Vol. 14, No. 3, pp. 49–60.

24. Jones, Alan and Hendry, Chris (1992). *The Learning Organization*. Coventry, U.K.: HRD Partnership, pp. 10–60; Dixon, Nancy (1992). "Organizational Learning: A Review of the Literature with Implications for HRD Professionals." *Human Resource Development Quarterly*. Vol. 3, No. 1, pp. 29–49; Senge, Peter (1990). "The Leader's New Work: Building Learning Organizations." *Sloan Management Review*. Vol. 32, No. 1, pp. 7–23.

25. Harrington, John (1991). *The Virtual Organization and Information Technology*. Englewood Cliffs, N.J.: Prentice-Hall, pp. 12–65; Rheingold, D. (1994). *The Virtual Community*. New York: Harper Collins, pp. 10–50; Davidow, William H. and Malone, Michael S. (1992). *The Virtual Corporation*. New York: Harper Business, pp. 1–72.

26. Handy, Charles (1989). *The Age of Unreason*. London: Basic Books, pp. 40–70.
27. Hammer, Michael and Champy, James (1993). *Reengineering the Corporation*. New York: Harper, pp. 10–39.
28. Sturner, William F. (1993). *Impact: Transforming Your Organization*. Buffalo, N.Y.: Creative Education Foundation; Fletcher, Beverly R. (1990). *Organization Transformation: Theorists and Practitioners*. Westport, Conn.: Greenwood Publishing Group; Jaccaci, August (1989). "The Social Architecture of a Learning Organization." *Training and Development Journal*. Vol. 43, No. 11, pp. 49–51.
29. National Geographic Society Research Group (1975). *The Craftsman in America*. Washington, D.C.: The National Geographic Society, pp. 164–166.
30. Skinner, Wickham (1981). "Big Hat—No Cattle: Managing Human Resources." *Harvard Business Review*. September–October, p. 109.
31. Singer, Marc G. (1990). *Human Resource Management*. Boston: PWS-Kent, pp. 5–7.
32. Roethlesberger, F.J. and Dickson, W.J. (1939). *Management and the Worker*. Cambridge, Mass.: Harvard University Press, pp. 20–80.
33. Maslow, Abraham (1954). *Motivational Personality*. New York: Harper and Row; Herzberg, F., Mausner, B., and Snyderman, B. (1959). *The Motivation to Work*. 2nd edition, New York: John Wiley & Sons; McGregor, Douglas (1960). *The Human Side of Enterprise*. New York: McGraw-Hill; Porter, Lyman W. and Lawler, Edward E. (1968). *Managerial Attitudes and Performance*. Homewood, Ill.: Irwin; Vroom, V.H. (1964). *Work and Motivation*. New York: John Wiley.
34. Vroom, V.H. (1964). *Work and Motivation*. New York: John Wiley, pp. 55–71; Porter, L.W. and Lawler, E.E. (1968). *Managerial Attitudes and Performance*. Homewood, Ill.: Irwin, pp. 107–139.
35. Singer, Marc G. (1990). *Human Resource Management*. Boston: PWS-Kent, pp. 11–14.
36. Skinner, B.F. (1953). *Science and Human Behavior*. New York: Free Press.
37. Skinner, B.F. (1971). *Beyond Freedom and Dignity*. New York: Bantam Books.
38. Blanchard, Kenneth and Johnson, Spencer (1982). *The One-Minute Manager*. New York: Avon.
39. Hackman, J. Richard and Oldham, Greg R. (1980). *Work Redesign*. Reading, Mass.: Addison-Wesley.
40. Evans, James R. and Lindsay, William M. (1995). *The Management and Control of Quality*. 3rd edition, Minneapolis: West Publishing, p. 299.
41. Trist, Eric L. and Bamforth, K.W. (1951). "Some Social and Psychological Consequences of the Lingwall Method of Goal-Setting." *Human Relations*. Vol. 4, No. 2, pp. 3–38; Katzenbach, Jon R. and Smith, Douglas K. (1993). *The Wisdom of Teams*. Boston: Harvard Business School Press, pp. 85–175.
42. Adapted from Ernery, Fred and Thorsrud, Einar (1976). *Democracy at Work: The Report of the Norwegian Industrial Democracy Program*. Leirden,

Netherlands: H.E. Stenfort Kroese, pp. 14–15; Vogt, Judith and Murrell, Kenneth (1993). *Empowerment in Organizations*. San Diego: Pfeiffer and Company; Lawler, Edward E. III (1992). *The Ultimate Advantage: Creating High-Involvement Organizations*. San Francisco: Jossey-Bass, pp. 51–172.

43. Katzenbach, Jon R. and Smith, Douglas K. (1993). *The Wisdom of Teams*. Boston: Harvard Business School Press, pp. 1–19; Orsburn, Jack D., Moran, Linda, Musselwhite, Ed, and Zenger, John H. (1990). *Self-Directed Work Teams*. Homewood, Ill.: Irwin, pp. 3–170.

44. Bounds, Gregory M. and Pace, Larry A. (1991). "Human Resource Management for Competitive Capability." In Michael J. Stahl and Gregory M. Bounds, Eds. *Competing Globally through Customer Value*. Westport, Conn.: Quorum Books, pp. 648–682.

45. Kanter, Rosabeth Moss, Stein, Barry A., and Jick, Todd D. (1992). *The Challenge of Organizational Change*. New York: Free Press; Kochan, Thomas A. and Useem, Michael, Eds. (1992). *Transforming Organizations*. New York: Oxford University Press; Nadler, David A., Gerstein, Marc S., and Shaw, Robert B. (1992). *Organizational Architecture*. San Francisco: Jossey-Bass; Mintzberg, Henry (1989). *Mintzberg on Management*. New York: Free Press.

46. Schuler, Randall S. and Jackson, Susan E. (1987). "Linking Competitive Strategies with Human Resource Management Practice." *Academy of Management Executive*. Vol. 1, No. 3, pp. 207–219.

47. Shenkar, Oded (1995). *Global Perspectives of Human Resource Management*. Englewood Cliffs, N.J.: Prentice-Hall, pp. 1–15; Marquardt, M.J. and Engel, D.W. (1993). *Global Human Resource Development*. Englewood Cliffs, N.J.: Prentice-Hall, pp. 11–90.

48. Emery, Fred E. and Trist, Eric (1973). *Towards a Social Ecology*. London: Plenum Publishers.

49. Yukl, Gary A. (1994). *Leadership in Organizations*. 3rd edition, Englewood Cliffs, N.J.: Prentice-Hall, pp. 120–190.

50. Watson, Gregory H. (1993). *Strategic Benchmarking*. New York: John Wiley & Sons.

51. Burke, W. Warner (1994). *Organizational Development: A Process of Learning and Changing*. 2nd edition, Reading, Mass.: Addison-Wesley; Pedler, Mike, Burogoyne, John, and Boydell, Tom (1991). *The Learning Company: A Strategy for Sustainable Development*. London: McGraw-Hill; Howard, Robert (1990). *The Learning Imperative: Managing People for Continuous Innovation*. Boston: Harvard Business Review Books; Senge, Peter M. (1990). *The Fifth Discipline*. New York: Doubleday.

52. Singer, Marc G. (1990). *Human Resource Management*. Boston: PWS-Kent, p. 3.

53. Rampey, J. and Roberts, H. (1992). "Perspectives in Total Quality." In *Proceedings of Total Quality Forum IV*. Cincinnati, November.

54. Voehl, Frank (1992). *The House of Total Quality*. Coral Springs, Fla.: Strategy Associates, p. 17.

55. Evans, James R. and Lindsay, William M. (1995). *The Management and Control of Quality*. 3rd edition, Minneapolis: West Publishing, pp. 170–171.

56. Zimmerman, Charles D. and Enell, John W. (1988). "Service Industries: Section 33." In J.M. Juran, Ed. *Juran's Quality Control Handbook*. 4th edition, New York: McGraw-Hill, pp. 47–53.

57. Schein, Edgar H. (1988). *Organizational Culture and Leadership*. San Francisco: Jossey-Bass, pp. 1–136.

58. Schein, Edgar H. (1988). *Organizational Culture and Leadership*. San Francisco: Jossey-Bass, p. 9.

59. Schein, Edgar H. (1988). *Organizational Culture and Leadership*. San Francisco: Jossey-Bass, p. 14.

60. Trice, Harrison M. and Beyer, Janice M. (1993). *The Cultures of Work Organizations*. Englewood Cliffs, N.J.: Prentice-Hall, p. 18.

61. Wilkins, Alan and Dyer, Jr., W. Gibb (1988). "Toward Culturally Sensitive Theories of Culture Change." *Academy of Management Review*. Vol. 13, No. 4, pp. 522–533; Wilkins, Alan (1989). *Developing Corporate Character: How to Successfully Change an Organization without Destroying It*. San Francisco: Jossey-Bass; Trice, Harrison M. and Morand, David (1991). "Cultural Diversity: Organizational Subcultures and Countercultures." In Gale Miller, Ed. *Studies in Organizational Sociology*. Vol. 10, Greenwich, Conn.: JAI Press, pp. 69–105. See also the following references cited in column 3 of Table 1.2: Ouchi, W.G. and Jaeger, A.M. (1978). "Type Z Organization: Stability in the Midst of Mobility." *Academy of Management Review*. Vol. 16, No. 3, pp. 305–313; Ouchi, W. (1981). *Theory Z: How American Business Can Meet the Japanese Challenge*. Reading, Mass.: Addison-Wesley; Deal, T.E. and Kennedy, A.A. (1982). *Corporate Cultures*. Reading, Mass.: Addison-Wesley; Mitroff, I. and Kilmann, R.H. (1975). "Stories Managers Tell: A New Tool for Organizational Problem Solving." *Management Review*. Vol. 17, No. 7, pp. 18–28; Sethia, N.K. and Von Glinow, M.A. (1985). "Arriving at Four Cultures by Managing the Reward Sytstem." In R.H. Kilmann et al., Eds. *Gaining Control of the Corporate Culture*. San Francisco: Jossey-Bass, pp. 400–420; Kets de Vries, M.F. and Miller D. (1984). *The Neurotic Organization*. San Francisco: Jossey Bass; Victor, B. and Cullen, J. (1988). "The Organizational Bases of Ethical Work Climates." *Administrative Science Quarterly*. Vol. 33, No. 4, pp. 101–125; Cooke, Robert A. and Szumal, Janet L. (1993). "Measuring Normative Beliefs and Shared Behavioral Expectations in Organizations: The Reliability and Validity of the Organizational Culture Inventory." *Psychological Reports*. Vol. 72, No. 3, pp. 1299–1330.

62. Kohlberg, Lawrence (1981). *The Philosophy of Moral Development*. San Francisco: Harper and Row. This model can incorporate the five-stage model proposed by Reidenback, R.E. and Robin, D.P. (1991). "A Conceptual Model of Corporate Moral Development." *Journal of Business Ethics*. Vol. 10, No. 4, p. 274; Rest, James R. and Narvaez, Garcia F., Eds. (1994). *Moral Development in the Professions: Psychology and Applied Ethics*. New York: Lawrence Erlbaum Associates, pp. 20–82.

63. Gilligan, Carol (1982). *In a Different Voice*. Cambridge, Mass.: Harvard University Press.

64. Petrick, Joseph A. And Manning, George E. (1990). "Developing an Ethical Climate for Excellence." *The Journal for Quality and Participation*. Vol. 14, No. 2, pp. 85–87.

65. Petrick, Joseph A. and Pullins, Ellen Bohman (1992). "Organizational Ethics Development and the Expanding Role of the Human Resource Professional." *The Healthcare Supervisor*. Vol. 2, No. 2, pp. 52–61; Jacob, Rahul (1995). "Corporate Reputations." *Fortune*. Vol. 131, No. 4, pp. 54–64.

66. Evans, W. and Freeman, E. (1988). "A Stakeholder Theory of the Modern Corporation: Kantian Capitalism." In T. Beauchamp. and N. Bowie, Eds. *Ethical Theory and Business*. Englewood Cliffs, N.J.: Prentice-Hall, pp. 112–130; Drucker, Peter (1993). *Post-Capitalist Society*. New York: Free Press, pp. 15–60.

67. Dunfee, Thomas and Gibson, F. (1993). *Modern Business Law*. New York: McGraw-Hill, pp. 90–95.

68. Goodpaster, K.E. (1991). "Business Ethics and Stakeholder Analysis." *Business Ethics Quarterly*. Vol. 14, No. 1, pp. 24–37; Petrick, Joseph A. and Wagley, Robert A. (1992). "Enhancing the Responsible Strategic Management of Organizations." *Journal of Management Development*. Vol. 11, No. 4, pp. 57–72.

69. Sheppard, Blair H., Lewicki, Roy J., and Minton, John W. (1992). *Organizational Justice: The Search for Fairness in the Workplace*. New York: Lexington Books, pp. 9–108.

70. Gilligan, Carol (1982). *In a Different Voice*. Cambridge, Mass.: Harvard University Press, pp. 24–63.

71. Etzioni, Amitai (1992). *The Moral Dimension*. New York: Oxford Books, pp. 5–10; Waterman, J.R. (1994). *What America Does Right*. New York: W.W. Norton. Waterman even states: "Corporate cultures that tend to put their three constituencies—shareholders, customers, and employees— on the same plane, as opposed to putting shareholders first, are perversely the ones that do best for shareholders" (p. 57).

72. Paine, Lynn S. (1994). "Managing for Organizational Integrity." *Harvard Business Review*. March–April, pp. 110–111; Fiorelli, Paul E. (1992). "Fine Reductions through Effective Ethics Programs." *Albany Law Review*. Vol. 56, No. 2, pp. 403–440.

73. To obtain lists of reputable organizational ethics consultants, contact Organizational Ethics Associates in Cincinnati, Ohio (513-984-2820) or The Center for Business Ethics in Waltham, Massachusetts (617-891-2000).

74. Wright, P.M. and McMahan, G.C. (1992). "Theoretical Perspectives for Strategic Human Resource Management." *Journal of Management*. Vol. 18, pp. 295–320.

75. Bowen, D.E., Ledford, G.E., and Nathan, B.N. (1991). "Hiring for the Organization, Not the Job." *Academy of Management Executive*. Vol. 5, No. 4, pp. 35–51; Dobbins, G.H., Cardy, R.L., and Carson, K. P. (1991). "Exam-

ining Fundamental Assumptions: A Contrast of Person and System Approaches to Human Resources Management." In G. Ferris, Ed. *Research in Personnel and Human Resource Management*. Vol. 4, Greenwich, Conn.: JAI Press, pp. 1–38.

76. Chatman, J.A. (1989). "Improving Interactional Organizational Research: A Model of Person–Organization Fit." *Academy of Management Review*. Vol. 14, pp. 333–349.

77. Conger, J.A. and Kanungo, R. (1988). "The Empowerment Process: Integrating Theory and Practice." *Academy of Management Review*. Vol. 13, pp. 471–482; Thomas, K.W. and Velthouse, B.A. (1990). "Cognitive Elements of Empowerment: An Interpretive Model of Intrinsic Task Motivation." *Academy of Management Review*. Vol. 15, pp. 666–681.

78. Bowen, D.E. and Lawler, E.E. III. (1992). "Total Quality-Oriented Human Resources Management." *Organizational Dynamics*. Spring, pp. 29–41; Lawler, E.E. III. (1988). "Choosing an Involvement Strategy." *Academy of Management Executive*, Vol. 2, pp. 197–204; Guzzo, R.A. and Salas, E., Eds. (1994). *Team Decision Making Effectiveness in Organizations*. San Francisco: Jossey-Bass.

79. McArdle, L., Rowlinson, M., Proctor, S., Hassard, J., and Forrester, P. (1994). "Employee Empowerment or the Enhancement of Exploitation." In A. Wilkinson and H. Willmott, Eds. *Making Quality Critical*. London: Routledge, pp. 110–124; Spencer, B.A. (1994). "Models of Organization and Total Quality Management: A Comparison and Critical Evaluation. "*Academy of Management Review*. Vol. 19, No. 3, pp. 446–471.

80. Bowen, D.E. and Lawler, E.E. III. (1992). "Total Quality-Oriented Human Resources Management." *Organizational Dynamics*. Spring, pp. 34–36; Hall, D.T. and Richter, J. (1990). "Career Gridlock: Baby Boomers Hit the Wall." *Academy of Management Executive*, Vol. 4, No. 3, pp. 7–22.

81. Waldman, David A. (1994). "The Contributions of Total Quality Management to a Theory of Work Performance." *Academy of Management Review*. Vol. 19, No. 3, pp. 510–536; Deming, W.E. (1986). *Out of the Crisis*. Cambridge, Mass.: MIT Press; Sashkin, M. and Kiser, K.J. (1993). *Total Quality Management*. San Francisco: Berett-Koehler, pp. 15–90.

82. Dobbins, G.H., Cardy, R.L., and Carson, K.P. (1991). "Examining Fundamental Assumptions: A Contrast of Person and System Approaches to Human Resources Management." In G. Ferris, Ed. *Research in Personnel and Human Resource Management*. Vol. 4, Greenwich, Conn.: JAI Press, pp. 2–20; Waldman, David A. (1994). "The Contributions of Total Quality Management to a Theory of Work Performance." *Academy of Management Review*. Vol. 19, No. 3, pp. 516–518.

83. Ashforth, B.E. (1992). "The Perceived Inequity of Systems." *Administration and Society*, Vol. 24, pp. 375–408; Blumberg, M. and Pringle, C.C. (1982). "The Missing Opportunity in Organizational Research: Some Implications for a Theory of Work Performance." *Academy of Management Review*. Vol. 7, pp. 560–569.

84. Heneman, Herbert G. III and Heneman, Robert L. (1994). *Staffing Organizations*. Homewood, Ill.: Austen Press-Irwin; Campbell, J. P. (1990). "Modeling the Performance Prediction Problem in Industrial and Organizational Psychology." In M.D. Dunette and L.M. Hough, Eds. *Handbook of Industrial and Organizational Psychology*. 2nd edition, Vol. 1, Palo Alto, Calif.: Consulting Psychologists Press, pp. 687–732.

85. Jackson, Susan E. and Schuler, Randall S. (1995). "Understanding Human Resource Management in the Context of Organizations and Their Environments." *Annual Review of Psychology*. In press.

86. Chatman, J.A. (1989). "Improving Interactional Organizational Research: A Model of Person–Organization Fit." *Academy of Management Review*. Vol. 14, pp. 333–349.

87. Dobbins, G.H., Cardy, R.L., and Carson, K.P. (1993). "Total Quality Management and Work Characteristics: Behavior and Personality Measures." Paper presented at the Annual Meeting of the Academy of Management, Atlanta; Moorman, R.H. and Blakely, G.L. (1993). "Individualism–Collectivism as an Individual Difference Predictor of Organizational Citizenship Behavior." Paper presented at the Annual Meeting of the Academy of Management, Atlanta; Hayes, T.L., Roehm, H.L., and Castellano, J. (1994). "Personality Correlates of Success in Total Quality Manufacturing." *Journal of Business and Psychology*. Vol. 8, No. 4, pp. 397–410.

88. Iaffaldano, M.T. and Muchinsky, P.M. (1985). "Job Satisfaction and Job Performance: A Meta-Analysis." *Psychological Bulletin*. Vol. 97, pp. 251–273.

89. Campbell, J.P. (1990). "Modeling the Performance Prediction Problem in Industrial and Organizational Psychology." In M.D. Dunette and L.M. Hough, Eds. *Handbook of Industrial and Organizational Psychology*. 2nd edition, Vol. 1, Palo Alto, Calif.: Consulting Psychologists Press, p. 689.

90. Organ, D.W. (1988). *Organizational Citizenship Behavior: The Good Soldier Syndrome*. Lexington, Mass.: Lexington Books; Van Dyne, L., Graham, J.W. and Dienesch, R.N. (1994). "Organizational Citizenship Behavior: Construct Redefinition, Measurement and Validation." *Academy of Management Journal*. Vol. 37, No. 4, pp. 765–802.

91. Evans, James R. and Lindsay, William M. (1995). *The Management and Control of Quality*. 3rd edition, Minneapolis: West Publishing, p. 289.

92. Harari, Oreu (1993). "Ten Reasons Why TQM Doesn't Work." *Management Review*. Vol. 28, No. 1, pp. 33–38; see also the articles by Selwyn W. Beckerland Oreu Harari in *Management Review* (May 1993, pp. 30–36).

APPENDIX

ABSTRACT 1.1
THEORETICAL MODEL OF TOTAL QUALITY MANAGEMENT

Anderson, John C., Rungtusanatham, Manus, and Schroeder, Roger G. (1994). *Academy of Management Review.* Vol. 19, No. 3, pp. 472–509

The theoretical essence of the Deming management method uncovers the creation of an organizational system that fosters cooperation and learning to facilitate the implementation of process management practices. This, in turn, leads to continuous improvement of processes, products, and services and to employee fulfillment, both of which are critical to customer satisfaction and, ultimately, survival. The relational diagram of the theoretical model and the key conceptual definitions that underlie the method are treated in this article.

The relational diagram of the theory of total quality management underlying the Deming management method is illustrated as follows:

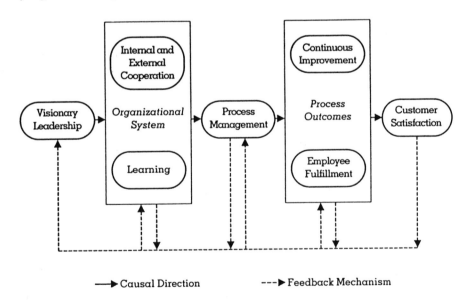

The key concepts underlying the Deming management method are as follow.

Visionary leadership is the ability of management to establish, practice, and lead a long-term vision for the organization, driven by changing customer requirements, as opposed to internal management control role. It is exemplified by clarity of vision, long-range orientation, a coaching management style, participative change, employee empowerment, and planning and implementing organizational change.

Internal and external cooperation is the propensity of the organization to engage in noncompetitive activities internally among employees and externally with respect to suppliers. It is exemplified by firm–supplier partnership, single-supplier orientation, collaborative organization, teamwork, organization-wide involvement, systems view of the organization, trust, and elimination of fear.

Learning is the organizational capability to recognize and nurture the development of skills, abilities, and knowledge base. It is exemplified by company-wide training, foundational knowledge, process knowledge, educational development, continuous self-improvement, and managerial learning.

Process management is the set of methodological and behavioral practices that emphasize the management of process, or means of actions, rather than results. It is exemplified by management of processes, prevention orientation, reduction of mass inspection, design quality, statistical process control, understanding variation, elimination of numerical quotas, elimination of management by objectives, elimination of merit-rating reward systems, understanding motivation, total cost accounting, and stable employment.

Continuous improvement is the propensity of an organization to pursue incremental and innovative improvements of its processes, products, and services. It is exemplified by continuous improvement.

Employee fulfillment is the degree to which employees of an organization feel that the organization continually satisfies their needs. It is exemplified by job satisfaction, job commitment, and pride of workmanship.

Customer satisfaction is the degree to which an organization's customers continually perceive that their needs are being met by the organization's products and services. It is exemplified by customer-driven focus.

ABSTRACT 1.2
NATURE AND SCOPE OF TOTAL QUALITY

Dean, James W. Jr. and Evans, James R. (1994). *Total Quality: Management, Organization, and Strategy.* Minneapolis: West Publishing, pp. 7–10

Most progressive organizations now define quality as meeting or exceeding customer expectations. The phrase *total customer satisfaction* is used to incorporate both meeting and exceeding customer expectations over time.

Quality, when defined as providing total customer satisfaction, forms a unifying perspective for treating quality in manufacturing and quality in services.

Quality in manufacturing products includes the following dimensions:

1. **Performance:** The primary operating characteristics of a product
2. **Features:** The "bells and whistles" of a product
3. **Reliability:** The probability of a product surviving over a specified period of time under stated conditions of use
4. **Conformance:** The degree to which physical and performance characteristics of a product match preestablished standards
5. **Durability:** The amount of use one gets from a product before it physically deteriorates or until replacement is preferable
6. **Serviceability:** The ability to repair a product quickly and easily
7. **Aesthetics:** How a product looks, feels, sounds, tastes, or smells
8. **Perceived quality:** Subjective assessment resulting from image, advertising, or brand name

Quality in providing services includes the following dimensions:

1. **Time:** How much time must a customer wait?
2. **Timeliness:** Will a service be performed when promised?
3. **Completeness:** Are all items in the order included?
4. **Courtesy:** Do frontline employees greet each customer cheerfully and politely?
5. **Consistency:** Are services delivered in the same fashion for every customer, and every time for the same customer?
6. **Accessibility and convenience:** Is the service easy to obtain?
7. **Accuracy:** Is the service performed right the first time?
8. **Responsiveness:** Can service personnel react quickly and resolve unexpected problems?

CUSTOMER SATISFACTION: STRATEGY DIMENSIONS

The focus of Chapter 2 is on two areas: the total quality business strategy and the total quality human resource (HR) strategy. Both are crucial in determining the strength of the first pillar of the House of Total Quality and clarifying the expanded strategic responsibilities of managers in a total quality system. The total quality business strategy is reciprocally interdependent with the total quality HR strategy in today's progressive firms; a successful business strategy requires a successful HR strategy.

THE TOTAL QUALITY BUSINESS STRATEGY

As indicated in Chapter 1, the first pillar of the House of Total Quality, total customer satisfaction, is based on the cornerstone of strategy planning

Figure 2.1 The First Pillar, Foundation, and Cornerstone of the House of Total Quality.

and the foundation of strategy management. As indicated in the appendix at the end of Chapter 1, total customer satisfaction incorporates both meeting and exceeding customer expectations over time.[1] The pillar of total customer satisfaction is the outcome of the coordination of sound design developed in the cornerstone of strategy planning with effective implementation delivered in the foundation of strategy management, as depicted in Figure 2.1.[2]

A generic definition of **strategy** *is the intended, emergent, and realized pattern of decision processes and actions employed to provide future organizational direction and achieve an organization's mission, objectives, and vision.* Effective strategy requires planning (i.e., environmental scanning and strategy formulation) and management (strategy implementation, evaluation, and control). Similarly, **total quality strategy** *is the intended, emergent, and realized pattern of decision processes and actions that produce total customer satisfaction;* to be effective, it requires adequate planning and management as described in the following model.

The Comprehensive Model of Total Quality Strategy Planning (SP) and Strategy Management (SM) involves four basic elements: (1) environmental scanning, (2) strategy formulation, (3) strategy implementation, and (4) strategy evaluation and control. How the four elements continuously interact is displayed in Figure 2.2.[3]

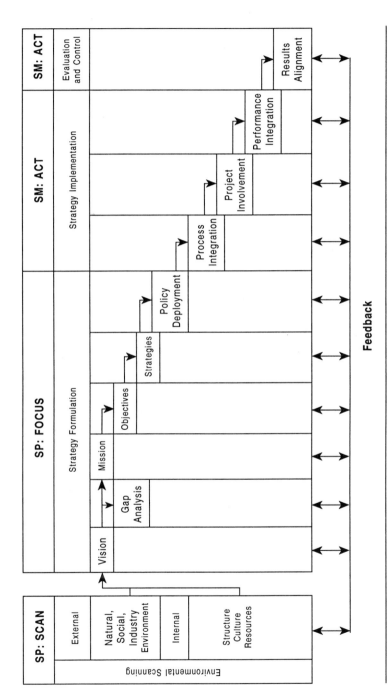

Figure 2.2 The Comprehensive Model of Total Quality Strategy Planning and Management.

TOTAL QUALITY BUSINESS STRATEGY PLANNING

Strategy Planning: Environmental Scanning

The first element of the strategic planning cornerstone, environmental scanning, is composed of two major divisions: the *external* environment assessment of the opportunities and threats that exist in the natural, social, and industry environments of the organization, and the *internal* environment assessment of the strengths and weaknesses that exist within the structure, culture, and resources of the organization. The goal of environmental scanning is to accurately assess the external opportunities and threats to the organization and its capacity to survive and adapt to its current reality, using its strengths and weaknesses.

The **external environment** includes the natural ecological systems and key physical and energy resources within which constraints the organization must function. Strategic planning processes that ignore the economic growth limits of natural ecosystems will ultimately fail in terms of long-term, sustainable development of the firm. The social environment includes the broad human factors that *indirectly* influence the organization's survival: economic, sociocultural, political–legal, demographic, labor market, transportation, energy infrastructure, and technology.[4] Finally, the industry environment includes those factors that *directly* impact the organization's survival: customers, employees, investors, suppliers, distributors, communities, governments, special interest groups, trade/professional/union organizations, and competitors.

An important total quality emphasis in external environment analysis is building strong customer–supplier partnerships that reduce the unnecessary market variations within which the organization must function. With regard to total customer satisfaction, quality strategists recommend extensive, incessant collection of data on and analysis of customer feedback. Applying market opportunity analysis tools, including sophisticated measures of buying and use processes, provides more refined and useful data on consumers than competitors normally attend to or collect.

Six different customer buying roles, for example, apply to purchasing processes for both consumer and industrial products:

1. **Initiator:** Identifies the need for the product
2. **Influencer:** Has informational or preference input to the decision
3. **Gatekeeper:** Does analysis and makes recommendations
4. **Decider:** Makes the final decision
5. **Purchaser:** Makes the actual purchase
6. **User:** Consumes the product or service[5]

Total quality strategic managers, unlike many traditional strategic managers, use this detailed role list continually to ensure that important customers are not ignored, repeat customers are sustained, and market share is increased.[6] In addition to more detailed and frequent customer information on the buying process, strategic quality managers focus on the entire range of the use process: all of the activities that customers go through in using a product or service.[7]

Again, the value of a product or service to a customer is more than the mere act of consumption; strategic quality managers consider the whole use process to better satisfy more customer needs simultaneously. Customers have to find, acquire, transport, store, use, dispose of, and stop the ongoing use of a product or service, as indicated below:

1. **Find:** A customer must locate a product or service to fulfill a need. This requires search, recognition, and choice resources.

2. **Acquire:** This process may entail ordering, paying for, financing, transferring, and registering the ownership.

3. **Transport:** Once acquired, the customer may have to move the product from where it is to where it can be further used.

4. **Store:** The customer may have to store the product prior to further use; the storage can be short or long term and may be repeated in different forms.

5. **Use:** At some point, the customer applies the product or service to fulfill an original need or desire.

6. **Disposal:** Once utilized, the customer may have to dispose of the remainder of the product.

7. **Stop:** The customer may decide to stop using the product and need to go through termination procedures.[8]

The acronym FATSUDS has been applied to this sequence of customer use processes.[9] One person may perform all or only some of the FATSUDS activities. In addition, other aspects of the use process, such as ease of availability, quality of the service, and congeniality of supplier, may impact the customer's perception of value, and the astute total quality strategy manager addresses all of these issues as well.

With regard to industry supplier relations, the traditional approach has been one of self-interested adversarial negotiation between customer and supplier, each trying to maximize his or her slice of the pie at the expense of the other.[10] The thrust of total quality strategy is to expand the pie rather than argue over its division. Juran's trend framework distinguishes the traditional adversarial supplier relationship from the total quality partnership and exhibits the total quality difference in Table 2.1.[11]

Table 2.1 Juran on Trends in Supplier Relations

Supplier relations element	Traditional adversary relationship	Total quality partnership relationship
Number of suppliers	Multiple, often many	Few, often single source
Duration of supply contracts	Annual	Three years or more
Criteria for quality	Conformance to specifications	Fitness for use
Emphasis of surveys	Procedures, data systems	Process capability, quality improvement
Quality planning	Separate	Joint
Pattern of collaboration	Arms length, secrecy, mutual supervision	Mutual visits, disclosures, assistance

The total quality strategic approach also emphasizes social responsibility as a leadership expectation. The Malcolm Baldrige National Quality Award criteria include a criterion on the public responsibility of organizational leaders to the external community, including specific responsibilities to the public for health, safety, environmental protection, and ethical business practices as they impact a wide range of stakeholders.

The **internal environment** includes organizational structure, ethical work culture, and functional resources. The structure is the way the organization is designed and run in terms of work flows, authority, communication channels, and decision-making processes. Although an organization structure can predispose its strategic managers toward the selection of one strategy over another, structure should normally follow strategy.[12] In particular, the adequacy and priority accorded measurement systems relating to financial performance, customer feedback, production efficiency, and employee contributions become a key feature of internal structure and strategy choice.[13] The **ethical work culture** is the collection of beliefs, values, and behaviors regarding organizational integrity shared and transmitted by the organization's members.[14] Organizational ethical work cultures can exhibit strategic myopia and become major deterrents to success at a time when the organization most needs to change strategic direction.[15] Assessment of internal customer satisfaction and ethical work culture levels is a nontraditional input into the quality internal environment analysis, but a key factor in enhancing the quality of work life for the organization's people. Organizational resources include those financial, physical, organizational system, and technological processes that constitute the raw material for the production of an organization's products and/or services. Assessment of internal process capabilities and improvement opportunities is another nontraditional input into the quality internal environment analysis.

An important total quality difference in internal environment analysis is that the refocused strategic priority of customer satisfaction drives a new alignment of processes, resources, and performance measures.[16] The traditional U.S. strategic planning approach reinforces hierarchic authority and accords highest priority to financial measures and resources. Total quality strategists, on the other hand, are flattening organizations and holding total customer satisfaction as the highest strategic priority. They regard profit or market share as the outcomes of meeting and exceeding customer needs, thereby requiring the full integration of quality into strategic planning, as depicted in Figure 2.3.

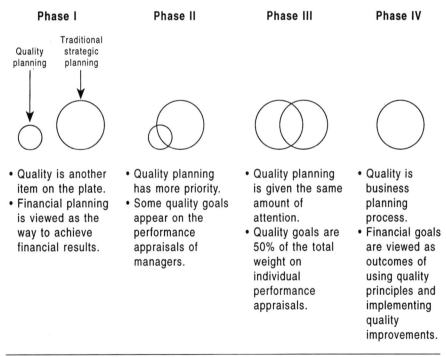

Phase I	Phase II	Phase III	Phase IV

Quality planning   Traditional strategic planning

• Quality is another item on the plate.
• Financial planning is viewed as the way to achieve financial results.

• Quality planning has more priority.
• Some quality goals appear on the performance appraisals of managers.

• Quality planning is given the same amount of attention.
• Quality goals are 50% of the total weight on individual performance appraisals.

• Quality is business planning process.
• Financial goals are viewed as outcomes of using quality principles and implementing quality improvements.

Figure 2.3 The Phased Transition from Traditional Strategic Planning to Total Quality Planning. (Source: Collins, Brendan and Huge, Ernest (1993). *Management by Policy*. Milwaukee: ASQC Quality Press, p. 138. Modified by the authors.)

Furthermore, this quality strategic priority elevates the importance of operating measures, customer feedback measures, and employee contribution measures relative to traditional financial measures of performance. Operating measures in particular are emphasized to quantitatively identify and eliminate defects, increase production reliability by meeting progressively higher standards, and reduce cycle time or time to market.[17]

Traditional financial and accounting measures are now widely recognized as inadequately reflecting, and even obscuring, actual operational effectiveness.[18] U.S. financial measures compare unfavorably with Japanese financial measures as reporting vehicles on critical strategic success factors in at least four ways. First, whereas U.S. firms initially develop a product and price it at whatever level is necessary to turn a profit, Japanese companies reverse the order through target costing. With target costing, the firm first decides what the consumer will be willing to pay for the new product and then works backward to drive design, production, distribution, marketing, and supplier costs down to the target figure.[19] Second, rather than using accountants to measure costs, the Japanese tend to use cost engineers who are experienced product developers. These individuals not only measure costs, but also have the expertise and responsibility to reduce them.[20] Third, in order to maintain flexibility across workers and products, Japanese accountants seek to minimize *total* costs (rather than *unit* costs, as do U.S. accountants), to keep staff specialists and other overhead costs to a minimum, and to calculate the value added at each stage of the production process, including supplier-based stages. Fourth, the Japanese do not make capital investment decisions primarily by anticipated profits or return on investment, but by business judgments that factor in operational, customer, supplier, and employee input. For the most part, however, internal U.S. business decisions are still driven by the strategic priority accorded financial accounting systems designed primarily for external reporting purposes rather than internal efficiency enhancement.[21]

The organizational ethical work culture in the internal environment also needs to be assessed by the total quality strategist. Routine ethical work culture assessments determine the organization's level of moral development and whether it is at a stage that is hospitable to the House of Total Quality, as described in Chapter 1.[22] Strategic planners who ignore the ethical work culture of an organization cannot accurately predict the kind and degree of resistance or support that employees will have for total quality initiatives. To ensure the mutually reinforcing strategic impact of both total quality and organizational ethics development, quality planners need to be sure that the organization is structured not around the old paradigm of detection/control but around the new paradigm of coordination/strategic impact, as depicted in Table 2.2.[23]

Because the sources of low-quality performance and unethical conduct

Table 2.2 Strategic Paradigm Shifts in Total Quality and Organizational Ethics Development

	Old paradigm		New paradigm	
	Detection	Control	Coordination	Strategic impact
Parties responsible for quality management	Inspection department	Engineering, manufacturing, and production departments	All functional departments	All functional departments with strong leadership from top management
Parties responsible for ethics development	Security department	Legal, accounting, and human resource departments	All functional departments	All functional departments with strong leadership from top management

are often systemic and not simply the result of rotten apples in an organizational barrel, the responsible quality strategic planner addresses the ethical work culture as an important element of the internal environment. Quality-oriented and ethical people can be compromised by working in a morally underdeveloped organization, just as people with questionable quality commitment and questionable moral integrity can be uplifted or at least prevented from unacceptable behavior in a morally developed one.[24]

Strategy Planning: Strategy Formulation

The second element of the strategic planning cornerstone, strategy formulation, is composed of six divisions that focus the strategic design: the enterprise vision, the gap analysis, the mission, the objectives, the strategies, and the policy deployment focus steps.

The Enterprise Vision

The first focus step is to create the **enterprise vision**. *The enterprise vision is the integrative synthesis, or conceptual crystallization, of the future desired result that both legitimizes and energizes stakeholders.*[25] The enterprise vision is not achieved through calculating, quantitative, analytic techniques; it is an imagi-

Table 2.3 Types and Scope of Enterprise Vision and
the Total Quality Enterprise Vision

Types of enterprise visions	Scope of enterprise visions
1. Investor	The corporation should maximize the interests of investors
2. Managerial prerogative	The corporation should maximize the interests of management
3. Restricted stakeholder	The corporation should maximize the interests of a narrow set of stakeholders such as employees, suppliers, or investors
4. Unrestricted stakeholder	The corporation should maximize the interests of all stakeholders
5. Unrestricted prioritized stakeholder	**The corporation should maximize the interests of all stakeholders, but should prioritize the interests of some, such as customers, employees, suppliers, investors, communities, society, and natural environments**

native, intuitive synthesis that evokes the committed response of stakeholders because it gives voice to their most cherished work aspirations.[26]

Although enterprise visions differ, they should provide directional momentum and key value priorities. Five types of enterprise vision are listed in Table 2.3, with the total quality enterprise vision in bold.[27]

The total quality enterprise vision seeks to add value to all stakeholders but accords strategic priority to customer satisfaction. The clear visualization, articulation, and endorsement of the vision, however, requires a strategic leadership style that is capable of generating ideas as well as involving people at all organizational levels in the creation and exchange of ideas. This iterative process of creating the vision through requesting and considering input, which results in joint commitment and joint ownership, has been called "conceptual catchball," as opposed to isolated, unilateral "conceptual hardball."[28]

Creation of the enterprise vision is an often-neglected strategic task in the traditional work environment and is a litmus test for the type of leadership style required in a total quality environment. Some differences between traditional and total quality leadership styles are indicated in Table 2.4.

To demonstrate collaborative rather than controlling leadership, a **quality council** with wide representation (not only senior management) provides

Table 2.4 Comparison of Traditional and Total Quality Leadership Styles

Traditional leadership style	Total quality leadership style
Commander, boss ("Do what you're told")	Coach, facilitator, teacher, mentor
Controller, by insistence on rigid compliance ("People need to be controlled.")	Leader, by shared purpose, vision, values, and beliefs; commitment to the purpose and values provides control
Internally competitive	Internally cooperative, externally competitive
Withholding information and communication	Open communication, always explaining why
Owner mentality ("It's my company. You work for me. I pay your salary. Do what you are told.")	Trustee mentality ("I don't own the company; I've been entrusted with it and am responsible for providing an environment in which people can have a fulfilled life.")
Independent individualist	Interdependent team builder
Says employees are the most valuable asset but acts differently	Consistently says and acts as if employees are the most valuable asset
Plays "conceptual hardball"	Plays "conceptual catchball"

an opportune vehicle for generating a shared vision and maintaining participative continuity throughout the strategic steps to ensure customer satisfaction. Leaders who encourage the advisory input of a quality council at the highest levels in order to generate, steer, monitor, and update quality concerns send a message to stakeholders that participatory leadership should be the norm.

The Gap Analysis

Once the enterprise vision of the desired future is shared and endorsed, the results of the environmental scanning of the current reality provide the basis for comparison between what exists and what should exist. The recognition, acknowledgment, and treatment of the perceived gap between the current reality and the desired future constitute the second focus step, **gap analysis.**

Organizations that engage in strategic planning by going directly to mission statements after environmental scanning bypass the enterprise vision and gap analysis steps and are likely to encounter strategy resistance from two sources: organizational inertia and organizational defensive patterns.[29]

Organizational inertia is a form of resistance to gap analysis because people refuse to acknowledge a performance gap and insist on relying on the tried and proven ways of doing things. As Hornstein[30] states: "When in doubt, do what you did yesterday. If it isn't working, do it twice as hard, twice as fast, and twice as carefully."

Organizational defensive patterns occur in a wide variety of forms, but they essentially come down to relying on defensive rather than productive reasoning. Defensive reasoning is a form of covert justification for faulty thinking that leads to anticipated or actual failure as opposed to productive reasoning which openly acknowledges its premises, inferences, and conclusions in order to responsibly resolve problems.[31] Defensive reasoning can be caused by (1) lack of personal and organizational virtues (honesty, courage, humility), (2) skilled incompetence in handling embarrassing or threatening situations maturely, (3) pervasive organizational defensive routines to bypass responsibility and cover up performance issues, (4) pervasive organizational fancy footwork to protect the defensive routines, (5) emergent organizational malaise (hopelessness, cynicism, distancing and blaming others), and (6) sustained mediocre performance that is organizationally acceptable. This organizational defensive pattern is diagrammed in Figure 2.4.[32]

The organizational defensive routines are policies and actions that prevent individuals or work units from experiencing embarrassment or threat. The strategic performance gap is just such a perceived embarrassment or threat. Predictably, many managers use face-saving devices and denials to

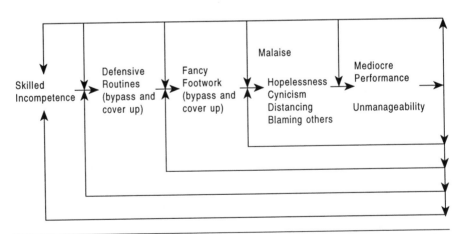

Figure 2.4 Organizational Defensive Pattern to Deny Performance Gaps and to Justify Mediocre Performance.

bypass or cover up performance gaps in order to protect their organizational image as a winner.

After overcoming these obstacles (many organizations never do and remain static or regress to institutional mediocrity), the successful gap analysis honestly and adequately provokes several responses: (1) a reassessment and reaffirmation of the vision, (2) a reassessment of current external and internal environments, (3) an assessment of the realistic challenges of bridging the gap between vision and the current reality, and (4) the development of "trigger themes" that need to be addressed in the mission. Some visions need to be "fleshed out"; others are excessively idealistic or insufficiently motivating and need to be modified. Total quality strategy planners need to be aware of the positive dimensions of the tension created by gap awareness. While there is a short-term temptation to "lower the bar," the long-term benefit of "raising the floor" (i.e., adopting challenging performance standards) is preferable to relapsing into mediocrity. Reassessment of the results of the environmental scan can detect new strengths and weaknesses as well as new opportunities and threats in light of the revised vision. The link between desired future and current reality should be reasonably challenging and worthy of organizational endorsement. Finally, if the gap analysis is done properly, it will result in "trigger themes" that the mission will address.

The Mission

The **mission** is the third focus step in strategy formulation. The enterprise vision addressed the question, "What do we as an organization stand for in the world?" The mission addresses the questions, "What industry or business are we in and why?" After the vision has determined what is socially worth doing, the mission is the institutional purpose for the already legitimized existence of the firm. The components and corresponding questions that the mission should answer are listed in Table 2.5.[33]

A well-conceived mission statement defines the distinctive purpose that sets an organization apart from others and identifies the scope of the organization's operations in terms of products/services offered and markets served. Corporations with a unifying set of prioritized values that integrate processes, projects, and people are better able to direct and administer their many activities.[34] A major challenge is to write a mission statement that is broad enough to facilitate quality growth yet narrow enough to focus the organization on what it does best.

In discussing the sixth component of the mission statement, the philosophy of the organization, an explicit statement of prioritized and shared core values is required.[35] In a total quality organization, service to stakeholders, dedication to continuous improvement, application of scientific tools to system measurement and control, empowerment and respect for people, and

Table 2.5 Components and Questions for a Mission Statement

Customers	Who are the enterprise's customers?
Products or services	What are the firm's major products or services?
Markets	Where does the firm compete?
Technology	What is the firm's basic technology?
Concern for survival, growth, and profitability	What is the firm's commitment toward economic objectives?
Philosophy	What are the basic beliefs, values, aspirations, and philosophical priorities of the firm?
Self-concept	What are the firm's major strengths and competitive advantages?
Concern for public image	What is the firm's public image?
Concern for employees	What is the firm's attitude toward employees?
Prioritization of stakeholders	What is the firm's prioritization of stakeholder concerns?

personal integrity are core values that form the bases for work community performance. The intense commitment to shared values distinguishes the total quality work community from other workplaces where values remain implicit or are only complied with in a grudging manner. Total quality organizations are value-driven, and these values are created by design and endorsed by consensus rather than by tacit default.

To meet that challenge, the quality council provides an open forum to elicit the diverse organizational voices that will produce a challenging and realistic mission statement. The content of the mission statement should factor in the results of the enterprise vision and the gap analysis, clearly prioritizing stakeholder interests for future decision guidance at all levels in the organization.

Objectives

In order to fulfill its mission, a total quality organization must complete the fourth step in strategy formulation, stating and achieving its **objectives**. *Objectives determine what is to be accomplished by when and should be quantified if possible.*[36] In contrast to an objective, a **goal** *is an open-ended statement of what one wants to accomplish with no quantification of what is to be achieved and* *no time criteria for completion.*[37] Goals for quality firms vary but include product quality/service, stakeholder welfare, market share, profitability, growth, research and development, financial stability, and efficiency. The ten major quality objectives to achieve total customer satisfaction are depicted in Figure 2.5.

Normally, the interdependence rooted in the enterprise vision and the mission requires cross-functional attention to each of the major objectives that affect total customer satisfaction. The cross-functional *quality* objective focuses on two areas: product/service design and meeting process standards in making products and/or providing services. Quality design dimensions in products (performance, features, reliability, conformance, durability, serviceability, aesthetics, and perceived quality) and quality design dimensions in services (time, timeliness, completeness, courtesy, consistency, accessibility and convenience, accuracy, and responsiveness) were mentioned in the appendix at the end of Chapter 1. The quality objective is concerned with emphasizing and documenting prevention rather than subsequent inspection and rework in obtaining defect-free performance. Both quality design and quality process standard performance are necessary to monitor and ensure total quality.

The aim of the *cost* objective is to ensure the right price for the customer and appropriate market share and profits for the organization. Target costing first determines what customers are likely to pay for a new product/service, which, in turn, drives design, administrative, production, distribution, marketing, and supplier costs down to meet the target figure.[38] Cost targets are developed by subtracting profit from the selling price until the desired market share is achieved. It is interesting to note that while the traditional Japanese corporate management style has provided lifetime employment and rewarded seniority, the current glut of white-collar Japanese employees, who are less productive than their blue-collar factory associates, is costing more than many companies can afford during recessionary times.[39] One inevitable result has been the dismissal or forced "retirement" of some inefficient office workers and middle managers.[40] In this case, increasing market share and wealth building through investing in productive resources and reducing inefficient administrative expenses are important aims of the cost objective.

The *delivery* objective maintains schedule adherence by ensuring that the right products/services are delivered at the right times and in the right quantities. This increased responsiveness and flexibility through supply–cycle time reduction is a key international objective.[41]

The *safety* objective focuses on product/service and employee safety as well as social/environmental protection and enhancement. While production/service safety guidelines are legally available, the human safety factor (i.e., accidents caused by employee error, equipment insufficiency, faulty

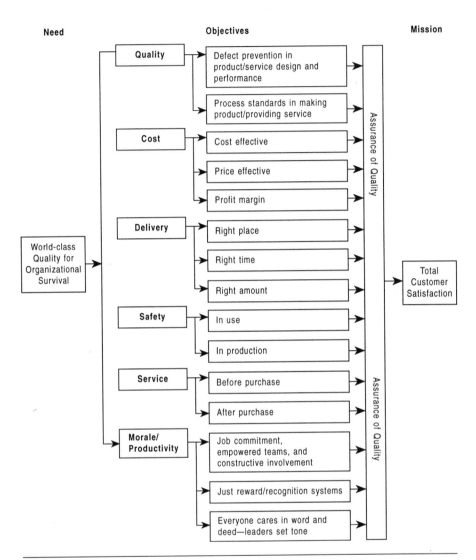

Figure 2.5 Organizational Strategic Objectives of Total Quality.

vehicles, and/or procedure insufficiency) needs to be properly monitored and addressed.[42] In addition, the social/environmental safety impact of new products/services is accorded strategic status by the safety objective.[43]

The aim of the *service* objective is to monitor and ensure continuously improving service before and after purchase.[44] External and internal customer perceptions of service can be surveyed and measured continuously to detect and/or correct undesirable service variance.

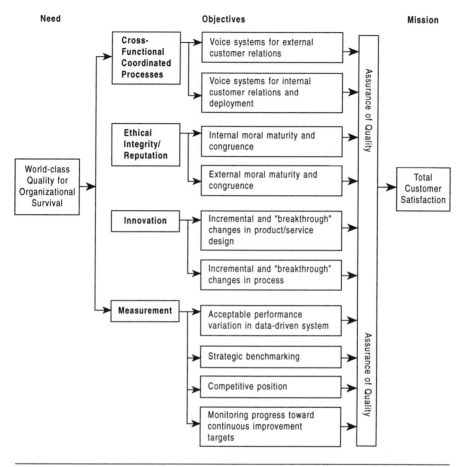

Figure 2.5 Organizational Strategic Objectives of Total Quality (continued).

The *morale/productivity* objective addresses the intricate relationship between morale factors and productivity increases.[45] Work attitude, job design, group dynamics, team improvement, employee development, and constructive employee involvement in appropriate contexts need to be monitored and addressed.[46] Balancing reward/recognition systems in terms of consistency, competitiveness, contributions, profit/gainsharing, and administration, along with procedural fairness, fall within the domain of this objective.[47] While changing the way employees are treated may boost productivity more than changing the way they are paid, developing structures to enhance the intrinsic work motivation of employees through team collaboration, meaningful work content, and empowered choice requires attention.[48] Finally, managerial leadership practices that demonstrate in word and deed respectful concern for the welfare of employees, the satisfaction of customers, and the impartial administration of justice (e.g., avoidance of favoritism) require monitoring and reinforcement.[49]

The *cross-functional coordinated process* objective aims to address system problems across traditional functional boundaries in an integrated manner.[50] Simultaneous engineering, for example, requires cross-functional coordinated participation processes to ensure that the voices of external and internal customers are heard in a timely and accurate manner, and that the strategic priority focus has been communicated throughout the organization. Coordinated system flexibility provides competitive advantage.

The *ethical integrity/reputation* objective aims to assess and continually develop an organization that expects, shapes, and supports ethically sound behavior, which strengthens internal customer relationships and builds a solid public reputation for external customer satisfaction and responsible citizenship.[51] While organizational legal compliance is normally included in this objective's domain, especially in light of the U.S. 1991 Federal Sentencing Guidelines, the intent of the objective is to enable more responsible conduct in the customer chain and not just prevent criminal misconduct.[52] Organizational moral maturity reflects the extent of habitual decision making and performance based on principled norms to sustain "organizational character"; over time, organizations of sound character are better able to attract and retain the resources they need to survive and thrive.[53]

The *innovation* objective aims to develop and coordinate incremental improvements and innovative breakthroughs in products/services, technology, and other processes.[54] To delight customers faster and better than competitors requires cross-functional attention to new product development and new service creation.

The *measurement* objective is focused on the systematic and continuous quantification and comparison of an organization's products/services and processes against global leaders both to gain information which will help the organization continuously improve its performance and to enhance its competitive position.[55] The committee monitors the use and results of statistical measuring tools to establish improvement targets and provide precise feedback on current organizational performance and competitive position.

Each of the ten organizational strategic objectives (quality, cost, delivery, safety, service, morale/productivity, cross-functional coordinated processes, ethical integrity/reputation, innovation, and measurement) is quantified and assigned timelines (e.g., reduce total manufacturing costs by 20% in five years and improve employee morale survey results by 30% in five years). The prioritization of objectives is dependent on mission priorities but needs to be clearly communicated throughout the organization.

Three critical drivers for prioritizing objectives are the importance to total customer satisfaction, the opportunity for competitive advantage, and the severity of the areas that have the greatest need for improvement. At certain times and places, one of the drivers may assume strategic priority, but sustaining continuity of prioritization provides the best avenue for coordinated internal effort to achieve objectives.

Strategies

To achieve objectives, the fifth focus step, the formulation of **strategies**, must occur. Strategies are comprehensive master plans that state how an organization will achieve its mission and objectives. They are usually divided into grand and generic strategies. **Grand strategies** *refer to an organization's coordinated macro efforts to achieve long-term success, whereas generic strategies refer to the most fundamental bases on which an organization's micro efforts are directed at success.*

A traditional matrix which organizes the major grand strategies based upon prior environmental scanning analyses is displayed in Figure 2.6.

In quadrant I, the four grand strategies usually recommended to capital-

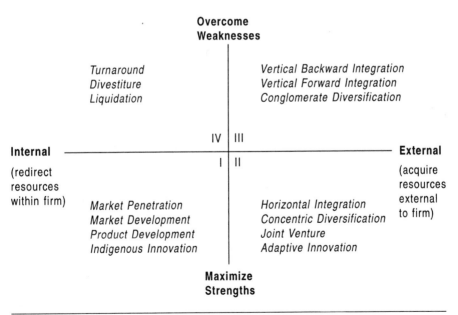

Figure 2.6   Grand Strategy Selection Matrix. (Source: Pearce, John A. II (1982). "Selecting Among Alternate Grand Strategies." *California Management Review.* Vol. 44, No. 4, p. 29. Modified by the authors.)

ize on a firm's strengths by addressing internal redirection of resources are market penetration (same products, same markets), market development (same products, new markets), product development (new products, same markets), and/or indigenous innovation (fast new product development using only internal resources, same and new markets).

In quadrant II, the four grand strategies usually recommended to exploit a firm's strengths by securing external resources are horizontal integration (buy competitor at same stage in activity chain), concentric diversification (acquire related products, markets, or technologies), joint ventures (form separate new organizations jointly owned), and/or adaptive innovation (fast new product development using external resources, same and new markets).

In quadrant III, the three grand strategies usually recommended to compensate for a firm's weaknesses and obtain external resources are vertical backward integration (buy operations with activities upstream), vertical forward integration (buy operations with activities downstream), and/or conglomerate diversification (obtain unrelated products, markets, or technologies).

In quadrant IV, the three grand strategies usually recommended to address a firm's weaknesses through internal redirection of resources are turnaround (downsize and improve), divestiture (sell assets as an operating concern), and/or liquidation (close operations and sell assets piecemeal or in aggregate).

Firms of average strength in medium-growth industries can adopt a holding grand strategy wherein they pause or proceed with caution.

The traditional approach to generic organizational strategies is to divide them into four categories: broad target cost leadership, broad target differentiation, narrow target focused low cost, or narrow target focused differentiation.[56] Broad and narrow targets refer to the competitive scope of business strategies, whereas focused refers to niche segments of quality features (differentiation) or low expenditure (cost leadership). According to Porter, using one of these generic strategies enables a firm to achieve superior competitive position and sustainable competitive advantage, while being "stuck in the middle" (i.e., combining strategies in an industry) lowers performance and may jeopardize survival.

The total quality approach toward generic strategies, however, differs from Porter's by advocating the combination of low cost and high quality for generic strategic integration, as indicated in Figure 2.7.[57]

In quadrant I, the two generic strategies usually recommended for a low-cost, low-differentiation position are cost leadership (broad competitive scope with low expenditure) and/or cost focus (narrow competitive scope with low expenditure).

In quadrant II, the two conjoint generic strategies usually recommended by total quality strategists for a low-cost, high-differentiation position are the

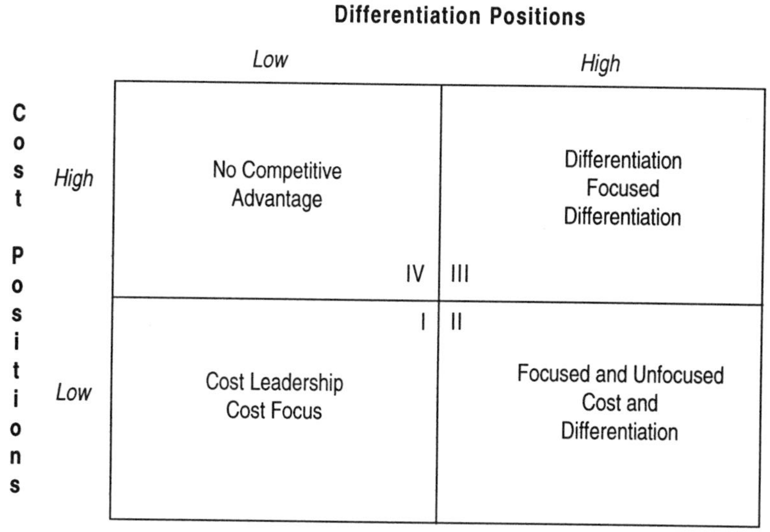

Differentiation Positions

		Low	High
C o s t *High* **P o s i**		No Competitive Advantage	Differentiation Focused Differentiation
		IV | III	
		I | II	
t i o n s *Low*		Cost Leadership Cost Focus	Focused and Unfocused Cost and Differentiation

Figure 2.7 Total Quality Generic Strategy Selection Matrix. (Source: White, R.E. (1986). "Generic Business Strategies, Organizational Context and Performance: An Empirical Investigation." *Strategic Management Journal.* Vol. 47, No. 4, p. 226. Modified by the authors.)

combination of cost leadership and differentiation and/or the combination of focused cost and focused differentiation. For the quality planners, the strategic goal is to simultaneously and continuously lower costs and improve quality, whether a firm is in a broad or narrow competitive arena. Achieving best quality by statistical management of external and internal systems and empowerment of people often results in lowest delivered cost as inferior input, redesign, scrap, rework, field failures, and customer complaints are eliminated. Further, superior quality leads to repeat purchases and differentiation based on customer feedback satisfaction. The combination of lowest delivered cost and highest quality, of course, usually provides best value to consumers when pricing is based on cost.

In quadrant III, the two generic strategies usually recommended for a high-cost, high-differentiation position are differentiation (broad competitive scope with distinctive features) and focused differentiation (narrow competitive scope with distinctive features).

In quadrant IV, there is no competitive advantage for a firm in a high-cost, low-differentiation position.

The clear and consistent combination of grand and generic strategies provides directional stability and coherent integration of organizational macro and micro efforts to achieve its prioritized objectives. If a firm's generic strategic position at the micro level is in quadrant IV (no competitive advantage), it normally is involved in quadrant IV of the grand strategy at the macro level (turnaround, divestiture, and/or liquidation) and vice versa. If a firm's generic position at the micro level is in quadrant III (differentiation or focused differentiation), it normally is engaged in quadrant III of the grand strategy at the macro level (vertical backward integration, vertical forward integration, and/or conglomerate diversification). If a firm's generic position at the micro level is in quadrant II (focused and unfocused cost and differentiation), it usually is engaged in quadrant II of the grand strategy at the macro level (horizontal integration, concentric diversification, joint venture, and/or adaptive innovation). If a firm's generic position at the macro level is in quadrant I (cost leadership and cost focus), it normally is involved in quadrant I of the grand strategy at the macro level (market penetration, market development, product development, and/or indigenous innovation). Congruent, rather than conflicting, grand and generic strategies are most likely to maximize and improve total customer satisfaction.

Policy Deployment

The sixth focus step in strategy formulation is **policy deployment**, which is the systematic spreading, integration, and adaptation of organizational resources to support policies.[58] After establishing the contours of policy (the broad guidelines for decision making throughout the organization), the next step is linking strategy formulation with strategy implementation. To ensure feasible consistency of direction, the quality organization engages in several deployment processes: catchball analysis; coordination of targets, means, and budgets; and selection/training of functional, cross-functional, process, and project teams and their leaders.

Catchball analysis *is the iterative, two-way communication process designed to operationally analyze opportunities and problems in order to assure realistic feasibility, joint commitment, and joint ownership of objectives at all organizational levels.* One-way issuance of memoranda to announce changes in objectives is not the total quality way. The catchball analysis provides critical concrete data and facts on operational capabilities, key measurement indicators (control points for desired outcomes and checkpoints for process parameters), support resources available, and prioritized causes of problems. This is quite different from the arbitrary imposition of a required contribution from an isolated top management team.

The catchball analysis results in the feasible coordination of performance targets, means, and budgets which cascade throughout the organization into a series of interrelated control points and checkpoints (i.e., the means at one level of the organization become the objectives at the next lower management level). For example, the means to achieve the objectives/targets selected by top management become the objectives/targets of middle managers. Middle managers, in turn, select the means to achieve their objectives/targets, and these means become the means/targets of lower level managers. Attention to detail and "speaking with facts," rather than blaming and scapegoating, bring focus and alignment to the process of honing strategic objectives, allocating budgetary support, and building organizational commitment.

Finally, the selection and training of functional, cross-functional, process, and project teams and their leaders spreads competent involvement throughout the organization as implementation is about to occur.

TOTAL QUALITY BUSINESS STRATEGY MANAGEMENT

Strategy Management: Strategy Implementation

The first element of the strategy management foundation is **strategy implementation.** *Total quality strategy implementation is the operational system by which strategies and policies are put into action through process integration, project involvement, and individual performance integration.* The goals of process integration, project involvement, and individual activity completion are, respectively, continuous improvement, speaking with facts, and self-respect and respect for people. These three goals constitute the remaining three pillars of the House of Total Quality. Since each will be accorded detailed treatment in subsequent chapters, only a preliminary overview is offered at this time. It is important to note, however, that there is a stronger emphasis on strategy implementation and feedback in total quality organizations than in most traditional organizations.

Process Integration

As the first step in quality strategy implementation, **process integration** *is the identification, coordination, measurement, and systematic development of the flow of core sets of linked activities in order to continuously improve organizational performance.* Structuring ongoing programs around processes that correspond to core organizational objectives strongly aligns strategy formulation and implementation. A **process** *is any set of linked activities that take an input and transform it to create an output.*[59] Processes can be physical, involve paperwork, occur within computers, or simply be a logical or standard operational sequence of events. However, by conceptualizing organizations as processes through quality function deployment, instead of compilations of functions, managers can focus on designing, streamlining, and measuring processes in order to create more customer value with less effort as opposed to focusing on reducing the size of functions in order to simply cut costs.[60] From the total quality perspective, cost cuts will naturally occur as non-value-adding activities are identified and removed from the core processes and as the processes increase their level of effectiveness as measured by an organization-wide indicator system. Identifying and linking the critical measuring points of organizational processes in turn permits system accountability and acceptable variation ranges while avoiding well-intentioned but counterproductive process interventions.

Process integration is driven by three different goals: internal incremental cost reduction, external competitive renewal, and external breakthrough dominance.[61] Managers must differentiate these goals when determining the direction of process integration, since not all companies are able or willing to invest in external breakthrough dominance. The cross-functional coordinated process teams and innovation teams collaborate to determine the appropriate direction of efforts. Process integration with a cost reduction focus in noncore processes (i.e., *kaizen* in Japan) can lead to incremental advantages over time.[62] Process integration that focuses on external competitive renewal may attain either parity or best-in-class status for the company.[63] This effort directs process integration to match or exceed the processes of those who have in the past set the competitive standards and made the rules. Finally, external breakthrough dominance through reengineering or other breakpoint methods attempts to rewrite the rules and create a new definition of best-in-class for all others to achieve in the future.[64]

In order to manage process integration, certain process assessment and improvement tools need to be mastered. The interrelationship digraph, tree diagram, matrix diagram, arrow diagram, process decision program chart, and matrix data analysis are the major process management tools that competent strategy implementers need to master. They are treated in detail in Chapter 3, along with six supplemental process management tools. Essentially, process mapping delineates current and possible future processes to enhance customer satisfaction. If those processes depend on widely distributed data, data modeling is used to manage data as an asset and radically alter business processes to coincide with state-of-the-art information technology. The remaining tools refine different aspects of process integration management.

The results of process integration include clear ongoing program designations, cross-functional coordination for system flexibility, realistic budget estimates, and feedback to strategy formulators about the feasible process capacities of the firm. Process integration clarifies system dynamics and prepares the way for team projects.

Project Involvement

The second step in quality strategy implementation is **project involvement**. While process integration designs the stream of linked activities, project involvement focuses on the single pulse of work flow. Projects *are normally regarded as single, nonrecurring events that implement organizational changes through structured phases and specified outcomes and require teamwork for successful completion.*[65] Projects are forms of nonstandard implementation work that meet the challenges posed by complex changes in today's environment. Standard implementation work is best addressed through ongoing programs, uniform procedures, and fixed routines. **Project involvement** *is the team assessment and resolution of single, nonrecurring problems through the development of employee involvement.*[66]

The structural relationship of project leadership to functional and executive leaders is a key determinant of the success of project initiatives. Sometimes, the project sponsor is either a functional or executive leader, and formal authority and informal influence are conjoined in project involvement; more often, there are different structural preferences which require strong influencing skills from the project leader. Studies have shown that traditional executives in companies that are developing new products tend to favor the functional matrix structure, which accords project managers limited authority while functional managers retain responsibility and authority for their specific segments of the project.[67] Project managers, on the other hand, in companies developing new processes or services prefer the project matrix structure, which accords project managers primary responsibility and authority for project completion while functional managers provide personnel and technical expertise as needed.[68]

The quality units or teams usually occur in three forms: steering committee teams, problem-solving teams, and self-managed teams.[69] Their full treatment will be provided in Chapter 4, but it is important to recognize at this time that although project teams come in various forms, they are needed to enhance the multifunctional, objective, factual implementation of strategy, using the integrated processes of the organization and prioritized objectives as guides.

In addition, project management teams need to master project scheduling, work breakdown, operational estimation, progress monitoring, and control tools, as well as the seven major project management tools: cause-and-effect diagrams, check sheets, display graphs, histograms, Pareto charts, scatter diagrams, and control charts. These major tools will be examined in detail in Chapter 4, along with six supplemental project management tools. Mastery of these tools provides organizational stakeholders with the reliable factual bases for effective strategy implementation and accurate feedback.[70]

Performance Integration

The third step in quality strategy implementation is **performance integration**. *Performance integration is the daily implementation of continuous improvement in personal task and relational activity within an employee's own scope of responsibility.*[71] It occurs at the intrapersonal and interpersonal levels. At the former level, it requires individuals to demonstrate both task and relational skills in job performance; it is not enough to be technically competent but rudely uncommunicative in a total quality firm. At the latter level, performance integration requires respectful and sincere relations between persons so that process commitment rather than mere system compliance occurs in the daily activity sphere. While the organization's motivational system must be supportive of high individual and group performance, each person's self-respect and work pride grow with competent performance in meeting unit and company quality objectives. In turn, respect for other people who are similarly committed to integrated performance builds and team project involvement escalates.

Strategy implementation, therefore, requires process, project, and personal coordinated activities. Personal performance integration is enhanced through the use of two tools: performance planning by using the Personal Process Planning Chart and performance management by using the Quality Performance Management Journal.[72] The former tool identifies personal activities/tasks to complete, suppliers and customers to satisfy, quality indicators and defect measurement, and opportunities for individual process improvement. The latter tool defines each problem (opportunity) in detail, analyzes and responds to the causes of the problem, studies the results of the intervention, standardizes acceptable solutions, and provides lessons for future role occupants.

Strategy Management: Evaluation and Control

Total quality **evaluation and control** is the strategic stage in which organizational activities are monitored so that alignment of actual results can be compared with planned results, as indicated in Figure 2.8.[72] **Results alignment** *is the process of measuring and comparing organizational and societal results to determine the extent to which formulated and implemented strategies are adequate or in need of corrective intervention.*

Organizational results include both enroute results, such as products or services, and **outputs**, *which are the aggregated products of the system that are delivered or deliverable to society.* External societal results include **outcomes,** *which are the effects of outputs on society and the community.* Evaluation and control systems measure and determine the strength of the "results chain" that extends from organizational inputs and processes to organizational and

	Inputs (raw material)	Processes (how to do it)	Products (enroute result)	Outputs (the aggregated products of the system that are delivered or deliverable to society)	Outcomes (the effects of outputs in and for society and the community)
Examples	Existing human resources; existing needs, goals, objectives, regulations, laws, money, values, societal & community characteristics; current quality of life; natural resources	Means, methods, procedures; searching for "excellence," teaching; learning; human resource development, training, managing	Course completed; competency test passed; competency acquired; learner accomplishments; instructor accomplishments; production quota met; the performance "building blocks"	Delivered automobiles, sold computer systems; program completed; job placements; certified licenses	Safety of outputs; profit; dividends declared; continued funding of agency; self-sufficient, self-reliant, productive individual; socially competent and effective, contributing to self and to others; no addictive relationship to others or to substances; financial independence
Scope		Internal (Organization)			External (Societal)
Cluster	Organizational Efforts		Organizational Results		Societal Results/Impact

Figure 2.8 Organizational Efforts and Results Model (Source: Kaufman, Roger (1988). "Preparing Useful Performance Indicators." *Training and Development Journal.* Vol. 10, No. 4, p. 81.)

societal consequences. Without results alignment, organizations could get better and better at doing what should not be done at all to meet customer needs.

Regular process reviews and audits ensure that quality strategy remains focused on priority objectives, reduces duplication of efforts, limits non-value-added activities, and streamlines work processes.

For quality evaluation and control to be effective, however, managers must obtain clear, prompt, and unbiased feedback on an ongoing basis from all sectors of the strategic planning and management system, as indicated by the double-pointed arrows at the bottom of Figure 2.2. The ongoing feedback, detailed progress reviews, process indicator measurements, and audit reports warrant continual organizational leadership attention to ensure strategic success.

THE TOTAL QUALITY HUMAN RESOURCE STRATEGY

It has been estimated that less than 20% of HR strategic plans in the United States are formulated and integrated into the total business strategy of organizations.[74] Yet research studies indicate that 80% of U.S. executives would like to see HR considerations have more than a moderate impact on strategy formulation.[75] This expectation is gradually being met as more firms, like American Express and SmithKline Beecham Corporation, include senior HR professionals, who are also accomplished business managers, in business strategic planning sessions.[76]

In total quality organizations, there is more of a recognition of the reciprocal interdependence of successful business and HR strategies.[77] However, there are still perceived shortcomings that prevent HR executives from being as effective as they could be in total quality business strategy committees. First, the legalistic, inflexible bent of long-standing HR practices, such as judicial and legislative compliance, job analyses, job descriptions, job evaluations and merit increase grids, often blind HR professionals to strategic business growth opportunities. *Keeping legal is not the main strategic priority of any organization.*[78] Total quality strategic planners need HR executives who accord priority to envisioning a preferred future, accurately forecasting HR impacts of policies, and performing change agent roles rather than emphasizing the legal control function. Second, the overwhelming predominance of an individualistic orientation in all major HR subfunctions—selection based on individual accomplishments, evaluation based on independent contributions, and rewards packaged as individualized pay increases—runs counter to the group and team project emphasis in total quality strategic planning and organizational design.[79] Third, the shortfalls in the business knowledge and skill base of HR executives combined with functional isolation from mainstream operations prevent many practitioners from making substantive recommendations on business strategy issues and tactically handling the wide range of human resource services needed by the line managers.[80] Fourth, the failure of HR professionals to routinely collect and evaluate data for improved future decision making (i.e., underutilization of the tools available to the HR function) runs counter to the total quality principles which use statistical measures to reduce variability and increase understanding of covariances among activities and outcomes.[81] Finally, the failure to recognize the cross-functional financial implications of HR strategic recommendations makes these recommendations appear to have an air of unreality about them.[82]

If HR executives are to assume critical roles in business strategic planning, these shortcomings must be remedied. In brief, the strategic role of the HR function in a total quality organization needs to be clearly delineated, as indicated in Figure 2.9.[83]

The HR role can fall into four categories: strategic/high profile (change agent), strategic/low profile (hidden persuader), operational/high profile (internal contractor), or the operational/low profile (facilitator). The change agent role involves high visibility for the HR function in strategically plan-

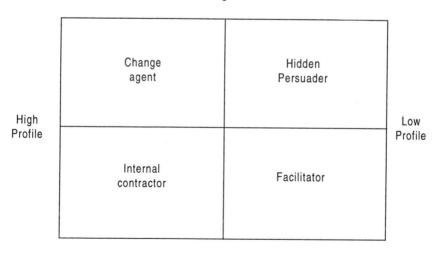

Figure 2.9   The Roles of the Human Resource Functions in Total Quality Organizations. (Source: Wilkinson, Adrian, Marchington, Mick, and Dale, B. (1993). "Enhancing the Contribution of the Human Resource Function to Quality Improvement." *Quality Management Journal.* Vol. 1, No. 1, p. 40.)

ning and preparing the groundwork (structure, measurements, ethical work culture, reward and recognition, and feedback systems) for total quality changes in all phases, introductory to review. The hidden persuader role is a less risky strategic posture wherein the HR function acts as a mentor or behind-the-scenes sounding board for senior management planners regarding the approach to and feasibility of total quality initiatives. The internal contractor role is a high-visibility operational orientation without strategic responsibility and focuses on providing timely personnel products and services to improve internal customer decision making (e.g., advisory services on all aspects of safe employment conditions within three working days for all employees). The facilitator role is one of providing hands-on support for line manager operations, without being involved in strategic planning (e.g., quality training courses, newsletters to publicize total quality, accurate record keeping on traditional human resource data).

TOTAL QUALITY HUMAN RESOURCE STRATEGY PLANNING

Because the change agent and hidden persuader roles provide the highest HR impact on the strategic direction of the firm, HR practitioners who plan to have that strategic impact need to address all five of the previous shortcomings and be prepared to shift HR paradigms from the traditional approach to the total quality approach, as indicated in Table 2.6.[84]

The eight HR subfunctional areas listed in the left column of Table 2.6 provide the conceptual comparison categories for the traditional and total quality HR paradigms. In the first three subfunctional areas (management practices), the shift from internal/external control focus to internal/external flexibility focus, from compliance priority to customer satisfaction priority, from implementing policy to shaping/developing/implementing policy, and from suggestion systems to continuous improvement systems requires that HR practitioners attend to different forms of information to achieve strategic partnership (e.g., more attention to internal and external customer satisfaction surveys).

Subfunctional areas four through eight point toward additional processes, measurements, and outcomes that a total quality HR paradigm entails. These subfunctional areas will be addressed in more detail in Chapter 3, but the cross-functional, team empowerment, continuous improvement, and extensive measurement for organizational effectiveness trends point toward a wider scope of HR responsibility than the traditional HR domain.

This wider scope of responsibility is warranted because of the reciprocal interdependence that a proactive total quality HR strategy has with the organizational/business competitive strategy. The formation of total quality

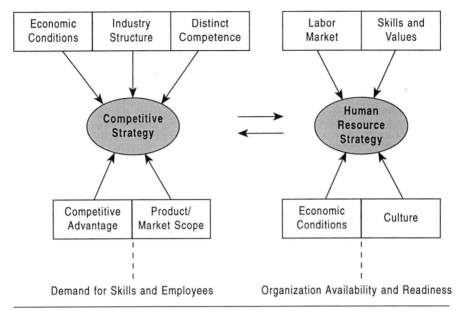

Figure 2.10 Reciprocal Interdependence of Total Quality Organizational Competitive Strategy and Total Quality Human Resource Strategy. (Source: Anthony, W.P., Perrewe, P.L., and Kacmar, K.M. (1993). *Strategic Human Resource Management*. New York: Dryden Press, p. 92.)

corporate competitive advantage not only influences but is influenced by total quality HR strategies, as indicated in Figure 2.10.[85]

The crucial interaction is between the corporate multidimensional (economic conditions, industry structure, distinct competence, competitive advantage, product/market scope) demand for skills and employees and multifaceted HR (labor market, skills and values, economic conditions, culture) availability and readiness. Each is an input to and a constraint on the other in order to achieve total quality organizational effectiveness.[86]

Just as corporate strategic planning requires environmental scanning, so does HR strategic planning. Labor market, domestic/international economic conditions, legal/political factors, social/demographic factors, industry competition, technological trends, and end-user market demands are all part of responsible HR environmental scanning. Strategic benchmarking of HR systems is also an important part of total quality HR environmental scanning. The results of environmental scanning may indicate the extent to which HR strategy formulations will be plan-based, project-based, or population-based.[87]

Plan-based HR planning is the logical approach that integrally links grand and generic corporate and HR strategies. Project-based HR planning

Table 2.6 Selected Comparison of Traditional and Total Quality Human Resource Paradigms

HR professional certification/ subfunctional areas	Traditional paradigm	Total quality paradigm
1. Management practices: leadership priorities	Professional specialization Individual contributions Internal/external control focus Compliance priority Operational support	Cross-functional generalist work Collective contributions Internal/external flexibility focus Customer satisfaction priority Strategic/operational involvement
2. Management practices: organizational communications/planning	Top-down communication Planning information available on a "need-to-know" basis Implement policy	Multidirectional communication Planning information widely shared Shape/deploy/implement policy
3. Management practices: voice and involvement	Detect and control Reactive legal grievance procedures Suggestion systems No explicit whistleblower protection Morale measurements Control through power, not principle, which breeds fear	Coordinate and build Proactive legal/ethical problem-prevention procedures Continuous improvement systems Explicit whistleblower protection Morale/ethical climate surveys Drive fear out of workplace by institutionalizing organizational ethics program development
4. Staffing and placement	Selection by manager Narrow job/task skills Promotion based on individual accomplishment Knowledge, skills, and/or abilities testing	Selection by peers Wide problem-solving skills Promotion based on group facilitation Knowledge, skills, and/or abilities and integrity testing
5. Training and development	Develop a regulatory mindset (enforce compliance) Job-related skills	Develop statistical mindset (manage variation) Organizational skills

	Functional departmental focus	Cross-functional focus
	Technical skills Unit-specific skill training Short-term training Learning for individual productivity Linear career path Productivity	Process skills Firm/industry-specific skill training Lifelong learning Learning for organizational effectiveness Horizontal career path Productivity and quality
6. Compensation, benefits, and job design	Competition for individual financial merit increases and benefits Job design: narrow span of control Specific job description with limited responsibility Employee expected to do job only by adhering to standard procedures Employee rewards linked with "doing the job" Cost savings shared with management	Team/group-based rewards; financial rewards, financial and nonfinancial recognition Job design: wide span of control Autonomous, empowered work teams with wide responsibility Employee expected to accomplish results and improve procedures Employee rewards linked with "getting results for customer" Cost savings shared with all employees
7. Performance appraisal, employee and labor relations	Individual goals Supervisory review Employment-at-will Emphasize financial performance Adversarial union relations Limited, occasional measurement and feedback	Team goals Customer, peer, supervisory, and self-review Due process Emphasize quality and service Partnership union relations Extensive, incessant measurement and feedback
8. Health, safety, and security	Only hold others accountable Treat problems Hold individuals accountable for noncompliance with mandated health, safety, and security standards Only meet legal/regulatory minimum requirements	Assume personal responsibility and hold others accountable Prevent problems Hold individuals and systems accountable for noncompliance Exceed legal/regulatory minimum requirements

is the response to either sudden changes in the environment or urgent cross-functional organizational needs requiring systematic and uninterrupted HR attention. Population-based HR planning focuses on identifying and obtaining a critical group of employees normally in short supply (e.g., nurses in health care organizations).

In addition, total quality strategic HR objectives are also parallel to the ten organizational strategic objectives and include alignment with quality, cost, delivery, safety, service, morale/productivity, cross-functional, coordinated processes, ethical integrity/reputation, innovation, and measurement objectives at the HR level. In particular, a total quality organization, which accords highest priority to customer satisfaction, requires that a priority HR objective be selecting and developing human resources that are customer satisfaction oriented. One quality HR policy to achieve this objective is employee selection based on good citizenship behavior and service orientation.

Recent studies indicate that total quality HR practitioners can enhance selection success by screening for good citizenship behavior and service orientation. **Good citizenship behavior**, which is the tendency to be helpful to others, loyal, and considerate of the whole organization, can be ascertained from background checks, reference checks, and behavior-based interviews.[88] **Service orientation**, which is the psychological predisposition to be helpful to customers, can be predicted by conducting behavior-based interviews, using the Service Orientation Index psychological test, and performing background checks.[89]

To short-circuit the good citizenship behavior and service orientation, some theorists maintain that desirable employee performance and customer satisfaction can best be accomplished by enforcing appropriate affect display behaviors (feeling rules) to ensure that the interaction between employee and customer appears to be pleasant.[90] "Feeling rules" are formal and informal norms that require employees to display emotions appropriate to their jobs (e.g., salesclerks are expected to smile frequently, establish eye contact, and thank customers for purchasing). These feeling rules can be extended to internal customers as part of the responsibility of all employees.[91] However, the imposition of feeling rules on anyone, even persons with the attitude of a "conscripted employee," is an inappropriate means to the end of total quality service. There is no substitute for commitment to shared strategic values and sincere regard for the customer; this spirit of service cannot be coerced but must be voluntarily given. While it is important to recognize the emotional labor entailed in customer satisfaction, there are alternatives to feeling rule enforcement to achieve the desired result (e.g., careful selection processes to screen out potential attitude problems, frequent training mini-sessions on commitment to shared values, and/or more frequent breaks from heavy customer contact).

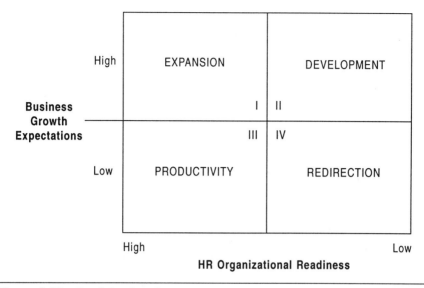

Figure 2.11   Total Quality Grand Human Resource Strategies.

Given a plan-based HR approach, the interdependent congruence between total quality grand business strategies and total quality grand HR strategies is illustrated in Figure 2.11.[92]

The vertical axis in Figure 2.11, business growth expectations, is a proxy for the goals of the organization as a whole, while the horizontal axis, organizational readiness, measures availability or obtainability of HR knowledge, skills, and/or abilities needed for strategy implementation. The business and HR grand strategy quadrants remain the same (although quadrant category names are different), and the following correlated total quality HR strategies apply to the four quadrants.

In quadrant I, expansion (high growth expectations and high HR level of readiness), the total quality HR grand strategy options include: (1) HR investment to maintain desired growth and continued readiness, (2) allocation decisions regarding the proportion of resources to be devoted to growth and to managing the effects of growth (e.g., updating systems), and/or (3) balance the costs of expansion with the benefits that additional growth is expected to provide.

In quadrant II, development, (high growth expectations and low level of HR readiness), the total quality HR grand strategy options include: (1) invest heavily in existing human resources to improve implementation feasibility of strategic and operational goals, (2) adjust business goals to reflect the lack of current HR readiness, and/or (3) keep strategic goals and change business operating strategy to capitalize on existing unit-, firm-, and industry-specific HR skills in order to generate new products services. For total quality HR programs that attempt to commit to employment security and promotion from within, firm-specific rather than unit-specific skill development provides greater flexibility to enhance readiness of HR resources.

In quadrant III, productivity (low growth expectations and high HR readiness), the total quality HR grand strategy options include: (1) focus on how to best channel the results of productive activities that are no longer required to extend a market or establish a position, (2) prepare for anticipated changes by investing in HR resources from related or unrelated businesses, and/or (3) optimize the unit, firm, and industry skill mix to facilitate business diversification and/or integration.

In quadrant IV, redirection (low growth expectations and low HR readiness), the total quality HR grand strategy options include: (1) evaluate the industry condition to determine turnaround feasibility with current human resources, (2) assess the firm's competitive position given the current HR skill mix and/or timely acquisition of necessary competitive skills, and/or (3) HR strategies suitable for exit, either through divestiture or liquidation.

Again, there is a parallel correlation between each of the business and HR grand strategies. The HR grand strategy in quadrant I (expansion) supports quadrant I of the business strategy by redirecting resources to maximize strengths in market penetration, product development, and indigenous innovation. The HR grand strategy in quadrant II (development) supports quadrant II of the business grand strategy by acquiring resources external to the firm to maximize strengths in horizontal integration, concentric diversification, joint venture, and adaptive innovation; all the business options require highly developed human resources to succeed. The HR grand strategy in quadrant III (productivity) channels high-quality human resources to support quadrant III of the business grand strategy by acquiring resources external to the firm that overcome weaknesses by utilizing backward integration, vertical forward integration, and conglomerate diversification. The HR grand strategy in quadrant IV (redirection) aligns with quadrant IV of the business grand strategy by redirecting resources within the firm that overcome weaknesses by relying on turnaround, divestiture, and/or liquidation.

Selected total quality tactical strategies that parallel the HR total quality grand strategies are indicated in Table 2.7. The HR tactical strategies in Table 2.7 provide intermediate range translations of total quality grand strategies into more operational terms. Total quality HR tactics always involve extensive organizational communication, team involvement, training services, and the possibility of organization development (OD) interventions to facilitate organization change.

In addition, there are generic total quality HR strategies that are correlated with the generic business strategies to ensure appropriate employee

Table 2.7 Total Quality Human Resource Grand
and Selected Tactical Strategies

Total quality HR grand strategies	Selected total quality HR tactical strategies
Expansion	• Aggressive hiring, training, and promotion • Promotion of successful experienced personnel • R&D recruitment • Expansion advisory teams • Rapidly rising wage ranges • Job creation • OD interventions for expansion • Communication of tactical strategy throughout organization
Development	• Job redesign and job combinations • Retraining • Job creation • Acculturation training • Expand training and development • External growth teams • OD interventions for development • R&D recruitment • Selective layoffs, if required • Communication of tactical strategy throughout organization
Productivity	• Productivity increases • Acculturation training • Early retirement • OD interventions for productivity • Continuous training and development • Managed turnover • Efficiency improvement teams • Communication of tactical strategy throughout organization
Redirection	• Retraining • Job redesign • Reassignments • Restructuring • Redirection teams • Early retirement • OD interventions for redirection • Renegotiated labor agreements • Transition training and services • Layoffs and terminations, when required • Communication of tactical strategy throughout organization

role behaviors for each strategy, as indicated in Table 2.8. Each generic business strategy quadrant requires a generic total quality HR strategy for organizational congruence. HR practitioners who want to make substantive contributions to total quality strategy formulation need to be aware of the appropriate strategic employee role behaviors and align policies, processes, project measurements, and outcomes to ensure that HR strategy formulation implementation and evaluation are congruent with organizational directions.

TOTAL QUALITY HUMAN RESOURCE STRATEGY MANAGEMENT

Total quality HR strategy management is also reciprocally interdependent with business strategy management.[93] This insight is probably the most important contribution of the quality orientation to HR practitioners. Organization design input, interventions at implementation and evaluation stages, and application of total quality processes to the HR unit performance are ways that enhance the strategic role of human resources and distinguish total quality HR programs from traditional ones. The role of implementation is so significant that the identity of total quality HR units is shaped by the statement: "we implement fully, therefore we are." Traditional HR programs, on the other hand, often follow the Cartesian statement: "we think (design HR policies), therefore we are." HR strategy planning without the implementation required by HR strategy management will likely result in a flashy launch of a quality initiative without the concrete follow-through to ensure the full functioning of the quality HR approach.

Total quality organizations require a different design than traditional hierarchies in order to be effective. In general, they organize around processes (instead of tasks), flatten hierarchies, use teams to manage everything, let customer satisfaction drive output, reward team results, maximize supplier and customer contact, and inform and train all employees. Creating and sustaining this type of organization requires the collaboration of HR and corporate strategic managers to focus on the following actions:[94]

1. *Identify* strategic objectives.

2. *Analyze* key competitive advantages to fulfilling objectives.

3. *Define* core processes, focusing on what is essential to achieve objectives.

4. *Organize* around processes, not functions. Each process should link related tasks to yield a competitive product or service to a customer.

Table 2.8 Alignment of Generic Business and Human Resource Strategies for Employee Role Behaviors

Generic business Quadrant I: Cost leadership	Generic business Quadrant II: Low cost and high differentiation	Generic business Quadrant III: Differentiation	Generic business Quadrant IV: High cost/low differentiation
1. Highly repetitive and predictable behaviors	1. Moderate creative and predictable behaviors	1. High degree of creative behavior	1. High repetitive and predictable behavior
2. Short-term focus	2. Long-term focus	2. Long-term focus	2. Short-term focus
3. Primarily autonomous or individual activity	3. High level of cooperative and interdependent behavior	3. Moderate level of cooperative, interdependent behavior	3. Dependent level of interaction
4. Modest concern for quality	4. High concern for quality	4. Moderate concern for quality	4. Low concern for quality
5. High concern for quantity of output	5. Moderate concern for quantity of output	5. Moderate concern for quantity of output	5. Low concern for quantity of output
6. Primary concern for results	6. High concern for process (*how* goods and services are made and delivered)	6. Equal moderate degree of concern for process and results	6. Equal low degree of concern for process and results
7. Low degree of risk taking	7. Moderate risk taking	7. High degree of risk taking	7. Low degree of risk taking
8. Commitment to organizational stability and moderate tolerance for change	8. Commitment to organizational goals with moderate tolerance for change	8. Commitment to creative process and high tolerance for ambiguity and change	8. Commitment to individual comfort and low tolerance for change
9. Extensive use of "virtual" employees, outsourcing temporaries	9. Avoidance of "virtual" employees, e.g., outsourcing temporaries	9. Moderate use of "virtual" employees, e.g., outsourcing temporaries	9. Extensive use of "virtual" employees, e.g., outsourcing temporaries
10. Reduce wage levels as far as possible for individuals and groups	10. Keep wage level range competitive for individuals and groups	10. Keep wage levels very high to attract innovative individuals	10. Reduce wage levels as far as possible for individuals and groups

5. *Determine* key process indicators and performance measurement variations.

6. *Eliminate* all activities that fail to add value or contribute to the key objectives.

7. *Cut* function and staff departments to a minimum, preserving key expertise.

8. *Appoint* a manager or team as the "owner" of each core process.

9. *Create* multidisciplinary teams to run each process and specific projects.

10. *Determine* performance standards for processes, projects, and persons.

11. *Empower* employees with the authority, resources, and information to achieve quality goals.

12. *Revamp* planning, staffing, training/development, appraisal, reward, and budgeting systems to support the new structure and link it to customer satisfaction.

The interdependence of organization design and HR strategy management as well as the dramatic differences between total quality company/HR configurations and others are indicated in Table 2.9.[95]

The three types of organization structures (pyramid, delayered restructured pyramid, and networks/alliances) indicate corporate strategic priorities and require integrated HR strategy implementation for success. The last alternative approximates the ideal total quality organization structure and, therefore, entails different HR strategy management activities than the traditional pyramid-based HR approaches. HR practitioners who want total quality strategic impact must be willing to engage in organization redesign at the implementation stage.

Furthermore, total quality HR strategy managers must be willing to engage in the shaping, introduction, maintenance, and review of total quality initiatives.[96]

Total quality HR strategy managers *shape* total quality management (TQM) by being actively involved in the following activities:

1. Preparing and synthesizing reports from other organizations that have experience in TQM, in conjunction with the management team

2. Assisting with choices about which TQM approach to adopt and, in particular, helping to identify which, if any, external consultants may be able to offer appropriate advice

3. Identifying any internal sources of expertise

Table 2.9 Organization Design and Human Resource
Strategy Implementation

Organization structure	Strategic priorities	HR strategy implementation
Pyramid 	• Command and control	• Hierarchical, specified career paths • Specific, detailed job descriptions • Pay supports, merit promotions, and commitment • Training is job specific • Information in hands of top managers
Delayered restructured pyramid 	• Remove layers • Enrich jobs • Team focus • Empower employees	• Limited career paths, horizontal promotions • Share career responsibility with employee • Generic job descriptions • Pay emphasizes individual and team performance • Training emphasizes generalist and flexibility • Information shared with teams on need-to-know basis
Networks/ alliances 	• Recreate boundaries to suppliers and customers • De-emphasize functional specialties • Emphasize customers • Team as basic building block	• Careers primarily individual responsibility • Generic job descriptions • Training options at individual discretion • Pay emphasizes individual knowledge and team performance • Information is widely accessible

Source: Milkovich, George T. and Boudreau, John W. (1994). *Human Resource Management*. 7th ed., Burr Ridge, Ill.: Irwin, p. 122.

4. Utilizing the expertise of practitioners from other organizations by gaining access to local TQM networks

5. Ensuring that an appropriate infrastructure for TQM is put into place and takes sufficient account of both customer feedback and people-management issues

6. Reviewing current practices, behavior, and attitudes in the organization and assessing their degree of fit with TQM

7. Shaping the type of organizational structure, culture, and ethical climate appropriate for introducing and sustaining TQM

8. Designing and delivering senior management development courses that set the proper tone for TQM

9. Developing a TQM directory of internal resources and expertise

Total quality HR strategy managers *facilitate the introduction and adoption* of TQM by being actively involved in the following activities:

1. Encouraging and facilitating a total quality partnership between company and union leadership in order to establish collaboration to benefit all stakeholders

2. Training all formal leaders (including union officers) in the principles of TQM, advising them of the best means of developing a process of continuous improvement within their areas of influence, encouraging them to persuade everyone to take personal responsibility for their own quality assurance, and being prepared to seek improvements

3. Identifying the conditions necessary for the successful use of quality management tools and techniques

4. Providing guidance on what is necessary for the successful employment of teams that focus on quality improvement and how they fit into the organizational structure

5. Training and coaching facilitators, mentors, and team members in interpersonal skills and how to manage the improvement process

6. Designing communication events and vehicles to publicize the launch of TQM and early successes

7. Consulting with employees about the introduction and development of TQM

8. Institutionalizing organizational ethics development programs

9. Proactively contributing to vision and mission statements and preparing quality objectives for dissemination to staff, customers, and suppliers

Next, total quality HR strategy managers *maintain and reinforce* TQM within the organization by being actively involved in the following activities:

1. Adopting selection processes that target and screen for conceptual, technical, ethical, and social skills that support a TQM environment

2. Introducing or upgrading the quality awareness and TQM component within orientation courses

3. Identifying the most appropriate mechanisms for recognizing and rewarding achievements, in particular looking at nontraditional reward systems

4. Ensuring that training in quality management tools, techniques, and processes continues to be provided within the organization and that the knowledge imparted in such training is being used in the workplace

5. Redesigning appraisal procedures so that they contain criteria relating to specific TQM objectives, appropriate social relations skills, and support personal responsibility, self-assessment, and 360-degree performance feedback

6. Preparing and overseeing special newsletters or team briefs on TQM and improvement initiatives and the outcome of quality improvement team projects

7. Assisting continuous improvement and project teams to work effectively and innovate

Finally, the total quality HR strategy managers *review* TQM implementation progress by being actively involved in the following activities:

1. Contributing to or leading the preparation of an annual TQM report

2. Assessing the effectiveness of the TQM infrastructure, including steering committees, quality councils, quality improvement teams, improvement facilitators, project teams, and individual performance

3. Preparing and administering employee attitude and ethical climate surveys and disseminating their results

4. Coordinating customer comments on the organization's progress

5. Benchmarking the effectiveness of the organization's TQM with that of competitors and global best practices

6 Facilitating the operation of internal reviews using criteria such as ISO 9000, the Malcolm Baldrige National Quality Award, or the Deming Prize

7. Identifying the barriers to continuous quality improvement

8. Conducting HR, quality, and ethics audits

Total quality HR strategic management would not be complete if HR practitioners do not *review their own activities* as they do all other areas. Some of the more typical self-review total quality activities include:

1. Undertaking a department mission analysis of the functional contribution of human resources to the organization, which could include the following:

   - Identifying internal customers and suppliers

   - Agreeing to performance measures as part of service-level agreements

   - Tracking such measurements

   - Identifying non-value-added activities

   - Taking part in cross-functional project teams to resolve interface problems with customers and suppliers

2. Selecting new HR employees only with peer and customer involvement

3. Appraising and rewarding HR staff for teamwork, ethical integrity, and customer satisfaction

4. Training and developing HR employees on a regular basis

5. Surveying and distributing the results of HR staff satisfaction and ethical climate surveys

6. Providing advice on ethical problem analysis and conflict resolution within a specified and agreed-upon time period

7. Benchmarking HR policies and processes with world-class models

In summary, total quality HR strategic management expands the strategic responsibilities of HR practitioners and challenges them to change from "professional whiners" (because they are excluded from strategy input) into "total quality winners" as productive members of the strategy team.

REVIEW QUESTIONS

2.1. How does total quality strategy differ from traditional strategy planning and management?

2.2. What essential factors in the external and internal environments set the context for total quality strategy and, therefore, should be scanned, analyzed, and influenced?

2.3. In what four ways do U.S. financial measures compare unfavorably with Japanese financial measures as reporting vehicles on critical success factors?

2.4. What are the four types of enterprise vision, and how does the total quality enterprise vision differ from the others?

2.5. What ten key questions should the organization's mission answer?

2.6. What are the ten strategic objectives of total quality, and what is the specific aim of each objective?

2.7. What are the major grand and generic strategies that an organization can employ?

2.8. What roles do process integration, project involvement, and performance integration play in strategy management?

2.9. Elaborate on the four possible roles of the human resource function in total quality management.

2.10. Discuss the reciprocal interdependence of total quality business competitive strategy and total quality human resource strategy.

2.11. How does the total quality human resource paradigm differ from the traditional paradigm in the six human resource professional certification areas?

2.12. What ten generic quality human resource strategies are correlated with the generic business strategy of high cost/low differentiation?

DISCUSSION QUESTIONS

2.1. Compare and contrast the five types of organizational defense patterns and indicate how they are used to deny performance gaps and justify mediocre performance.

2.2. Assess the benefits and risks of creating a total quality partnership with suppliers. Do you agree that this is a wise move, regardless of industry and/or ethical work culture? Why or why not?

2.3. Describe the best and worst ethical work cultures you have personally experienced. What did you learn from the impact of those work cultures on people and performance that you believe will serve you well in the future?

2.4. In what ways has U.S. strategic leadership in the private and public sectors violated total quality objectives, and how has this strategic incompetence impacted human resources?

2.5. Discuss the factors to consider in responsible organizational total quality and human resource total quality strategy planning and management.

2.6. Discuss the relationship between total quality business and human resource grand strategies.

2.7. Discuss the ways in which total quality human resource strategy managers must be willing to shape, introduce, maintain, and review total quality initiatives.

ENDNOTES

1. See Horovitz, J. and Panak, M.J. (1994). *Total Customer Satisfaction.* Burr Ridge, Ill.: Irwin; Barsky, Jonathan D. (1994). *World-Class Customer Satisfaction.* Burr Ridge, Ill.: Irwin; Whiteley, Richard C. (1991). *The Customer-Driven Company.* Reading, Mass.: Addison-Wesley.

2. There are at least five approaches to strategic planning and management: (1) the *rational/analytic* approach relies on a conscious, "top-down," linear flowchart model (Pearce, John A. II and Robinson, Richard B. Jr. (1994). *Strategic Management.* 5th edition, Burr Ridge, Ill.: Irwin; Thompson, Arthur A. Jr. and Strickland, A. III (1992). *Strategic Management.* 6th edition, Homewood, Ill.: Irwin; Wheelen, Thomas L. and Hunger, J. David (1992). *Strategic Management and Business Policy.* 4th edition, Reading, Mass.: Addison-Wesley); (2) the *intuitive/inductive* approach emphasizes a more imaginative, empirical, incrementally emergent "bottom-up" model (Quinn, J.B., Mintzberg, H., and James, R.M. (1988). *The Strategy Process.* Englewood Cliffs, N.J.: Prentice-Hall; Quinn, J.B. (1980). *Strategies for Change: Logical Incrementalism.* Homewood, Ill.: Irwin); (3) the *political/behavioral* approach emphasizes the power and influence factors in strategic decision making (Cyert, R.M. and March, J.G. (1963). *A Behavioral Theory of the Firm.* Englewood Cliffs, N.J.: Prentice-Hall); (4) the *customer value* approach relies on detailed market opportunity analysis that emphasizes a customer-driven rather than competition-driven model (Bounds, G., Yorks, L., Adams, A., and Ranney, G. (1994). *Beyond Total Quality Management.* New York: McGraw-Hill); and (5) the *unconscious/drift* approach focuses on individual and/or collective unconscious factors that lead to strategy utilization (Kets de Vries, M.F. and Miller, D. (1984). *The Neurotic Organization.* San Francisco: Jossey-Bass; Mitroff, I. (1983). "Archetypal Social System Analysis: On the Deeper Structure of Human Systems." *Academy of Management Review.* Vol. 9, No. 2, pp. 207–224). The authors' approach is a creative hybrid version of these five approaches.

3. This model is adapted with modifications from Wheelen, Thomas L. and Hunger, J. David (1992). *Strategic Management and Business Policy.* 4th

edition, Reading, Mass.: Addison-Wesley. Strategic quality planning (SQP) differs from traditional strategic planning in four ways: (1) the role of quality in strategy is accorded more preeminence for total quality practitioners than traditional strategic planners since quality is broadly conceived as meeting or exceeding customer expectations by total quality advocates and narrowly conceived by traditional strategists as one form of differentiation; (2) strategy implementation is emphasized by SQP whereas strategy formulation is emphasized by traditional strategists; (3) the strategic focus of SQP is on customer expectations and aligning the organization accordingly, whereas traditional strategists realize that there are multiple ways of satisfying customer expectations which are dependent on the core strengths and weaknesses of organizations, thereby pointing to the need (addressed in this book) to conduct quality and ethics audits to measure and improve organizational capability; and (4) the strategic process is regarded by total quality advocates as more important than strategic content and as uniform, whereas traditional strategists emphasize content over process and explain strategic process variation in terms of size, structure, and other variables. See Dean, James W. Jr. and Bowen, David E. (1994). "Management Theory and Total Quality: Improving Research and Practice Through Theory Development." *Academy of Management Review*. Vol. 19, No. 3, pp. 403–406.

4. See Willig, John T., Ed. (1994). *Environmental TQM*. 2nd edition, New York: McGraw-Hill; Stead, W.E. and Stead, J.G. (1992). *Management for a Small Planet: Strategic Decision Making and the Environment*. Newbury Park, Calif.: Sage; and Dechant, K. and Altman, B. (1994). "Environmental Leadership: From Compliance to Competitive Advantage." *Academy of Management Executive*. Vol. 8, No. 3, pp. 7–27 for detailed treatment of sustainable development as an important natural consideration in SQP. Total quality organizations also react to and influence their social environments by proactively building international, national, and regional societal learning networks that share information about new quality practices and, in turn, place social pressure on other organizations to meet new quality standards. In Japan, for example, the extended institutional infrastructure of societal learning includes six elements: (1) national promotional organizations, (2) national training in existing quality methods, (3) national knowledge dissemination of new quality methods, (4) societal learning and promotion activities, (5) national and international standard certification, and (6) sustained research and development of new total quality methods. Among the national promotional organizations are the Ministry of International Trade and Industry (MITI), the Japanese Industrial Standards (JIS), the Union of Japanese Scientists and Engineers (JUSE), and the Japanese Standards Association (JSA). The primary roles of JUSE and JSA are national training, national knowledge dissemination, societal learning, promotional activities, and new research and development efforts. JIS, in conjunction with the International Standards Organization

(ISO), certify national and international quality standards. While the United States has somewhat of a social network infrastructure (the American Society for Quality Control, GOAL/QPC, Center for Quality Management, Department of Labor Office of the American Workplace, and others), it is not as integrated and mutually reinforcing as the Japanese network. For more detailed information on total quality strategic networking to influence the social environment, see Shiba, Shoji, Graham, Alan, and Walden, David (1993). *A New American TQM: Four Practical Revolutions in Management.* Cambridge, Mass.: Productivity Press, pp. 505–557; Reich, Robert B. (1992). *The Work of Nations: Preparing Ourselves for 21st Century Capitalism.* New York: Vintage, pp. 268–282; Reich, Robert B. (1994). "Leadership and the High Performance Organization." *Journal for Quality and Participation.* Vol. 17, No. 2, pp. 6–11.

5. Lehmann, D.R. and Winer, R.S. (1991). *Analysis for Marketing Planning.* 2nd edition, Homewood, Ill.: Irwin, pp. 119–120.

6. Rust, Roland T., Zahorik, Anthony R., and Keininghan, Timothy L. (1994). *Return on Quality.* Chicago: Probus Publishing, pp. 105–107.

7. Bounds, G., Yorks, L., Adams, A., and Ranney, G. (1994). *Beyond Total Quality Management.* New York: McGraw-Hill, pp. 181–182.

8. Bounds G.M. and Dobbins, G. (1993). "Changing the Managerial Agenda." *Journal of General Management.* Vol. 8, No. 3, pp. 77–93.

9. Bounds, G., Yorks, L., Adams, A., and Ranney, G. (1994). *Beyond Total Quality Management.* New York: McGraw-Hill, p. 182.

10. Tenner, Arthur R. and DeToro, Irving J. (1992). *Total Quality Management: Three Steps to Continuous Improvement.* Reading, Mass.: Addison-Wesley, p. 197.

11. Juran, J.M. (1989). *Juran on Leadership for Quality: An Executive Handbook.* New York: Macmillan, p. 38. Copyright by Juran Institute, Inc.

12. Frederickson, J.W. (1986). "The Strategic Decision Process and Organizational Structure." *Academy of Management Review.* Vol. 16, No. 4, pp. 280–297; Miller, D. (1986). "Configurations of Strategy and Structure: Towards a Synthesis." *Strategic Management Journal.* Vol. 11, No. 5, pp. 233–249.

13. Primozic, K., Primozic, E., and Leben, J. (1991). *Strategic Choices.* New York: McGraw-Hill, pp. 83–108.

14. Petrick, Joseph A. and Quinn, John F. (1995). *Management Ethics and Organization Integrity.* Thousand Oaks, Calif.: Sage, pp. 15–17.

15. Lorsch, J. (1985). "Strategic Myopia: Culture as an Invisible Barrier to Change." In R.H. Kilmann, M.J. Saxton, and R. Serpa, Eds. *Gaining Control of the Corporate Culture.* San Francisco: Jossey-Bass, pp. 84–102; Ansoff, H.I. and Baker, T.E. (1986). "Is Corporate Culture the Ultimate Answer?" In R. Lamb and P. Shrivastava, Eds. *Advances in Strategic Management.* Vol. 4, Greenwich, Conn.: JAI Press, p. 84.

16. Olian, Judy D. and Rynes, Sara L. (1991). "Making Total Quality Work: Aligning Organizational Processes, Performance Measures, and Stakeholders." *Human Resource Management.* Vol. 30, No. 3, pp. 303–333.

17. Stalk, G. Jr. and Hart, T.M. (1990). *Competing Against Time: How Time-Based Competition Is Reshaping Global Markets.* New York: Free Press; Meredith, J., McCutcheon, D., and Raturi, A. (1994). "The Customization-Responsiveness Squeeze." *Sloan Management Review.* Vol. 18, No. 1 (Winter), pp. 89–99.

18. Kaplan, R.S. (1984). "Yesterday's Accounting Undermines Production." *Harvard Business Review.* Vol. 62, No. 3, pp. 95–101.

19. Sakurai, M. (1992). "Target Costing and How to Use It." In B.J. Bunker, Ed. *Emerging Practices in Cost Management.* Boston: Warren, Gorham and Lamont, pp. 65–72.

20. Olian, Judy D. and Rynes, Sara L. (1991). "Making Total Quality Work: Aligning Organizational Processes, Performance Measures, and Stakeholders." *Human Resource Management.* Vol. 30, No. 3, p. 319.

21. Johnson, H.T. (1990). "Professors, Customers and Value: Bringing a Global Perspective to Management Accounting Education." In P. Turney, Ed. *Performance Excellence in Manufacturing and Service Organizations.* Sarasota, Fla.: American Accounting Association, pp. 95–111; Turney, P.B. (1991). "Using Activity-Based Costing to Achieve Manufacturing Excellence." In B.J. Brinker, Ed. *Emerging Practices in Cost Management.* Boston: Warren, Gorham, Lamont, pp. 47–58.

22. Petrick, Joseph A. and Wagley, Robert A. (1992). "Enhancing the Responsible Strategic Management of Organizations." *Journal of Management Development.* Vol. 11, No. 4, pp. 57–72; Paine, Lynn Sharp (1994). "Managing for Organizational Integrity." *Harvard Business Review.* Vol. 75, No. 4, pp. 106–117.

23. Petrick, Joseph A. and Manning, George E. (1993). "Paradigm Shifts in Quality Management and Ethics Development." *Business Forum.* Vol. 18, No. 4, p. 17.

24. Hoffman, Michael (1986). "Developing the Ethical Corporation." *Bell Atlantic Quarterly.* Vol. 3, No. 1, pp. 18–21.

25. Anthony, W., Maddox, T., and Wheatley, M. (1988). *Envisionary Management.* New Haven, Conn.: Greenwood Press, pp. 10–15.

26. Mintzberg, Henry. (1994). "The Rise and Fall of Strategic Planning." *Harvard Business Review.* Vol. 76, No. 1, pp. 107–115.

27. Modified from Freeman, R. Edward and Gilbert, Daniel R. Jr. (1988). *Corporate Strategy and the Search for Ethics.* Englewood Cliffs, N.J.: Prentice-Hall, pp. 72–73; Ansoff, H. Igor (1984). *Implanting Strategic Management.* Englewood Cliffs, N.J.: Prentice-Hall, pp. 129–151.

28. Collins, Brendan and Huge, Ernest. (1993). *Management for Policy: How Companies Focus Their Total Quality Efforts to Achieve Competitive Advantage.* Milwaukee: ASQC Quality Press, pp. 83–84. The latest empirical comparison of Baldrige winner leadership styles with those in the same U.S. industry is enlightening. Clearly, senior executive total quality involvement and visibility and operational leadership that consistently reinforces quality processes at lower levels is strategically greater in the Baldrige winner than elsewhere. See Petrick, Joseph A., Scherer, Robert A., Wilson,

J.C., and Westfall, F. (1994). "Benchmarking and Improving Core Competencies." *Journal for Quality and Participation.* Vol. 17, No. 4, pp. 72–77.

29. Argyris, Chris. (1990). *Overcoming Organizational Defenses: Facilitating
Organizational Learning.* Boston: Allyn and Bacon, pp. 5–25.

30. Hornstein, Harvey. (1986). *Managerial Courage.* New York: John Wiley, pp.
18–19.

31. Argyris, Chris. (1985). *Strategy, Change and Defensive Routines.* Boston:
Ballenger, pp. 6–40.

32. Argyris, Chris. (1985). *Strategy, Change and Defensive Routines.* Boston:
Ballenger, p. 64.

33. Modified from David, Fred R. (1989). *Concepts of Strategic Management.*
2nd edition, Columbus, Ohio: Merrill Publishing, pp. 104–105.

34. Ansoff, H.I. (1988). *The New Corporate Strategy.* New York: John Wiley &
Sons, pp. 75–77; Snyder, N.H., Dowd, J.J. Jr. and Houghton, D.M. (1994).
Vision, Values and Courage. New York: Free Press, pp. 153–204.

35. Wheelen, Thomas L. and Hunger, J. David. (1992). *Strategic Management
and Business Policy.* Reading, Mass.: Addison-Wesley, p. 15.

36. Richards, M.D. (1987). *Setting Strategic Goals and Objectives.* 2nd edition, St.
Paul, Minn.: West Publishing, p. 12.

37. Richards, M.D. (1987). *Setting Strategic Goals and Objectives.* 2nd edition, St.
Paul, Minn.: West Publishing, p. 18.

38. Sakurai, M. (1992). "Target Costing and How to Use It." In B.J. Bunker, Ed.
Emerging Practices in Cost Management. Boston: Warren, Gorham and
Lamont, pp. 66–68.

39. Schlender, Brenton R. (1994). "Japan's White-Collar Blues." *Fortune.* Vol.
129, No. 6, pp. 97–104.

40. Schlender, Brenton R. (1994). "Japan's White-Collar Blues." *Fortune.* Vol.
129, No. 6, p. 98.

41. Northey, Patrick (1993). *Cycle Time Management: The Fast Track to Time-
Based Production.* Portland, Ore.: Productivity Press, pp. 5–85; Stalk, George
and Hout, Thomas (1990). *Competing Against Time: How Time-Based Competition Is Reshaping Global Markets.* New York: Free Press, pp. 10–70.

42. Scherer, Robert F., Brodzinski, James D., and Crable, Elaine A. (1993).
"Human Factors in Workplace Accidents." *HR Magazine.* Vol. 21, No. 4,
pp. 92–97.

43. Buchholz, Rogene A. (1993). *Principles of Environmental Management.*
Englewood Cliffs, N.J.: Prentice-Hall, pp. 15–35.

44. Albrecht, Karl and Zemke, Ronald E. (1985). *Service America.* Homewood,
Ill.: Dow Jones-Irwin, pp. 10–24; Band, William A. (1991). *Creating Value
for Customers.* New York: John Wiley & Sons, pp. 14–40.

45. Lindsay, William H., Manning, George E., and Petrick, Joseph A. (1992).
"Work Morale in the 1990's." *SAM Advanced Management Journal.* Vol.
57, No. 31, pp. 43–48; Petrick, Joseph A. and Manning, George E.
(1990). "How to Manage Morale." *The Personnel Journal.* Vol. 69, No. 10,
pp. 82–88.

46. Lawler, Edward E. (1994). "Total Quality Management and Employee Involvement: Are They Compatible?" *Academy of Management Executive.* Vol. 8, No. 1, pp. 68–76; Lawler, E.E. (1992). *Employee Involvement and Total Quality Management.* San Francisco: Jossey-Bass, pp. 14–74; Katzenbach, Jon R. and Smith, Douglas K. (1993). *The Wisdom of Teams: Creating the High-Performance Organization.* Boston: Harvard Business School Press, pp. 212–293; Scholtes, Peter (1988). *The Team Handbook.* Madison, Wisc.: Joiner Associates, pp. 5–44.

47. Milkovich, George T. and Newman, Jerry M. (1992). *Compensation.* 4th ed., Homewood, Ill.: Irwin, pp. 2–30; McCaffery, Robert M. (1988). *Employee Benefit Programs: A Total Compensation Perspective.* Boston: PWS-Kent, pp. 14–37; Lawler, E.E. (1990). *Strategic Pay: Aligning Organizational Strategies and Pay Systems.* San Francisco: Jossey-Bass, pp. 25–60; Sheppard, Blair H., Lewicki, Roy J., and Minton, John W. (1992). *Organizational Justice: The Search for Fairness in the Workplace.* New York: Lexington Books, pp. 109–138.

48. Blinder, Alan S., Ed. (1990). *Paying for Productivity: A Look at the Evidence.* Washington, D.C.: Brookings Institution, pp. 5–60; Kohn, Alfie (1993). *Punished by Rewards.* Boston: Houghton Mifflin, pp. 179–198.

49. Yukl, Gary (1994). *Leadership in Organizations.* 3rd edition, Englewood Cliffs, N.J.: Prentice-Hall, pp. 252–462; Cohen, Allan R. and Bradford, David L. (1990). *Influence without Authority.* New York: John Wiley & Sons, pp. 1–25; Block, Peter (1992). *Stewardship: Choosing Service Over Self-Interest.* San Francisco: Berrett-Koehler, pp. 2–23; Rost, J.C. (1991). *Leadership for the Twenty-First Century.* New York: Praeger, pp. 15–80.

50. Ishikawa, K. and Lu, D. (1985). *What Is Total Quality Control? The Japanese Way.* Englewood Cliffs, N.J.: Prentice-Hall, pp. 40–60; Hammer, M. and Champy, J. (1993). *Reengineering the Corporation.* New York: Harper Collins, pp. 5–49; GOAL/QPC Research Committee (1991). *Cross-Functional Management.* Methuen, Mass.: GOAL/QPC, pp. 1–15; Akao, Yoji, Ed. (1991). *Hoshin Kanri: Policy Deployment for Successful TQM.* Cambridge, Mass.: Productivity Press, pp. 10–70; Withey, M.J. and Cooper, W.H. (1989). "Predicting Exit, Voice, Loyalty and Neglect." *Administrative Science Quarterly.* Vol. 34, No. 11, pp. 521–539.

51. Petrick, Joseph A. and Quinn, John F. (1995). *Management Ethics and Organization Integrity.* Thousand Oaks, Calif.: Sage, pp. 9–16; Petrick, Joseph A. and Manning, George E. (1990). "Developing an Ethical Climate for Excellence." *The Journal for Quality and Participation.* Vol. 14, No. 2, pp. 84–90; Paine, Lynn Sharp (1994). "Managing for Organizational Integrity." *Harvard Business Review.* Vol. 82, No. 3, pp. 106–117; Cohen, Deborah Vidaver (1993). "Creating and Maintaining Ethical Work Climates." *Business Ethics Quarterly.* Vol. 3, No. 4, pp. 343–358.

52. Sigler, Jay A. and Murphy, Joseph E. (1988). *Interactive Corporate Compliance: An Alternative to Regulatory Compulsion.* New York: Quorum Books, pp. 169–199; Fiorelli, Paul E. (1992). "Fine Reductions through Effective

Ethics Programs." *Albany Law Review.* Vol. 56, No. 2, pp. 403–440; Paine, Lynn Sharp (1994). "Managing for Organizational Integrity." *Harvard Business Review.* Vol. 82, No. 3, p. 113.

53. Petrick, Joseph A. and Manning, George E. (1990). "Developing an Ethical Climate for Excellence." *The Journal for Quality and Participation.* Vol. 14, No. 2, p. 88; Wilkins, A.L. (1989). *Developing Corporate Character.* San Francisco: Jossey-Bass, pp. 10–60; Weber, James (1993). "Institutionalizing Ethics into Business Organizations." *Business Ethics Quarterly.* Vol. 3, No. 4, pp. 419–436.

54. Imai, Masaaki (1986). *Kaizen: The Key to Japan's Competitive Success.* New York: Random House, pp. 15–66; Foster, Richard (1986). *Innovation: The Attacker's Advantage.* New York: Summit Books, pp. 165–285; Hammer, M. and Champy, J. (1993). *Reengineering the Corporation.* New York: Harper Collins, pp. 148–214; Utterback, James M. (1994). *Mastering the Dynamics of Innovation.* Boston: Harvard Business School; Main, Jeremy (1994). *Quality Wars: The Triumphs and Defeats of American Business.* New York: Free Press; Boulton, William R. (1993). *Resource Guide for Management of Innovation and Technology.* Auburn, Ala.: AACSB and Auburn University.

55. Watson, Gregory H. (1993). *Strategic Benchmarking.* New York: John Wiley & Sons; Camp, Robert C. (1989). *Benchmarking: The Search for Industry Best Practices that Lead to Superior Performance.* Milwaukee: Quality Press/American Society for Quality Control, pp. 25–75; Liebfried, K.H. and McNair, C.J. (1992). *Benchmarking: A Tool for Continuous Improvement.* New York: Harper Collins, pp. 40–77.

56. Porter, Michael (1980). *Competitive Strategy.* New York: Free Press, pp. 40–45.

57. Reitsperger, Wolf D., Daniel, Shirley J., Tallman, Stephen B., and Chisman, William G. (1993). "Product Quality and Cost Leadership: Compatible Strategies?" *International Management Review.* Vol. 33, No. 5, pp. 7–22; Porter, M.E. (1985). *Competitive Advantage: Creating and Sustaining Superior Performance.* New York: Free Press, pp. 80–95.

58. Sheridan, Bruce M. (1993). *Policy Deployment: The TQM Approach to Long-Range Planning.* Milwaukee: ASQC Quality Press, pp. 25–35.

59. Johansson, Henry J., McHugh, Patrick, Pendleburg, A. John, and Wheeler William A. III (1993). *Business Process Reengineering.* New York: John Wiley & Sons, pp. 210–212.

60. Akai, Yoji, Ed. (1990). *Quality Function Deployment.* Cambridge, MA: Productivity Press, pp. 47–55.

61. Johansson, Henry J., McHugh, Patrick, Pendleburg, A. John, and Wheeler William A. III (1993). *Business Process Reengineering.* New York: John Wiley & Sons, pp. 61–65; Hammer, Michael and Champy, James (1993). *Reengineering the Corporation.* New York: Harper Business, pp. 31–65; Moody, Patricia E. (1993). *Breakthrough Partnering.* Essex Junction, Vt.: Oliver Wright, pp. 3–33.

62. Imai, Massaki (1986), *Kaizen: The Key to Japan's Competitive Success.* New York: Random House, pp. 12–32.

63. Watson, Gregory H. (1992). *The Benchmarking Workbook: Adapting Best Practices for Performance Improvement.* Cambridge, Mass.: Productivity Press, pp. 15–25; Balm, Gerald J. (1992). *Benchmarking: A Practitioner's Guide for Becoming and Staying Best of the Best.* Schaumberg, Ill.: Quality and Productivity Management Association, pp. 6–18.

64. Wallace, Thomas F. and Barnard, William (1994). *Quantum Leap: Achieving Strategic Breakthroughs with QFD.* Essex Junction, Vt.: Oliver Wright, pp. 25–60.

65. Leavitt, Jeffrey S. and Nunn, Philip C. (1994). *Total Quality through Project Management.* New York: McGraw-Hill, pp. 47–50; Rosenau, Milton D. Jr. (1992). *Successful Project Management.* 2nd edition, New York: Van Nostrand Reinhold, pp. 18–40; Meredith, J. and Mantel, J.W. (1995). *Project Management.* New York: John Wiley, pp. 5–19; Lewis, James P. (1991). *Project Planning, Scheduling and Control.* Chicago: Probus, pp. 12–85; Collins, Brendan and Huge, Ernest (1993). *Management by Policy.* Milwaukee: ASQC, pp. 161–164.

66. Lawler, Edward E. (1994). "Total Quality Management and Employee Involvement: Are They Compatible?" *The Academy of Management Executive.* Vol. 8, No. 1, pp. 68–76; Lawler, E.E., Mohrman, S.A., and Ledford, G.E. (1992). *Employee Involvement and Total Quality Management: Practices and Results in Fortune 1000 Companies.* San Francisco: Jossey-Bass. Evidence supports the view that the most effective organizations are those that have integrated or coordinated TQM and employee involvement programs.

67. Gobeli, D.H. and Larson, E.W. (1987). "Relative Effectiveness of Different Project Structures." *Project Management Journal.* Vol. 18, No. 2, pp. 82–83.

68. McCollum, J.K. and Sherman, J.D. (1993). "The Matrix Structure: Bane or Benefit to High Tech Organizations?" *Project Management Journal.* Vol. 23, No. 2, pp. 44–46.

69. Elmes, M. and Wilemon, D. (1988). "Organizational Culture and Project Leader Effectiveness." *Project Management Journal.* Vol. 19, No. 4, pp. 54–60; Katzenbach, Jon R. and Smith, Douglas K. (1993). *The Wisdom of Teams.* New York: Harper Business, pp. 27–84; Wellins, Richard S., Byham, William C., and Wilson, Jeanne M. (1991). *Empowered Teams: Creating Self-Directed Work Groups that Improve Quality.* San Francisco: Jossey-Bass, pp. 10–90.

70. Leavitt, Jeffrey S. and Nunn, Philip C. (1994). *Total Quality through Project Management.* New York: McGraw-Hill, pp. 50–53; Klein, Ralph L. and Ludin, I.S. (1992). *The People Side of Project Management.* Brookfield, Vt.: Gower Publishing, pp. 72–78.

71. Roberts, Harry V. and Sergesketter, Bernard F. (1993). *Quality Is Personal: A Foundation for Total Quality Management.* New York: Free Press, pp. 1–27; Schultz, Louis (1991). *Personal Management: A System for Individual Performance Improvement.* Minneapolis: Process Management International.

72. Roberts, Harry V. and Sergesketter, Bernard F. (1993). *Quality Is Personal: A Foundation for Total Quality Management.* New York: Free Press, pp. 27–

60; Schultz, Louis (1991). *Personal Management: A System for Individual Performance Improvement.* Minneapolis: Process Management International, pp. 6–9.

73. Kaufman, Roger (1988). "Preparing Useful Performance Indicators." *Training and Development Journal.* Vol. 10, No. 4, pp. 80–83.

74. Burach, Elmer H. (1985). "Linking Corporate Business and Human Resources Planning: Strategic Issues and Concerns." *Human Resource Planning.* Vol. 8, No. 3, pp. 133–145; Nkomo, Stella M. (1986). "The Theory and Practice of HR Planning: The Gap Still Remains." *Personnel Administrator.* Vol. 31, No. 8, pp. 71–84.

75. Fombrun, Charles J., Tichy, Noel M., and Devanna, M.A. (1984). *Strategic Human Resource Management.* New York: John Wiley & Sons, pp. 22–23.

76. Gordon, George C. (1987). "Getting in Step." *Personnel Administrator.* Vol. 32, No. 14, pp. 44–48; Jarrell, Donald W. (1993). *Human Resource Planning: A Business Planning Approach.* Englewood Cliffs, N.J.: Prentice-Hall, pp. 51–61.

77. Blackburn, Richard and Rosen, Benson (1993). "Total Quality and Human Resource Management: Lessons Learned form Baldrige Award-Winning Companies." *Academy of Management Executive.* Vol. 7, No. 3, pp. 49–66.

78. Olian, Judy D. and Rynes, Sara L. (1991). "Making Total Quality Work: Aligning Organizational Processes, Performance Measures, and Stakeholders." *Human Resource Management.* Vol. 30, No. 3, p. 324; Fitz-Enz, J. (1990). *Human Value Management.* San Francisco: Jossey-Bass, pp. 10–70; Schuler, R.S. (1990). "Repositioning the Human Resource Function: Transformation or Demise?" *Academy of Management Executive.* Vol. 4, No. 5, pp. 49–60.

79. Dobbins, G., Cardy, R.L., and Carson, K. (1991). "Examining Fundamental Assumptions: A Contrast of Person and System Approaches to Human Resource Management." In G. Ferris and K. Rowlands, Eds. *Research in Personnel and Human Resource Management.* Vol. 9, New York: John Wiley & Sons, pp. 1–38.

80. Bellmay, G.M. (1986). *The Quest for Staff Leadership.* Glenview, Ill.: Scott, Foresman, pp. 10–60; Olian, Judy D. and Rynes, Sara L. (1991). "Making Total Quality Work: Aligning Organizational Processes, Performance Measures, and Stakeholders." *Human Resource Management.* Vol. 30, No. 3, pp. 315–318.

81. Fitz-Enz, J. (1990). *Human Value Management.* San Francisco: Jossey-Bass, pp. 55–69; Olian, Judy D. and Rynes, Sara L. (1991). "Making Total Quality Work: Aligning Organizational Processes, Performance Measures, and Stakeholders." *Human Resource Management.* Vol. 30, No. 3, pp. 321–322.

82. Gordon, George C. (1987). "Getting in Step." *Personnel Administrator.* Vol. 32, No. 14, p. 46.

83. Wilkinson, Adrian, Marchington, Mick, and Dale, B. (1993). "Enhancing the Contribution of the Human Resource Function to Quality Improvement." *Quality Management Journal.* Vol. 1, No. 1, pp. 35–46.

84. Adapted from Blackburn, Richard and Rosen, Benson (1993). "Total Quality and Human Resources Management: Lessons Learned from Baldrige Award-Winning Companies." *Academy of Management Executive.* Vol. 7, No. 3, p. 51; Weinberg, R.B., Mathis, R.L., and Cherrington, D.J. (1991). *Human Resource Certification Institute Certification Study Guide.* Alexandria, Va.: HRCI Institute, pp. 23–64.

85. Lengnick-Hall, C.A. and Lengnick-Hall, M.L. (1988). "Strategic Human Resource Management: A Review of the Literature and a Proposed Typology." *Academy of Management Review.* Vol. 13, No. 3, pp. 454–470.

86. Lengnick-Hall, C.A. and Lengnick-Hall, M.L. (1988). "Strategic Human Resource Management: A Review of the Literature and a Proposed Typology." *Academy of Management Review.* Vol. 13, No. 3, p. 467.

87. Heneman, H.G. III and Heneman, R.L. (1994). *Staffing Organizations.* Burr Ridge, Ill.: Irwin, pp. 192–194.

88. Smith, Ann C., Organ, D.W., and Near, J.P. (1983). "Organizational Citizenship Behavior: Its Nature and Antecedents." *Journal of Applied Psychology.* Vol. 68, No. 4, pp. 653–663; Van Dyne, L., Graham, J.W., and Dienesch, R.M. (1994). "Organizational Citizenship Behavior: Construct Redefinition, Measurement and Validation." *Academy of Management Journal.* Vol. 37, No. 4, pp. 765–802; Schnake, M. (1991). "Organizational Citizenship: A Review, Proposed Model, and Research Agenda." *Human Relations.* Vol. 44, No. 2, pp. 735–759.

89. Hogan, J., Hogan, R., and Busch, C.M. (1984). "How to Measure Service Orientation." *Journal of Applied Psychology.* Vol. 69, No. 1, pp. 167–173.

90. Hochschild, A.R. (1983). *The Managed Heart.* Berkeley: University of California, pp. 35–46.

91. Rafaeli, A. (1989). "When Clerk Meets Customer: A Test of Variables Related to Emotional Expressions on the Job." *Journal of Applied Psychology.* Vol. 74, No. 3, pp. 385–393.

92. Lengnick-Hall, C.A. and Lengnick-Hall, M.L. (1988). "Strategic Human Resource Management: A Review of the Literature and a Proposed Typology." *Academy of Management Review.* Vol. 13, No. 3, pp. 461–466.

93. See Schuler, R.S. and Jackson, S.E. (1987). "Linking Competitive Strategies with Human Resource Management Practices." *Academy of Management Executive.* Vol. 1, No. 3, pp. 207–219.

94. Byrne, John A. (1993). "The Horizontal Corporation." *Business Week.* No. 3351, December 20, pp. 76–81.

95. Milkovich, George T. and Boudreau, John W. (1994). *Human Resource Management.* 7th edition, Burr Ridge, Ill.: Irwin, p. 122.

96. Dale, B.G. and Cooper, C.L. (1992). *Total Quality and Human Resources.* London: Blackwell, pp. 10–60; Wilkinson, Adrian, Marchington, Mick, and Dale, B. (1993). "Enhancing the Contribution of the Human Resource Function to Quality Improvement." *Quality Management Journal.* Vol. 1, No. 1, pp. 42–44.

EXERCISES

PRACTITIONER ASSESSMENT INSTRUMENT 2A: CUSTOMER SATISFACTION PROFILE

DIRECTIONS

For each characteristic, rate the extent to which the statement is true about your own organization, using the following scale:

    1 = Not at all
    2 = To a small extent
    3 = To a moderate extent
    4 = To a great extent
    5 = To a very great extent

Then add up the scores for each cluster in the space entitled "Your Score." Next, calculate your percentage rating by dividing your score by the highest possible score.

A. CUSTOMER SATISFACTION COMMITMENT PRIORITY

1. Our organization accords strategic priority to satisfying customers. _____

2. Our leadership demonstrates by word and deed that customer satisfaction is the strategic priority. _____

3. Being customer-focused is a major factor in determining who gets ahead in our organization. _____

4. My work unit demonstrates by word and deed that customer satisfaction is its strategic priority. _____

5. I demonstrate by word and deed at work that customer satisfaction is my top priority. _____

YOUR SCORE _____

Divided by a possible 25 (your percentage score) = _____ %

B. ALIGNING OURSELVES WITH OUR CUSTOMERS

6. When it comes to selling, we play a consultative or partnership role with our customers. _____

7. In our advertising and promotional materials, we avoid promising more than we deliver. _____

8. We know which attributes of our products or services our customers value most. _____

9. Information from customers is used in designing our products/ _____
   services.

10. We competitively benchmark our products/services to provide _____
    the best value for customers.

YOUR SCORE   _____

Divided by a possible 25 (your percentage score) =   ___ %

C. READINESS TO FIND AND ELIMINATE CUSTOMER PROBLEMS

11. We monitor customer complaints.

12. We regularly ask customers to give us feedback about our _____
    performance.

13. Customer complaints are regularly analyzed in order to _____
    identify quality problems.

14. We look for ways to eliminate internal procedures and _____
    systems that do not add value to our customers.

15. I solicit customer feedback on a regular basis to improve _____
    my performance.

YOUR SCORE   _____

Divided by a possible 25 (your percentage score) =   ___ %

D. READINESS TO ADDRESS CUSTOMER EXPECTATIONS

16. We provide opportunities for employees at various levels _____
    and functions to meet with customers.

17. We clearly understand the nature and extent of the market _____
    demand for our product/service.

18. We regularly give information to customers that helps _____
    shape realistic expectations.

19. Within the organization, there is agreement about who our _____
    top-priority customers are.

20. My work unit clearly understands current customer _____
    expectations.

YOUR SCORE   _____

Divided by a possible 25 (your percentage score) =   ___ %

E. REACHING OUT FOR OUR CUSTOMERS

21. We make it easy for our customers to do business with us. _____

22. Employees are encouraged to go above and beyond to serve _____
    customers well.

23. We try to resolve all customer complaints. _____

24. We make it easy for customers to complain to us about our _____
    products and services.
25. My work unit actively solicits customer feedback. _____

    YOUR SCORE _____

    Divided by a possible 25 (your percentage score) = ___ %

F. COMPETENCE, CAPABILITY, AND EMPOWERMENT OF PEOPLE

26. We treat employees with respect. _____
27. Employees at all levels have a thorough understanding of our _____
    products/services.
28. Employees who work with customers are supported with _____
    resources that are sufficient for doing the job well.
29. Even at lower levels of our organization, employees are _____
    empowered to use their judgment when quick action is needed
    to make things right for a customer.
30. Employees are cross-trained so that they can fill in for each _____
    other when necessary to maintain continuous customer
    satisfaction.

    YOUR SCORE _____

    Divided by a possible 25 (your percentage score) = ___ %

G. CONTINUOUSLY IMPROVING OUR PROCESSES AND PRODUCTS

31. We study the best practices of other companies to get ideas. _____
32. We work to continuously improve our products/services. _____
33. We systematically try to reduce our research and _____
    development cycle times.
34. When problems with quality are identified, we take quick _____
    action to solve them.
35. We invest in the development of innovative ideas. _____

    YOUR SCORE _____

    Divided by a possible 25 (your percentage score) = ___ %

INTERPRETATION

After calculating your percentage score in each cluster, look at the high and low
percentages. This calculation will point your organization toward opportunities (low
percentage sectors) for improvement in providing customer satisfaction.

Source: Adapted from Whitely, Richard C. (1991). *The Customer Driven Company*.
Reading, Mass.: Addison-Wesley, pp. 221-225.

PRACTITIONER ASSESSMENT INSTRUMENT 2B: STRATEGY COMPETENCE PROFILE

DIRECTIONS

For each characteristic, rate the extent to which the statement is true about your own organization, using the following scale.

1 = Not at all
2 = To a small extent
3 = To a moderate extent
4 = To a great extent
5 = To a very great extent

Then add up the scores for each cluster in the space entitled "Your Score." Next, calculate your percentage rating by dividing your score by the highest possible score.

A. STRATEGY PLANNING: ENVIRONMENTAL SCANNING

1. Our organization engages in an ongoing comprehensive scan   _____
   of external opportunities and threats in the natural environment.

2. Our organization engages in an ongoing comprehensive scan   _____
   of external opportunities and threats in the social environment.

3. Our organization engages in an ongoing comprehensive scan   _____
   of external opportunities and threats in the industry environment.

4. Our organization establishes collaborative partnerships with   _____
   suppliers to ensure timely, quality input.

5. Our organization routinely assesses the ethical climate of the   _____
   work culture.

YOUR SCORE   _____

Divided by a possible 25 (your percentage score) =   ___ %

B. STRATEGY PLANNING: STRATEGY FORMULATION

6. Our organization has explicitly articulated an enterprise vision   _____
   of a desired future.

7. Our organization has a clear mission statement with prioritized   _____
   and shared values.

8. Our organization explicitly endorses all ten quality strategic   _____
   objectives.

9. Our organization explicitly aligns its grand and generic   _____
   strategies to coherently provide the highest quality, low-cost
   products/services available.

10. Our organization regularly solicits employee input on the   _____
    feasibility of and commitment to formulated strategies.

YOUR SCORE   _____

Divided by a possible 25 (your percentage score) =   ___ %

C. STRATEGY MANAGEMENT: STRATEGY IMPLEMENTATION

11. Our organization understands and streamlines its processes to efficiently implement strategies. _____

12. Our organization utilizes cross-functional teams to solve cross-organizational problems. _____

13. Our organization trains people in the proper use of total quality tools. _____

14. Our organization expects individuals to apply total quality tools to enhance personal performance. _____

15. Our organization expects individuals to actively contribute to team projects and process improvements. _____

YOUR SCORE _____

Divided by a possible 25 (your percentage score) = _____ %

D. STRATEGY MANAGEMENT: EVALUATION AND CONTROL

16. Our organization certifies or guarantees the quality of its products/services. _____

17. The *output* (aggregated products/services of the system) that is delivered to society by our organization is regarded as high quality _____

18. The *outcome* (effect of output on society and the community) of our organization is regarded as beneficial. _____

19. Our organization performs total quality strategic audits on a timely basis. _____

20. Our organization conducts ethical work culture audits on a timely basis. _____

YOUR SCORE _____

Divided by a possible 25 (your percentage score) = _____ %

INTERPRETATION

After calculating your percentage score in each cluster, look at the high and low percentages. This calculation will point your organization toward opportunities (low percentage sectors) to enhance total quality strategic competence.

CONTINUOUS IMPROVEMENT: PROCESS DIMENSIONS

The focus of Chapter 3 is in two areas: the total quality business processes and the total quality human resource (HR) processes. Both are crucial in determining the strength of the second pillar of the House of Total Quality and clarifying the expanded process responsibilities of employees in a total quality system. Both total quality business and HR processes need to be aligned to ensure organizational effectiveness and efficiency.

THE TOTAL QUALITY BUSINESS PROCESSES

As indicated in Chapter 1, the second pillar of the House of Total Quality, continuous improvement, is based on the cornerstone of process planning and the foundation of process management. In Chapter 2, process was defined as a set of linked activities that take an input and transform it to create an output.[1] The pillar of continuous improvement is the outcome of the

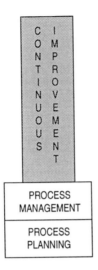

Figure 3.1 The Second Pillar, Foundation, and Cornerstone of the House of Total Quality.

continuation of sound design developed in the cornerstone of process planning with effective implementation delivered in the foundation of process management, as depicted in Figure 3.1.[2]

The first step in strategy implementation in Chapter 2 was process integration. It is this strategy implementation step that is now being treated as the process dimensions that ensure continuous improvement. **Total quality continuous improvement** *is the range of system innovation designed and implemented to produce total customer satisfaction on an ongoing basis.* The types of continuous improvement are listed in Table 3.1.[3]

The first type of continuous improvement, *kaizen,* has been used extensively in Japan.[4] Individuals, process and project teams, and cross-units are incrementally improving procedures to reduce costs and increase efficiency. The second type of continuous improvement, competitive parity, is aimed at reaching the "best-in-class" status to match the existing market leaders. The third type of continuous improvement, breakthrough dominance, is oriented toward outdistancing competitors by reengineering or restructuring processes to achieve quantum breakthrough advantages.

The basis of world competition is changing; reduced time to market, flexibility, service, rapid customization, and market differentiation via value metric excellence are now required, as indicated in Figure 3.2.[5]

Because the price of admission to world-class status is constantly increasing, attention to business process improvement is essential for global competitive success. Making work processes effective (producing desired

Table 3.1 Types of Continuous Improvement

	Kaizen: cost reduction	Competitive parity	Breakthrough dominance
1. Effect	Long term and long-lasting, but undramatic	Short term, but dramatic to match best-in-class	Long term and long-lasting to rewrite the rules
2. Pace	Small steps to cut costs	Big steps to catch up	Quantum leaps to outdistance
3. Time frame	Continuous and incremental	Continuous and nonincremental	Intermittent and nonincremental
4. Change	Gradual and constant	Abrupt and externally focused	Revolutionary restructuring
5. Involvement	Driven by everybody	Driven primarily by external competition scanning "champions"	Driven primarily by R&D, leadership from the top and process change agents
6. Approach	Individual and group efforts, collective systems approach	Strategists and key business process "owners"	R&D and key business processes, cross-functional collaboration and accountability
7. Mode	Maintenance and improvement	Scrap and rebuild to catch up	Start over, create from scratch
8. Spark	Conventional know-how and state-of-the-art	Competitor challenges, technological breakthroughs, matching market changes	Reinvent to meet envisioned future needs using technology as the essential enabler
9. Practical requirements	Requires little investment but great effort to maintain	Requires large investment but little effort to maintain	Requires large investment and great effort to maintain
10. Effort orientation	People and current daily practices	Competitive benchmarking processes	Reengineering breakthrough business processes
11. Evaluation criteria	Process and efforts for better results on reducing costs and improving efficiency	Results demonstrated by competitive process parity in the marketplace	"Order-of-magnitude" performance improvements—in key business indicators (cost, timeliness, quality)
12. Advantage	Works well in slow-growth economy	Better suited to fast-growth economy where keeping pace is crucial	Used when radical redesign is necessary to rapidly outdistance the competition

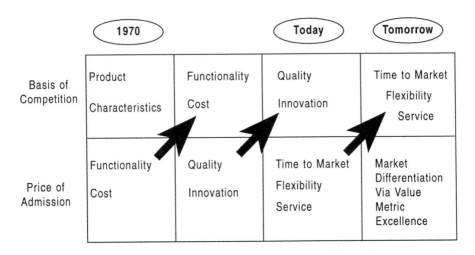

Figure 3.2 The Basis of Global Competition Is Changing. (Source: Johansson, Henry J., McHugh, P., Pendlebury, A. John, and Wheeler, W.A. III (1993). *Business Process Reengineering: Breakpoint Strategies for Market Dominance*. New York: John Wiley & Sons, p. 9.)

results), efficient (minimizing the resources used), and adaptable (able to flexibly meet changing customer and business needs) reduces costs, achieves competitive parity, and eventually provides the basis for sustained competitive advantage, as indicated in Figure 3.3.[6]

In the organizational life cycle (from entrepreneurial birth, to growth, maturity and eventual decline), the prospect of renewal is necessary to sustain competitive advantage. Five steps to achieve that advantage are depicted in Figure 3.3: restructuring, bureaucracy "bashing," employee empowerment, continuous improvement, and strategic cultural change.

Step 1: Restructuring. Through downsizing and delayering from early retirements, reorganizations, consolidation, plant closings, and greater spans of control, leaders focus on the right work (essential processes that add value to an internal and/or external customer) to be done.

Step 2: Bureaucracy "Bashing." Unnecessary reports, procedures, and other bureaucratic barriers to meeting customer needs are eliminated. To facilitate this step, a work process audit containing at least two questions is conducted: (1) To what extent does this work activity add value to customers? and (2) To what extent are these activities performed as effectively as possible?[7] Leaders need to encourage and reinforce, rather than punish, risk taking among employees who initiate bureaucracy-busting activities.

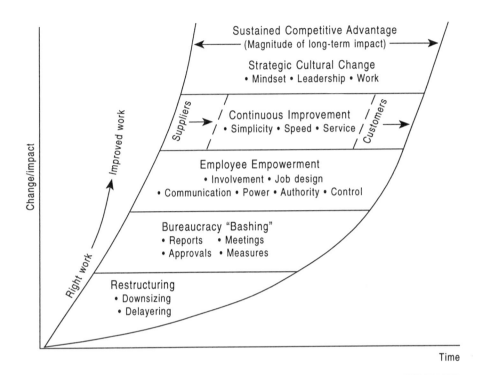

Figure 3.3 The Role of Continuous Improvement in Achieving Sustained Competitive Advantage. (Source: Beatty, Richard W. and Ulrich, David O. (1991). "Re-Energizing the Mature Organization." *Organizational Dynamics*. Vol. 25, No. 4, p. 22.)

Step 3: Employee Empowerment. Empowerment results in part from bureaucracy bashing, because bureaucracies primarily empower top managers. Real empowerment, however, occurs when position, status, and seniority are no longer the bases of power and authority in a firm and are replaced by competency relationships, trust, and solid expertise. Enlarging the horizontal communication channels, dialogue opportunities, and employee involvement processes assists leaders in sharing power in order to build widespread organizational capacities for commitment to change. Pepsico, for example, has involved and empowered employees by announcing profit-sharing benefits for everyone and challenging its employees to assume a corporate responsibility mindset. Federal Express guarantees all employees access to weekly senior management meetings. Saturn, Inc. and numerous public and nonprofit organizations have cost-saving and gainsharing programs to align employee and organizational empowerment interests.

Table 3.2 Comparison of Traditional Organizational
and New Process Mindsets

Traditional organizational focus	New process focus
• Employees are the problem	• The process is the problem
• Doing my job	• Help to get things done
• Understanding my job	• Knowing how my job fits into the total process
• Measuring individuals	• Measuring the process
• Change the person	• Change the process
• Can always find a better employee	• Can always improve the process
• Motivate people	• Remove barriers
• Controlling employees	• Developing people
• Don't trust anyone	• We're all in this together
• Who made the error?	• What allowed the error to occur?
• Correct errors	• Reducing variation
• Bottom-line driven	• Customer driven

Step 4: Continuous Improvement. Work process integrations that simplify, speed, and increase service to internal and external customers represent effective continuous improvement activities. While restructuring increases productivity, bureaucracy busting increases flexibility, and employee involvement increases empowerment, continuous improvement is the outcome of these prior steps and leads to responsive customization.

Step 5: Strategic Cultural Change. The cultural change required by continuous improvement ushers in a new employee mindset, leadership style, and work design. Among the mindset shifts is a change from the traditional organizational to the new process focus, as indicated in Table 3.2.[8]

A completely different thought pattern in the assessment, resolution, and prevention of strategic and operational problems emerges over time to improve systemic effectiveness to maintain competitive advantage when the new process focus rather than the traditional organizational focus is used.

TOTAL QUALITY BUSINESS PROCESS PLANNING

Business process planning begins with a clarification of the meaning of relevant concepts, including the following: process, system, structure, and technique. A **process** is any set of linked activities that take an input, add value to it, and provide an output to an internal or external customer. A **system** is an interrelated set of plans, policies, processes, procedures, people, and technology needed to reach the objectives of an organization. Thus, a set of processes may be seen as making up a system. A process usually will cross organizational boundaries within an operating unit and require coordination across those boundaries. A **structure** *is a formal or informal organization entity that is developed to perform a certain process or set of tasks that are part of a process.* Functional structures are common in both manufacturing and service organizations at all levels. From the total quality perspective, however, functional structures are undesirable for at least three reasons: (1) they distance employees from customers and insulate them from customer expectations, (2) they promote complex and wasteful processes and inhibit cross-functional process improvement, and (3) they separate the quality function from the rest of the organization, providing employees with an excuse not to worry about quality. Finally, a **technique** *is a systematic approach, procedure, tool, and/or associated technology required to carry out a task.*[9]

Using an airplane analogy, a system is seen at the 35,000-foot level as a "big picture" view of the organization and its processes. Zooming in to the 5000-foot level enables us to see the details of process, which may cross some organizational boundaries. At the 500-foot level, the structure of organizational departments and groups that carry out processes or tasks becomes clear. Finally, at the 50-foot level, the techniques used by individuals and small groups to accomplish work (and sometimes to improve processes) can be easily seen.

Process planning is the cornerstone of the continuous improvement, as shown in Figure 3.1. According to Voehl, the purpose of process planning is to ensure that all key processes work in harmony to maximize organizational effectiveness and efficiency.[10] The goal is to achieve a competitive advantage through superior customer satisfaction. A principal activity at this level is to develop a total quality improvement process, frequently labeled continuous quality improvement (CQI), that uses effective and efficient problem-solving techniques. If effectively implemented, three major outcomes typically result: (1) a common language for documenting and communicating activities and decisions for key CQI processes is established, (2) an organization-wide system of linking CQI indicators is developed, and (3) both initial and long-term gains due to the elimination of waste, rework, and bottlenecks are realized.

The scope of business process planning extends to both the cross-unit and organizational domains.[11] The cross-unit has, in effect, become the new unit of competition in Japan, replacing the corporation as the primary unit of competition. The thirteen major components of the cross-unit are illustrated in Figure 3.4.[12]

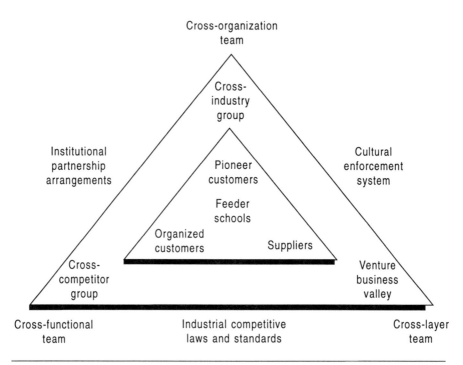

Figure 3.4 The Thirteen Principal Components of the New Unit of Competition: The Cross-Unit. (Source: Greene, R.T. (1993). *Global Quality: A Synthesis of the World's Best Management Methods*. Milwaukee: ASQC Quality Press, p. 147. Modified by the authors.)

The cross-unit consists of four layers of components. The outermost layer consists of two types of crossovers. The first set consists of intra-organizational teams (i.e., cross-functional, cross-layer, and cross-organization teams), and the second set of crossovers consists of inter-organizational arrangements (i.e., institutional partnerships, cultural enforcement of policies and industrial competitive laws and standards). The third layer includes crossovers among units of the supplier–customer chain: suppliers, organized customers, and pioneer customers. The fourth layer consists of feeder schools and educational institutions that supply employees, training, and research to the cross-unit.

Managing the process linkages between the four layers of organizations and their environments requires an array of skills that exceeds traditional production/manufacturing process expertise. It involves environmental scanning skills, collaborative and competitive networking skills, and intercompany partnership building skills to form the web of process linkages that sustain the cross-unit. In addition, leaders in cross-units must work on three primary links: (1) use customer and competitor data to drive all decisions and **process empowerment rooms** (*rooms equipped with high technology to enable live data transmission and analysis by process team members assisted by HR and technical facilitators*)[13] to create and disseminate information in a timely manner, (2) institute a system of copying and adapting the best practices of intra-cross-unit and extra-cross-unit models, and (3) cultivate employees with the developed alignment of cognitive (rational/scientific), affective (emotional), behavioral (psychological), social (norm-sensitive, likability), and moral (ethically mature) qualities to strengthen cross-unit links.[14]

To obtain timely information within the cross-unit, organizations are being viewed as collections of process empowerment rooms, consisting of a trio of facilitators (group dynamics and technical), information appliances (electronic work spaces, data walls, intelligent electronic whiteboards, shared meeting walls), and groupware technology (networked, interactive computer links with teams within and across organizations).[15] Furthermore, cross-unit best practices are rapidly disseminated through systematic copying and adaptation to local conditions of use. Finally, the importance of competent, sincere relations in building and nurturing trust within and between organizations is treated as an important human process in any cross-unit success. It is not enough to have the best groupware technology and copied best practices if people are not expected to exhibit integrity (thinking, feeling, saying, and doing what one promises to others in the cross-unit). The building of cross-unit trust creates intrinsic rewards and builds momentum for carrying out one's linkage promises to more people beyond formal, legal contractual obligations. Process integration, therefore, requires both reliable impersonal technical systems and trustworthy interpersonal relationship networks to be successful.

One of the primary technical tools for business process planning within an organization, however, is quality function deployment (QFD).[16] QFD is a planning methodology used to ensure that customer requirements are met throughout the product design process and in the design and operation of production systems. A set of matrices is used to relate the voice of the customer to technical features and production planning and control requirements. Because of its structure, the first phase of QFD is often referred to as the House of Quality (Figure 3.5), not to be confused with the House of Total Quality in Chapter 1. The latter is the conceptual framework for this book; the former is one phase of a business process improvement tool.

Building the House of Quality requires six basic steps:[17]

1. Identify customer and consumer attributes.
2. Identify technical features.
3. Relate the customer attributes to the technical features.

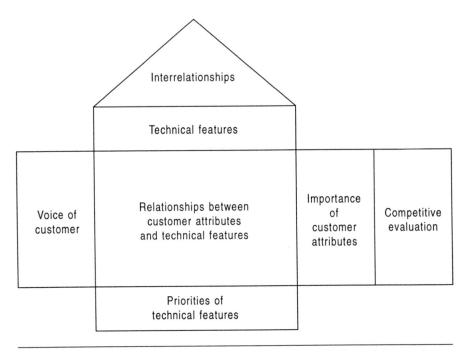

Figure 3.5 The House of Quality. (Source: Dean, James W. Jr. and Evans, James R. (1994). *Total Quality: Management, Organization and Strategy*. Minneapolis: West Publishing, p. 70.)

4. Conduct an evaluation of competing products.

5. Evaluate technical features and develop targets.

6. Determine which technical feature to deploy in the production process.

The first step is correctly identifying customer and consumer attributes. This requires ongoing market research to stay in touch with changing demand.

The second step is listing the technical features that are necessary to meet customer requirements. These technical features are design attributes expressed in that technical language of the designer and engineer. They form the basis for subsequent design, manufacturing, and service process activities. They must be measurable, because the output will be controlled and compared to objective targets.

The roof of the House of Quality shows the interrelationships between any pair of technical features. Various symbols are used to denote these relationships. A typical scheme is to use the symbol ⊙ to denote a very strong relationship, ○ for a strong relationship, and △ for a weak relationship. These notations help determine the effects of changing one product feature and enable planners to assess the tradeoffs between features. This process enables designers to focus on features collectively rather than individually.

Third, a relationship matrix between the customer attributes and the technical features is developed. Customer attributes are written down the left column, and technical features are listed across the top. In the matrix itself, the same symbols (as those used in the roof of the house) are utilized to indicate the degree of relationship. The purpose of the relationship matrix is to show whether the final technical features adequately address the customer attributes. This assessment may be based on expert experience, customer responses, or controlled experiments.

Technical features can relate to customer attributes in a variety of ways. The lack of a strong relationship between a customer attribute and any of the technical features suggests that either the attributes are not being addressed and the final product will have difficulty meeting customer needs or more market research on customer attributes is necessary. Similarly, if a technical feature does not affect any customer attribute, it may be unnecessary, redundant, or the designers may have missed an important customer attribute.

The fourth step is adding market evaluation and key selling points. This step includes rating the importance of each customer attribute and evaluating existing products with respect to each of the attributes. Customer importance ratings represent the areas of greatest interest and highest expectations to the customer. Competitive evaluation helps highlight the absolute strengths and weaknesses of competing products/services. This step enables designers to see opportunities for improvement. It also links QFD to a company's strategic position and allows priorities to be set in the design process. For example, focusing on a high-priority attribute that receives a low evaluation on all competitors' products can help a company gain a competitive advantage. Such attributes become key selling points and help establish promotion strategies.

Fifth, the evaluation of the technical features of competitive products and the development targets is produced. This is usually accomplished through in-house testing and is translated into measurable terms. These evaluations are compared with the competitive evaluation of customer attributes to detect any inconsistencies. If a competing product best satisfies a customer attribute, but the evaluation of the related technical feature indicates otherwise, then either the measures used are faulty or the product has an image difference (either positive toward the competitor or negative toward the product) that affects customer perceptions. In either case, the findings can guide future company action. Targets for each technical feature are determined on the basis of customer importance ratings and existing product strengths and weaknesses.

The sixth and final step in building the House of Quality is selecting technical features to be deployed in the remainder of the process. This means identifying the characteristics that have a strong relationship to customer needs, have poor competitive performance, or are strong selling points. These characteristics, in turn, need to be deployed—or translated into the language of each function—in the design and production process, so that proper actions and controls are taken to address the voice of the customer.

The House of Quality provides marketing with an important tool to understand customer needs and gives top management strategic direction. However, it is only the first of four stages in the QFD process. The other houses of quality are:

- The **technical features deployment matrix**, which translates technical features of the final product into design requirements for critical components

- The **process plan and quality control charts**, which translate component features into critical process and product parameters and control points for each

- The **operating instructions**, which identify operations to be performed by plant employees to assure that important process and product parameters are achieved

Most of the QFD activities represented by the first two houses of quality are performed by people in the product development and engineering functions. At the next stage, the planning activities begin to involve supervisors and production-line operators. This represents the transition from planning to implementation. If a product component parameter is critical and is created or affected during the process, it becomes a control point. The linkage of critical indicators provides the basis for measurement, monitoring, and improvement of the business process system to achieve customer satisfaction. The last house relates the control points to specific requirements for system quality assurance. This includes specifying control methods, sample sizes, and related technical operations to achieve the necessary level of quality.

It has been estimated that the majority of QFD applications in the United States concentrate on the first, and to some extent the second, house of quality. Lawrence Sullivan, who brought QFD to the West, suggests that the third and fourth houses offer far more significant benefits, especially in the United States.[18] Japanese employees are more naturally cross-functional and tend to promote group effort and consensus thinking. U.S. employee are more vertically oriented and tend to suboptimize for individual and/or departmental achievements. Beginning to emphasize effective cross-functional processes as supported by QFD will enable U.S. firms to be more competitive with foreign rivals. The third and fourth houses of quality utilize the knowledge of about 80% of a company's employees; if they are not used, this potential is wasted.

An excellent example of the application of QFD in the United States is Florida Power and Light (FPL), the first non-Japanese company ever to win the Deming Prize.[19] FPL is the fourth largest and fastest growing electric utility in the United States. Currently the primary investor-owned subsidiary of FPL Group, Inc. (a diversified holding company organized in 1984), the utility was established in 1925 to supply reliable electric light and power to parts of southeastern Florida.

The present-day service area, broken into five major divisions (northeastern, eastern, southeastern, southern, and western), encompasses the east coast of Florida and virtually the entire lower half of the state (27,650 sq. mi.), providing power to 6 million residents (3 million customer accounts). With its General Office in Miami, the company operates 13 power plants (total capacity 16,000 megawatts), two of which are nuclear (St. Lucie and Turkey Point). It also runs 45 customer service offices and 72 service centers and pays nearly 15,000 employees from an operating budget of $4.75 billion.

The company's rapid growth between the 1940s and 1970s led to an unwieldy expansion of management ranks and a lack of rapid response capability to a changing customer base. Although FPL had a limited, team-based quality program, there was no internal comprehensive process system that could achieve its expanded vision of becoming the best-managed electric utility in the United States. After examining domestic and global management process models, FPL decided to adapt the Japanese total quality process system used by the Kansai Electric Power Company in Osaka, Japan. Dr. Tetsiuchi Asaka, an eminent total quality management process educator in Japan who was affiliated with the Union of Japanese Scientists and Engineers (JUSE), served as the lead counselor to FPL from Kansai Electric.

The basic QFD model was adapted to more precisely detect the voices of diverse customers. This led to the focus on eight general customer attributes: reduce customer dissatisfaction, increase customer satisfaction, reduce service unavailability, reduce transmission-line-forced outages, increase nuclear availability, reduce fossil-forced outages, improve nuclear safety, and improve employee safety. Technical features related to these customer attributes were identified, and measurement indicators to scientifically determine critical changes were set up. Competing utilities were benchmarked for process and outcome results. Detail process records were kept, increased numbers of employee suggestions were encouraged, Plan-Do-Study-Act cycle iterations continued to hone the focus on process improvements, and extensive training in quality techniques was provided.

FPL's coordinated efforts resulted in stunning results:[20]

1. Overall customer complaints dropped from 0.9 per 1000 in 1984 to 0.23 in 1989. FPL went from the one of the worst utilities in Florida to one of the best in the state of Florida in terms of number of customer complaints.

2. The percentage of time when improvement was needed in caring and concern for the customer dropped from 13% to 3.5% by the end of 1988. Monitored positive interactions registered customer delight and noted the reduction of times when customer contact was not as pleasant and courteous as possible.

3. Service unavailability dropped from an average of 75 minutes per year per customer in 1983 to 47 minutes in 1989.

4. The number of transmission-line-forced outages dropped from an average of 730 in 1983 to 604 in 1989.

5. The number of unplanned days nuclear plants were off-line dropped from 310 in 1983 to 267 in 1989.

6. The percentage of time the fossil-fueled plants were not available to make electricity dropped from 5.95% in 1983 to 3.62% in 1989. In 1990 this indicator went below 3%—the best record for a utility company in the United States.

7. With regard to nuclear safety, the occurrence of nuclear plant shutdowns dropped from 0.85 shutdowns per 1000 critical hours in 1983 to 0.20 shutdowns per 1000 critical hours in 1989.

8. With regard to employee safety, the lost-time injuries per 100 employees dropped from 1.17 per 100 employees in 1983 to 0.40 lost-time injuries per 100 employees in 1989.

The aggregate bottom-line impact of these goal-linked efficiency efforts was to reduce the cost of electricity to FPL customers. From the mid-1970s to 1985, FPL was never able to keep the price of electricity below the rate of the Consumer's Price Index. From 1985 to 1989, however, when the total quality processes were operational, the price of electricity in normal dollars was down 10%. In constant dollars, the price was down 30%. Furthermore, for the years 1985 through 1989, FPL earned the full amount allowed by the Florida Public Service Commission and provided a refund to customers.

These findings are not unique to process improvements at FPL. For the period 1965 to 1985, the Deming Prize winners had increases in sales and profits of 14%. By comparison, other Japanese companies during the same period averaged 12%. For the same period, U.S. companies averaged only 8%.[21]

While senior leadership has changed at FPL and the extensive, detailed processes required for the Deming Prize have been severely reduced, the commitment to a total quality orientation persists today.[22] An important lesson was learned at FPL—if a firm wants to achieve a quality prize, it must be sure that winning the prize is organizationally perceived as worth the sustained effort, that the award criteria are suited to organizational HR capacities, and that the quality challenge will not overstrain resources and prompt a backlash.

The Deming Prize emphasizes the JUSE penchant for detailed statistical process documentation. As in Japan, individuals are expected to provide extensive, ongoing statistical documentation for all incremental improvements to operational systems. This prize emphasis, however, may not be as well suited to *sustainable commitment* in U.S organizations as one that accords more weight to individual interaction with systems. In the United States, the Baldrige Award emphasizes that interaction between individuals and systems, with much less focus on statistical documentation for incremental improvements and more on the need for visible, involved leadership.[23] In Europe, the ISO 9000 standards and the European Quality Award emphasize detailed policies and standards, with a broad environmental concern, not typical of either the Japanese or the U.S. award criteria.

While FPL's success demonstrates that QFD can work elsewhere, perhaps adopting regionally appropriate award criteria might facilitate sustained organizational commitment, and more recognition/celebration rituals along the way would maintain the morale and momentum for change.

TOTAL QUALITY BUSINESS PROCESS MANAGEMENT

Business process management is a systematic approach to helping an organization make significant advances in the way its business processes operate.[24] The main rationale is to ensure that the organization has business processes that:

- Eliminate errors
- Minimize delays
- Maximize the use of assets
- Promote understanding
- Are easy to use
- Are customer friendly
- Are adaptable to customers' changing needs
- Provide the organization with a competitive advantage
- Reduce excess head count

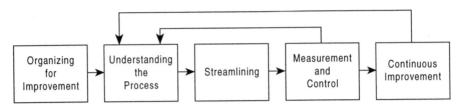

Figure 3.6 Five Phases of Business Process Improvement. (Source: Harrington, H. James (1991). *Business Process Improvement*. New York: McGraw-Hill, p. 23.)

One widely used model for managing business process improvement (BPI) identifies five specific phases: organizing for improvement, understanding the process, streamlining, measurement and control, and continuous improvement.[25] These five phases are illustrated in Figure 3.6.

The objective of the first phase of BPI (organizing for improvement) is to ensure success by building understanding, leadership, and commitment. To achieve this aim, the following ten activities are recommended: (1) establish an executive improvement team (EIT) to oversee business process reengineering or improvement; (2) appoint a BPI champion to drive the process reengineering or improvement; (3) establish an ethical work culture team (EWCT) with a champion to coordinate and drive the assessment and development of the human side of process reengineering or improvement; (4) develop a process reengineering or improvement model that clarifies the relationship between processes and strategic objectives as well as between process hierarchies (macro process, subprocesses, activities, and tasks) and process linkages; (5) review the entire business process–strategy objectives linkage in light of current and anticipated external and internal customer expectations; (6) provide executive education on business process reengineering or improvement and ethical work culture development; (7) identify critical business processes in light of prioritized strategic objectives and select the key processes for improvement; (8) communicate goals, approach, and progress to employees; (9) select key process owners—those who are most impacted have power to act on the process, have leadership ability, and have process knowledge; and (10) select the process improvement team (PIT) cross-functional members to participate in, conduct, and implement BPIs in designated areas.

While there may be a need for widespread reengineering of business processes, the HR impact needs to be addressed. The design and implementation of a reengineering effort should take into account the implications for the organization's people and should be carried out in such a way as to balance bottom-line cost reduction objectives with morale/productivity, ethical integrity/reputation, and safety objectives. Organizations that ignore these pluralistic objectives in the interest of gaining short-term financial results may jeopardize, if not permanently damage, the resiliency, sustainable commitment, and contribution of employees to total customer satisfaction and company success.

The objective of the second phase of BPI (understanding the process) is to understand all the dimensions of the current business process. To achieve this aim, the following ten activities are recommended: (1) define the process scope and mission in light of strategic objectives; (2) define process boundaries, including department improvement team (DIT) and specific task team (TT) responsibilities; (3) provide PIT, DIT, EWCT, and TT training on process improvement and ethical work culture development; (4) establish a business process and ethical work culture overview for long-range guidance of improvement efforts; (5) define customer and business measurements and expectations for the process; (6) flow diagram the entire process;[26] (7) collect cost, time, and value-added data to ensure that action is based on facts instead of guesses; (8) perform process walk-throughs to determine any variances between flowcharting diagrams and actual operations and identify as chronic or occasional any problems that lead to ineffectiveness, inefficiency, or lack of adaptability; (9) identify appropriate process measurements and resolve process disparities between diagram and practice in the areas of effectiveness, efficiency, cycle time, and costs; and (10) update process documentation to conform to new findings.

In the case of reengineering, which seeks to achieve a radical process redesign without being limited to the approach currently in place, steps one through five of phase 2 still set the appropriate context for change. The additional steps in phases 2 and 3, however, would be modified to enable breakthrough thinking through a "clean sheet of paper" approach to process design. This approach essentially ignores the existing process and asks the question: "If we were to design this process today, given what we know about our customers, our market, our associates, and the technology that is available, how would we design it"?

The objective of the third phase of BPI (streamlining) is to improve effectiveness, efficiency, and adaptability of business processes. To achieve this objective, the following 13 activities are recommended: (1) provide team training on process improvement sequencing: streamlining by eliminating waste, then preventing errors by process redesign, then correcting specific problems only after the basic process design is stable and prevents most problems, and finally, excelling in setting up processes to sustain customer delight; (2) identify and prioritize improvement opportunities in business processes and the ethical work culture; (3) eliminate bureaucracy by removing unnecessary administrative tasks, approvals, and paperwork; (4) eliminate duplication of activities; (5) identify the real value-added activities (those customers pay you to do) and eliminate non-value-added activities;

(6) simplify and reduce the complexity of the business process and the language used to communicate it; (7) reduce process cycle time through parallel rather than serial activities by changing activity sequences, reducing interruptions, improving timing, assessing movement and location, and setting priorities; (8) error-proof the process; (9) update the non-human resources and upgrade the technical and relational vitality of human resources; (10) standardize the work procedures to ensure that all current and future employees uniformly use the best practices; (11) automate, computerize, or mechanize whenever possible;[27] (12) document the streamlined process; and (13) select, train, and/or retrain the employees who are implementing the business process.

The objective of the fourth phase of BPI (measurement and control) is to implement the system to control the process for ongoing improvement. To achieve this objective, the following six activities are recommended: (1) develop appropriate in-process measurements and targets by answering the 11 W's:[28]

1. Why should you measure?
2. Where should you measure the process, HR, and ethics systems?
3. What should you measure in each system?
4. When should you measure each system?
5. Who should be measured in each system?
6. Who should do the measuring in each system?
7. Who should provide feedback in each system?
8. Who should perform the business process, HR, and ethics audits?
9. Who should set business, HR, and ethics targets (standards) in each system?
10. Who should set challenge targets in each system?
11. What should be done to locate, solve, and prevent problems in each system?

(2) establish a process and ethics system for timely positive and negative feedback, utilizing improvement chart indicators; (3) utilize statistical process control procedures whenever possible to identify upper control limits and lower control limits for critical business processes; (4) perform process and ethics audits periodically; (5) establish a poor-quality cost system to detect and control direct and indirect costs to the organization; and (6) establish a routine correction procedure that includes awareness, desire to eliminate errors, training in problem solving, failure analysis, follow-up practices, and liberally giving credit and recognition to all who participate.

The objective of the fifth phase of BPI (continuous improvement) is to implement a continuous improvement process. To achieve this objective, the following six activities are recommended: (1) certify individual contributors and qualify the entire business process and ethical work culture development systems; (2) perform periodic qualification reviews; (3) continuously find, define, and eliminate process problems; (4) evaluate the change impact in the business and on customers; (5) benchmark the process over time and across competitor/industry/political boundaries; and (6) provide ongoing advanced team training.

The six-level process qualification provides an effective assessment guide for BPI activities. These levels lead the PITs from an unknown process status to world-class status, as indicated in Table 3.3.

Until the BPI methodology has been applied, all business processes are considered to be at level 1. As the process improves, it progresses logically up to level 6 *as long as the ethical work culture is simultaneously developed.* This qualification system enables the organization to quickly evaluate its business process status and determine the stage of ethical work culture that would sustain it.

All processes in all organizations may not need to be able to progress through all six levels. Often, there are considerable costs involved in becoming the best. In most cases, organizations have many business processes that need to be improved. Because of the magnitude of this job, it may be wise to use PITs to bring some of the key prioritized processes under control and then direct the limited remaining resources to secondary critical business processes. Once all the critical processes are under control, PITs, DITs, and TTs can be assigned to bring other processes up to level 6.

When the EIT decides that something less than a world-class perfor-

Table 3.3 The Six Levels of Business Process Qualification

Level	Status	Description
1	Unknown	Process status has not been determined
2	Understood	Process design is understood and operates according to prescribed documentation
3	Effective	Process is systematically measured, streamlining has started, and end-customer expectations are met
4	Efficient	Process is streamlined and is more efficient
5	Error-free	Process is highly effective (error-free) and efficient
6	World-class	Process is world-class and continues to improve

Source: Harrington, H. James (1991). *Business Process Improvement.* New York: McGraw-Hill, p. 206. Numerical order reversed by the authors.

Table 3.4 Parallels Between Levels/Stages of
Business Process and Ethical Work Culture

Level/stage	Business process status	Ethical work culture status
1	Unknown	Social Darwinism
2	Understood	Machiavellianism
3	Effective	Popular conformity
4	Efficient	Allegiance to authority
5	Error-free	Democratic participation
6	World-class	Principled integrity

mance level is acceptable, it should communicate this information to the PIT immediately. Ideally, this decision should be made prior to forming the PIT. When management decreases its expectations late in the process cycle, it can negatively impact the PIT's morale by being interpreted as management's loss of faith.

The obvious parallel between the six business process levels and the six ethical work culture stages treated in Chapter 1 needs to be emphasized since the quality process context can either inhibit or support ethical conduct and vice versa, as indicated in Table 3.4.

Organizations that want a level 6 (world-class) business process status to operate in the House of Total Quality require an institutionalized ethical work culture operating at stage 6 (principled integrity). Designing an organizational ethics development system that includes integrity testing in its selection process, ethical behavior expectations in employee performance, ethics training and development, ethical impact of employee conduct in appraisals, whistleblower protection from retaliation, vehicles for reporting ethics violations, organizational justice processes and outcomes for ethics offenders, commendation rituals for exemplary ethical behavior, and ethical climate assessments and ethical audits for system improvement are important processes to institute if world-class principled integrity is to become an organization performance standard.

Organizations that settle for a level 4 (efficiency) business process status to operate in the House of Compliance only require an institutionalized ethical work culture operating at stage 4 (allegiance to authority). The traditional hierarchy in most organizations, which relies on the chain of command, legal compliance and control measures, and rapid dismissal for any ethical offenses, can obtain short-term employee compliance. Nevertheless, process and ethics compliance is not commitment; people may abide by the letter of the law but the spirit of community dedication to creating and improving a world-class workplace will be absent. Managers need to recognize this fact. Traditional managers in conventional organizations often try to implement total quality business processes without developing the ethical work culture and then are surprised by the cultural resistance to their quality initiatives. Total quality business processes necessitate ethical work culture development processes to engender commitment to organizational change. In particular, the sharing of power and authority, based upon total quality competence and organizational compatibility, is an important business process and ethical work culture shift that managers need to be able to risk in order to achieve world-class status.

Organizations that are mired at level 1 (unknown) business process status to operate in the House of Manipulation are stagnating in an ethical work culture operating at stage 1 (Social Darwinism). Organizations that have unknown processes rely upon fear to control behavior, and in the absence of direct or indirect power, employees will resort to unethical and dysfunctional work behavior. Driving fear out of the workplace is essential for total quality implementation.[29] Attempting to introduce total quality processes in such an ethical work culture is doomed to failure.

TOTAL QUALITY HUMAN RESOURCE PROCESSES

Total quality HR processes involve five key elements: *selection, performance, appraisal, rewards*, and *development*. The total quality HR processes are the result of the business strategy involvements and paradigm shifts referred to in Chapter 2 applied across and within organizations. The paradigm shifts from a traditional to a total quality HR approach entail HR process changes in selection, performance, appraisal, rewards, and development that reflect the total quality emphasis.[30]

In the traditional human resource management (HRM) model, job performance is seen as a function of the HR components of selection, individual performance, appraisal, rewards, and development. These elements of HRM suggest generic activities that are performed by HR managers. These elements have been described as *selecting* people who are best able to perform the jobs defined by the structure, *appraising* their *performance* to facilitate the equitable distribution of *rewards*, motivating employees by linking rewards to high levels of performance and *developing* employees to enhance their current performance at work as well as to prepare them to perform in positions they may hold in the future. Marginal and unacceptable individual performers are dismissed from the system.[31]

Traditionally, HRM systems have focused on the individual. An individual job is designed, as part of broader organizational design, with specific tasks and duties prescribed. Individuals typically specialize in training and education to master a narrow domain of work. Focused criteria define the basis for evaluating performance on the tasks and duties. Superiors appraise individual performance in accord with the specified criteria and render judgment as to the adequacy or inadequacy of the performance. Contingent rewards are then administered for the individual, in accord with the individual's performance appraisal. Developmental needs are identified in relationship to the appraisal, and action is taken to correct any deficiencies in current performance or to avoid any anticipated deficiencies in future performance.

There are at least six implicit and explicit questionable assumptions on which this individualistic HRM approach rests. Key among these assumptions are the following:[32]

1. The individual is completely (or largely) in control of his or her own performance variation.

2. Supervisors can accurately judge individual performance with current tools.

3. Individual contributions to system performance are accurately reflected by current HR criteria.

4. The administration of contingent rewards and punishments exclusively at the individual level is motivational and ensures that future organizational performance will be satisfactory.

5. Differentiating among individuals with regard to level of performance, level of compensation, and level of status serves important organizational purposes.

6. Existing HR systems that select, appraise, reward, and develop individuals are adequate vehicles for managing organizational change and creating customer value.

The total quality HR approach calls into question all of these assumptions and offers alternatives for managers of human resources based on systems and management team performance, combined with jobs and individual performance. The traditional HR approach ignores the impact of systems on individual performance and reflects a reductionist managerial viewpoint which assumes that aggregated individual performances ensure overall system performance.

In reality, an individual's performance is impacted by the methods, rules, materials, technologies, equipment, and other constraints on facilitators provided by the larger system of which an individual is only a part. Individual performance also depends on the timing and consistency of the work execution of other individuals within the system. Thus, individual performance reflects the system performance of a larger team. Conversely, system performance reflects individual contributions and the synergistic and interactive effects of team contributions. While it is theoretically possible to separate the job/individual performance from the team/system performance, in practice they are two sides of the same productivity coin. Just as a coin provides its owner no expendable currency unless it has two sides, a viable and competitive organization must manage individuals in conjunction with systems, as indicated in Figure 3.7.[33]

The critical linkages between the individual and system sides of the HRM coin must be managed to ensure competitive capability. HR managers and the HRM subsystem of the organization must ensure these linkages.

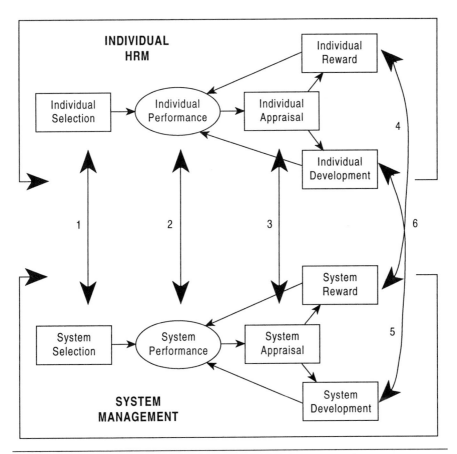

Figure 3.7 Critical Individual–System Linkages for Total Quality Management of Human Resources. (Source: Bounds, G.M. and Pace, L.A. (1991). "Human Resource Management for Competitive Capability." In Michael J. Stahl and Gregory M. Bounds, Eds. *Competing Globally through Customer Value.* New York: Quorum Books, p. 658.)

These linkages suggest that (1) individual selection criteria must match system improvement criteria, (2) individual performance must be integrated with system performance, (3) individual performance appraisal must be tied to system performance appraisal, (4) individual reward must be linked to system performance, (5) individuals must be developed to practice system improvement, and (6) results of executing these cycles should be linked to renewing of these cycles for continuous improvement.

Failure to recognize these linkages can cause strategic deficiencies and diminish organizational competitiveness. For example, consider the customary incongruity and compensation inequity inherent in the reward practice of dramatically increased executive compensation while the organization suffers severe declines in market share, customer satisfaction, quality measures, costs, and delivery schedules.[34]

The importance of clarified, aligned, and internalized roles in a total quality HR system is also evident. Roles represent the axis around which the two domains of individual and system performance spin. A **work role** *is the summation of the requirements, the set of activities, or the expected behaviors associated with a position in an organization.* The inclusion of both individual and system responsibilities in total quality HR role expectations is a necessary expansion of the traditional HR approach.

The prescribed "role" of managerial leaders defines the learning and developmental needs of these human resources. For example, managing for incremental improvement of organizational systems through the study and understanding of variation in systems means that HR managers must develop skills for, and learn about, studying variation through statistical methods. In addition, HR managerial leaders should convey that part of their role is to continuously improve the systems of the organization for internal and external customer value. They do so by role modeling, coaching, asking process questions in progress reporting meetings, and creating appropriate appreciation and reward systems for the organization.

Attempts to make an organization more competitive will fail if HR managers choose to operate on only one side of the coin, either on the system side (for example, through structural modifications which amount to shuffling the chairs on the *Titanic*) or on the individual side (for example, through massive dosages of individual training that amount to preparing an athlete for a foot race when the competitive system is an auto race track).

TOTAL QUALITY HUMAN RESOURCE PROCESS PLANNING

Total quality HR process planning involves consideration of all the HR elements: selection, performance, appraisal, rewards, and development. The first total quality HR process is **selection**. *Selection is the mutual process* *by which the individual and the organization become matched to form the employ-ment relationship.* Total quality selection emphasizes rigorous procedures and budgets for recruiting, selecting, orienting, and placing people at all organizational levels.[35] For example, Hampton[36] reports that Mazda and Diamond-Star Motors (a Chrysler-Mitsubishi joint venture) spend about $13,000 per production employee hire. Although specifics vary slightly across the two firms, each includes written tests, drug tests, medical exams, and several rounds of interviews, problem-solving exercises, and work sample tryouts.

Multiple methods have been used in quality firms to responsibly select human resources in as complete and unbiased a manner as possible.[37] These methods include application forms, reference checks, biographical data, in-terviews, integrity tests, cognitive ability tests, skills tests, personality assess-ment, peer assessment, subordinate assessment, and behavioral assessment through work sampling, simulation, business games, and group exercises. An example of an innovative selection process is the peer screening for auditor and investigator positions in the Inspector General's Office of the Tennessee Valley Authority. Internal candidates and external applicants for these positions were interviewed by their potential co-workers, who then made recommendations to management. The job incumbents assisted their managers in developing both the criteria and the screening process itself. Another example is Diamond-Star, which uses a realistic preview video that warns applicants that they must learn several jobs, change shifts, work overtime, make and take constructive criticism, and submit a constant stream of suggestions for improving efficiency.

The importance of teams and teamwork is also reinforced in a number of ways. First, in many companies, ongoing teams play a large (or even solo) role in new employee recruitment and selection. Interpersonal skills, moral maturity, and willingness to be a team player also form a large part of the interviewing and testing procedures. Finally, these characteristics are rein-forced through general orientation and socialization which often lasts several months even for production workers. At Mazda, line workers receive several days of general philosophy training, followed by five to seven weeks of technical skills training, followed by three to four weeks of supervision when first placed on the assembly line. Thus, recruitment, selection, and orienta-tion all work in concert to produce dedicated, team-oriented, and highly skilled employees.

Despite their screening rigor and demanding work requirements, em-ployers such as Honda, Mazda, and Diamond-Star can afford to be very selective because they are widely regarded as good places to work. Selection ratios (number of hires relative to the size of the applicant pool) of 0.04 are reported at Diamond-Star, 0.13 at Mazda, 0.095 at Honda (Marysville), and 0.025 at Honda Power Equipment.[38]

The second element in total quality HR process planning is **performance.** *Performance is the contribution both individuals and systems make to the accomplishment of the objectives of the organization.* Performance is more broadly conceived in the total quality approach than in the traditional approach. The traditional model focuses on individual performance in a job. In contrast, total quality performance focuses on team and individual performance in the system process and project successes. Total quality models consider both individual/job and team/system performance. Some companies are starting to make changes in the way they balance individual and system performance expectations. For example, in some new quality plant startups, 80% of the individual's performance appraisal is weighted toward team contribution and only 20% toward individual contribution.[39]

Individual performance involves both task completion and relationship development for individuals in a total quality environment. Balancing both conceptual competence to complete technical tasks with moral/emotional process competence to build the work community is a dual performance responsibility for total quality employees. The moral/emotional competence is exhibited by sincere communication styles that nurture trust and respect; empathic interactions such as pain sharing in meetings sustain a solace system when adjusting to the technical system changes and raise team stress thresholds. Pain sharing builds community at work because after resolving technical problems in a meeting, it is important to get all employees to see who is paying a price and who is not in any new work initiative. This acknowledgment of differential impact on quality of work life builds the work unit social memory of who is sacrificing and who is benefiting, which is later used as an informal organizational justice process in balancing the books among employees in future work decisions.[40]

The second performance area is union relations.[41] It is important to note that the most competitive national economies (Japan and Germany) seem to combine technologically advanced and highly competitive companies with far higher levels of unionization than in the United States. The very success of U.S. industrial unionism has sowed the seeds of its own decline. In order to defend workers from the early abuses of Taylorism, union leaders implicitly accepted the separation of "managing" from "working," thereby cutting off workers from decision-making responsibilities. The job control unionism that followed (i.e., multiple job classifications, wage rates linked to the job instead of a worker's skills, seniority as the basis for promotion) gave unions the negative power to hamstring management but not the positive power to influence strategy or operations. With international competition, however, flexible manufacturing, flattened hierarchies, and blurred boundaries among functions and jobs all demanded that workers make critical decisions at the lowest possible levels.

Total quality union relations performance can best be determined by the nature and extent to which an active partnership is formed with union officers and membership to include them in the design, implementation, and evaluation stages of any competitive initiative. Total quality HR performance should address four areas: training, work redesign, employee ownership, and new HR issues. First, unions can be helpful in emphasizing the value of employability training; union involvement in "skill formation" can play an equivalent role in the new U.S. economy to "wage formation" in the mass production era. Second, unions can constructively represent employee interests and concerns in work restructuring or work redesign projects in order to streamline operations with employee involvement. There needs to be continual awareness of the need for aligning quality product/service improvement processes with quality labor relations and HR policies, as well as sharing the recognition and reward for joint quality achievements.[42] Third, as employee ownership of companies increases (by the year 2000 it is estimated that more than a quarter of publicly traded companies will be at least 15% employee owned), unions can give voice to employee-owner interests and interact with HR professionals as owner representatives.[43] Fourth, as the new diverse work force emerges with women and minorities leading the way, unions can gain jobs and justice for the unorganized and help to train and stabilize the new work force. In effect, total quality HR performance is demonstrated to the extent that constructive partnerships with unions are facilitated to achieve organizational objectives.

The third area of performance is health, safety, and security.[44] Total quality HR professionals need to demonstrate awareness and control of the adverse impacts to health, safety, and security generated by inadequate processes/procedures, equipment insufficiency, faulty vehicles, and employee error. The aftermath of the Exxon Valdez oil spill incident is one recent case that indicates the extent to which company patterns of overwork scheduling and systemic pressures to meet unrealistic deadlines contributed to poor performance that damaged the health, safety, and security of multiple stakeholders. The legal ploy of separating oil transport financial risks from other oil-related production risks still does not address the fundamental health, safety, and security issues in the global oil and maritime industries. Having tankers registered under foreign flags of small Third World countries (African and Latin American nations), where health, safety, and security standards are relatively low, simply transfers legal and financial risks without addressing the fundamental total quality safety concerns. Total quality HR performance, therefore, in some industries requires challenging policies that are likely to adversely impact health, safety, and security and proactively involving employees in wellness, safety, and security programs.

The third element of total quality HR process planning is **appraisal**. *Appraisal is the feedback process of evaluating and improving individual and system performance.* Traditional performance appraisal systems tend to rely on an appraisal system, with unilateral flow of information from a single source, wherein the immediate superior passes judgment and informs the subordi-

Table 3.5 Appraisal Systems

	Traditional appraisals	Total quality appraisals
Guiding value	Individual accountability	System and individual accountability
Primary goals	Control, documentation	Development, solving problems
Input range	Immediate superior	360-degree input from all key internal and external customers
Leadership practices	Directional, evaluative	Developmental, coaching
Appraisal frequency	Occasional	Frequent
Degree of formality	High	Low
Focus	Individual/job	Team/systems and individual/job

nate. In contrast, Deming argued that individually based appraisals are fundamentally harmful and unfair because if the system in which people work is predictable, then over time most employees will perform at about the same level. The influence of variation is such that it is impossible to accurately measure the overall performance of individuals within a variable process. In fact, it is impossible to separate the performance of the individual from that of the system.[45] The need to factor in both system and individual inputs into appraisals is a key obligation of total quality HR professionals.

A comparison between traditional and total quality appraisal systems is provided in Table 3.5.

The difference between a traditional and a total quality approach to appraisal is analogous to the difference between the traditional approach to quality control through inspection and quality improvement through the statistical study of variation. The orientations and attitudes that accompany these two approaches are very different. Total quality appraisal is more like the statistical approach to continuous improvement rather than the inspection-oriented approach to quality control. The inspection-oriented approach spends too much time trying to screen out defects or subpar performers (i.e., individuals not pulling their weight). With this orientation, inspectors miss the opportunities to continuously improve and develop all employees and the systems within which they contribute to customer value.

For behavioral feedback and development, 360-degree appraisals should be gathered from peers, subordinates, internal and external customers, and superiors (plural). Each of these sources possesses strengths and weaknesses, but the biases in one will be balanced by the others. Multiple perspectives give a more accurate and comprehensive appraisal. In addition, self-feed-back and self-appraisal should be used. Individual self-assessment is some-what automatic in an organization in which the managers use statistical methods to monitor and improve their processes and systems.[46]

Reward systems are the fourth HR total quality process. *Rewards are all forms of financial and nonfinancial returns to individuals, teams, and the system for contributions as part of the employment relationship.* Rewards have traditionally been distributed exclusively in an individually contingent manner (i.e., re-wards are given out to individuals on the basis of individual merit or judged individual performance), and individuals come to expect extrinsic rewards for any contribution. Unfortunately, when rewards are administered to indi-viduals, competition between individuals for limited rewards results rather than the collaboration crucial for quality team and system performance. In addition, when rewards are viewed as extrinsic returns for instrumental work activities, the intrinsic motivation to take pride in a job well done is jeopardized.[47]

The challenge for total quality HR managers is to design a reward system that takes advantage of the extrinsic and intrinsic motivational effects of rewards, satisfies norms for equity, meets external market competitiveness challenges, complies with appropriate laws and regulations, is consistently and efficiently administered, and encourages collaboration for team and system success.

The extrinsic and intrinsic reward system includes the full range of financial and nonfinancial returns: direct and indirect compensation, ben-efits, and recognition. On the side of extrinsic financial rewards for individu-als and teams, progressive firms support quality achievements and employee involvement through profit-sharing and cost-saving/gainsharing plans. For example, Nucor Steel has implemented profit sharing plus a variety of small group incentives, and PepsiCo, Inc. provides stock options for all of its roughly 100,000 permanent employees to involve everyone in the fate of the company.[48] On the side of extrinsic nonfinancial rewards for individuals and teams, quality approaches to recognition/appreciation systems are verbal, visible, and public; have a strong next and final customer bias; focus on teams first and individuals second; are active and frequent; and ensure consistency.[49] For example, Milliken, the Baldrige Award-winning textile manufacturer, has "Alcoves of Excellence," "Walls of Fame," and a company news magazine filled with recognition stories and photos of both individuals and team accomplishments. At Xerox, the Team Celebration Day turns into a "happening," with over 12,000 employees, customers, and suppliers at-tending a huge quality fair at one of four U.S. or international locations, all linked via satellite.[50]

On the side of intrinsic rewards for individuals and teams, total quality

HR professionals need to maximize the meaningful content of work, interdependent collaboration in the work flow process, and choice and control over work activities.[51] These are the key ingredients in sustaining intrinsic work motivation. For total quality HR professionals, it is important to heed Blinder's conclusion in his anthology entitled *Paying for Productivity: A Look at the Evidence:* "Changing the way workers are *treated* may boost productivity more than changing the way they are paid.[52] The degree of emphasis on intrinsic rewards is correlated with the adequacy of the selection process. Individuals who are likely to be strongly internally motivated would normally indicate high customer service orientations, high moral maturity from integrity testing, and a record of good citizenship behavior. These are the type of people who are ready, able, and willing to demonstrate the reciprocal altruism necessary to enjoy contributing to personal, team, and system advancement.

Reward systems also need to exhibit visible vertical and horizontal remuneration equity.[53] Companies such as Nike, Herman Miller, and Ben & Jerry's limit the number of pay grades in the hierarchy as well as the ratio of executive to lowest level employee pay. Other companies (e.g., Mars, Inc.) have increased horizontal equity by not differentiating the pay of same-level managers in different functions or teams. Excessive executive rewards not linked with skill acquisition, quality performance, and/or increased customer satisfaction are rightly perceived as equity problems and should be eliminated by total quality HR professionals.[54] Equitably sharing burdens (downsizing, restructuring, dismissals) at all organizational levels also enhances the perception of systemic, procedural, and outcome justice that operates in a total quality firm dedicated to moral integrity in the workplace and, in turn, strengthens commitment to current and future strategic HR decisions.[55]

Furthermore, both the Conference Board and KPMG Peat Marwick surveys show that as companies mature along the total quality cycle, they increasingly shift their reward and recognition practices toward teams and broader workplace units, as indicated in Table 3.6.[56]

Table 3.6 Frequency of Distributing Rewards to Individuals, Teams, and Broader Work Units

Years total quality process in place	To individuals		To teams		Unit-wide	
	Cash	Noncash	Cash	Noncash	Cash	Noncash
8 years or more	10%	58%	10%	53%	10%	53%
1 year or less	15%	23%	8%	31%	4%	11%

Rewarding collaboration and community-building choices provides the system incentives needed in a total quality organization.

Development is the fifth HR total quality process. *Development is the ongoing process of planned and structured activities designed to improve individual, team, and organizational performance.* Total quality HR development normally includes individual and team training and development, organization development, and career development.[57] The identification and nurturance of potential is a never-ending enabling responsibility of total quality HR professionals. Because systems both constrain and enhance the performance of individuals and teams, and are thus an important part of total quality performance, total quality HR professionals must attend to various aspects of system development, such as structure, policies, methods, procedures, and ethical work culture.

Formal quality training appears to be the most common technique for initiating and sustaining employee involvement, at least during the early stages of total quality implementation. According to the Conference Board, 90% of manufacturing companies and 75% of service corporations report using some sort of training in their total quality efforts.[58] However, the KPMG Peat Marwick survey found that while training was the most important initiative in the early stages of total quality implementation, cross-functional quality teams and work process redesign became relatively more important in more mature implementations.[59] Across total-quality-practicing companies, the median number of hours devoted to quality training (per employee) was 20, with a larger commitment in corporations just launching their total quality efforts.

According to the General Accounting Office of the U.S. government, total quality training is typically a two-stage process.[60] The first stage consists of general awareness training to create a common frame of reference and a sense of the leadership commitment. The second stage focuses on concrete skill-based training designed to prepare individuals to become effective members of quality improvement teams. For example, in a small convenience sample of Fortune 199 firms, Olian and Rynes found the most common training content to be (in descending order of frequency) personal interaction skill, quality improvement process and problem solving, team leading, team building, running meetings, statistical process control, supplier qualification training, and benchmarking.[61]

Team training normally evolves from short-term single-issue teams. Over time, teams tend to become longer standing, more cross-functional, multi-issue, and increasingly self-managed. For example, KPMG Peat Marwick found that only 15% of its total sample used completely self-managing work teams as a primary total quality tool.[62] However, this figure rose to 50% in companies with the most developed total quality cultures.

Organization development *is the system-wide change process designed to* *enhance the effectiveness, efficiency, and ongoing improvement of an organization and the well-being of its members through planned interventions.* Total quality HR professionals are to be engaged in system-wide changes to build and sustain a world-class learning community that competes effectively and develops interdependencies within and outside its four walls.[63] The total quality HR professional needs to develop system design and redesign competencies, ethical work culture assessment techniques, human resource information system research skills, and command of statistical control tools to make substantive contributions to organization development.

Career development *is the process by which individuals progress through a series of work-related stages, each of which is characterized by a relatively unique set of issues, themes, and tasks.*[64] Career development activities in a total quality firm encompass a spectrum from person-centered (self-directed workbooks and tapes), to team-centered (team enrichment exercises), to organization-centered (corporate succession planning). Total quality HR professionals need to be sensitive to the job insecurity and career gridlock concerns of many contemporary U.S. employees. One set of guidelines for total quality HR professionals in the career development of current U.S. employees is provided in Table 3.7.

TOTAL QUALITY HUMAN RESOURCE PROCESS MANAGEMENT

Total quality HRM involves the systematic implementation of the five HR processes. To accomplish this aim, total quality HR professionals need to master a wide range of new process improvement tools.[65] While the number of such tools runs into the hundreds, seven "higher level" process management and planning tools are provided. The term "higher level" is not meant to imply that only top managers should be involved in the use of such tools, nor does it mean that the tools are only applicable to corporate-wide change efforts. However, these tools are most useful where reorganization, process changes, or improvements involve several groups or departments, require coordination with other organizations or partners, and are above the small project level in size and scope.

The seven major process improvement tools include affinity diagram/KJ method, interrelationship digraph, tree diagram, matrix diagram, arrow diagram, process decision program chart, and matrix data analysis.

1. Affinity Diagram/KJ Method. *This tool organizes pieces of information into groupings based on the natural relationships that exist among them.* It is used when large numbers of ideas, issues, and other items are being collected.

Table 3.7 Total Quality Human Resource Career Development Actions

Employee profile	Recommended total quality/HR action
1. Concern for basic values	1. a. Replace promotion culture with psychological success culture b. Examine, change corporate career criteria c. Focus on corporate ethics
2. Freedom to act on values	2. a. Support protean career paths b. More lateral mobility c. Decouple rewards and the linear career path
3. Focus on self	3. Build ongoing development into the job through: • Self-development • Lifelong learning
4. Need for autonomy	4. More flexible careers
5. Less concern with advancement	5. More diversity in career paths More change • within present job • within present function • within present location • across function and locations
6. Crafting	6. Reward quality performance, not potential
7. Entrepreneurship	7. a. Create internal entrepreneurial assignments b. Encourage employee career exploration (internally and externally)
8. Concern for work–home balance	8. a. More organizational sensitivity to home life b. Training for managing the work–home interface c. Inclusion of spouse in career discussions d. Career assistance for employed spouse e. Flexible benefits to help meet family needs (e.g., child care, elder care, care for sick children) f. More flexible work arrangements

Source: Hall, D.T. and Richter, J. (1990). "Career Gridlock: Baby Boomers Hit the Wall." *The Executive.* Vol. 14, No. 4, p. 19.

The affinity diagram/KJ method was developed in the 1960s in Japan by Kawakita Jiro (the "KJ" is a registered trademark owned by the Kawayoshida Research Center). For a HRM application, it may be extremely helpful to use this tool in the early stages of a large-scale process or reengineering project to consider responses and ideas generated by questions such as "What are our *essential* products or processes?" "How might departments be rearranged if we went from a functional to a process orientation?" "What system might we use for assessing individual and group effectiveness if we eliminate performance reviews?"

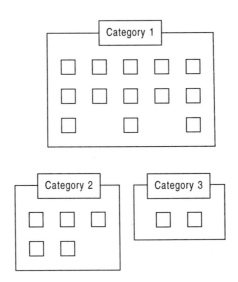

2. Interrelationship Digraph. *This tool displays the cause-and-effect relationship between factors relating to a central issue.* Factors that have a high number of relationships (arrows going into and emanating from) are usually the most fundamental or critical. A HRM application would be delineating the multiple causes for turnover and diagramming responses to the question "Why is this happening?" The following diagram shows both the strength (indicated by the boldness of the arrow) and direction of causes.

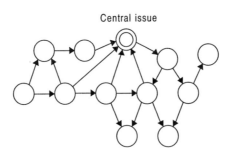

3. Tree Diagram. *This tool shows the complete range and sequence of subtasks required to achieve an objective.* Tree diagrams have been used for many years in decision analysis. They have been called "decision trees" in operations research literature. One of the best-known models of leadership, the Vroom Jago model,[66] uses a decision tree to show the degrees of participation that leaders can and should use in making decisions. This model is referenced in many organization behavior and HRM texts today.

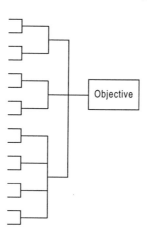

4. Matrix Diagram. *This tool shows the relationships among various data.* For example, QFD is a process to understand the voice of the customer and translate it into technical design parameters, subsystems, parts, components, processes, and process controls. The House of Quality matrix, used in QFD, is shown below. It depicts a diagram showing the relationship between primary, secondary, and tertiary customer needs and the technical design parameters or substitute quality characteristics which, if met, would ensure that the customer's needs will be satisfied. This type of diagram could be used by HRM practitioners in planning union collective bargaining sessions by anticipating and soliciting initial union demands.

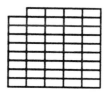

5. Arrow Diagram. *This tool is used to develop the best schedule and appropriate controls to accomplish an objective.* It answers "when" questions. It is very similar to the program evaluation review technique (PERT) and the critical path method (CPM).

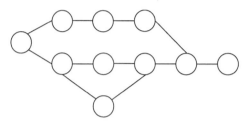

6. Process Decision Program Chart (PDPC). *This tool is used to plan the implementation of new or revised tasks that are complex.* The PDPC maps out all conceivable events that can go wrong and contingencies for these events. HRM applications are evident in forecasting contingencies for labor shortages, downsizing effects, and/or new compensation and benefits plans.

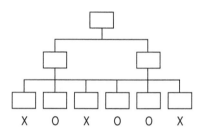

X   O   X   O   O   X

X = Impossible/difficult to do
O = Selected events

7. Matrix Data Analysis. *This tool is a mathematical analysis of numerical data arranged as matrices (e.g., "where in the data do we find various patterns?").* There are many methods, often called multivariate analysis, including cluster, multiple regressions, and principle component analysis. Matrix data analysis can be applied to all five of the major HRM processes to quantitatively detect and analyze patterns; this is a useful check on qualitative intuitions about problem identification and causal analysis.

$$w_j = \sum_{i=1}^{p} [i_j \, x]_j$$

In addition to the seven major process management tools, six supplemental process tools include competitive benchmarking, flowcharts, nominal group technique, structured surveys, trend charts, and Excelerator.

1. Competitive Benchmarking. *This tool measures process, product, and/or service against those of recognized leaders.* It helps establish priorities and targets, which lead to a competitive advantage.

The concept of benchmarking was developed and used extensively by Xerox.[67] When Xerox was attempting to regain market share that had been lost to Japanese copier manufacturers in the late 1970s and early 1980s, Xerox undertook a study of competitors' products in terms of quality, features, and costs in comparison with Xerox's products. The company was shocked to learn that its unit manufacturing costs were equal to the Japanese makers' selling price in the United States, the number of suppliers used by Xerox was nine times the number used by the best competitors, assembly line rejects were ten times higher, product lead times were two times longer, and defects per 100 machines were seven times higher. After a second benchmarking study confirmed the results of the first one, the company assembled its top 25 managers to begin planning their HRM/total quality management efforts that eventually brought about the turnaround.

2. Flowchart. *A flowchart is a pictorial diagram of the steps in a process and is useful for finding out how a process works.*

Flowcharting is actually a term that may be used to describe a family of useful techniques that can be applied at many levels within an organization. A comprehensive approach was developed by Harrington,[68] who advocates using flowcharting as the basic tool for *business process improvement.* In addition to being used to "map" existing processes, flowcharts can also be used to develop proposed new systems and processes within organizations. HR managers and practitioners frequently use flowcharts during their process of examining current systems and proposing new ones for implementation in organizations.

3. Nominal Group Technique (NGT). *This tool is a structured group decision-making process used to assign priorities or rank order groups of ideas.*

Nominal group technique is used where agreement about a decision is lacking or where group members have incomplete knowledge of the details of a problem. It was developed by Delbecq and his colleagues in the 1970s[69] and has been used for a wide variety of organizational development and HRM improvement activities since then. For example, one of the authors used it to obtain responses from a focus group of business faculty on the type and relative importance of changes that were needed in a comprehensive revision of an MBA program at a state university.

The process for performing the NGT is as follows:

- Silent (written) generation of ideas in response to a focused question

- Round-robin recording (usually on a flip chart) of one idea at a time from each group member by a designated recorder

- Clarifying ideas through questions from group members on the meaning of various listed items

- Voting on ideas to prioritize importance; uses a one- or two-stage process

- Closure around a decision of what to do about the prioritized items

4. Structured Surveys. *This tool consists of written questionnaires in which survey questions are designed to address anticipated quality problems.*
As pointed out in Chapter 1, one of the earliest tools used by HR practitioners was survey research. There are many standardized survey instruments that can be used to assess organizational climate, morale, leadership characteristics, and other measure of organizational health and performance. This information can be extremely valuable in pinpointing the need for organization change and quality improvement and can point to the direction in which the change should take place. The survey questionnaire generally has a number of questions, followed by a point scale that usually ranges from low to high, indicating some perceived degree of disagreement to agreement for each item. It is easy to quantify the results of such an instrument, but it is difficult to determine whether the results reflect the true opinions of the respondents.

5. Trend Chart. *This tool is used to monitor shifts in long-range averages and graph results of a process such as defect reduction, admissions increases, machine downtime, or phone calls.*
Trend charts have also been used for many years to graphically depict data. HR practitioners can use them in planning for organizational interventions by observing the trends in survey results from period to period and perhaps comparing them on the same graph with changes in grievances and employment levels over a period of months or even years. The advantage of doing this is that it provides HR specialists and managers with a common basis for understanding and "speaking from facts."

6. Excelerator. *This tool is a personal computer software program for systems analysis, design, and documentation.* It is available from Index Tech Corp., 1 Main Street, Cambridge, MA 02142.
This computerized software package contains various tools, which make it easy for an analyst to enter data and to have that data summarized in chart, graph, or other form so that it can be distributed and discussed in order to draw conclusions on courses of action.

REVIEW QUESTIONS

3.1. What are the five steps of organizational renewal that lead to sustained competitive advantage?

3.2. How does a "process focus" mindset differ from the traditional "organizational focus"? Why is this distinction significant?

3.3. What are the four layers of the "cross-unit," the new unit of competition in Japan?

3.4. What is quality function deployment, and what six basic steps are required to build its House of Quality?

3.5. What benefits and pitfalls did Florida Power & Light experience in its pursuit and achievement of the Deming Prize?

3.6. What are the five phases of business process improvement, and what are the major activities involved in each?

3.7. How does performance appraisal differ in a total quality environment from the appraisal that has occurred traditionally in organizations?

3.8. Define and elaborate on the five elements of the total quality human resource process planning.

3.9. Briefly discuss the role of unions and total quality human resource process planning.

3.10. Define each of the seven major process management tools and demonstrate how each could be used in human resource problem solving.

DISCUSSION QUESTIONS

3.1. Compare and contrast the three types of total quality continuous improvement: *kaizen*, competitive parity, and breakthrough dominance.

    A. In what competitive situations would each one be most beneficial for a corporation to pursue?

    B. What internal organizational capabilities must be present in order to achieve success with each one?

3.2. "Total quality human resource performance is demonstrated to the extent that constructive partnerships with unions are facilitated to achieve organizational objectives."

A. Do you agree with this assertion? Why or why not?

B. What current examples can you cite from U.S. business to support or contradict this assertion?

3.3. Drawing upon your own experience, what difficulties might an organization encounter in shifting from an evaluative approach to an improvement approach in its appraisal of performance? Would managers have more or less difficulty than employees in making the shift? Why?

3.4. What major barriers and opportunities would need to be addressed in order to successfully apply the cross-unit concept in the United States?

ENDNOTES

1. Harrington, H. James (1991). *Business Process Improvement*. New York: McGraw-Hill, pp. 9–14; Harrington, H. James (1995). *Total Improvement Management*. New York: McGraw-Hill, pp. 6–19; Davenport, T. (1993). *Process Innovation*. Boston: Harvard Business School Press, pp. 45–90; Lillrank, P. and Kano, N. (1989). *Continuous Improvement*. Ann Arbor: University of Michigan Press, pp. 15–26; Johnson, Richard S. (1995). *TQM: Management Processes for Quality Operations*. Milwaukee: ASQC Quality Press, pp. 27–41.

2. Voehl, Frank W. (1992). *Total Quality: Principles and Processes within Organizations*. Coral Springs, Fla.: Strategy Associates, pp. 4–7.

3. Imai, Masaaki (1986). *Kaizen: The Key to Japan's Competitive Success*. New York: Random House, pp. 10–70; Hammer, Michael and Champy, James (1993). *Reengineering the Corporation*. New York: Harper Business, pp. 31–158; Moody, Patricia E. (1993). *Breakthrough Partnering*. Essex Junction, Vt.: Oliver Wight, pp. 49–132.

4. Imai, Masaaki (1986). *Kaizen: The Key to Japan's Competitive Success*. New York: Random House, pp. 20–40; Kume, Hitoshi (1985). *Statistical Methods for Quality Improvement*. Tokyo: AOTS Press, pp. 10–60.

5. Johansson, Henry J., McHugh, P., Pendlebury, A. John, and Wheeler, W.A. III (1993). *Business Process Reengineering: Breakpoint Strategies for Market Dominance*. New York: John Wiley & Sons, pp. 8–12; Camp, Robert C. (1994). *Business Process Benchmarking*. Milwaukee: ASQC Quality Press, pp. 5–45; Harrington, H. James (1995). *Total Improvement Management*. New York: McGraw-Hill, pp. 41–79.

6. Beatty, Richard W. and Ulrich, David O. (1991). "Re-Energizing the Mature Organization." *Organizational Dynamics*. Vol. 25, No. 4, pp. 16–30.

7. Mills, Charles A. (1989). *The Quality Audit: A Management Evaluation Tool*. New York: McGraw-Hill, pp. 20–64; Mills, David (1993). *Quality Auditing*. New York: Chapman and Hall, pp. 30–71.

8. Shiba, Shoji, Graham, A., and Walden D. (1993). *A New American TQM: Four Practical Revolutions in Management.* Cambridge, Mass.: Productivity Press, pp. 107–188; Tenner, Arthur R. and DeToro, Irving J. (1992). *Total Quality Management.* Reading, Mass.: Addison-Wesley, pp. 97–124; Torbert, William R. and Fisher, Dalmer (1995). *Personal and Organizational Transformations.* New York: McGraw-Hill, pp. 87–98.

9. Evans, James R. and Lindsay, William M. (1995). *The Management and Control of Quality.* 3rd edition, Minneapolis: West Publishing, p. 16.

10. Voehl, Frank W. (1992). *Total Quality: Principles and Processes within Organizations.* Coral Springs, Fla.: Strategy Associates, pp. 20–25.

11. Greene, R.T. (1993). *Global Quality: A Synthesis of the World's Best Management Methods.* Milwaukee: ASQC Quality Press, pp. 146–156; Shiba, Shoji, Graham, A., and Walden D. (1993). *A New American TQM: Four Practical Revolutions in Management.* Cambridge, Mass.: Productivity Press, pp. 505–558.

12. Greene, R.T. (1993). *Global Quality: A Synthesis of the World's Best Management Methods.* Milwaukee: ASQC Quality Press, p. 147.

13. Greene, R.T. (1993). *Global Quality: A Synthesis of the World's Best Management Methods.* Milwaukee: ASQC Quality Press, pp. 498–504; Galegher, J., Kraut, R., and Egido, C. (1990). *Intellectual Teamwork.* Hillsdale, N.J.: Lawrence Erlbaum, pp. 30–75; Greenberg, S., Ed. (1991). *Computer-Supported Cooperative Work and Groupware.* New York: Academic Press, pp. 90–115.

14. Greene, R.T. (1993). *Global Quality: A Synthesis of the World's Best Management Methods.* Milwaukee: ASQC Quality Press, pp. 152–158; Johnson, Richard S. (1993). *TQM: Leadership for the Quality Transformation.* Milwaukee: ASQC Quality Press, pp. 265–294.

15. Olson, J. and Olson, G. (1991). "User-Centered Design of Collaboration Technology." *Journal of Organizational Computing.* Vol. 4, No. 1, pp. 61–62; Greene, R.T. (1990). *Implementing Japanese A.I. Techniques.* New York: McGraw-Hill, pp. 10–60.

16. Brossert, James L. (1991). *Quality Function Deployment: A Practitioner's Approach.* Milwaukee: ASQC Quality Press; Sullivan, L.P. (1988). "Policy Management through Quality Function Deployment." *Quality Progress.* Vol. 10, No. 6, pp. 20–25; Akao, Yoji, Ed. (1990). *Quality Function Deployment.* Cambridge, Mass.: Productivity Press.

17. This section relies on material from Dean, James W. Jr. and Evans, James R. (1994). *Total Quality: Management, Organization and Strategy.* Minneapolis: West Publishing, pp. 70–74.

18. Sullivan, L.P. (1990). "Quality Function Deployment: The Latent Potential of Phases III and IV." In Richard A. Shores, Ed. *A TQM Approach to Achieving Manufacturing Excellence.* Milwaukee: ASQC Quality Press, pp. 47–59.

19. Hudiburg, John (1991). *Winning with Quality: The FPL Story.* White Plains, N.Y.: Quality Resources, pp. 5–80.

20. Hudiburg, John (1991). *Winning with Quality: The FPL Story.* White Plains, N.Y.: Quality Resources, pp. 81–87.

21. Hudiburg, John (1991). *Winning with Quality: The FPL Story.* White Plains, N.Y.: Quality Resources, p. 88

22. Shiba, Shoji, Graham, A., and Walden D. (1993). *A New American TQM: Four Practical Revolutions in Management.* Cambridge, Mass.: Productivity Press, p. 524.

23. Petrick, J., Scherer, R., Wilson, J.C., and Westfall, F. (1994). "Benchmarking and Improving Core Competencies." *Journal for Quality and Participation.* Vol. 17, No. 4, pp. 76–78.

24. Johansson, Henry J., McHugh, P., Pendlebury, A. John, and Wheeler, W.A. III (1993). *Business Process Reengineering: Breakpoint Strategies for Market Dominance.* New York: John Wiley & Sons, p. 10; Harrington, H. James (1995). *Total Improvement Management.* New York: McGraw-Hill, pp. 16–29.

25. Harrington, H. James (1991). *Business Process Improvement.* New York: McGraw-Hill, p. 23; Harrington, H.J. (1989). *The Quality/Profit Connection.* Milwaukee: ASQC Quality Press, pp. 38–59; Harrington, H. James (1995). *Total Improvement Management.* New York: McGraw-Hill, pp. 55–71.

26. Modell, M.E. (1988). *A Professional Guide to Systems Analysis.* New York: McGraw-Hill, pp. 40–71; Jeffrey, D.R. and Lawrence, M.J. (1984). *Systems Analysis and Design.* Englewood Cliffs, N.J.: Prentice-Hall, pp. 65–80; Bruno, Gerard (1994). *The Process Analysis Handbook for Government.* Milwaukee: ASQC Quality Press, pp. 10–38; Galloway, Diane (1994). *Mapping Work Processes.* Milwaukee: ASQC Quality Press, pp. 3–13.

27. Hammer, Michael and Champy, James (1993). *Reengineering the Corporation.* New York: Harper Business, pp. 83–102.

28. Harrington, H. James (1991). *Business Process Improvement.* New York: McGraw-Hill, p. 164–165.

29. Ryan, Kathleen D. and Oestreich, Daniel K. (1991). *Driving Fear Out of the Workplace.* San Francisco: Jossey-Bass, pp. 3–102.

30. Blackburn, Richard and Rosen, Benson (1994). "Human Resource Management Practices and Total Quality Management." Paper presented at the 1994 Academy of Management Meeting, Atlanta; Blackburn, R. and Rosen, B. (1993). "Total Quality and Human Resources Management: Lessons Learned from Baldrige Award-Winning Companies." *Academy of Management Executive.* Vol. 7, No. 3, pp. 49–66; Schmidt, W.H. and Finnigan, J.P. (1993). *TQ Manager.* San Francisco: Jossey-Bass, pp. 45–138; Snell, S. and Dean, J. (1992). "Integrated Manufacturing and Human Resource Management: A Human Capital Perspective." *Academy of Management Journal.* Vol. 35, No. 3, pp. 467–504; Schuler, R.S. and Harris, D. (1992). *Managing Quality.* Reading, Mass.: Addison-Wesley, pp. 89–140; Lawler, E., Mohrman, S., and Ledford, G. (1992). *Employee Involvement and Total Quality Management: Practices and Results in Fortune 1000 Compa-*

nies. San Francisco: Jossey-Bass; Olian, J. and Rynes, S. (1991). "Making Total Quality Work: Aligning Organizational Processes, Performance, Measures and Stakeholders." *Human Resource Management.* Vol. 30, No. 3, pp. 303–333; Hart, C. and Schlesinger, L. (1991). "Total Quality Management and the Human Resource Professional: Applying the Baldrige Framework to Human Resources." *Human Resource Management.* Vol. 30, No. 4, pp. 433–454; Dobbins, G., Cardy, R.L., and Carson, K. (1991). "Examining Fundamental Assumptions: A Contrast of Person and System Approaches to Human Resource Management." In G. Ferris and K. Rowlands, Eds. *Research in Personnel and Human Resource Management.* Vol. 9, pp. 1–38; KPMG Peat Marwick (1991). *Quality Improvement Initiatives through the Management of Human Resources.* Short Hills, N.J.: KPMG Peat Marwick; Bounds, G.M. and Pace, L.A. (1991). "Human Resource Management for Competitive Capability." In M.J. Stall and G.M. Bounds, Eds. *Competing Globally through Customer Value: The Management of Strategic Supersystems.* New York: Quorum Books, pp. 648–684.

31.　Olian, J. and Rynes, S. (1991). "Making Total Quality Work: Aligning Organizational Processes, Performance, Measures and Stakeholders." *Human Resource Management.* Vol. 30, No. 3, p. 305.

32.　Bounds, G.M. and Pace, L.A. (1991). "Human Resource Management for Competitive Capability." In M.J. Stall and G.M. Bounds, Eds. *Competing Globally through Customer Value: The Management of Strategic Supersystems.* New York: Quorum Books, pp. 652–655.

33.　Bounds, G.M. and Pace, L.A. (1991). "Human Resource Management for Competitive Capability." In M.J. Stall and G.M. Bounds, Eds. *Competing Globally through Customer Value: The Management of Strategic Supersystems.* New York: Quorum Books, p. 656.

34.　Crystal, Graef S. (1992). *In Search of Excess: The Overcompensation of American Executives.* New York: W.W. Norton, pp. 10–79.

35.　Blackburn, Richard and Rosen, Benson (1994). "Human Resource Management Practices and Total Quality Management." Paper presented at the 1994 Academy of Management Meeting, Atlanta, pp. 6–7; Olian, J. and Rynes, S. (1991). "Making Total Quality Work: Aligning Organizational Processes, Performance, Measures and Stakeholders." *Human Resource Management.* Vol. 30, No. 3, p. 314.

36.　Hampton, W.J. (1988). "How Does Japan, Inc. Pick Its American Workers?" *Business Week.* October 3, pp. 84–88.

37.　Olian, J. and Rynes, S. (1991). "Making Total Quality Work: Aligning Organizational Processes, Performance, Measures and Stakeholders." *Human Resource Management.* Vol. 30, No. 3, p. 314; Heneman, Herbert G. III and Heneman, R.L. (1994). *Staffing Organizations.* Homewood, Ill.: Austen Press-Irwin, pp. 331–430.

38.　Shook, R.L. (1988). *Honda: An American Success Story.* New York: Prentice-Hall, pp. 6–45.

39. Olian, J. and Rynes, S. (1991). "Making Total Quality Work: Aligning Organizational Processes, Performance, Measures and Stakeholders." *Human Resource Management.* Vol. 30, No. 3, p. 313.

40. Greene, R.T. (1993). *Global Quality: A Synthesis of the World's Best Management Methods.* Milwaukee: ASQC Quality Press, pp. 215–216.

41. Cohen-Rosenthal, E., Ed. (1995). *Unions, Management and Quality: Opportunities for Innovation and Excellence.* Chicago: Irwin, pp. 3–85; Hoerr, J. (1991). "What Should Unions Do?" *Harvard Business Review.* Vol. 42, No. 6, pp. 30–45; Weiler, Paul C. (1990). *Governing the Workplace: The Future of Labor and Employment Law.* Cambridge, Mass.: Harvard University Press; Rankin, T. (1990). *New Forms of Work Organization: The Challenge for North American Unions.* Toronto, Canada: University of Toronto; Blasi, J.R. and Kruse, D.L. (1991). *The New Owners.* New York: Harper Business; Turner, L. (1991). *Democracy at Work: Changing World Markets and the Future of Labor Unions.* Ithaca, N.Y.: Cornell University; Mishel, L. and Voos, P., Eds. (1991). *Unions and Economic Competitiveness.* New York: M.E. Sharpe.

42. Lawler, E., Mohrman, S., and Ledford, G. (1992). *Employee Involvement and Total Quality Management: Practices and Results in Fortune 1000 Companies.* San Francisco: Jossey-Bass, pp. 10–40; Turner, L. (1991). *Democracy at Work: Changing World Markets and the Future of Labor Unions.* Ithaca, N.Y.: Cornell University, pp. 44–79; Cohen-Rosenthal, E. (1995). "Thinking about Quality and Unions. In E. Cohen-Rosenthal, Ed. *Unions, Management and Quality.* Chicago: Irwin, pp. 17–19.

43. Blasi, J.R. and Kruse, D.L. (1991). *The New Owners.* New York: Harper Business, pp. 60–85.

44. Scherer, Robert F., Brodzinski, J.D., and Crable, E.A. (1993). "The Human Factor in Workplace Accidents." *HR Magazine.* Vol. 21, No. 4, pp. 92–97; Scherer, R., Petrick, J., and Quinn, J. (1995). "Non-Human Factors in Workplace Accidents." Research paper under revision.

45. Gabor, A. (1990). *The Man Who Discovered Quality.* New York: Random House, pp. 26–28; Harrington, H. James (1995). *Total Improvement Management.* New York: McGraw-Hill, pp. 15–16.

46. Anthony, W.P., Perrewe, P., and Kacmar, K.M. (1993). *Strategic Human Resource Management.* New York: Dryden Press, pp. 442–443; Kohn, Alfie (1993). *Punished by Rewards.* Boston: Houghton Mifflin, pp. 183–186; Schuler, R.S. and Harris, D. (1992). *Managing Quality.* Reading, Mass.: Addison-Wesley, pp. 113–127; Masterson, S. and Taylor, S. (1994). "Total PA: The Value-Added Contribution of Performance Appraisal to TQM." Unpublished manuscript. College of Business and Management, University of Maryland.

47. Kohn, Alfie (1993). *Punished by Rewards.* Boston: Houghton Mifflin, pp. 49–67, 270–276.

48. Schonberger, R.J. (1990). *Building a Chain of Customers.* New York: Free Press, pp. 95–107; Kanter, R.M. (1989). *When Giants Learn to Dance.* New York: Touchstone, pp. 55–90.

49. Schonberger, R.J. (1990). *Building a Chain of Customers*. New York: Free Press, pp. 88–90.
50. Schonberger, R.J. (1990). *Building a Chain of Customers*. New York: Free Press, pp. 86–87.
51. Kohn, Alfie (1993). *Punished by Rewards*. Boston: Houghton Mifflin, pp. 181–197.
52. Blinder, Alan S., Ed. (1990). *Paying for Productivity: A Look at the Evidence*. Washington, D.C.: Brookings Institution, p. 3.
53. Greene, R.T. (1993). *Global Quality: A Synthesis of the World's Best Management Methods*. Milwaukee: ASQC Quality Press, pp. 137–140; Sheppard, B.H., Lewicki, R.J., and Minton, J.W. (1992). *Organizational Justice: The Search for Fairness in the Workplace*. New York: Lexington Books, pp. 9–108; Olian, J. and Rynes, S. (1991). "Making Total Quality Work: Aligning Organizational Processes, Performance, Measures and Stakeholders." *Human Resource Management*. Vol. 30, No. 3, p. 312.
54. Crystal, Graef S. (1992). *In Search of Excess: The Overcompensation of American Executives*. New York: W. W. Norton, pp. 15–70; Eccles, R.G. (1991). "The Performance Measurement Manifesto." *Harvard Business Review*. Vol. 69, No. 1, pp. 131–137.
55. Sheppard, B.H., Lewicki, R.J., and Minton, J.W. (1992). *Organizational Justice: The Search for Fairness in the Workplace*. New York: Lexington Books, pp. 109–201; Ewing, D.W. (1989). *Justice on the Job*. Boston: Harvard Business School Press, pp. 5–70; Withey, M.J. and Cooper, W.H. (1989). "Predicting Exit, Voice, Loyalty and Neglect." *Administrative Science Quarterly*. Vol. 34, No. 4, pp. 521–539; Korsgaard, M.A., Schweiger, D.M., and Sapienza, H.J. (1995). "Building Commitment, Attachment and Trust in Strategic Decision-Making Teams: The Role of Procedural Justice." *Academy of Management Journal*. Vol. 38, No. 1, pp. 60–84.
56. The Conference Board (1991). *Employee Buy-in to Total Quality*. New York: The Conference Board, Report No. 974, pp. 11–17; KPMG Peat Marwick (1991). *Quality Improvement Initiatives through the Management of Human Resources*. Short Hills, N.J.: KPMG Peat Marwick, pp. 15–20.
57. Harris, David M. and De Simone, R.L. (1994). *Human Resource Development*. New York: Dryden Press, pp. 430–450; McCormack, S.P. (1992). "TQM: Getting It Right the First Time." *Training and Development Journal*. Vol. 41, No. 1, pp. 25–27; Schonberger, R.J. (1992). "Total Quality Management Cuts a Broad Swath through Manufacturing and Beyond." *Organizational Dynamics*. Vol. 20, No. 4, pp. 16–28; Bowen, D.E. and Lawler, E.E. III (1992). "Total Quality-Oriented Human Resources Management." *Organizational Dynamics*. Vol. 20, No. 4, pp. 29–41; Tollison, P. (1992). "Assessing TQM Training Needs." *Journal for Quality and Participation*. Vol. 15, No. 1, pp. 50–54.
58. The Conference Board (1991). *Employee Buy-in to Total Quality*. New York: The Conference Board, Report No. 974, pp. 15–17; Blackburn,

R.S. and Rosen, B. (1994). "Human Resource Management Practices and Total Quality Management Paper." Paper presented at the Annual Meeting of the Academy of Management, Dallas, August (argues that nonexecutive quality training is the most effective utilization of quality training expenditures).

59. KPMG Peat Marwick (1991). *Quality Improvement Initiatives through the Management of Human Resources.* Short Hills, N.J.: KPMG Peat Marwick, pp. 29–32.

60. General Accounting Office (1990). *Management Practices—U.S. Companies Improve Performance through Quality Efforts.* Washington, D.C.: U.S. General Accounting Office, pp. 7–12.

61. Olian, J.D. and Rynes, S.L. (1991). "Survey of U.S. Quality Practices." Unpublished manuscript. College of Business and Management, University of Maryland.

62. KPMG Peat Marwick (1991). *Quality Improvement Initiatives through the Management of Human Resources.* Short Hills, N.J.: KPMG Peat Marwick, pp. 30–31.

63. Spencer, Barbara A. (1994). "Models of Organization and Total Quality Management: A Comparison and Critical Evaluation." *Academy of Management Review.* Vol. 19, No. 3, pp. 446–471; Lindsay, William M. and Petrick, Joseph A. (1995). *Total Quality in Organization Development.* Delray Beach, Fla.: St. Lucie Press.

64. Hall, D.T. and Richter, J. (1990). "Career Gridlock: Baby Boomers Hit the Wall." *The Executive.* Vol. 14, No. 4, p. 19.

65. Shiba, Shoji, Graham, A., and Walden D. (1993). *A New American TQM: Four Practical Revolutions in Management.* Cambridge, Mass.: Productivity Press, pp. 158–159; Evans, James R. and Lindsay, William M. (1995). *The Management and Control of Quality.* 3rd edition, Minneapolis: West Publishing, pp. 253–269.

66. Vroom, V.H. and Jago, A.G. (1988). *The New Leadership: Managing Participation in Organizations.* Englewood Cliffs, N.J.: Prentice-Hall, pp. 20–65; Rost, Joseph C. (1993). *Leadership for the Twenty-First Century.* Westport, Conn.: Praeger, pp. 97–152.

67. Watson, Gregory H. (1993). *Strategic Benchmarking.* New York: John Wiley & Sons, pp. 31–77; Camp, Robert C. (1994). *Business Process Benchmarking.* Milwaukee: ASQC Quality Press, pp. 20–46; Kearns, D.T. and Nadler, D.A. (1992). *Prophets in the Dark: How Xerox Reinvented Itself and Beat Back the Japanese.* New York: Harper Business, pp. 201–267.

68. Harrington, H.J. (1989). *The Quality/Profit Connection.* Milwaukee: ASQC Quality Press, pp. 40–49; Harrington, H. James (1995). *Total Improvement Management.* New York: McGraw-Hill, pp. 44–47.

69. Delbecq, A.L., Van de Ven, A.H., and Gustafson, D.H. (1975). *Group Techniques for Program Planning: A Guide to Nominal and Delphi Processes.* Glenview, Ill.: Scott Foresman.

EXERCISES

PRACTITIONER ASSESSMENT INSTRUMENT 3A: ORGANIZATION PROCESS CLIMATE

DIRECTIONS

Read each dimension of organization process climate and consider the descriptions at both ends of the scale. Circle the number on the scale that reflects your evaluation of conditions in your organization at this time. (1 is the lowest evaluation possible and 20 is the highest evaluation possible.)

1. **Reward System:** The degree to which employees, as individuals and as teams, feel they are being recognized and rewarded for good work rather than being ignored, criticized, or punished when something goes wrong.

Rewards are not in line with effort and performance	1 2 3 4 5	6 7 8 9 10	11 12 13 14 15	16 17 18 19 20	Employees are recognized and rewarded positively

2. **Standards of Performance:** The emphasis placed upon quality performance and achieving results, including the degree to which employees feel meaningful and challenging goals are being set at every level of the organization.

Performance standards are low	1 2 3 4 5	6 7 8 9 10	11 12 13 14 15	16 17 18 19 20	Performance standards are high

3. **Warmth and Support:** The feeling that friendliness is a valued norm and that employees trust, respect, and offer support to one another. The feeling that good human relationships prevail in the day-to-day work of the organization.

There is little warmth and support in the organization	1 2 3 4 5	6 7 8 9 10	11 12 13 14 15	16 17 18 19 20	Warmth and support are characteristic of the organization

4. **Leadership:** As needs for leadership arise, people feel free to take leadership roles and are rewarded for shared successful leadership. The organization is not dominated by or dependent upon just one or two individuals.

Leadership not respected or rewarded; organization dominated by or dependent upon just 1 or 2 individuals					Leadership is accepted and rewarded based on expertise of individuals and teams
	1 2 3 4 5	6 7 8 9 10	11 12 13 14 15	16 17 18 19 20	

5. **Organizational Clarity:** The feeling among employees that things are well organized and goals and responsibilities are clearly defined rather than being disorderly, confused, or chaotic.

The organization is disorderly, confused, and chaotic					Organization is well organized, with clearly defined goals and responsibilities
	1 2 3 4 5	6 7 8 9 10	11 12 13 14 15	16 17 18 19 20	

6. **Communications:** Important information is shared quickly and accurately—up, down, and sideways—in the organization.

Information is wrong, censored, or unavailable					Information is accurate, open, and available
	1 2 3 4 5	6 7 8 9 10	11 12 13 14 15	16 17 18 19 20	

7. **Creativity:** New ideas are sought and used in all areas of the organization. Employee creativity is encouraged at every level of responsibility.

The organization is closed and unresponsive to change					The organization is innovative and open to new ideas
	1 2 3 4 5	6 7 8 9 10	11 12 13 14 15	16 17 18 19 20	

8. **Job Stress:** Employees are neither overworked nor underworked. Stress levels are appropriate for the job.

Stress levels are harmful					Stress levels are optimum
	1 2 3 4 5	6 7 8 9 10	11 12 13 14 15	16 17 18 19 20	

9. **Ethics:** The emphasis the organization places upon high standards of moral behavior at all levels of responsibility.

Double standards exist; ethics are low					High standards of conduct are expected at all levels
	1 2 3 4 5	6 7 8 9 10	11 12 13 14 15	16 17 18 19 20	

10. **Tolerance:** The degree of open-mindedness that exists toward different people, ideas, and customs in the organization.

Prejudice and discrimination are the norm					Nonprejudice and nondiscrimination are the norm
	1 2 3 4 5	6 7 8 9 10	11 12 13 14 15	16 17 18 19 20	

11. **Feedback and Controls:** The use of reporting, comparing, and correcting procedures, such as employee evaluations and financial audits.

Controls are used for policing and punishment					Controls are used to provide guidance and solve problems
	1 2 3 4 5	6 7 8 9 10	11 12 13 14 15	16 17 18 19 20	

12. **Resources:** Sufficient financial and physical resources are available to accomplish the job.

Insufficient funds, equipment, and supplies					Supplies, equipment, and funds are sufficient
	1 2 3 4 5	6 7 8 9 10	11 12 13 14 15	16 17 18 19 20	

13. **Employee Growth:** Personal and professional development is emphasized at all levels and in all classifications in the organization.

Employee growth is a low priority in the organization					Employee growth is a high priority in the organization
	1 2 3 4 5	6 7 8 9 10	11 12 13 14 15	16 17 18 19 20	

14. **Physical Working Conditions** (lighting, space, heat, washroom facilities, etc.): Safe and comfortable working conditions exist throughout the organization.

Working conditions are poor					Working conditions are good
	1 2 3 4 5	6 7 8 9 10	11 12 13 14 15	16 17 18 19 20	

15. **Teamwork:** The amount of understanding and cooperation between difference levels and work groups in the organization.

Teamwork is poor					Teamwork is high
	1 2 3 4 5	6 7 8 9 10	11 12 13 14 15	16 17 18 19 20	

16. **Employee Pride:** The degree of pride that exists—pride of individual workmanship and pride of organization goals and accomplishments.

Pride is low					Pride is high
	1 2 3 4 5	6 7 8 9 10	11 12 13 14 15	16 17 18 19 20	

17. **Employee Involvement:** Responsibility for decision making is broadly shared in the organization. Employees are involved in decisions that affect them.

Low employee participation in decision making					High employee participation in decision making
	1 2 3 4 5	6 7 8 9 10	11 12 13 14 15	16 17 18 19 20	

SCORING

Total all the scores you gave to all the dimensions of organization climate and divide by 17. Place this number on the following scale:

Types of Organization Process Climates

1 2 3 4 5	6 7 8 9 10	11 12 13 14 15	16 17 18 19 20
Exploitive	Impoverished	Supportive	Total Quality

INTERPRETATION

Exploitive (1–5.9): Organizational process climate is autocratic and hierarchical, with virtually no participation by employees. Managers show little confidence or trust in employees, and employees do not feel free to discuss job-related problems with their managers. Exploitive climates rarely survive for any length of time because employees avoid them as much as possible. Where they do exist, they are characterized by a lack of employee loyalty, substandard performance, and recurrent financial crises.

Impoverished (6–10.9): Organizational process climate attempts to avoid being completely autocratic, but power remains at the top and employees are given only occasional opportunities for participation. Impoverished process climates fall into two categories: benevolent autocracy, in which those at the top of the organization have genuine concern for the welfare of their employees, and neglectful autocracies, in which concern for employees and worker participation is perfunctory. Impoverished process climates rarely excel because employees are never encouraged to do so. Managers may invest only in what will keep employees minimally contented and avoid investments in employee empowerment.

Supportive (11–15.9): Organizational process climate maintains power in the hands of managers, but there is good communication, encouragement, and participation throughout the organization. Employees understand the goals of the organization, feel free to discuss job-related problems with their managers, and are committed to achieve organization goals as long as the external reward and recognition system compensates them adequately. There is no sense of employee ownership of process and/or product improvement, nor is there a sense of autonomous interdependence between fully mature parties. Supportive process climates create productive but dependent followers and underutilize the intellectual capital of an organization relative to total quality organizations.

Total quality (16–20): Organizational process climate is one in which a high degree of work empowerment maturity exists in all parties. Employees have a high degree of autonomy to initiate, coordinate, and implement plans to accomplish goals. Communication between employees and managers is open and honest; employees are treated with trust and respect rather than suspicion. Employees have a sense of process ownership and pride in continually improving and learning. Power resides in the logical focus of interest and concern for a process problem rather than in the hierarchical chain of command. Total quality process climates result in the highest work productivity for an organization and the highest quality of work life for responsible employees.

Sources Adapted from Likert, Rensis (1967). *The Human Organization*. New York: McGraw-Hill, pp. 119–125; Manning, George and Curtis, Kent (1988). *Morale: Quality of Work Life*. Cincinnati: South-Western Publishing, pp. 74–81.

PRACTITIONER ASSESSMENT INSTRUMENT 4B: ORGANIZATIONAL EXCELLENCE BENCHMARKING

DIRECTIONS

Listed below are eight attributes and their characteristics common among excellent companies. Rate your organization on each characteristic using the following scale:

> 5 = *Always* present
> 4 = Present *most of the time*
> 3 = *Sometimes* present
> 2 = *Rarely* present
> 1 = *Never* present

Total the scores of the characteristics of each attribute. Then divide by the number of characteristics under that attribute. This will give an overall rating for each attribute.

I. RISK AND EXPERIMENTATION (A Bias for Action)

1. ____ Concrete action is taken early.
2. ____ Prototypes are provided for customers; they can experiment.
3. ____ Risk taking is supported by a tolerance for failure.
4. ____ Physical layout and tools, such as conference rooms, blackboards, and flip charts, invite interaction, impromptu problem solving, and "good-news-story swapping."
5. ____ Resources are willingly shifted as required to get the job done.
6. ____ Small teams solve problems or develop new products and then are dissolved.
7. ____ A freewheeling informality prevails, and the "glue" is a common purpose.
8. ____ "One page only" memos, five-page new product proposals, and an aversion to planning documents and reports create an action-oriented environment.

____ **TOTAL**

____ **Divide the total by 8**

Mark your score on the scale below:

1	2	3	4	5

1.5	2.5	3.5	4.5

There is *not* a bias toward action.   There *is* a bias toward action (things get done)

II. CUSTOMERS ARE FULL PARTNERS (Close to the Customer)

1. ____ Quality and service are the number one priority.
2. ____ Proposals are cost justifiable from the customer's standpoint.
3. ____ People put themselves in the customer's shoes.
4. ____ "Satisfaction guaranteed" is the company philosophy.

5. ____ Senior leaders know and care about customers.
6. ____ Customers participate in experiments with prototypes.
7. ____ Inventions and improvement ideas come from customers.
____ **TOTAL**
____ **Divide the total by 7**
Mark your score on the scale below:

1	2	3	4	5
1.5	2.5	3.5	4.5	

Customers receive   Customers are treated
little consideration   as full partners

III. INNOVATION THROUGH ENTREPRENEURSHIP
(Autonomy and Entrepreneurship)
1. ____ Self-initiated, self-directed experimentation is encouraged.
2. ____ The creative fanatic is tolerated.
3. ____ People who have the know-how, energy, daring, and staying power to implement ideas (the champions) are rewarded positively.
4. ____ Rewards and a share of success are provided.
5. ____ Support systems exist to get the job done.
6. ____ The burden of proof is transferred to those who want to prove that an idea will *not* work.
____ **TOTAL**
____ **Divide the total by 6**
Mark your score on the scale below:

1	2	3	4	5
1.5	2.5	3.5	4.5	

Innovation is *not*   Innovation *is* encouraged
encouraged   within the organization

IV. MOTIVATING PEOPLE TO CHOOSE PRODUCTIVITY
(Productivity Through People)
1. ____ Respect for the individual is the number one operating philosophy.
2. ____ There is a dedication to training people.
3. ____ Reasonable, clear expectations are established for each person.
4. ____ Lots of feedback and celebrating are done.
5. ____ There is a great deal of positive reinforcement.
6. ____ There is an everyday commitment to helping people become winners.
7. ____ People are treated as adults.
____ **TOTAL**
____ **Divide the total by 7**

Mark your score on the scale below:

1	2	3	4	5

1.5   2.5   3.5   4.5
There is a lack of   People are motivated
motivation within the   to be productive
organization

V. SHAPING A POWERFUL ETHICAL WORK CULTURE
(Hands-On, Integrity-Driven Approach)

1. ____ There is a principled, clear, compelling description of what the organization stands for.

2. ____ People respect the personal and professional integrity of their leaders.

3. ____ People feel that they become better persons at work.

4. ____ People feel they are fairly treated at work.

5. ____ People feel that managers respond to feedback.

6. ____ Ethical work culture assessments and audits are performed annually.

____ **TOTAL**

____ **Divide the total by 6**

Mark your score on the scale below:

1	2	3	4	5

1.5   2.5   3.5   4.5
A powerful ethical work   A meaningful ethical
culture to guide behavior   work culture operates
is lacking   throughout the organization

VI. STRUCTURE IS SIMPLE AND LEADERS LEAD
(Simple Form, Lean Support Staff)

1. ____ Bureaucratic layers are minimal, with little red tape required to get things done.

2. ____ People are provided with a fairly stable organizational structure that makes sense and works for them.

3. ____ Flexibility is fostered by creating small units and by designing short-term groups to address problems and develop innovations.

4. ____ Resources are focused on the action line. The organization is not top heavy.

5. ____ First-line leaders are not afraid to resolve conflicts or delegate authority.

____ **TOTAL**

____ **Divide the total by 6**

Mark your score on the scale below:

1	2	3	4	5
1.5	2.5	3.5	4.5	

There is a complex structure, with first-line leaders having little influence	The basic structure is simple and the driving force comes from first-line leaders

VII. LIBERATING TALENT WITHIN PARAMETERS
(Simultaneous Tight–Loose Properties)

1. ____ Stable, well-defined expectations are provided from the top.

2. ____ A meaningful value system is promoted throughout the organization which inherently defines appropriate behavior.

3. ____ Employee involvement is encouraged to function as a powerful productivity force.

4. ____ "Quality versus cost" and "efficiency versus effectiveness" arguments are defined in favor of liberating ordinary people to invest and produce the highest quality product every time.

____ **TOTAL**

____ **Divide the total by 4**

Mark your score on the scale below:

1	2	3	4	5
1.5	2.5	3.5	4.5	

People feel personally constrained; at the same time, they feel organizational direction is lacking	Central direction co-exists with maximum individual autonomy

INTERPRETATION
Add the average scores for each of the seven attributes:

If the total equals:	The evaluation is:
29–35	Excellent; outstanding; conditions reflect those in the best run companies
22–28	Very good; solid; however, more work is needed to attain excellence
14–21	Below par; unsatisfactory; improvement is needed
1–13	Poor; failing; much work is needed to solve basic problems

Adapted from Peters, Thomas J and Waterman, Robert H. Jr. (1982). *In Search of Excellence: Lessons from America's Best-Run Companies.* New York: Warner Books.

SPEAKING WITH FACTS: PROJECT DIMENSIONS

The focus of Chapter 4 is on two areas: the total quality business projects and the total quality human resource (HR) projects. Both are crucial in determining the strength of the third pillar of the House of Total Quality and clarifying the expanded project responsibilities of employees in a total quality system. Both total quality business and HR projects need to be aligned to ensure organizational effectiveness and efficiency.

THE TOTAL QUALITY BUSINESS PROJECTS

As indicated in Chapter 1, the third pillar of the House of Total Quality, speaking with facts, is based on the cornerstone of project planning and the foundation of project management. In Chapter 2, a *project was defined as a single, nonrecurring event that implements organizational changes through structured phases and specified outcomes, requiring teamwork for successful completion.*[1]

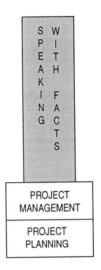

Figure 4.1   The Third Pillar, Foundation, and Cornerstone of the House of Total Quality.

The pillar of speaking with facts is the outcome of sound design developed in the cornerstone of project planning with effective implementation delivered in the foundation of project management, as depicted in Figure 4.1.[2]

Quality project involvement is undertaken for many reasons (e.g., monitoring and maintaining existing processes, new product, service or process design, assessing and improving standards, process certification, and/or quality audits). Regardless of the range of quality project involvement, its purpose is to implement strategy by operationalizing quality processes. To achieve world-class quality project success requires that teams enable the organization to **speak with facts**. *To speak with facts means that the organization has the resources and methods to determine what is factually true and structures itself to ensure members give voice to the truth.*

To appreciate the importance of speaking with facts, it is useful to consider it in the context of four alternatives: (1) speaking without facts, (2) knowing the facts but not speaking with facts, (3) not knowing the facts and not speaking with facts, and (4) speaking with facts. With the first option, individuals or groups make themselves heard in the organization through various voice mechanisms (e.g., committees, policy meetings, newsletters, open-door policies, training sessions, and suggestions).[3] Voice mechanisms promote organizational loyalty and vitality.[4] They normally preserve and protect the power of those who currently govern the organization.[5] Giving voice to ideas is a form of empowerment, and some persons delight in the use of voice power, even when they "do not know what they are talking about." Persuasive personalities and powerful groups that speak without facts (and either intentionally or unintentionally deceive or make decisions with inadequate statistical justification) put the survival and success of the organization at risk for their own benefit.

With the second option, individuals or groups may know the truth and have adequate statistical documentation, but there is no voice mechanism in the organization for them to be heard. Often nonmanagerial employees who are close to the actual operations know what causes problems and how to fix them, but their knowledge is discounted by those with more voice power.[6] In fact, in many organizations where "shooting the messenger" is routine, the fear of factually confronting those with more voice power with the truth inhibits any expression of dissent from stated policy.[7] Again, the survival and success of the organization are put at risk because the organization's internal voice systems do not empower those who could most help it.

With the third option, individuals and/or groups do not know the truth or do not have adequate statistical documentation and do not speak up. In general, these individuals and groups flounder and eventually fail; their personal fears and the fear in the workplace paralyze them and prevent them from obtaining the facts and assertively voicing them.[8] Sometimes, they tacitly know what needs to be done but do not have the self-esteem or the training in statistical methods to transform their intuition into knowledge that decision-makers would regard as credible.[9]

Finally, speaking with facts is the option advocated by total quality business projects. It entails the disciplined use of tools and techniques to obtain factual knowledge and the responsibility to voice those findings, whether they be good news or bad news, to help the organization survive and succeed. It requires that barriers to fact finding be eliminated, that people accurately and honestly report the truth on a timely basis, and that the organization proactively place all the relevant voice mechanisms at the disposal of those who are ready to speak with facts. It means that incompetent fact finding, unwillingness to use statistical tools, dishonest reporting, uncommunicative hoarding of information, and uncooperative relations with internal and/or external customers will not be tolerated. Learning from successes and failures occurs when voice mechanisms are routinely used. In turn, employees can expect a total quality firm that wants the facts to provide ongoing training in technical, teamwork, and communication skills and a reward and recognition process that reinforces that aim.

The importance of speaking with facts is further emphasized by the most recent nationwide survey of human resource management (HRM) practice and total quality management.[10] The survey statistically confirms that firms with higher levels of total quality management (TQM) commitment and effectiveness can be distinguished from firms with lower levels of commitment and effectiveness on the basis of more substantive communication practices (toward more and different types of multidirectional voice systems) and changes in job design (toward employees more empowered to obtain facts).[11] In addition, firms reporting higher levels of TQM commitment and effectiveness tended to make changes in a number of HR key processes rather than changing only one or two such key processes.[12]

TOTAL QUALITY BUSINESS PROJECT PLANNING

To speak with facts further requires a total quality business project plan to identify how and what facts are to be determined. In a total quality environment, the process of obtaining facts is as important as the facts themselves. The major steps, key fact-finding cycles, and appropriate tools to speak with facts are identified in Table 4.1.

In column A of Table 4.1, the seven quality control steps provide the macro procedure for fact finding. The first step is theme selection, which is the result of sensing a problem at the cognitive level and experientially exploring the situation and formulating the problem. It means honestly acknowledging any perceived weaknesses (e.g., defects, mistakes, delays, waste, accidents/injuries, performance gaps) and using the appropriate management and planning tools in column C (which were treated in Chapter 3). The second and third steps entail collecting and analyzing data and analyzing causes without jumping to solutions, but instead using the appropriate tools in column D (which will be treated at the end of this chapter). The remaining steps follow to arrive at a standard solution with appropriate process documentation conjoined with the appropriate tools along the way.

The key to achieving and maintaining quality project success, however, is the alternating repetition of cycles of process control to standardize routine daily work and structure improvement activities, as indicated in Figure 4.2.

The basic cycle of process control to maintain routine daily work is often called the SDCA cycle. In the SDCA cycle, there is a standard (S), and it is used to do the process (D). Then the results of the process are checked (C), and appropriate action is taken (A). If the results are within specification, the appropriate action is to continue to use the standard and repeat the cycle. If the results are beginning to drift or are actually out of specification (i.e., not meeting customer needs, standard corrective actions are to be taken).

However, from time to time, project teams may decide that the specifications are not stringent enough and that they must improve the process (reduce the variance) so that tighter specifications can be met. When this happens, they use a form of PDCA to find the source of the greatest natural variation and improve the process by eliminating it. This alternating interac-

Table 4.1 Fact-Finding Steps, Cycles, and Tools

(A) Seven quality control steps	(B) PDCA/SDCA cycles	(C) Seven process management/ planning tools	(D) Seven quality control project tools
1. Select theme	Plan	KJ method Matrix data analysis Relations diagram	
2. Collect and analyze data		Matrix diagram	Check sheet, display graphs, Pareto chart, histogram, scatter diagram, cause-and-effect diagram, control chart
3. Analyze causes			
4. Plan and implement solution	Do	Tree diagram Matrix diagram Arrow diagram PDPC diagram	
5. Evaluate effects	Check		Check sheet, display graphs, Pareto chart, histogram, scatter diagram, cause-and effect diagram, control chart
6. Standardize solution	Act	Arrow diagram PDPC diagram	
7. Reflect on process (and next problem)		KJ method	
(Provides steps)	(Provides repetitions)	(Provides tools)	(Provides tools)

Source: Shiba, Shoji, Graham, A., and Walden D. (1993). *A New American TQM: Four Practical Revolutions in Management.* Cambridge, Mass.: Productivity Press, p. 159. Modified by the authors.

tion between the SDCA and the PDCA cycles for initiating improvements can be depicted in the following scenario:

SDCA   Run an existing process for a while. Compute the natural variation, thus highlighting uncontrolled variation.

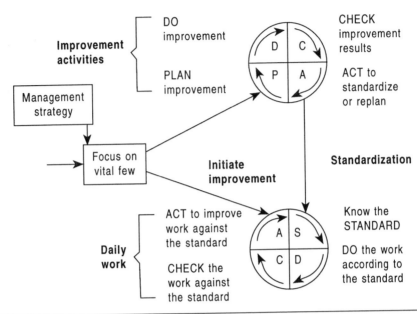

Figure 4.2 Alternation of SDCA and PDCA Process Control Cycles. (Source: Shiba, Shoji, Graham, A., and Walden, D. (1993). *A New American TQM: Four Practical Resolutions in Management*. Cambridge, Mass.: Productivity Press, p. 67.)

PDCA Find and eliminate the sources of uncontrolled variation.

SDCA Continue running the new or now accurately followed process. Eliminate the source of any out-of-control condition that begins to occur.

PDCA Use the seven quality control steps to find and reduce the largest source of controlled variation.

SDCA Continue running the new process. Eliminate the source of any out-of-control condition that begins to occur.[13]

Speaking with facts, therefore, is different than speaking with feelings or speaking with power. Speaking with facts requires disciplined application of quality control steps, cycles, and tools to the system itself.

Once the method of fact finding is mastered, project teams decide on which facts to obtain and in what order. Engaging in a **quality audit** is one form of determining which facts to address. *A quality audit provides a comprehensive and systematic examination of the extent to which formulated plans and implemented processes are successful.*[14] While domestic and international award criteria (Baldrige, Deming, or ISO 9000) provide a convenient checklist for a quality audit, project teams are expected to certify system processes.

The six levels of system processes were identified in Chapter 3. To determine whether each process has evolved to the next level, project teams need to ascertain the facts in eight major change areas:[15]

- End-customer-related measurements
- Process and/or performance measurements
- Supplier partnerships
- Documentation
- Training
- Benchmarking
- Process adaptability
- Continuous improvement

Harrington addresses each of the levels in detail as the process moves from meeting customer requirements to expectations and, finally, latent desires. The following is a detailed list of project team tasks to obtain factual documentation for each level.

Factual Requirements to Be Qualified at Level 2

All processes are classified as level 1 (*unknown status*) until sufficient data have been collected to determine their true status. Normally, processes move from qualification level 1 to qualification 2 level (*understood status*). Qualification level 2 signifies that the process design is understood by the process improvement team (PIT) and is operating to the prescribed documentation. To be qualified at any level, all the criteria in each of the eight major change areas (for example, supplier partnerships, process measurements, and/or performance) must be met and factually documented. Those for level 2 are:

End-customer-related measurements
- Measurements reflect the end customer's view of the process.
- End-customer requirements are documented.
- End-customer feedback system is established.
- End-customer effectiveness charts are posted and updated.

Process and/or performance measurements
- Overall effectiveness and efficiency are measured and posted where they can be seen by employees.

- Effectiveness and efficiency targets are set.
- Process operational and/or control weaknesses are evaluated and meet minimum requirements.
- Overall ethical climate assessment is completed and development targets set.
- Overall organization process analysis is completed and development targets set.

Supplier partnerships
- All suppliers are identified.

Documentation
- Process is defined and flowcharted.
- Flowchart accuracy is verified.
- Documentation is followed.
- Quality council or executive improvement team (EIT) members are named.
- PIT members and process owners are named.
- PIT mission is documented.
- Process boundaries are defined.
- Ethics council members and ethical work culture team (EWCT) members are named.

Training
- PIT is trained in the basic tools and the fundamental business process improvement (BPI) tools.
- In-process training needs are evaluated and documented.
- Resources are assigned to support training needs.
- EWCT is trained in the basic tools of the ethical work culture assessment.
- Quality council (or EIT) members are trained in the basic tools of total quality organization development (OD).

Benchmarking
- Not required.

Process adaptability
- Not required.

Continuous improvement
- Basics of BPI are in place.
- All major exposures are identified, and action plans are in place.

- A detailed plan to improve the process to level 3 is agreed to and funded.
- A detailed plan to improve the ethical work culture to stage 3 is agreed to and funded.
- A detailed plan to develop the organization to the next stage is agreed to and funded.

Factual Requirements to Be Qualified at Level 3

When a process evolves to qualification level 3, it is called an *effective process*. Processes qualified at level 3 have a systematic measurement system in place that ensures that end-customer expectations are met. The process has started to be streamlined. To be qualified at level 3, the process must be able to meet all the requirements for qualification level 2, plus the following requirements:

End-customer-related measurements
- End-customer requirements are met.
- End-customer expectations are documented.

Process and/or performance measurements
- Overall effectiveness targets are met, and challenge targets are established by the PIT.
- Some internal efficiency measurements are established.
- Internal effectiveness measurements and targets are 50% complete and posted.
- Overall process cycle time and cost are defined.
- No significant effectiveness, efficiency, or control exposures exist.
- Substantial improvement activities are under way.
- Value priorities and code of ethics are developed.
- All work units are operating at least in a stage 3 ethical work culture.

Supplier partnerships
- Meetings are held with critical suppliers, and agreed-to input requirements are documented.
- Feedback systems to critical suppliers are in place.

Documentation
- Process is flowcharted, and documents are updated.
- Overall process is fully documented.
- Documentation of subprocesses starts.

- Readability is evaluated.
- Ethical impacts of all key HRM and OD processes are determined and institutionalized as decision factors.

Training

- In-process job training procedures are developed for all critical activities.
- People are assigned to conduct advanced job and process training.
- PIT is trained in statistical process control.
- EWCT and total quality advanced training conducted.

Benchmarking

- Plan exists to benchmark end-customer requirements.
- Preliminary ethics audit is formulated.

Process adaptability

- Data that identify problems with present process adaptability are collected.
- Ethics reporting and enforcement mechanisms are established.

Continuous improvement

- Process is operational, and control weaknesses are assessed and deemed containable.
- A plan for improving the process to level 4 is prepared, approved, and funded.
- A plan for improving the ethical work culture to stage 4 is prepared, approved, and funded.
- A plan for improving HRM and OD to the next stage is prepared, approved, and funded.
- The process philosophy accepts that people make mistakes, provided everyone works relentlessly to find and remove causes of errors.

Factual Requirements to Be Qualified at Level 4

When a process evolves to qualification level 4, it is called an *efficient process*. Processes qualified at level 4 have completed the streamlining activities, and there has been a significant improvement in the efficiency of the process. To be qualified at level 4, the process must be able to meet all the requirements for qualification levels 2 and 3, plus the following:

End-customer-related measurements
- End-customer expectations are met.
- Challenge targets are set by the PIT.

Process measurements and/or performance
- There is a significant improvement in process quality control.
- Internal effectiveness and efficiency measurements are in place and are posted, with targets set by the affected areas.
- There is a significant reduction in cycle time and bureaucracy.
- Overall efficiency targets are met.
- Most measurements show an improvement trend.
- Key process control points are identified.
- Tangible, measurable results are realized.
- Ethical work culture measures show improvements.
- OD measures show improvements.

Supplier partnerships
- Meetings are held with all suppliers, and agreed-to input requirements are documented.
- All critical suppliers meet input requirements.
- Ethical work culture expectations are communicated to suppliers to extend integrity network.

Documentation
- Subprocesses are documented.
- Training requirements are documented.
- Software controls are in place.
- The readability level of all documents is at a grade level less than the minimum education of the people using them.
- Employees understand their job descriptions.
- The impact of ethical measures in all key HRM and OD processes is documented.
- Department improvement team (DIT) and task team (TT) members and process owners are named.

Training
- All people performing critical jobs are trained in the new procedures, including job-related training.

- In-process job training procedures are developed for all activities.
- Plans are in place to train all employees who are part of the process in team methods and problem-solving tools.
- PIT understands one or more of the advanced total quality tools.
- All employees in the process receive training in the total process operation.
- EWCT advanced training is conducted in ethical conflict resolution.

Benchmarking

- End-customer requirements are benchmarked.
- Plan exists to benchmark critical activities.
- Plan exists to benchmark the process.
- Ethics audit is finalized and implemented.

Process adaptability

- Employees are trained to distinguish how far they can deviate from the established procedures to meet a customer's special needs.
- Future process change requirements are projected to correct process adaptability problems.
- A proactive internal and external customer complaint system is established.
- The end customer reviews the process change plan and agrees that it meets his or her needs over the strategic period.

Continuous improvement

- A plan to improve the process to level 5 is developed, approved, and funded.
- A plan to improve the ethical work culture to stage 5 is developed, approved, and funded.
- A plan to improve HRM and OD to the next stage is developed, approved, and funded.

Factual Requirements to Be Qualified at Level 5

When a process has evolved to qualification level 5, it is called an *error-free process*. Processes qualified at level 5 are highly effective and efficient. Both external and internal customer expectations are measured and met. Rarely is there a problem within the process. Schedules are always met, and stress levels are low. To be qualified at level 5, the process must be able to meet all the requirements for the previous qualification levels, plus the following requirements:

End-customer-related measurements

- End-customer expectations are updated.
- Performance for the last six months never fell below end-customer expectations.
- The trend lines show continuous improvement.
- World-class targets are established.
- End customers are invited to regular performance reviews.
- End-customer desires are understood.

Process and/or performance measurements

- All measurements show an improvement.
- Benchmark targets are defined for external customers and critical in-process activities.
- Feedback systems are in place close to the point at which the work is being done.
- Most measurements are made by the person doing the job.
- There is tangible and measurable improvement in the in-process measurements.
- No operational inefficiencies are anticipated.
- An independent quality process audit plan is in place and working.
- The process is error-free.
- Formal and informal voice systems to convey ethics and OD feedback are institutionalized.
- Organizational ethics handbook is routinely used in the socialization process.

Supplier partnerships

- All supplier inputs met requirements for the last three months.
- Regular meetings are held to ensure that suppliers understand the changing needs and expectations of the quality process, ethical work culture, and OD standards.

Documentation

- Change level controls are in place.
- Documents are systematically updated.
- Ethical conflicts are resolved fairly and in a timely manner and standards are widely disseminated.
- Recognition and/or commendation rituals for exemplary individual and/or team ethical conduct become routine.

Training

- All employees in the process are trained and scheduled for refresher courses.
- Employee evaluation of the training process is complete, and the training meets all employee requirements.
- Team and problem-solving courses are complete. Employees are meeting regularly to solve problems.
- Quality council (or EIT), EWCT, DIT, and PIT continue advanced training.

Benchmarking

- Process is benchmarked, and targets are assigned.
- PIT understands the keys to the benchmark organization's performance.
- DITs and TTs begin benchmarking.

Process adaptability

- Employees are empowered to provide the required emergency help to their customers and are measured accordingly.
- Resources are committed to satisfy future customer needs.
- Process adaptability complaints are significantly reduced.

Continuous improvement

- The process philosophy evolves to the point at which errors are unacceptable. Everyone works relentlessly to prevent errors from occurring even once.
- Surveys of the employees show that the process is easier to use.
- Plans to improve the process to level 6 are prepared, approved, and funded.
- Plans to improve ethical work culture to stage 6 are prepared, approved, and funded.
- Plans to improve HRM and OD to the next stage are prepared, approved, and funded.

Factual Requirements to Be Qualified at Level 6

Qualification level 6 is the highest qualification level. It indicates that the process is one of the ten best processes of its kind in the world or is in the top 10% of like processes, whichever has the smallest population. Processes that reach qualification level 6 are called *world-class processes*. Processes qualified at level 6 have proven that they are among the best in the world. These processes are often benchmark target processes for other organizations. As a rule, few processes in an organization ever get this good. Processes that reach level 6 truly are world-class and continue to improve so that they keep their world-class status. To be qualified at level 6, the process must be able to meet all the requirements for the previous levels, plus the following:

End-customer-related measurements

- End-customer expectation targets are regularly updated and always exceeded.
- World-class measurements are met for a minimum of three consecutive months.
- Many of the end-customer desires are met.

Process measurements and/or performance

- All measurements exceed those of the benchmark company for three months.
- Effectiveness measurements indicate that the process is error-free for all end-customer and in-process control points.

Supplier partnerships

- All suppliers meet quality process expectations.
- All suppliers meet quality process, ethical work culture, and OD requirements for a minimum of six months.

Documentation

- All documents meet world-class standards for the process, ethical work culture, and OD being improved.

Training

- Employees are regularly surveyed to define additional training needs, and new training programs are implemented based on these surveys in process, ethics, and OD skills.

Benchmarking

- Ongoing benchmarking plan is implemented for quality processes, ethical work cultures, and OD.

Process adaptability

- In the last six months, no customers complained that the process did not meet their needs.
- Present process handles the exceptions better than the benchmark company's process.

Continuous improvement

- A comprehensive quality audit, ethics audit, and HR audit verifies world-class status.
- Plans are approved and in place to become even better.

It is important to note that the goal for all level 6 processes is to go beyond world-class status to become the *best-of-breed process*. Although some processes become best-of-breed for short periods of time, it is very difficult to stay number one. It requires a great deal of work and creativity, but the personal, team, and organizational satisfaction is well worth it.

It is important to note the wide range of fact finding that quality project teams must engage in to complete a quality audit. It is also important to note, however, that the focus of project attention is on the system, not persons. Project teams are focused on improving the system instead of scapegoating people. Too often in organizations that do not speak with facts, special project teams are formed to justify a predetermined executive decision or build a case of incompetence against personnel whom the administration has targeted as marginal.

TOTAL QUALITY BUSINESS PROJECT MANAGEMENT

In addition to business project planning, effective project management that allows all stakeholders to "speak with facts" requires reliable information gathering across different organizational subcultures. The savvy project management leader is aware of the four basic subcultures in most organizations: *clan subculture, adhocracy subculture, market subculture,* and *bureaucratic subculture*.[16] These subcultures and their distinctive features are depicted in Figure 4.3. This pluralistic reality calls upon different leadership roles to direct a successful project and gather accurate information for decision making.

The clan, adhocracy, market, and bureaucratic subcultures are the organizational "homes" for employees who need to become involved in quality project teams. Good project leadership recognizes these differences and weaves appropriate aspects of home organization subcultures into the project team subculture. Information gathering behavior tends to separate subcultures by their focus on individual details and organizational patterns, whereas decision-making behavior tends to separate subcultures into short-term and long-term thinkers. Adhocracy and market cultures have goals and emphases naturally attuned to participation in project teams. On the other hand, team members from clans and bureaucracies normally have the greatest difficulty in joining the project team because of their focus on individuals. Project leaders need to integrate diverse skills, personalities, and subcultural

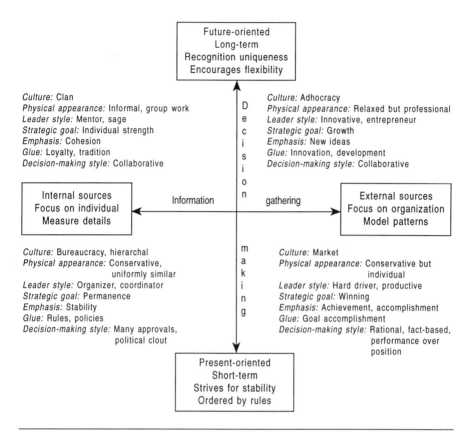

Figure 4.3 Organizational Subcultures and Project Leadership Styles for Information Gathering. (Source: Elmes, M. and Wilemon, D. (1988). "Organizational Culture and Project Leader Effectiveness." *Project Management Journal*. Vol. 19, No. 4, p. 57.)

orientations into a focused, fact-finding implementation unit able to weather attacks from functional departments wary of domain infringement.[17] The basic thrust of the project management team, however, is to reduce the organizational impact of the bureaucratic subculture over time.

Effective total quality project management also requires competency in coordinating the phases and stages of the project life cycle, as depicted in Figure 4.4.[18] Lack of this coordination may lead to either the premature death of a worthwhile project or, at the very least, the inefficient utilization of resources. Given external competition and the need to make the best use of limited internal resources, project managers must orchestrate internal and external support to successfully complete a worthwhile project on time and

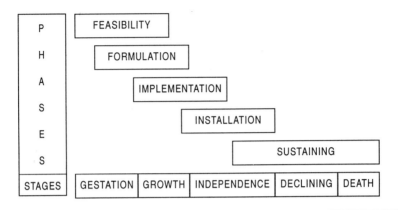

Figure 4.4   The Phases and Stages of a Project Life Cycle. (Source: Kliem, Ralph L. and Ludin, Irwin S. (1992). *The People Side of Project Management.* Brookfield, Vt.: Gower Publishing, p. 40.)

under budget. Committed project teams that invest a great deal of time and energy on worthwhile projects only to find them underfunded due to a lack of organizational support become frustrated. On the other hand, if organizational leaders external to the project team are not kept well informed, they may perceive the project as incongruent with organizational priorities and become overtly or covertly resistant to the success of the project.

The **phases** *of a project life cycle (feasibility, formulation, implementation, installation, and sustaining) represent all of the processes and practices required for the successful planning and implementation of the project by the leader and/or the team* (i.e., the *internal* momentum of the project). The **stages** *of a project life cycle (gestation, growth, independence, declining, and death) represent the external organizational and/or extra-organizational support for the project over time* (i.e., the kind and degree of assistance provided to the project by key external stakeholders).

Project stages will typically lag behind project phases because the project team is closer to and more familiar with the needs of the project and what can and cannot be done. The project team's challenge, therefore, is to speak with facts about the operational feasibility of a project in such a way as to develop and sustain support from other key stakeholders over time. Ideally, a competent project leader keeps internal phases and external stages aligned to ensure a successful outcome for the project leader, the project team, and the organization(s) involved.

When they become misaligned, the responsible project leader must diagnose the cause(s) and take appropriate action. A project, for example, may exist in the gestation stage for a long time but may be in the implementation phase in the project leader's agenda. This is due to a lack of support for the project, either by senior management or even the client department. The project manager must assertively justify the project to key external parties.

A project may be in the growth stage while simultaneously in the implementation phase. In this case, senior management recognizes the importance of the project and is willing to allocate whatever resources are required for its successful completion. Management may even expand the project's purview. The project may start to have all the features of a standing program due to its level of magnitude relative to other projects. It receives more than all the resources it needs to succeed while other projects are neglected. Again, a project may be in the independence stage while in the sustaining phase. Because the project was so successful, senior management and the client department are willing to treat the continued support of the project in the sustaining phase as an ongoing endeavor that has the same level of status as a project in the earlier phases.

A project may be in the decline stage regardless of phase. Senior management may feel that more important projects exist which demand attention. Management may also decide to trim existing resources. The project quickly loses legitimacy. This requires prompt action by the project leader to regain legitimacy and momentum. In addition, a project may be in the death stage during any phase. Senior management may make the decision to cut all support, in which case the project becomes nonexistent. Premature project death is a tragedy that every project leader wants to avoid and requires steady communication, interim progress reports, and sustained advocacy of the merits of the project.

To overcome dysfunctional subcultural propensities and capitalize on project management coordination skills, a project management leader must form a strong project team. While organizations have traditionally been formed around task or work groups, the concept of **teams** and **teamwork** is crucial for total quality organizations.[19] *A team is a small number of people with complementary skills who are committed to a shared purpose, collective performance goals, and a common approach for which they hold themselves mutually accountable.*[20] The basic ingredients of teams are graphically depicted in Figure 4.5. Teams outperform individuals acting alone or in larger organizational groupings—especially when performance requires diverse skills, broad experience, informed judgment, complex coordination and multiple accountabilities.

Teams normally consist of fewer than 25 people with complementary technical/functional, problem-solving, and interpersonal skills. Complementary technical/functional skills might include marketing and engineering skills for new product development. Complementary problem-solving skills might include quantitative analysis skills to assess computer printouts of company progress reports and decision-making skills regarding new prac-

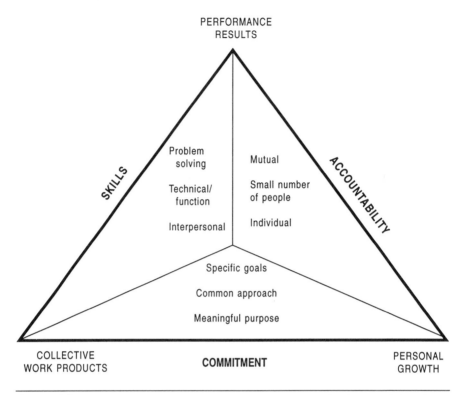

PERFORMANCE
RESULTS

Problem
solving

Mutual

Technical/
function

Small number
of people

Interpersonal

Individual

SKILLS

ACCOUNTABILITY

Specific goals

Common approach

Meaningful purpose

COLLECTIVE
WORK PRODUCTS

COMMITMENT

PERSONAL
GROWTH

Figure 4.5 Basic Ingredients of Teams. (Source: Katzenbach, J. and Smith, D. (1993). *The Wisdom of Teams*. New York: Harper Business, p. 8.)

tices to follow in light of the statistical data. Complementary interpersonal skills might include helpful criticism, risk taking, objective feedback, active listening, giving the benefit of the doubt, emotional encouragement, respecting the needs of others, and celebrating the achievement of others.

Teams also develop a commitment to a shared, meaningful purpose that they own and translate that purpose into specific and actionable goals. Groups that fail to become teams often do not coalesce around a challenging purpose for various reasons (i.e., insufficient focus on performance, lack of effort, or poor leadership). Specific goals that define team work products that are different from both organization-wide missions and the sum of individual objectives are essential. The specificity of group goals facilitates clear communication, constructive conflict, and a democratic leveling effect because all members are working for the same end. When intermediate goals are reached, the celebration of small "wins" builds renewed membership commitment. In addition, teams are committed to a common approach. They must agree on who will do particular jobs, how schedules will be set and adhered to, what skills need to be developed, how continuing membership is to be earned, and how the group will make and modify decisions. A working approach, for example, that delegates all the real work to a few members (or staff outsiders) and thus relies on review and discussion meetings for the only "work together" aspects of the approach cannot sustain a real team.

Finally, teams require individual and joint accountability for performance. At the least, team accountability is about sincere promises we make to ourselves and others for which we pledge committed action. When we follow through on our promises, we preserve and extend the trust upon which the team is built. We earn the right to express our own views about all aspects of the team's efforts and to have our judgments receive a fair, respectful, and constructive hearing. Specific performance goals and agreed-upon approaches provide clear yardsticks for mutual accountability.[21]

The success of every total quality organization rests fully on the effectiveness of each work group and each team. A **group** *is a collection of individuals who are in an interdependent relationship with one another.*[22] A **nonworking group** *is simply a loose affiliation of individuals without a task focus.* A **working group** *is one for which there is no significant incremental performance need or opportunity that would require it to become a team.* The members interact primarily to share information, best practices, or perspectives and to make decisions to help each individual perform within his or her area of responsibility. Beyond that, there is no realistic or truly desired "small group" common purpose, incremental performance goals, or joint work products that call for either a team approach or mutual accountability. Groups can be productive, but it is becoming increasingly evident that just bringing a group of people together to complete specific tasks is often unproductive and ineffective. Members of real teams develop strong feelings of allegiance that go beyond the mere grouping of individuals. The productive outcome is synergistic, and the accomplishments often can exceed even the original goals of the group or its sponsor.

There is a collective performance improvement as groups transition through four phases: pseudo-teams, potential teams, real teams, and high-performance teams.[23] A **pseudo-team** *is a group for which there could be a significant incremental performance need or opportunity, but it has not focused on collective performance and is not trying to achieve it.* It has no interest in shaping a common purpose or set of performance goals, even though it may call itself a team. Pseudo-teams almost always contribute less to company performance needs than effective working groups because their interactions detract from each member's individual performance without delivering any joint benefit. In pseudo-teams, the sum of the whole is less than the potential of the individual parts.

The **potential team** *is a group for which there is a significant incremental performance need and that really is trying to improve its performance impact.* Typically, however, it requires more clarity about its purpose, goals, or work products and more discipline in hammering out a common working approach. It has not yet established collective accountability. Potential teams abound in most organizations.

A **real team** *is a small number of people with complementary skills who are equally committed to a common purpose, goals, and working approach for which they hold themselves mutually accountable.* Real teams are the *real power* in total quality organizations, i.e., *they have the ability to energetically guide their own conduct, influence the conduct of others, and resist unwanted influence.* Real teams are the basic operating units of performance in total quality organizations. They require task, psychosocial, and moral maturity to exist, sustain regular interactions, and develop. Real project teams are the models to which pseudo- and potential teams aspire. *Members of pseudo- and potential teams may demand empowerment as an entitlement; members of real teams deserve empowerment because they are the operational backbone of any successful total quality organization.* **Empowerment readiness** determinations for individuals, groups, and teams become crucial decisions because diversion of valuable scarce resources to "squeaky wheel" groups that are unable or unwilling to shoulder the commensurate responsibilities of power deprives real teams of the fuel they need to continue productive contributions. (See Practitioner Assessment Instrument 4C at the end of this chapter to assist in the *empowerment readiness determination.*)

The **high-performance team** *meets all the conditions of real teams and has members who are also deeply committed to one another's personal growth and success.* That commitment usually transcends the team. The high-performance team significantly outperforms all other like teams and outperforms all reasonable expectations given its membership. It is as powerful as it is rare, but it remains an excellent model for all real teams.

Consider the rewarding experience of working on a team where a strong sense of unity and commitment toward accomplishing a highly motivating goal prevails. The achievement of putting astronauts on the moon and the defeat of the Russians by the U.S. Olympic hockey team are often cited as readily recognized examples of highly focused team efforts. Most people have at some time had the opportunity to enjoy the experience of participating in a team effort that was highly focused and driven by a shared vision. Every team member spent countless hours working on the task, and the result may have even surpassed the original goal.

The story of "Team Taurus," which designed the original model of the Taurus/Sable automobile at Ford Motor Company, is one recent example of superb teamwork from a business organization.[24] According to various accounts, the unique approach of gathering together representatives from design, engineering, purchasing, marketing, quality assurance, sales, and service had never been done at Ford until Team Taurus was formed in 1980. From this effort came innovations of over 1400 significant design improvements that were culled from suggestions by customers, employees, and suppliers. Engineers tore down over 50 comparable cars in seeking the "best-in-class" features. Of some 400 such features, Ford claimed that the final Taurus-Sable product met or exceeded 80% of them in design quality. The final result of this team effort was that Taurus and Sable were the number 1 and number 2 choices for *Motor Trend's* Car of the Year award in 1986. Later versions of the Taurus outsold the Honda Accord to recapture first place in the mid-sized car market in the United States in 1993.

Such experiences are very fulfilling but may be short-lived. It is the goal of total quality HR project planning to create these or similar experiences within organizations by empowering each group to exercise and continuously develop its skills and talents within the framework of real teams.

TOTAL QUALITY HUMAN RESOURCE PROJECTS

The thrust of HR projects in most organizations, however, has traditionally been focused on individuals. Thus, project assignments, opportunities, and rewards have been designed around *individual* people rather than groups or teams. It has become apparent that this contributes to rivalries, competition, favoritism, and self-centeredness, which collectively counter the focus of two of the most important functions of quality organizations: customer satisfaction and continuous improvement.

The central role of teams, and the need for such team skills as cooperation, interpersonal communication, cross-training, and group decision making, represents a fundamental shift in how the work of public and private organizations is performed in the United States and many other countries in the world. Presently, cooperation between such departments as design and manufacturing in automotive firms, doctors and administrators in hospitals, and business managers and orchestra conductors is not the norm. The predominant practices encourage individual advancement. This is built into the management system by such practices as management by objectives, individual performance evaluation, professional status and privileges, and individual promotion.

To counter these mainstream dysfunctional trends, total quality HR projects need to be focused on fact finding regarding its key processes: selection, performance, appraisal, rewards, and development. Through the use of the seven quality control scientific procedure steps, the alternating SDCA/PDCA cycles, and appropriate total quality tools, the certification of all HR processes can take place. If the selection process, for example, is at stage 4 (efficient) and it needs to be at least at stage 5 (error-free), facts need to be secured in the eight process subcategories (end-customer-related measurements, process measurements and/or performance, supplier partnerships, documentation, training, benchmarking, process adaptability, and continuous improvement). The best way for HR departments to lead quality project initiatives is to make sure that their function has certified and is improving its own processes using the total quality steps, cycles, and tools. How many HR departments, for example, systematically benchmark their policies and procedures with the best practices in their industry, nation, or the world? For most HR professionals, it would mean additional training in statistics and applying quality practices to HR processes.

A **human resource audit** is one professionally endorsed way to assess current policies and practices.[25] It provides a way to keep up with changes, avoid litigation, and incorporate new techniques to improve performance. Supplementing the HR audit with both a quality audit and an ethics audit would provide the organization with valuable information regarding its current stage of quality process certification and its current level of ethical work culture development.[26] If, for example, current HR audit procedures are primarily geared to regard the organization as only a House of Compliance (i.e., assessing policies and practices to avoid litigation), whereas the rest of the organization has reached a quality process stage and an ethical work culture level ready for the House of Total Quality, the HR function might well be perceived as unable to provide leadership in total quality initiatives.

To avoid that organizational perception, HR professionals can begin to capitalize on their conventional strengths in delivering quality training and development programs. The emphasis of the training and development efforts would be to shift current project leadership styles from the traditional, hierarchic supervisory approach toward participative leadership and finally team leadership within a total quality context, as illustrated in Figure 4.6.[27]

The movement toward team leadership is necessary in a total quality firm, and HRM has an important role to play in that transition. It is possible to offer training in both team building and team development; the former would emphasize intense short-term attention to remedial relationship issues to unblock performance, whereas the latter would emphasize diffused long-term attention to positive growth opportunities for sustaining superior team performance.[28] Effective real teams improve quality within a reasonable time frame and strengthen working relationships both inside and outside the team.[29] HR departments must contribute to the building and development of effective real teams by planning to facilitate the transition from supervisory leadership to team leadership, or they will be marginalized.

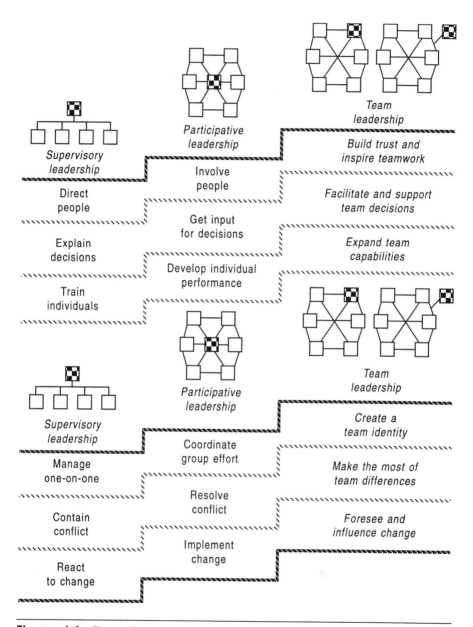

Figure 4.6 From Supervisory to Team Leadership. (Source: Zenger, J., Musselwhite, E., Hurson, K., and Perrin C. (1994). *Leading Teams: Mastering the New Role.* Burr Ridge, Ill.: Irwin, p. 29.)

TOTAL QUALITY HUMAN RESOURCE PROJECT PLANNING

To respond to the quality project planning challenge, HR practitioners need to realize that in most total quality firms there are at least three types of teams: guidance teams (quality councils or EITs, ethics councils, steering committees, and/or lead teams), problem-solving teams (PITs, EWCTs, and other cross-functional project teams and DITs and other departmental project teams), and self-managed teams (TTs).[30] The building and development of those teams must be the key objective of total quality HR project planning.

The HR team development project will necessarily entail the balancing of empowerment and responsibility/authority issues in the organization as a whole as well as within the evolution of each team. In fact, a **team empowerment continuum** with specific responsibilities can help determine how much empowerment each team is able and willing to assume, as indicated in Figure 4.7.[31] Teams may move progressively through four levels of empowerment, taking on more responsibility and authority.

The process of responsible team empowerment, however, does not occur automatically and in isolation, but rather is the result of the managed convergence of three factors: (1) the stage of system development along the involve-

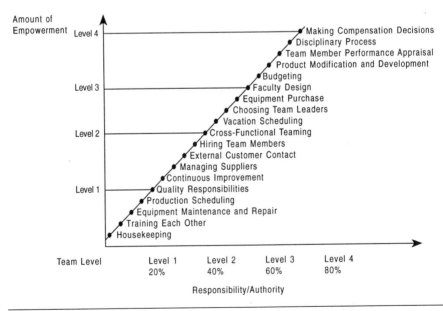

Figure 4.7 The Team Empowerment Continuum. (Source: Wellins, R.S., Byham, W.C., and Wilson, J.M. (1991). *Empowered Teams.* San Francisco: Jossey-Bass, p. 26. Modified by the authors.)

ment/empowerment continuum, (2) the maturity (task, psychosocial, and moral) levels of followers, and (3) the extent of adequate and accurate information sharing. The first factor is depicted in Table 4.2.[32] At the micro-system level, process involvement steps that project teams need to take, from defining problems through implementing solutions and conducting evaluation, can entail different ranges of employee involvement and ownership, from awareness with low involvement to empowered ownership. Patterns of business process improvements become part of the micro-system decision-making tradition and determine at the operational level whether empowered ownership becomes a daily work reality for line employees.

At the macro-system level, the organizational dimensions of structure, focus, authority, idea sources, and stakeholder intensity can also entail different ranges of employee involvement and ownership, from compliant involvement to empowered ownership. The macro-system structure and dynamics determine at the strategic design level whether empowered ownership will be supported. Responsible team empowerment, therefore, is the managed alignment of micro- and macro-system support for empowered ownership. *Without this alignment, the gap between empowerment rhetoric and reality will widen, leading to a form of organizational cynicism that erodes the ethical work culture necessary for world-class productivity. Responsible managers cannot preach teamwork without providing and monitoring the actual micro and macro systems that support it.*

The second factor in responsible team empowerment is the empowerment readiness demonstrated by the task, psychosocial, and moral maturity levels of followers, as indicated in Figure 4.8. As followers mature, the leader's behavior is normally characterized by a decreasing emphasis on task structuring and an increased emphasis on consideration. As the followers continue to mature, there should be an eventual decrease in consideration. Since *leadership is an influence relationship among leaders and followers who intend real changes that reflect their mutual purposes,* the work empowerment maturity of leaders and followers is a crucial factor to consider.[33] **Work empowerment maturity** *is a condition characterized by high task competence and wide experience, high psychosocial motivation to achieve and share power and high moral commitment to use power to enhance justice, trust, and care in the workplace.* Premature empowerment of leaders and/or followers can lead to poor business decisions being made more quickly and more often, to people in top positions doing the wrong thing well—a recipe for disaster.

To avoid premature team empowerment disaster, the situational leadership style grid in Figure 4.8 provides a road map for the four appropriate contexts for managerial directing, coaching, participating, and finally delegating in order to promote responsible team empowerment.[34] The four leadership styles are placed within a two-dimensional grid of supportive and directive actions and are placed on a time line which starts at the top left and

Table 4.2 Micro- and Macro-System Phases of the Involvement/Empowerment Continuum

Micro-system improvement phases	Awareness with low involvement	Some involved commitment	Empowered ownership
1. Define problem	Manager defines customers, requirements, and necessary processes	Group proposes opportunity; manager approves	Team defines opportunity as next stage in improvement
2. Identify and document process	Manager or staff documents processes	Group works with staff to document	Team documents and flow-charts processes
3. Measure performance	Manager collects data but shares little	Manager defines data for group to collect	Team determines what data to collect and gets them
4. Understand why	Manager analyzes data and draws conclusions	Manager suggests causal factors and group confirms	Team analyzes data, determines root causes, and understands variation
5. Develop and test ideas	Manager defines improvements	Manager suggests alternatives for group to evaluate	Team identifies and tests alternative solutions
6. Implement solutions and evaluate	Manager drives implementation and evaluates outcome	Group implements solution and shares evaluation with manager	Team has responsibility and authority to implement solution and track results

Macro-system organizational phases	Compliant involvement	Participative involvement	Empowered ownership
7. Structure	Hierarchical Precise job descriptions Functional units	Less hierarchical Loose job descriptions Matrix management	Flat No job descriptions Self-directed teams
8. Focus	Internal targets Preservation Costs Problem-solving Find-and-fix	Competition Adaptation Quality and productivity Product service improvement Detection	Customers' needs Flexible, responsive Customer satisfaction Process improvement Prevention
9. Authority	Top-down command Inflexible Controlling Rank and title	Special assignments Open to challenge Sharing Committee	Consensus Seeks challenge Trusting Knowledge
10. Idea sources	Work measurement Suggestion systems	Staff studies Quality circles	Work teams Customers and employees
Micro-system improvement phases	Awareness with low involvement	Some involved commitment	Empowered ownership
11. Morale	Occasional morale assessment Acceptance of low morale levels as long as system objectives achieved	Regular morale assessment Acceptance only of moderate morale levels as long as system objectives are achieved	Regular morale assessment and development Acceptance only of high morale levels and achievement of system objectives
12. Stakeholder	Apathetic compliance No ownership	Participative involvement Some ownership	Committed dedication Full ownership

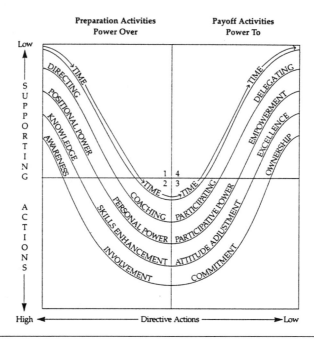

Figure 4.8 Total Quality Situational Leadership Styles and Team Empowerment. (Source: Johnson, Richard S. (1993). *TQM: Leadership for the Quality Transformation.* Milwaukee: ASQC Quality Press, p. 92.)

works its way through all four styles, ending at the top right quadrant. TQM followers should progress along this time line, which is a measure of training effectiveness and ownership of the TQM process as time progresses. In fact, *total quality leadership and team empowerment must be a blend of both situational (system) adaptability and transformational leadership styles.*[35]

The second line on the chart places the four leadership styles along the time line. This shows the expected progression of people from their initial introduction into any work situation, from beginning employment to new process deployment under the directing style, through coaching and participating, to the ultimate payoff style afforded by delegation. In the directive style, a high level of support either is not required or there is not time. The coaching style becomes a natural progression as training and awareness of need take hold. In the participating style, high-level direction is not needed and may interfere with the team's initiative. When the delegating plateau is reached, the team is willing and able to handle the situation facing them with little support or direction; providing either generally would be undesirable. Since the greatest performance potential exists under the delegating style, the leader's goal must be to bring the team up to speed rapidly so it can effectively operate in this self-directed, delegating mode.

The third line shows the activating force that powers each of these leadership styles. Positional power generally is the prime mover during the directing stages. Initial relationships with new employees do not produce personal power to any great degree, and the deployment of new processes requires the leader to create and sell his or her vision of work excellence. When coaching is used, the followers have been progressing long enough that the skilled coach usually has gained considerable personal power, which becomes the motivating force. The leader's influence is enough in most cases when participative leadership styles are employed and empowerment fuels the delegative style.

The fourth line illustrates the progression of training and development that supports the various leadership styles. Knowledge acquisition is the initial phase of training, which introduces the participants to the task at hand and provides them with the basics to begin their efforts in that tasking. This is followed by skills enhancement, which helps people become productive. Under proper leadership, most people become more willing to perform as their ability to do the job well increases. This leads us to participation, which requires prosocial, psychosocial, and moral attitude adjustments, organization citizenship behavior, and teamwork skills for maximum effectiveness. Fine-tuning the process on an ongoing basis requires the delegation style and demands attention to task, psychosocial, and moral excellence in every dimension of the work environment.

The fifth line exhibits employee attitudes and contributions to the TQM process in part and the organization as a whole. People are initially aware of organizational needs and quality processes. As they progress in working with solid leaders, they become involved in TQM and the organization. Participation demands commitment to excellence and the organization if there is to be a payoff. The ultimate is TQM and organizational ownership as teams are empowered through the delegating leadership style. Responsible team empowerment, therefore, is the result of work empowerment maturity in task, psychosocial, and moral dimensions between leader and followers. The Empowerment Readiness Assessment instrument at the end of this chapter can be of use in this determination.

The situational leadership flow from quadrant 1 to quadrant 4 is dependent on the work empowerment maturity of leaders and employees in the first quadrant. Leaders who have positional power without commensurate work empowerment maturity (i.e., inadequate task competence and experience, low psychosocial motivation to achieve, inability or unwillingness to accept responsibility, or low moral commitment to use power to enhance justice, trust, and care in the workplace) will impede employee empowerment. Employee reactions to leaders with low work empowerment maturity are likely to include (1) lack of respect for leadership direction, position, knowledge, and awareness; (2) active or passive resistance; (3) compliance accompanied by resentment; or (4) exit from the organization. To avoid the prior negative sequence of outcomes, employees must be able to speak with facts (i.e., voice the truth about leadership inadequacies with impunity).

The flow of empowerment reflected in this model is not leader-controlled as it is in a traditional organization. Employee empowerment readiness may exceed the leader's readiness to delegate and share power. Leader reactions to employees with higher work empowerment maturity may include (1) unwillingness to acknowledge obvious employee capability, (2) active or passive resistance to employee empowerment, (3) resignation and abdication of responsibility appropriate to each stage, or (4) exit from the organization. To avoid this negative sequence of outcomes, leaders must be able to create and adjust to new role responsibilities which relinquish traditional positional power prerogatives. Empowerment is a reallocation of responsibilities for both leaders and employees. If work force empowerment does not result, both parties have failed.

The third factor in achieving responsible team empowerment is the extent of adequate and accurate HR information sharing that occurs.[36] Responsible team empowerment cannot occur in an information vacuum. Blocking fact-finding inquiries, neglecting to collect key team project-related information, delaying timely release of necessary information, underutilizing computer technology applications, and/or hoarding HR information relevant to project team activities are all counterproductive measures that detract from HR total quality project involvement.

Yet all of these measures have been taken by some HR departments to protect their job security and professional/staff status when line workers are empowered to perform typical HR subfunctions, such as selection and performance appraisal, in a team setting.[37]

A more proactive HR response to total quality project involvement and team empowerment is to develop, use, and share human resource information system (HRIS) technology to strategically and operationally contribute to team empowerment. In Table 4.3, the linking of total quality HR strategic objectives with HRIS traditional computer, expert systems, and decision support systems broadens the ways in which HR departments can share accurate, adequate, and timely information that will support team empowerment, without risking job security or professional/staff status.[38] This means, however, that HR practitioners need to conduct work outside private offices, in consultation with line workers in teams on or near the shop floor, which is common practice in Japanese firms. It is this very committed involvement and useful contribution to team empowerment that provides the *prima facie* evidence for retaining HR services in the total quality organization's future.

Table 4.3 Total Quality Human Resource Strategic Objectives and Human Resource Information System Total Quality Computer Applications

Total quality HR strategic objectives	Transaction processing/ reporting/tracking systems	Expert systems	Decision support systems
Cost leadership: People working harder	• Reduces paper handling • Standardizes entry and reporting • Increases processing accuracy • Increases report turnaround • Early warning of goal deviations	• Decreases need for HR experts • Helps spread database and training costs over entire work force	• Increases chance of innovation for HR cost controls
Quality/customer satisfaction: People working smarter	• Increases time for HR quality initiatives • Enables custom reports and data entry • Increases awareness of HR information and can lead to its improvement	• Enables line employees to make HR decisions informed by HR expertise • Increases customizing of HR programs • Increases line satisfaction	• Increases chance of innovations for HR quality/ customer satisfaction
Innovation: People working with vision	• Increases time for HR innovation • Awareness of goal deviations sparks discoveries	• Increases time for HR innovation • Line understanding of HR sparks collaboration and discovery	• Powerful team support for discovery • Shortens team discovery process • Fast testing, reporting, and documentation of new team finds

Source: Broderick, R. and Boudreau, J. (1992). "Human Resource Management, Information Technology, and the Competitive Edge." *Academy of Management Executive.* Vol. 6, No. 2, p. 12. Modified by the authors.

TOTAL QUALITY HUMAN RESOURCE PROJECT MANAGEMENT

Quality Project Management Tools

The HR practitioner needs to develop competency in the following major total quality project tools: cause-and-effect diagrams, check sheets, display graphs, histograms, Pareto charts, scatter diagrams, and control charts.

Cause-and-Effect Diagrams

A cause-and-effect diagram is a problem identification tool that organizes potential causes of a desirable or undesirable effect. It assists in identifying root causes by asking, five times, why a cause exists.

To identify and solve a problem, it is important to know the real causes and the interrelations among causes. One can then identify the major causes to solve the problem. A cause-and-effect diagram is used to guide data collection and analysis to find the root cause of a problem. A cause-and-effect diagram shows an effect at the right and the main causes of that effect off the horizontal axis. These main causes are in turn effects that have subcauses, and so on, down many levels. This is not basically a statistical tool; it enumerates the variety of causes rather than the frequency of events. However, it is a useful tool for noting the frequency of events once one has the data.

Cause-and-effect diagrams were developed by Dr. Kaoru Ishikawa in Japan in the 1960s.[39] By diagramming a relatively simple problem, it is sometimes found that there are a number of factors that contribute to the problem but have not been carefully considered. For example, callers to an HR group office may be upset by the fact that they cannot reach someone to discuss the impact of a proposed "reengineering" project. Instead, they either get a busy signal or are switched to a recorder. Initially, a problem-solving team can meet and discuss the factors that contribute to this problem of "unsatisfactory handling of phone calls to the HR group." Factors might include the number of HR representatives that are available at specific times, the number of phone lines available and in use, peak period calls, printed information that is available to be sent out, etc. A cause-and-effect diagram would clarify which factors of materials (printed information, etc.), personnel (number of representatives), methods (training in handling questions and problems, messages on recorders, etc.), and machinery (telephone lines and recorders, etc.) contribute in a negative way to the problem.

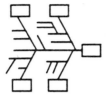

Check Sheets

Check sheets are forms that are used for easy collection of data to represent the facts. To analyze problems, the HRM practitioner must collect data that represent the facts. Check sheets are used to take data systematically regarding the frequency of various effects (e.g., racial, gender, and age data for all organizational employees or work accidents reported by causes). They are much like a set of tally marks on the back of an envelope. However, they are usually marked on forms prepared in advance, according to expected effects. Also, they are calibrated so that when someone takes the data, a running plot of frequency of effects is created; the check marks create a histogram.

Check sheets are simple forms that have been used to record and categorize data for many years. In the HR group telephone problem mentioned above, check sheets could be used to classify the nature of the calls to an HR office according to how they were handled (by machine or human operator) and/or how they were resolved, according to several predetermined categories listed on the sheet.

A	X X
B	X X X X
C	X X X
D	X X
E	X

Display Graphs

Display graphs visually delineate data. There are many kinds of display graphs: bar graphs, line graphs, circle graphs, and radar graphs, among others. Most people are familiar with the first three types (see the following sample line and radar graphs).[40]

A radar graph compares several items on multiple dimensions. Suppose that for three competitive products, $e1$ is performance, $e2$ is cost, $e3$ is reliability, and $e4$ is delivery; in all four dimensions, the good direction is out from the center. The following example shows that one of the products is inferior in all dimensions. Of the other two products, one wins slightly in performance and the other wins slightly in all other dimensions. This is useful for HRM practitioners who compare vendors of benefit packages.

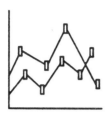 

Histogram

A histogram is a graph that shows dispersion of data. From this graph, the characteristics of the data and the cause of dispersion can be analyzed. Typically, a histogram is a bar graph that shows the statistical distribution over equal intervals of some measure of quality, such as computer literacy skills, high moral maturity ratings, and/or gaps in technical training. Histograms are used in analysis for *stratification* to create hypotheses for why defects are occurring. For example, when a piece of computer equipment used in an HR office has too much dispersion (i.e., uneven quality indicators) and it was made from two machines, it is possible to stratify or segregate the data corresponding to each machine. Thus, it is possible to find the difference between machine A and B and easily make adjustments.

A histogram could be used to display the data taken from a check sheet on the frequency of calls received by an HR group according to time of day or day of the week. After analysis of the data, it might suggest that a possible solution would be to increase the staff available to answer the phones for peak periods of the day, such as lunchtime.

Pareto Chart

A Pareto chart organizes causes by frequency. By using it, the significant few causes that account for most of the effect can be identified.

At any given time, many kinds of problems surround the HRM practitioner. It is not feasible to attack all these problems at the same time. Therefore, arranging the problems in order of importance and attacking the bigger problems first is important. A bar graph that shows the biggest problem on the left followed by the lesser problems is called a Pareto chart. Pareto charts *help one focus on the vital few effects or causes.*

Use of the Pareto concept of "the significant few items and the insignificant many" for quality problem analysis was first suggested by quality guru Joseph Juran. The Pareto principle is sometimes called the 80–20 rule and suggests that 80% of the items are accounted for by 20% of the causes or issues. A Pareto chart is simply a histogram in which frequency data are shown by bars on the chart that are arranged from highest to lowest, in order by cause. For the HR office telephone problem, data from a check sheet on the most frequent questions that are asked by callers could be displayed. If the phones are overloaded by calls, the problem-solving team might recommend that printed materials listing frequently asked questions and their answers could be distributed to all employees who would be interested.

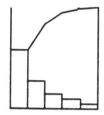

Scatter Diagram

A scatter diagram depicts the relationship between variables. Thus, it helps to substantiate whether a potential root cause is related to the effect.

The relationship between cause and effect (e.g., between illumination level at a worksite and inspection mistakes at the worksite) may be drawn on a graph called a scatter diagram. A scatter diagram plots many data points, typically with a measure of quality on one axis and a variable hypothesized to influence quality on the other axis. Used in analysis to test hypotheses on cause-and-effect relations, a scatter diagram is a visual representation of a two-dimensional correlation. A diagram such as this is often very useful because it illustrates patterns of data that are not otherwise obvious.

The scatter diagram might be set up to show the relationship between the number of hours of training for an HR telephone representative and the average number of minutes required to respond to each call. The premise that would be tested by this diagram would be that the more training (up to a certain point) that the representative received, the faster she or he would be able to respond to questions received from callers.

Control Chart

A control chart shows whether variation is due to common or special causes. Upper and lower control limits are easily calculated using the averages and ranges of the data observed. Control charts are used only to determine the nature of variation. They are much more precise than run charts relative to indicating whether variation is due to common or special causes.

Once training had been completed, and the system is stable, the average time to complete phone calls to the HR group should be stable and could be plotted on a control chart to determine if there have been significant changes in the average time to handle a call.

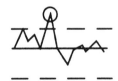

Supplemental Tools

In addition to the seven major quality project management tools, six supplemental tools include force-field analysis, prioritization matrix, run charts, block diagram, customer/supplier relations checklist, and quality mapping.

Force-Field Analysis

Force-field analysis is used to identify problems, their causes, and the driving and restraining forces that affect the problem.

Problem causes are shown as arrows restraining or opposing the driving forces needed to successfully accomplish a task or project. For example, a company may want to develop a TQM process in one of its divisions. The driving forces would be such things as leadership, competitiveness, cost, and need for greater employee involvement and commitment. The restraining forces might be a hostile union environment, lack of familiarity with TQM principles and processes, perceived high start-up costs, and employee skepticism over the benefits versus the efforts required. The political strength of the respective forces can be quantified and analyzed.

Prioritization Matrix

In a prioritization matrix, a diagram of alternatives and a list of weighted criteria are used to quantitatively determine the preferred option. Prioritization matrices are used to reduce the number of alternatives to those that are most significant in a structured, quantitative way. In HR settings, disciplinary alternatives for employees could be determined, evaluated, and justified. This tool can be computerized and input solicited and collectively tallied prior to a meeting to determine the level of support for an option *before* meeting face to face.

Run Chart

A run chart shows the results of a process plotted over time. It is useful to see the dynamic aspects of a process and identify cyclical patterns.

Again, data on the frequency of calls to the HR group might be plotted day by day on a run chart. If the printed materials mentioned earlier were distributed, a run chart would help to show if the number of calls concerning frequently asked questions declined after the materials reached the affected employees.

Block Diagram

A block diagram traces the paths that materials and/or information take between the point of input and final output.

A block diagram can frequently be used in the preliminary stages of process analysis to classify the system. For example, the major activities of a purchasing system could be shown on a block diagram. They might include issuing a request for proposals from potential vendors, receiving proposals, selecting the vendor, developing and signing the contract, receiving the goods, assuring compliance, closing out the contract, and verifying payment. If the purpose of the study was to simplify and/or improve the system, each of these activities, or the entire process, might be studied by one or more project teams.

Customer/Supplier Relations Checklist

This checklist is used to assess the relationship with customers and suppliers within and outside the organization.

It is a specialized form of check sheet that may be used to classify customers or suppliers into categories. For example, although it is not certain that such checklists were used, Hewlett Packard (HP) may have, or could have, done so in a case study reported in a recent article. HP was experiencing a large number of defects of a critical computer component that it received from a vendor. Instead of replacing the vendor, the company formed a three-person project team to investigate the feasibility of eliminating incoming inspection and establishing direct shipments of the parts from the vendor. By gathering and analyzing data, it was determined that the reasons for the vendor's problems were (1) a misinterpretation of the product specifications, (2) lack of consistency in the vendor's production and quality assurance capabilities, and (3) need for the development of a system to eliminate the need for HP to perform incoming inspection on the parts. Eventually the vendor was able to meet all of HP's requirements, thus retaining the HP account, while HP received the benefits of lower costs, shorter lead time, and elimination of 100% inspection and associated rework returns.

Quality Mapping

This tool refers to Q-Map (Quality Map), which is a personal software program for developing measures of process and project performance. It is available from

Table 4.4 Problem-Solving Steps and Useful Quality Control Tools

Problem-solving step	Useful quality control tools
Understanding the mess	Flowcharts
Understanding facts	Check sheets
Identifying problems	Pareto chart
	Histograms
	Force-field analysis
Generating ideas	Cause-and-effect diagrams
Developing solutions	Scatter diagrams
	Prioritization matrix
Implementation	Control charts

Source: Evans, James R. and Lindsay, William M. (1995). *The Management and Control of Quality.* 3rd edition, Minneapolis: West Publishing, p. 261. Modified by the authors.

Pacesetter Software, P.O. Box 5270, Princeton, NJ 08540. This proprietary software makes charting and analysis of various processes/projects easier and faster, once an HRM analyst becomes familiar with how to use the package.

In order to facilitate both the appropriate application of the quality control process and project tools that have been introduced and efficient, creative problem solving, Table 4.4 is provided to suggest one practical format to link problem-solving steps with useful quality control tools.[41]

REVIEW QUESTIONS

4.1. Distinguish "speaking with facts" from three alternatives, and describe how each impacts project success.

4.2. Identify the major steps, key fact-finding cycles, and appropriate tools to speak with facts in a total quality environment.

4.3. Describe how the factual requirements of an "efficient" process (level 4) differ from those of an "effective" process (level 3). How do they both fall short of creating a *total* quality environment?

4.4. Elaborate on the skills a total quality project manager must have to deal with organizational subcultures and the phases/stages of project life cycles.

4.5. Describe the basic ingredients of teams in detail and distinguish real teams from pseudo-, potential, and high-performance teams.

4.6. Elaborate on the transition from supervisory to team leadership and the team empowerment continuum.

4.7. Elaborate on total quality situational leadership styles and responsible team empowerment.

4.8. How can human resource professionals develop, use, and share human resource information system technology to strategically and operationally contribute to team empowerment?

4.9. Define and apply the seven major total quality project management tools to a human resource issue.

4.10. Using a real human resource issue, elaborate on Evans and Lindsay's problem-solving sequence and the total quality tools linked to each step.

DISCUSSION QUESTIONS

4.1. Drawing on your own experience, make a case for the importance of "speaking with facts" in an organization. Discuss the challenges and obstacles that may be present in successfully creating an organization that speaks with facts.

4.2. Compare and contrast four basic subcultures found in most organizations and the implications of these subcultures for information sharing and fact-based decision making.

4.3. Discuss the process of responsible team empowerment, considering it from three points of view: the organization, the employee, and the human resources professional. From each point of view, what factors might "disable" empowerment, and how might these disablers be overcome?

4.4. Identify at least one current business example of a real team *and* a high-performance team. Distinguish each team's characteristics and how those characteristics contributed to the team's results. Discuss what you think is required—from team leaders and team members—to make each kind of team work.

4.5. Discuss the ways in which traditional human resources systems or practices have tended to reinforce only individual effort and not team effort. Using real case examples, identify system, policy, or practice innovations you believe will be required to foster cross-functional team collaboration. Drawing on both the successes and failures in your case examples, what advice would you offer as keys to success?

4.6. Discuss the ways in which human resource practices contribute to the micro- and macro-system phases of the involvement/empowerment continuum (see Table 4.2).

4.7. What would (should) you do if you are offered a high-paying leadership position in a Machiavellian ethical work culture and are expected to lead a group with very low empowerment readiness? What would (should) you do if you are an employee with a high level of empowerment readiness but your immediate manager is overdirecting you?

ENDNOTES

1. Leavitt, Jeffrey S. and Nunn, Philip C. (1994). *Total Quality through Project Management*. New York: McGraw-Hill, pp. 45–46; Kliem, Ralph L. and Ludin, Irwin, S. (1992). *The People Side of Project Management*. Brookfield, Vt.: Ashgate Publishing.

2. Voehl, Frank F. (1992). *Total Quality: Principles and Processes within Organizations*. Coral Springs, Fla.: Strategy Associates, pp. 5–7.
3. Gordon, W.I., Infante, D.A., and Graham, E.E. (1988). "Corporate Conditions Conducive to Employee Voice: A Subordinate Perspective." *Employee Rights and Responsibilities Journal*. Vol. 1, No. 3, pp. 101–111; Saunders, D.M., Sheppard, B.H., Knight, V.E., and Roth, J. (1992). "Employee Voice to Supervisors." *Employee Rights and Responsibilities Journal*. Vol. 8, No. 4, pp. 85–94.
4. Minton, J.W. (1988). *Justice, Satisfaction and Loyalty: Employee Withdrawal and Voice in the Din of Inequity*. Unpublished doctoral dissertation. Durham, N.C.: Duke University; Spencer, D.G. (1986). "Employee Voice and Employee Retention." *Academy of Management Journal*. Vol. 29, No. 3, pp. 488–502.
5. Sheppard, B.H., Lewicki, R., and Minton, J.W. (1992). *Organizational Justice: The Search for Fairness in the Workplace*. New York: Lexington Books, pp. 154–155.
6. Rusbelt, C.E., Farrell, D., Rogers, G., and Mainous, A.G. (1988). "Impact of Exchange Variables on Exit, Voice, Loyalty, and Neglect: An Integrative Model of Responses to Declining Job Satisfaction." *Academy of Management Journal*. Vol. 31, No. 2, pp. 599–627.
7. Sheppard, B.H., Lewicki, R., and Minton, J.W. (1992). *Organizational Justice: The Search for Fairness in the Workplace*. New York: Lexington Books, pp. 156–158.
8. Ryan, Kathleen D. and Oestrich, D.K. (1991). *Driving Fear Out of the Workplace*. San Francisco: Jossey-Bass, pp. 29–102.
9. Alexander, Phil (1992). "Self-Esteem and Empowerment." *Journal for Quality and Participation*. Vol. 12, No. 6, pp. 26–28.
10. Blackburn, Richard and Rosen, Benson (1994). "Human Resource Management Practices and Total Quality Management." Paper presented at the 1994 Academy of Management Meetings, Atlanta.
11. Blackburn, Richard and Rosen, Benson (1994). "Human Resource Management Practices and Total Quality Management." Paper presented at the 1994 Academy of Management Meetings, Atlanta, pp. 12–15.
12. Blackburn, Richard and Rosen, Benson (1994). "Human Resource Management Practices and Total Quality Management." Paper presented at the 1994 Academy of Management Meetings, Atlanta, pp. 9–11. See also Seraph, J., Benson, P., and Schroeder, R. (1989). "An Instrument for Measuring the Critical Factors of Quality Management." *Decision Sciences*. Vol. 20, No. 5, pp. 810–829 for a precursor of the survey instrument used in the most recent study.
13. Shiba, Shoji, Graham, A., and Walden, D. (1993). *A New American TQM: Four Practical Revolutions in Management*. Cambridge, Mass.: Productivity Press, p. 65.
14. Mills, Charles A. (1989). *The Quality Audit: A Management Evaluation Tool*. New York: McGraw-Hill, pp. 10–70; Mills, David (1993). *Quality Auditing*. New York: Chapman and Hall, pp. 25–81.

15. The material in this subsection relies heavily on Harrington, H. James (1991). *Business Process Improvement.* New York: McGraw-Hill, pp. 206–215 and Harrington, H. James (1995). *Total Improvement Management.* New York: McGraw-Hill, pp. 339–354.

16. Elmes, M. and Wilemon, D. (1988). "Organizational Culture and Project Leader Effectiveness." *Project Management Journal.* Vol. 19, No. 4, pp. 54–63; Phillips, M.E., Goodman, R.A., and Sackmann, S.A. (1992). "Exploring the Complex Culture Milieu of Project Teams." *PM Network.* Vol. 6, No. 8, pp. 79–88; Ouchi, William (1987). "Bureaucratic, Market and Clan Control." *Academy of Management Journal.* Vol. 24, No. 5, pp. 120–129.

17. Leavitt, Jeffrey S. and Nunn, Philip C. (1994). *Total Quality through Project Management.* New York: McGraw-Hill, pp. 48–53; Hutton, D.W. (1995). *The Change Agents' Handbook: A Survival Guide for Quality Improvement Champions.* Milwaukee: ASQC Quality Press, pp. 16–50.

18. Kliem, Ralph L. and Ludin, Irwin, S. (1992). *The People Side of Project Management.* Brookfield, Vt.: Ashgate Publishing, pp. 38–42.

19. Scholtes, Peter R. (1988). *The Team Handbook.* Madison, Wisc.: Joiner Associates, pp. 14–30; Hirschhorn, L. (1991). *Managing in the New Team Environment.* Reading, Mass.: Addison-Wesley, pp. 39–52.

20. Katzenbach, J.R. and Smith, D.K. (1993). *The Wisdom of Teams: Creating the High-Performance Organization.* New York: Harper Business, p. 45. Modified by authors.

21. The material in this subsection relies heavily on Katzenbach, J.R. and Smith, D.K. (1993). *The Wisdom of Teams: Creating the High-Performance Organization.* New York: Harper Business, pp. 43–92.

22. Mears, P. and Voehl, F. (1994). *Team Building: A Structured Learning Approach.* Delray Beach, Fla.: St. Lucie Press, p. 62; Dimock, Hedley G. (1987). *Groups: Leadership and Group Development.* La Jolla, Calif.: University Associates, pp. 26–36.

23. Katzenbach, J.R. and Smith, D.K. (1993). *The Wisdom of Teams: Creating the High-Performance Organization.* New York: Harper Business, pp. 87–129.

24. Evans, James R. and Lindsay, William M. (1995). *The Management and Control of Quality.* 3rd edition, Minneapolis: West Publishing, pp. 492–493.

25. Hartsfield, William E. (1990). *HR Audit: How to Evaluate Your Personnel Policies and Practices.* Madison, Conn.: Business and Legal Reports.

26. Reidenbach, R.E. and Robin, D.P. (1989). *Ethics and Profits.* Englewood Cliffs, N.J.: Prentice-Hall, pp. 200–203; contact Organizational Ethics Associates in Cincinnati, Ohio (513-984-2820) for additional information.

27. Zenger, J., Musselwhite, E., Hurson, K., and Perrin, C. (1994). *Leading Teams: Mastering the New Role.* Burr Ridge, Ill.: Irwin, pp. 27–53; Johnson, R.S. (1995). *Quality Training Practices.* Milwaukee: ASQC Quality Press.

28. Aubrey, C.A. and Felkins, P.K. (1988). *Teamwork: Involving People in Quality and Productivity Improvement.* Milwaukee: ASQC Quality Press, pp. 10–40.

29. Dean, James W. Jr. and Evans, James R. (1994). *Total Quality: Management, Organization, and Strategy.* Minneapolis: West Publishing, p. 182.
30. Orsburn, J.D., Moran, L., Musselwhite, E., and Zenger, J.H. (1990). *Self-Directed Work Teams: The New American Challenge.* Homewood, Ill.: Irwin, pp. 20–62.
31. Wellins, R.S., Byham, W.C., and Wilson, J.M. (1991). *Empowered Teams.* San Francisco: Jossey-Bass, pp. 24–63.
32. Tenner, A.R. and DeToro, I.J. (1992). *Total Quality Management.* Reading, Mass.: Addison-Wesley, pp. 190–191. Modified by authors.
33. Hersey, P. (1984). *The Situational Leader.* New York: Warner Books; Johnson, Richard S. (1993). *TQM: Leadership for the Quality Transformation.* Milwaukee: ASQC Quality Press, pp. 88–99; Joiner, C.W. (1987). *Leadership for Change.* Cambridge, Mass.: Ballinger, pp. 15–85; Rost, Joseph C. (1991). *Leadership for the Twenty-First Century.* Westport, Conn.: Praeger, pp. 97–152.
34. Johnson, Richard S. (1993). *TQM: Leadership for the Quality Transformation.* Milwaukee: ASQC Quality Press, pp. 90–92.
35. Bass, Bernard M. (1990). *Bass and Stogdill's Handbook of Leadership.* 3rd ed., New York: Free Press, pp. 339–361, 488–494, 595–612; Schein, E.H. (1992). *Organizational Culture and Leadership.* 2nd ed., San Francisco: Jossey-Bass, pp. 35–75; Bass, B.M. (1985). *Leadership and Performance Beyond Expectations.* New York: Free Press, pp. 10–88; Trice, H.M. and Beyer, J.M. (1991). "Cultural Leadership in Organizations." *Organization Science.* Vol. 2, No. 2, pp. 149–169; Tichy, N.M. and Devanna, M.A. (1986). *The Transformational Leader.* New York: John Wiley & Sons, pp. 5–75; Rost, Joseph C. (1991). *Leadership for the Twenty-First Century.* Westport, Conn.: Praeger.
36. KPMG Peat Marwick (1988). *Computer Usage in Human Resources: A Competitive Advantage.* Dallas: KPMG Peat Marwick; Broderick, R. and Boudreau, J.W. (1992). "Human Resource Management, Information Technology and the Competitive Edge." *Academy of Management Executive.* Vol. 6, No. 2, pp. 7–17.
37. Olian, J. and Rynes, S. (1991). "Making Total Quality Work: Aligning Organizational Processes, Performance, Measures and Stakeholders." *Human Resource Management.* Vol. 30, No. 3, pp. 325–327.
38. Broderick, R. and Boudreau, J.W. (1992). "Human Resource Management, Information Technology and the Competitive Edge." *Academy of Management Executive.* Vol. 6, No. 2, pp. 9–16.
39. Ishikawa, Kaoru and Lu, D. (1985). *What Is Total Quality Control? The Japanese Way.* Englewood Cliffs, N.J.: Prentice-Hall, pp. 45–62.
40. Shiba, Shoji, Graham, A., and Walden, D. (1993). *A New American TQM: Four Practical Revolutions in Management.* Cambridge, Mass.: Productivity Press, pp. 102–105.
41. Evans, James R. and Lindsay, William M. (1995). *The Management and Control of Quality.* 3rd edition, Minneapolis: West Publishing, pp. 241–246.

EXERCISES

PRACTITIONER ASSESSMENT INSTRUMENT 4A: LEADER, MEMBER, AND GROUP FEEDBACK

PURPOSE

The purpose of this assessment instrument is to provide a framework to discuss ways to maintain or improve total quality team performance by collecting data about internal customer satisfaction concerning the effectiveness of the leader, each member, and the overall team. The instrument consists of two parts: Leader Feedback Form (Part 1) and Member/Group Feedback Form (Part 2).

PART 1: LEADER FEEDBACK FORM

DIRECTIONS

Circle the position on the poor to excellent range that represents your opinion about this leader's effectiveness in each area. Give reasons or examples to support your assessment.

Group: _____   Date: _____

Leader: _____

1. Is prepared for meetings

Poor	Fair	Adequate	Good	Excellent

Reasons or examples:

a. _____

b. _____

2. Is effective in conducting meetings

Poor	Fair	Adequate	Good	Excellent

Reasons or examples:

a. _____

b. _____

3. Encourages a cooperative atmosphere

Poor	Fair	Adequate	Good	Excellent

Reasons or examples:

a.

b.

4. Helps each person make contributions

Poor	Fair	Adequate	Good	Excellent

Reasons or examples:

a.

b.

5. Considers each person's needs

Poor	Fair	Adequate	Good	Excellent

Reasons or examples:

a.

b.

6. Assigns responsibilities for follow-through

Poor	Fair	Adequate	Good	Excellent

Reasons or examples:

a.

b.

7. Is willing to listen to others

Poor	Fair	Adequate	Good	Excellent

Reasons or examples:

a.

b.

8. Is open in expressing own ideas

Poor	Fair	Adequate	Good	Excellent

Reasons or examples:

a.

b.

9. Follows through on commitments

Poor	Fair	Adequate	Good	Excellent

Reasons or examples:

a.

b.

10. Supports the group with higher management

Poor	Fair	Adequate	Good	Excellent

Reasons or examples:

a.

b.

11. Creates a group-centered rather than a leader-centered atmosphere

Poor	Fair	Adequate	Good	Excellent

Reasons or examples:

a.

b.

12. Finds common areas of agreement among different people and ideas

Poor	Fair	Adequate	Good	Excellent

Reasons or examples:

a.

b.

13. Focuses attention on common goals

Poor	Fair	Adequate	Good	Excellent

Reasons or examples:

a.

b.

14. Generates enthusiasm among group members

Poor	Fair	Adequate	Good	Excellent

Reasons or examples:

a.

b.

15. Sees project(s) through to completion

| Poor | Fair | Adequate | Good | Excellent |

Reasons or examples:

a.

b.

16. Overall effectiveness of the leader

| Poor | Fair | Adequate | Good | Excellent |

Reasons or examples:

a.

b.

Additional Comments: _____

_____

_____

_____

SCORING
Assign five points for each "excellent," four for each "good," three for each "adequate," two for each "fair," and one for each "poor" rating that you circled on the Leader Evaluation Form. Total all points: _____

INTERPRETATION
Find your total on the following chart:

Total score	Leader evaluation
64–80	Good to excellent
48–63	Adequate to good
32–47	Fair to adequate
16–31	Poor to fair

Scores in the good to excellent range indicate maintenance activities to sustain leader effectiveness. Scores in the adequate to good range indicate areas for incremental improvements to enhance leader effectiveness. Scores in the two lower ranges (fair to adequate and poor to fair) signal the need for substantial improvement to achieve leader effectiveness.

Source: Stattler, William M. and Miller, N. Edd. (1968). *Discussion and Conference.* 2nd ed., Englewood Cliffs, N.J.: Prentice-Hall, pp. 476–488.

PART 2: MEMBER FEEDBACK FORM
DIRECTIONS
Evaluate each team member in two areas: problem-solving skills and group participation skills. Rate each item according to the following scale:

5 = Excellent   4 = Good   3 = Adequate   2 = Fair   1 = Poor

Group: _____   Date: _____

Feedback provider: _____

Names of Members
A. _____   D. _____   G. _____

B. _____   E. _____   H. _____

C. _____   F. _____   I. _____

FEEDBACK	A	B	C	D	E	F	G	H	I	AVG
I. Problem-solving (PS) skills										
1. Is knowledgeable about the subject										
2. Is complete and accurate in gathering information										
3. Understands basic issues and the relationship among parts or phases of the problem										
4. Reaches conclusions based on sound evidence										
5. Sees probable consequences of solutions										
6. Is objective										
7. Is creative										
TOTAL PS SKILL POINTS										
II. Group participation (GP) skills										
1. Shows consideration for the views of others										
2. Shows interest in free exchange of ideas										
3. Understands how others feel										
4. Listens respectfully										
5. Communicates clearly										

FEEDBACK	A	B	C	D	E	F	G	H	I	AVG
6. Brings together opposite points of view										
7. Actively participates in trying to solve problems										
TOTAL GP SKILL POINTS										
AGGREGATE POINTS (total PS and GP points)										

SCORING

Step 1: Add ratings in each vertical column (A-I) to obtain both total PS and GP skill points for each member.

Step 2: Add total PS and GP skill points for each member to arrive at the aggregate point total.

Step 3: In the column labeled AVG, which stands for average, add the horizontal row of ratings for each item and divide the total by the number of members.

INTERPRETATION

Step 1: Find each member's aggregate point total on the following chart.

Total score	Member evaluation
56–70	Good to excellent
42–55	Adequate to good
28–41	Fair to adequate
14–27	Poor to fair

Scores in the good to excellent range indicate maintenance activities to sustain member effectiveness. Scores in the adequate to good range indicate areas for incremental improvement to enhance member effectiveness. Scores in the two lower ranges (fair to adequate and poor to fair) signal the need for substantial improvement to achieve member effectiveness.

Step 2: Consider the group's average score for each skill factor in relation to the rating scale from 5 (excellent) to 1 (poor).

- Compare individual member ratings with team averages and discuss implications.
- Identify the three highest team average scores and discuss strengths to build on and celebrate.
- Identify the three lowest team average scores and discuss possible improvement needs.
- Given the scores, is the team more skilled at either problem solving or group participation? Discuss the implications of the skill mix and the improvements needed to achieve total quality performance.

Source: Stattler, William M. and Miller, N. Edd. (1968). *Discussion and Conference.* 2nd ed., Englewood Cliffs, N.J.: Prentice-Hall, pp. 476–488; Manning, George and Curtis, Kent (1988). *Group Strength: Quality Circles at Work.* Cincinnati: South-Western Publishing, pp. 107–112.

PRACTITIONER ASSESSMENT INSTRUMENT 4B: TOTAL QUALITY MORALE ASSESSMENT AND DEVELOPMENT

DIRECTIONS

The following instrument addresses a number of work-related issues. Answer each question as it relates to your current work experience. Check the appropriate response.

WORK	Strongly Disagree	Disagree	Undecided	Agree	Strongly Agree
1. I understand the responsibilities and importance of my work.					
2. I feel confidence and pride in competently performing my work responsibilities.					
3. I have a sense of personal autonomy and organizational support for quality work performance.					
GROUP					
4. I have confidence in the empowerment maturity of my co-workers.					
5. The people in my work group treat each other with respect and trust.					
6. My work group is a productive team and proud of it.					
MANAGEMENT					
7. Managers are respected for their competence.					
8. Managers provide accurate and timely feedback to improve employee performance.					
9. Managers treat employees fairly and respectfully.					
REWARD SYSTEM					
10. My personal compensation is satisfactory.					

	Strongly Disagree	Disagree	Undecided	Agree	Strongly Agree
11. The nonfinancial recognition my team and I receive is satisfactory.					
12. The reward system is fair and equitable.					

SCORING

Step 1:   For each question, score 1 for strongly disagree, 2 for disagree, 3 for undecided, 4 for agree, and 5 for strongly agree.

Step 2:   Add the total scores for each section of the questionnaire, divide by 3, and enter the averages in the spaces below.

Work	**Group**	**Management**	**Reward system**
_____	_____	_____	_____
Average for items 1, 2, 3	Average for items 4, 5, 6	Average for items 7, 8, 9	Average for items 10, 11, 12

INTERPRETATION

This exercise shows the relative impact of the four components of total quality morale. Assuming that a person has the basic knowledge and skills to perform a job, the quality of work and the quality of work life depend on commitment to do a good job. Regardless of the field—transportation, manufacturing, or medicine—and regardless of the level of responsibility—entry-level employee, middle manager, or president—commitment results from high morale in four key areas: the work itself, the work group, management practices, and the reward system.

The following is a description of what your scores mean.

Low total quality morale: Scores from 1.0 to 2.5 in any one or a combination of the four key areas—work, group, management, and reward system—indicate a low level of total quality morale. If you are doing good work, you are doing it because of personal qualities, not because of organizational support.

Average total quality morale: Scores between 2.6 and 3.4 in any one or a combination of these four areas indicate an average level of total quality morale, sometimes called a wait-and-see attitude. It is likely that your morale is neither helping nor hurting your work performance at this point. However, you lack a sense of full satisfaction and do not feel complete commitment to your work.

High total quality morale: Scores between 3.5 and 5.0 in all four areas indicate a high level of morale. You are fortunate in that you receive much satisfaction from your work. You are striving to do the best job possible and, with training and practice, your level of performance could be expected to be high and continually improving.

Managers who utilize this morale measurement are more likely to be aware of morale problems rather than delude themselves due to a lack of regular, structured feedback. Morale survey diagrams provide easy visual profiles of the workplace and isolate key variables that distinguish the morale profile of one work unit from another.

The transition from morale assessment to morale development can be facilitated by constructive actions that address the four components of morale: the work itself, the work group, management practices, and reward systems. Steps that improve total quality work include clarifying responsibilities, demonstrating significance of work, developing employee work competence through ongoing training, designing autonomy into work processes and job descriptions, and providing technical support for quality work performance. Steps that improve total quality work groups include ongoing team building and task competency training, human relations training, and team development/celebration activities.

Steps that improve total quality management practices include accurate and timely feedback to employees to coach and improve their performance, personal professional development programs that balance managerial effectiveness, and human relations/ethics training to sharpen skills/attitudes that result in the fair and respectful treatment of employees. Finally, steps that improve the total quality reward system include compensation systems that take advantage of extrinsic and intrinsic motivational effects of rewards, satisfy norms for equity, meet external market competitiveness challenges, comply with appropriate laws and regulations, are efficiently administered, and encourage collaboration for team and system success.

PRACTITIONER ASSESSMENT INSTRUMENT 4C: EMPOWERMENT READINESS ASSESSMENT

DIRECTIONS
This rating form considers the total quality empowerment readiness level of individuals and/or groups. It can be used as a personal or group self-assessment instrument, *or* by a manager considering another individual for promotion or group members for a project, *or* distributed for anonymous collective feedback about a prospective individual or group empowerment activity. For each of the dimensions listed below, circle the number that most closely represents your perception of the individual or group under consideration, using the rating scale below. Comments are optional.

High			Moderate			Low	
8	7	6	5	4	3	2	1

Dimensions   **Comments**

1. Job/project knowledge

Has job/project   Does not have job/
knowledge   project knowledge

8   7   6   5   4   3   2   1   _____

2. Achievement motivation

Has high desire   Has little desire
to achieve   to achieve

8   7   6   5   4   3   2   1   _____

3. Honesty

Always honest   Never honest

8   7   6   5   4   3   2   1   _____

4. Total quality problem-solving ability

Solves problems   Unable to solve
using total quality   problems using
tools   total quality tools

8   7   6   5   4   3   2   1   _____

5. Communication style

                               Does not commun-
Communicates   icate effectively at
effectively at work   work

8   7   6   5   4   3   2   1   _____

6. Trustworthy

Always trustworthy   Never trustworthy

8   7   6   5   4   3   2   1   _____

7. Past job/project experience

Has relevant   No relevant
experience   experience

8   7   6   5   4   3   2   1   _____

8. Sense of humor

Always exhibits an   Never exhibits an
appropriate sense   appropriate sense
of humor   of humor

8   7   6   5   4   3   2   1   _____

9. Justice/fairness

Always fair and just   Never fair and just

8   7   6   5   4   3   2   1   _____

Dimensions   **Comments**

10. Relevant computer literacy

Always uses   Never uses
computer   computer
effectively at work   effectively at work

8   7   6   5   4   3   2   1   _____

11. Work attitude

Has "can do-enjoy   Has "can't do–thank
making it happen"   goodness it's Friday
attitude   attitude

8   7   6   5   4   3   2   1   _____

12. Respectfully caring

Always respect-   Never respectfully
fully caring   caring

8   7   6   5   4   3   2   1   _____

13. Organization knowledge

Knows the   Does not know the
organization as a   organization as a
whole system   whole system

8   7   6   5   4   3   2   1   _____

14. Interdependent cooperation

Works cooper-   Does not work coop-
atively with others   eratively with others

8   7   6   5   4   3   2   1   _____

15. Good judgment

Always exhibits   Never exhibits
good judgment   good judgment

8   7   6   5   4   3   2   1   _____

16. Takes responsibility for an envisioned future

Envisions a future   Does not envision
and takes responsi-   a future and take
bility for it   responsibility for it

8   7   6   5   4   3   2   1   _____

17. Uses and shares power effectively

Uses and shares   Uses and shares
power effectively   power ineffectively

8   7   6   5   4   3   2   1   _____

18. Courage

Always exhibits courage   Never exhibits courage

8   7   6   5   4   3   2   1   _____

SCORING

1. **Task maturity:**   Add the numbers circled for questions 1, 4, 7, 10, 13, and 16, and divide the total by 6.

2. **Psychosocial maturity:**   Add the numbers circled for questions 2, 5, 8, 11, 14, and 17 and divide by 6.

3. **Moral maturity:**   Add the numbers circled for questions 3, 6, 9, 12, 15, and 18 divide by 6.

INTERPRETATION

Average scores for any of the factors:

0–4.0   =   Individual or group is not ready for total quality empowerment at this time.

4.1–7   =   Individual or group is ready for regular participation in total quality teamwork

7.1–8   =   Individual or group is ready for self-directed, high-performance total quality teamwork

Use your lowest average factor score as a place to begin preparing yourself or your group for responsible empowerment. Individuals or groups who are prematurely empowered (e.g., individual promoted without being ready to assume the commensurate responsibilities) eventually become problems for themselves, others, and the total quality system (i.e., "The Peter Principle" of institutionalized incompetence).

RESPECT FOR PEOPLE: PERFORMANCE DIMENSIONS

The focus of Chapter 5 is on two areas: total quality business individual performance and total quality human resource (HR) individual performance. Both are crucial in determining the strength of the fourth pillar of the House of Total Quality and clarifying the expanded daily performance responsibilities of individual employees in a total quality system. Both total quality business and HR individual performance need to be aligned to ensure organizational effectiveness and efficiency.

THE TOTAL QUALITY BUSINESS INDIVIDUAL PERFORMANCE

As indicated in Chapter 1, the fourth pillar of the House of Total Quality, respect for people, is based on the cornerstone of individual performance planning and the foundation of individual performance management. In Chapter 2, *individual performance* was defined as *the daily implementation of continuous improvement in personal tasks and relational activity within an employee's*

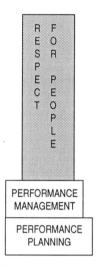

Figure 5.1 The Fourth Pillar, Foundation, and Cornerstone of the House of Total Quality.

own scope of responsibility.[1] The pillar of respect for people is the outcome of sound design developed in the cornerstone of individual performance planning with effective implementation delivered in the foundation of individual performance management, as depicted in Figure 5.1.[2]

While the previous total quality pillars involved system strategy, process, and project dimensions, the last pillar focuses on daily personal task and relational performance. Even the most innovative and sophisticated approaches to strategy, process, and project management will be unable to produce world-class results if respect for people is absent. Furthermore, respect for people is built—or eroded—every day in the planning and management of individual work performance.

Quality is personal because the individual choices people make every day as they work are critical to the outcomes they create.[3] Yet this personal commitment to quality will not come about by default; it must be nurtured by design. The fourth pillar, therefore, goes to the very heart of what makes or breaks total quality in any organization. **Respect for people** *is the fundamental positive regard for ourselves and for one another as people that grounds personal commitment to quality performance.* It plays out in how we treat ourselves and each other on a daily basis, how we view ourselves in relation to others, and how we view the value each person brings to every interaction. The characteristics of people who respect themselves and others and the implications these factors have in traditional and total quality work cultures are depicted in Table 5.1.[4]

Table 5.1 Characteristics and Work Culture Implications
of People Who Respect Themselves and Others

Characteristics of people who respect themselves and others	Implications in a traditional work culture	Implications in a total quality work culture
Less interested in seeking approval to bolster self-esteem	May be perceived as rebels, mavericks, "loose cannons," aloof, and self-serving	May be more likely to challenge status quo and take risks
More accepting of others	May be regarded with suspicion ("What's their hidden agenda?")	May foster collaboration and mutual support
Less likely to be driven by others' feedback	May be perceived as stubborn, closed, ineffective, with "blinders" on	May seek "best" solution, despite biases of tradition
High internal locus of control	May be perceived as resistant to the rightful authority of others	May hold self more accountable and take personal responsibility
Less likely to model others	May be perceived as devaluing heritage and past strengths	May envision and create needed innovations
Accept and feel good about themselves	May be seen as uncontrollable; may seem threatening to the insecure	May take more initiative to act with confidence even in the face of uncertainty
Driven to meet their own self-set goals which tend to be high and resistant to change	May be seen as troublemakers, making others "look bad"	May "raise the bar" and continuously seek improvement without settling for success of the past
Expect to succeed regardless of the context	May be perceived as unrealistic, naive	May help others achieve beyond self-imposed limitations
Emotionally well-adjusted	May be perceived as sensible and not easily manipulated or intimidated	May demonstrate emotional balance in handling success and coping with failure

Table 5.1 Characteristics and Work Culture Implications
of People Who Respect Themselves and Others (continued)

Characteristics of people who respect themselves and others	Implications in a traditional work culture	Implications in a total quality work culture
Avoids self-deception; has the courage and humility to face the truth	May be perceived as indecisive, self-critical, and/or weak	May openly acknowledge own improvement needs and seek both feedback and help from others in order to learn
Excellent empathic listeners	May be regarded as too considerate (emphasizing feelings over results)	May listen sincerely for genuine understanding of others' concerns or feedback, without being defensive, justifying self or imposing advice

Individuals at work who respect others but not themselves are incapable of relating in a collegial, interdependent manner because they undervalue their own worth, do not voice their own opinions, and rely on the approval of others for validation (e.g., managers or employees who allow others to verbally abuse them without setting boundaries for respectful discourse at work). Individuals at work who only respect themselves but not others alienate co-workers and are unable to learn from others or generate teamwork (e.g., managers who do not solicit input or ignore feedback from more knowledgeable employees because they (the managers) are too proud to learn from others). Some persons only feel or show honor for those who have higher rank or status in work organizations and treat peers and/or direct reports with contempt or neglect. Total quality firms require respect for all people in the organization, regardless of role, because each person is continually being empowered to enhance the effectiveness of the organization. Some persons profess respect for others but their behavior indicates that they always expect others to defer to their judgment; they regularly intrude upon others in conversations and decision-making processes. This gap between the rhetoric and reality of respect for people is exactly what is eliminated or severely reduced in a total quality organization because the system cannot improve without sincere respect and integrity.

Respect for people and social tolerance are particularly important in valuing diversity and achieving inclusivity in today's workplace.[5] Discrimination against people at work is not only illegal but violates the principles for which the fourth pillar of total quality stands. Disrespectful treatment at work is morally offensive and reduces the aggregate effectiveness of an organization by erecting barriers to equal access to information and training and by condoning prejudice against equal recognition for contributions to organizational success. On the other hand, people who respect themselves and others, whether or not they are in a protected class, are more likely to appreciate others' success and emulate it rather than resent it (e. g., when any co-worker has a successful achievement, respectful people acknowledge and celebrate that achievement, are inspired by their co-worker's example to honor their own talents and to do their personal best rather than allege favoritism or feel jealousy or envy). In total quality organizations, people earn respect through performance; emulation of success, rather than resentment against achievement, is the expected norm. Respect for people, therefore, includes both sincere self-respect and sincere respect for others to enhance personal performance integration in a total quality work culture.

TOTAL QUALITY BUSINESS PERFORMANCE PLANNING

In planning overall business quality performance, both system and personal factors need to be addressed, as indicated in Figure 3.7 in Chapter 3. However, a more detailed approach to work performance is warranted to clarify the most beneficial ways to enhance personal contributions in a total quality system.

Work performance can be defined as *behavior associated with the accomplishment of expected, specified, or formal role requirements on the part of individual organizational members.*[7] Total quality organizations are described in terms of norms, values, and reward procedures that emphasize holistic behavior oriented toward cooperation with fellow organizational members.[8] Work performance in such an environment includes accomplishing tasks and taking initiatives above and beyond the call of duty and sharing information with and helping co-workers. Moorman and Blakely regard such behaviors as falling under the rubric of organizational citizenship behavior (OCB).[9] In a total quality context, OCB is both expected and formally rewarded.[10] Inanimate systems, no matter how well reengineered, are no substitute for achieving total work performance through personal contributions.

Work performance, therefore, can be viewed as being influenced by four possible categories of factors: (1) *systematic system,* (2) *random system,* (3) *person,* and (4) *person/system interaction.*[11] Individual performance variation within a system results only from the latter three categories. Systematic system factors are those that affect persons equally (e.g., employees serving milk shakes in a fast-food restaurant using the same equipment and relying on identical procedures). Although systematic system factors may affect overall worker performance (e.g., through obsolete technology), they do not explain individual performance variations.

Random system factors, however, affect employees differentially. Variations in environmental conditions, raw materials, supplier relations, equipment maintenance, state-of-the-art technology, leadership styles, job design, and ethical work cultures affect individual performance. A sales representative assigned to a rapidly growing sales territory, as compared to other sales representatives who are not as fortunate, benefits from random system variation.[12] Both Deming and Juran argue that random system factors account for most performance variation and can eventually be brought under control.[13] The extent of random system influence, however, depends on the impact of factor 4 (i.e., the person–system interaction and, in particular, the work hierarchy level and autonomy of individual performers).

While it is necessary to address the systematic and random system factors, OCB work performance will not automatically result from these factors alone. The work-relevant knowledge, skills, and abilities (KSAs) of individuals and their motive patterns make them more or less disposed to constructively support total quality initiatives.[14] While this personal factor has been the preeminent concern of traditional HR management attention, the continuous training, development, and job redesign required in a total quality firm not only prevents worker obsolescence but so enriches work that it intrinsically motivates disposed persons toward OCB.[15]

Finally, the person/system interaction is crucial because even if systems are invariant, people interact differentially due to their work hierarchy level and autonomy, as indicated in Figure 5.2.[16]

Research has already established that managers at higher organizational levels shape and influence internal systems more effectively than lower level managers.[17] If **autonomy** is defined as *the degree of freedom or discretion a person has over the task domain regarding activities such as determining procedures and scheduling, research also demonstrates that increased autonomy varies inversely with powerlessness* (i.e., the state of "organizationally induced helplessness)."[18] Many work designs so tightly structure the work process that line employees feel incapable of process improvement. Deming's overattribution of system factors as exclusive causes of individual work performance is in part due to the prevailing lack of autonomy in work design in most industries. When industry workers are empowered, however, as was the case in the NUMMI automobile manufacturing facility in California or the Saturn automobile plant in Tennessee, significant work changes result from personal choices to effectively contribute.[19] In fact, individual factors will outweigh system constraints and demands in the determination of work performance at increas-

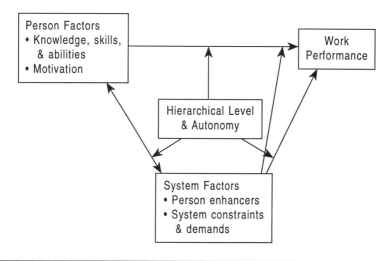

Figure 5.2 The Person/System Interaction Model of Work Performance. (Source: Waldman, David A. (1994). "The Contributions of Total Quality Management to a Theory of Work Performance." *Academy of Management Review.* Vol. 19, No. 3, p. 518. Title modified by the authors.)

ing hierarchical levels of management and when work is designed with a higher degree of autonomy, allowing for choice and personal control.[20]

Figure 5.2 delineates the connections between person and system factors as mediated by individual hierarchical level and autonomy to result in work performance. In total quality organizations, as individuals are empowered their increased autonomy can lead to heightened personal work performance and can reciprocally reduce the effects of system constraints and demands.[21] Because the advantages of increased empowerment and enhanced performance are to be maximized by design in a total quality firm, the model used to link individual empowerment and personal leadership becomes crucial for quality planners.

Individual empowerment has been described as intrinsic task motivation consisting of four dimensions: *choice, meaningfulness, competence,* and *impact.*[22] Choice involves causal responsibility for a person's actions and consists of an individual's belief, at a given point in time, in his or her ability to affect a change, in a desired direction, in the environment.[23] Field research has demonstrated that choice and personal control are related to intrinsic task motivation, job performance, and job satisfaction.[24] The central component of empowerment is choice. Meaningfulness concerns the value a task holds in relation to the individual's value system.[25] Competence refers to self-efficacy or the belief that one is capable of successfully performing a particular task

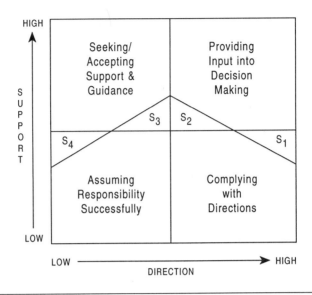

Figure. 5.3 Personal Leadership Styles and Respect Preferences. (Source: Beck, John D. and Yeager, Neil M. (1994). *The Leader's Window*. New York: John Wiley & Sons, p. 31.)

or activity.[26] Impact represents the degree to which the individual perceives his or her behavior as making a difference.[27] In essence, the personal control, job design, self-efficacy, and intrinsic motivation theories provide the basis for expected relations among the three dimensions of empowerment, work satisfaction, and job performance.[28] Individuals, in turn, are usually appreciative of organizations that provide them with opportunities for personal control, responsibility, and challenge in their work and will tend to reciprocate by being more committed to the organization.[29] As individuals demonstrate empowerment readiness, the choice of their personal leadership style will impact their performance, as indicated in Figure 5.3.[30]

Since the greatest performance potential exists when individuals assume responsibility successfully for their own learning and work contributions, the choice of a personal leadership style is important. This choice is usually influenced by what people respect in themselves and others. In Figure 5.3, the four personal leadership styles include high direction, low support (S1); high support, high direction (S2); high support, low direction (S3); and low support, low direction (S4). They are appropriate in different personal situations as respect preferences vary. For example, individuals who routinely respect themselves and others primarily for complying with directions (S1) are abdicating personal responsibility to initiate learning strategies to others who contribute to the organization. Individuals who regularly respect themselves and others primarily for providing input into decision making (S2) view their threshold of respectable performance as only being a contributor to group problem solving and not ultimately responsible for decisions made. Individuals who routinely respect themselves and others primarily for seeking/accepting support and guidance (S3) develop some personal responsibility for learning but rely on significant others to arrive at decisions. Finally, individuals who regularly respect themselves and others primarily for assuming responsibility successfully (S4) become self-empowered, confident people whose example of self-management inspires others to develop the leader within themselves.[31] A work force consisting of individuals who lead themselves is an empowered work force. It is committed and competent, with a sense of meaningful work, where people continually learn and build a sense of community.[32]

The dynamics of achieving individual empowerment and self-leadership include relying on two cycles: (1) when ample time exists, a natural development cycle (S1, S2, S3, S4) gives oneself and others increasing amounts of responsibility without feeling overwhelmed in the process, and (2) when time is of the essence, an empowerment cycle (S1, S4, S3, S2) surrounds responsibility assumption with up-front direction, ongoing development, and timely problem solving for rapid improvement, as indicated in Figure 5.4.[33]

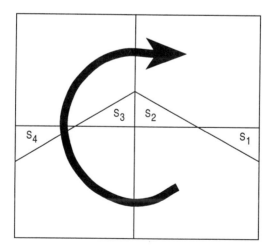

Figure 5.4 The S1-S4-S3-S2 Individual Empowerment Cycle. (Source: Beck, John D. and Yeager, Neil M. (1994). *The Leader's Window.* New York: John Wiley & Sons, p. 234.)

The empowerment cycle begins with clarifying and aligning personal/ organization visions and missions (S1) and then immediately requires trusting oneself to implement those goals (S4). When implementation of personal goals is blocked, the support of others and the development of personal skills is necessary (S3) in order to face and resolve problems (S2) for continual improvement. In a work setting, it is useful to initiate and conclude the empowerment cycle in a group setting to efficiently allocate your time as a leader. Some individuals try to use a S1-S4-S1 "shortcut" leadership cycle, which usually leads to personal frustration (i.e., premature assumption of individual responsibility without nondirectional support and guidance destroys confidence, perpetuates dependence on others, and eventually disempowers oneself). To prevent personal disempowerment, total quality managers need to encourage personal total quality performance contracting, which is the process of assuming personal responsibility for work performance by managing individual resources using total quality methods.

TOTAL QUALITY BUSINESS PERFORMANCE MANAGEMENT

Personal total quality performance management is particularly compelling in light of the most recent research on the relative productivity of total quality organizations.[34] *The most productive total quality firms are those whose employees "personalize" quality practices in their daily work.*[35] The internalization of quality standards and the daily use of quality procedures by employees contributes to superior work unit and organizational productivity.

Personal quality in daily work can be assessed and improved by routine application of the alternation of SDCA and PDCA cycles, as indicated in Figure 4.2 in Chapter 4. The process and project tools already delineated in Chapters 3 and 4 can be adapted from system use to personal use (e.g., check sheets can be used to tally defects in personal work habits and Pareto charts can be used to identify and prioritize individual task performance steps for personal improvement). In addition, however, the following four tools can facilitate and document total quality performance improvement: the *Organizational Integration Chart*, the *Leader Performance Matrix*, the *Personal Process Chart*, and the *Quality Journal*.[36]

The **Organizational Integration Chart** is the first tool and it *determines personal perceptions of individual and organizational congruence.* The chart consists of four columns: (1) current organizational, work unit, and personal vision, mission, ethical work culture (or personal moral development) level, and strategy; (2) ideal/desired organizational, work unit, and personal vision, mission, ethical work culture (or personal moral development) level, and strategy; (3) business significance of disparity between current and desired work reality (at the organizational, work unit, and personal levels) on a point scale of 1 to 10 (10 being most significant for the business); and (4) personal importance of disparity between current and desired work reality (at the organizational, work unit, and personal levels) on a point scale of 1 to 10 (10 being personally most important). The completed Organizational Integration Chart identifies the existence, or lack, of current strategic alignment among individual, work unit and organizational factors. The kind and degree of disparity or nonalignment is a useful indicator of the extent of committed personal performance at work. Quantitative disparity measures provide concrete discussion material for those internal stakeholders with whom one wishes to share this information and build alignment. The chart is an alternative to unfocused complaints and frustrations, a structured form of self-assessment, and an opportunity to determine stakeholder receptiveness to organizational change.

The **Leader Performance Matrix,** depicted in Figure 5.5,[37] is the second tool and *identifies the major activities (processes) of the individual and the functional responsibilities (objectives) of his or her work unit.* As with other personal performance enhancement tools, the respondent name and date are required to document change and progress over time. Two versions of this matrix are usually completed. One is completed from *the perspective of the individual as if he/she were the formal leader* of the work unit (e.g., what things I would do if I were the boss of the work unit). The second form is completed from *the*

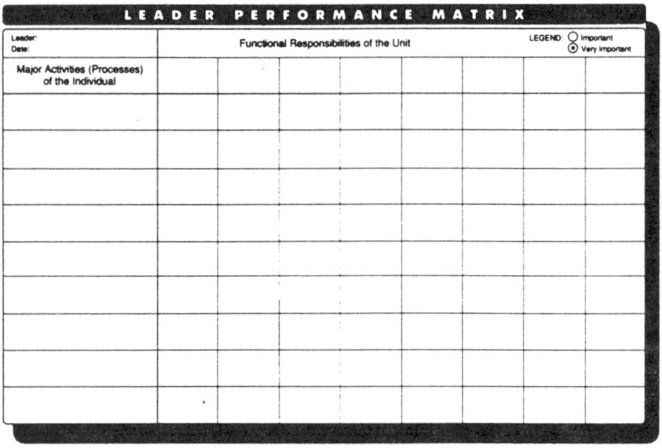
LEADER PERFORMANCE MATRIX
Leader:
Date:
Functional Responsibilities of the Unit
LEGEND: ○ Important ⦿ Very Important
Major Activities (Processes) of the Individual

Figure 5.5 Leader Performance Matrix. (Source: Schultz, Louis E. (1991). *Personal Management: A System for Individual Performance Improvement*. Minneapolis: Process Management International, p. 18.)

perspective of the empowered individual exercising leadership without formal authority (e.g., what things I would do in the work unit because they are the most important activities to be done, regardless of my rank, status, or position). Sometimes these two versions of the Leader Performance Matrix are identical (e.g., when the individual completing the matrix is the formal leader). Often they are slightly different, but the goal is to arrive at the six most important work unit leadership activities and transfer them to the next matrix. The steps for completing both versions of the matrix are as follows: (1) list functional responsibilities of the work unit in the horizontal axis of the matrix (e.g., increase quality output), (2) list major activities (processes) on the left side of the matrix in the form of a verb and object statement (e.g., provide state-of-the-art technology to employees), (3) draw a circle at intersections where leadership activity is important and a dot inside a circle to indicate extreme leadership activity is important in achieving a functional responsibility, (4) analyze what is currently being done and how well each activity supports each functional responsibility, and (5) transfer the six most important personal leadership activities to the next matrix, the Personal Process Chart.

The **Personal Process Chart**, displayed in Figure 5.6, is the third personal performance enhancement tool.[38] In order for individuals to demonstrate quality performance, they must not only know and fulfill their routine work output responsibilities, but they must also continually improve their work

PERSONAL PROCESS CHART

Major Activities (Processes) of the Individual	Specific Tasks	Objectives of Each Task	Internal/External Suppliers	Internal/External Customers	Quality Indicators	Opportunities for Improvement of the Process
A.	1. 2. 3. 4. 5.	1 2 3 4 5				
B.	1. 2. 3. 4. 5.	1 2 3 4 5				
C.	1. 2. 3. 4. 5.	1 2 3 4 5				
D.	1. 2. 3. 4. 5.	1 2. 3. 4 5				
E.	1. 2. 3. 4. 5.	1 2. 3. 4. 5.				
F.	1. 2. 3. 4. 5.	1 2 3 4 5				
REVIEW DATE:		SUPERVISOR:			LEADER:	

Figure 5.6 Personal Process Chart. (Source: Schultz, Louis E. (1991). *Personal Management: A System for Individual Performance Improvement.* Minneapolis: Process Management International, p. 19.)

processes in a documented manner. *The Personal Process Chart addresses this expanded performance responsibility by providing more detailed analyses of individual tasks, objectives, and relationships that can lead to the identification of opportunities for personal process improvement.*

The chart consists of seven columns, and the steps for completing it are as follows: (1) list and redefine operationally, if necessary, the six major individual leadership activities taken from the Leader Performance Matrix; (2) list specific tasks associated with each leadership activity; (3) identify one or two objectives (short and long term) related to each task; (4) identify internal and external suppliers and ways to enhance quality partnerships and productive relationships; (5) identify internal and external customers and solicit their input on improving personal quality work output; (6) determine and measure the quality indicators (critical factors) of individual performance (e.g., collect data to track progress on customer satisfaction results, supplier delivery schedules, and resource adequacy); (7) list several opportunities to improve each activity (e.g., streamline personal work habits or eliminate waste, defects, and rework in processing paperwork); and (8) regularly share results of chart analysis with immediate supervisor, co-workers, and/or direct reports, requesting feedback and cooperation and reporting progress.

The fourth personal performance enhancement tool is the **Quality Journal**, depicted in Figure 5.7.[39] Once the proposed opportunities for improve-

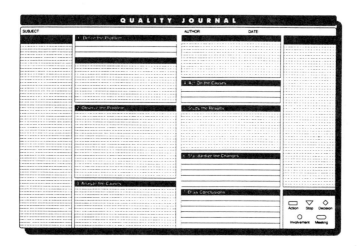

Figure 5.7 Quality Journal. (Source: Schultz, Louis E. (1991). *Personal Management: A System for Individual Performance Improvement*. Minneapolis: Process Management International, p. 20.)

ment are identified in the Personal Process Chart, *the Quality Journal adds value by providing a detailed analysis of the causes of process problems and a systematic approach to documenting improvement.* The journal consists of seven sections, and the steps for completing it are as follows: (1) clearly define each improvement opportunity using facts to demonstrate its significance and how it impacts personal performance, (2) observe the problem by examining it from different points of view (e.g., solicit input from others who are affected by your substandard performance), (3) determine the root causes and symptoms of the problem, (4) take short-term and long-term action to eliminate the root causes, (5) study the effectiveness (the results) of the actions taken and make any modifications necessary to achieve the desired results, (6) standardize the solution and cascade it throughout the appropriate work units, and (7) review the problem-solving and process improvement procedures to draw conclusions about and celebrate what was learned.

TOTAL QUALITY HUMAN RESOURCE PERFORMANCE

Total quality HR approaches to enhancing individual performance are designed to enable persons "from the inside out (i.e., tapping personal intrinsic motivation) and "from the outside in (i.e., providing an externally supportive work environment) to become highly motivated performers. To accomplish this consistently in a work organization requires a model that correlates individual motivation and performance, uniformly understood and applied in all HR contexts. A useful integrative model of motivation and performance that can be applied to HR total quality efforts is provided in Figure 5.8.

Motivation can be defined as *the pattern of factors that initiate, direct, and sustain human behavior over time.*[40] The model in Figure 5.8 is sequential and progressive and integrates both content theories of motivation (*what* motivates behavior) and process theories of motivation (*how* events and outcomes interact to motivate behavior). The four outcomes (desire to perform, effort, performance, and satisfaction), shown as rectangles, normally occur sequentially, and increased work satisfaction (the last outcome) normally leads to renewed desire to perform (the first outcome). HR total quality practitioners who want to enhance and sustain individual performance can, therefore, use this model to understand what and how to motivate total quality individual performance. The model contains six components in five steps and is used to explain four outcomes.

The six components, represented by circles in the model, include *valence, instrumentality, expectancy, ability, accuracy of role perceptions,* and *equity of rewards.* **Valence** *is the preference that a person has for a particular outcome.* If two

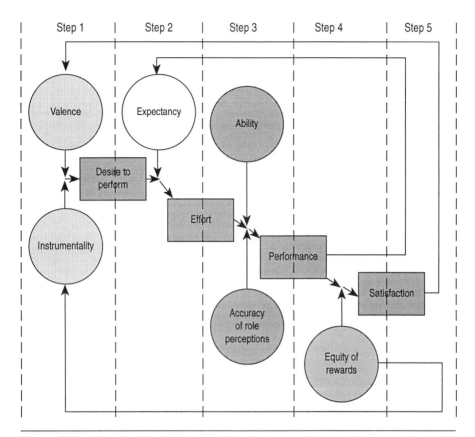

Figure 5.8 Model of Motivation and Performance. (Source: Wagner, John A. III and Hollenbeck, John R. (1992). *The Management of Organizational Behavior.* Englewood Cliffs, N.J.: Prentice-Hall, p. 204.)

outcomes are to be expected, a person may prefer a specific outcome (a positive valence), prefer *not* to attain that outcome (negative valence), or have no preference between the two possible outcomes (zero valence). A variety of need theories, including Maslow's need hierarchy, Alderfer's ERG theory, Murray's theory of manifest needs, and/or McClelland's theory of achievement motivation, explain intrinsic preferences of individuals and why they differ among people.[41] Alderfer's ERG theory, for example, proposes that people are internally motivated by the urge to fulfill three basic human needs: existence needs (physiological and safety needs), relatedness needs (belongingness and social esteem needs), and growth needs (self-esteem and self-actualization needs). Alderfer agreed with Maslow that need importance progresses up the hierarchy one step at a time. However, Alderfer maintained, and research has supported the claim, that individuals frustrated by failed attempts to satisfy some higher level growth needs will often regress to satisfying lower level relatedness and existence needs, thereby reducing their superior performance.[42] For HR total quality practitioners, this provides the challenge to assess and channel the strong intrinsic motivation of growth needs toward enhanced learning and performance for the organization. Enabling personal performance "from the inside" means acknowledging and endorsing growth needs, and enabling personal performance "from the outside" means removing barriers to growth need fulfillment that risk individual regression to lower performance standards.

Instrumentality *is the subjective belief that a person has about the relationship between performing an act and receiving an outcome.* A variety of learning theories, including Watson's classical conditioning, Skinner's reinforcement, and/or Bandura's social-learning, explain what people believe will lead to the attainment of desired outcomes.[43] Bandura's social-learning theory, for example, suggests that behavior to achieve desired outcomes is driven by the desire of an observer to model the behavior of persons deemed worthwhile, even to the extent of self-reinforcement of behavior in line with the learning role model.[44] For HR total quality practitioners, this provides the challenge to identify, develop, and broadcast role model behaviors and enable persons to reinforce their own emulation of role model behavior. To facilitate a total quality environment, HR practitioners must seek, find, and support their role models in both traditional and nontraditional places—not only within the ranks of formal management, but among employees at the front lines of operations as well. Internalization of total quality performance standards and self-reinforcement of those quality standards is exactly what constitutes the justification for worker self-control and self-inspection. In addition to self-reinforcement, reinforcement theory demonstrates the importance of environmentally shaping performance behavior by rewarding successive approximations of the behavior.[45] For total quality HR practitioners, developing the ethical work culture to the level of the House of Total Quality provides an organizational environment, in the form of an ethics development system, which shapes and supports OCB. Assessing and developing the ethical work culture becomes an expanded responsibility of HR total quality practitioners.[46]

Expectancy *is the set of beliefs regarding the link between making an effort and actually performing well.*[47] Whereas knowledge about valences and instrumentalities indicates what an individual *wants* to do, knowledge of expectancies indicates what an individual will *try* to do. Bandura's self-efficacy theory, for example, explains how expectancies are formed and can be changed.[48] People high in self-efficacy feel they can master, or have mastered, some specific task and feel empowered to exert the effort to take on new responsibilities. For

HR total quality practitioners, the importance of promulgating transformational leadership styles that build confidence and empowerment skills in employees is paramount to help employees develop the level of self-efficacy required to improve processes and continually innovate.[49]

Ability *is the set of physical, psychomotor, cognitive, social, affective, and moral capabilities an individual brings to bear on a situation.* People can only perform what they are capable of, although their abilities can be increased. Kanfer and Ackerman's interaction theory and Hunter's cognitive ability theory, for example, indicate that people high in cognitive ability learn more quickly and are able to attend to multiple responsibilities at any one time.[50] People high in demonstrated OCB dispositions are more capable and more likely to engage in cooperative, team performance behavior at work.[51] For total quality HR practitioners, therefore, selection criteria that include high cognitive ability, moral integrity, and OCB standards are more likely to result in a capable, cooperative work force.

Role perceptions *are people's beliefs about what they are supposed to be accomplishing on the job and how.*[52] Role perceptions are accurate when people facing a task know what needs to be done, how much needs to be done, and who will have the responsibility and authority to do it. Locke's goal-setting theory, Waldman's work performance theory, and Davenport's process innovation theory, for example, demonstrate that clear, unambiguous goals, goal commitment, hierarchy level, increased autonomy, and process change empowerment all enhance individual performance.[53] For total quality HR practitioners, clarifying the new responsibilities and authority of empowered employees is a major communication challenge that affects all the traditional HR processes: selection, performance, appraisal, reward, and development. Persuading middle managers to share power and line employees to assume more responsibility, or having all stakeholders held accountable for the quality of outputs, are major changes in role perceptions from the traditional organization. This is no less an employee role shift than viewing the employer as a partner rather than as a parent.

Equity *is a perceived standard whereby individuals and/or groups ought to receive outcomes (rewards) consistent with the quantity and quality of the results they produce.* The equity theories of Adams, Greenberg and McCarty, and Sheppard et al., for example, point toward the need for equity balance to ensure work satisfaction (i.e., the relationship between my inputs and outcomes matches).[54] The ratio relationship between a key reference person's inputs and outcomes should approximate one's own ratio relationship, in order to promote satisfaction.[55] If these ratios are not equal, the reward structure is perceived as unfair. In the face of perceived inequity of rewards, employees may alter their inputs (reduce performance contributions), alter their outputs (demand a raise or threaten to strike), distort the facts (rationalize or delude themselves about the reality of the inequity), change the behavior of the reference person (socially ostracize the superior or highest paid performer), and/or engage in sabotage (break equipment).[56] On the other hand, when people experience persistent justice at work through equitable rewards, several positive outcomes ensue: (1) persistent equitable pay improves performance, work satisfaction, and group morale; (2) persistent equitable pay enhances interpersonal trust, organizational loyalty, and OCB; and (3) persistent equitable pay lessens the likelihood of retaliation for occasional inadvertent injustice in the workplace.[57] For total quality HR practitioners, therefore, developing the ethical work culture to ensure outcome, procedural, and systemic justice in all reward decisions is crucial to achieving work satisfaction and organizational commitment. If the total quality HR practitioner wants to build a high-performance community at work, he or she must ensure organizational justice.

The five steps of the model in Figure 5.8 also show the key places where components combine to influence outcomes. The four outcomes, shown as rectangles, are *desire to perform, effort, performance,* and *satisfaction.* The first, **desire to perform**, is a function of valences and instrumentalities. A person's desire to perform well will be high when valences are associated with high performance. The second outcome, **effort**, is a function of desire to perform and expectancy. Effort will be forthcoming only when individuals want to perform well and when they believe they can do so. The third outcome, **performance**, is a function of effort, accurate role perceptions, and ability. Performance will be high only when individuals with the requisite abilities and knowledge of desired goals and strategies put forth their best effort. The model also shows how **satisfaction**, the fourth outcome, is a product of past performance and the perceived equity of rewards received for performing well. The dynamic nature of the motivation process is revealed in the way present levels of satisfaction, perceived equity of rewards, and performance affect future levels of valence, instrumentality, and expectancy.

A brief example may illustrate how this motivational model systematically applies to a HR total quality context. Imagine a compensation specialist who has been given the opportunity to design the compensation system for a new total quality company. She heads up a small team of people who have been given responsibility to complete the project within a specified time frame. She may feel that her efforts to lead the team are highly likely to have a major impact on the compensation design quality (high *instrumentality*). In addition, she also highly values the satisfaction and rewards that she anticipates receiving when the project is completed (high *valence*). This creates a high *desire to perform*, and, coupled with a high *expectancy* of success, she puts in a great deal of *effort* on the project, spending many hours interacting with and supporting her team members. Knowing that she has the *ability* to lead the team with success, together with *accurate role perception* of her autonomy and authority, she exhibits sustained *effort,* and the *performance* outcome is outstanding! The compensation design team leader completes her project on time, under budget, and with many features that will *delight the customer* due to innovative design quality. The feedback loop from *performance* to *expectancy* ensures that during the next project she will feel even more confident that she can meet future challenges. She and the team receive the anticipated *equitable reward*—a bonus, public recognition, and heartfelt appreciation from top management—and she reaps the *satisfaction* that she anticipated. With dynamic feedback loops to *instrumentality* of efforts, *valence* (anticipated satisfaction), and *expectancy,* there will be positive reinforcement to escalate motivational strength for future projects. This reinforced motivation to succeed empowers individuals and builds a high-performance work community. Of course, unsatisfactory combinations of components or violated psychological contracts for equitable reciprocity between employer and employee could have produced negative outcomes anywhere along the chain, adversely impacting both current and future individual performance.

TOTAL QUALITY HUMAN RESOURCE PERFORMANCE PLANNING

Total quality HR performance planning entails a balanced adaptation to external changes in employment relationships and adherence to internal commitments already made to employees. HR practitioners who want to enhance individual performance and build high-performance work communities must consciously address and honor the changing nature of the psychological contract between employee and employer.

The **psychological contract** *is the set of a beliefs regarding the terms and conditions of a reciprocal exchange agreement between a person and another party.*[58] Psychological contracts are conceptually distinct from both formal and implied contracts. Formal contracts are written agreements and are thus easy to identify; implied contracts are unwritten agreements that arise from repeated interactions between two parties. Psychological contracts, on the other hand, refer to an individual's *perception and understanding* of the reciprocal promises made between two parties.[59] In the context of the total quality employment relationship, each party has a unique psychological contract or a set of perceptions regarding the shared obligations between employee and employer.[60] The perceptual and personal nature of psychological contracts is their defining attribute, which makes them distinct from formal, implicit, and implied contracts.[61] Although psychological contracts are not written and formalized, they can impact performance and be as powerful as their legal counterparts.[62]

Empirical evidence supports the existence and significance of the psychological contract in employment relationships.[63] While maintained psychological contracts serve a variety of functions, they can also intensify psychological attachment to the organization.[64] They reduce uncertainty and increase predictability[65] by establishing the terms of the exchange and by specifying the appropriate behaviors and roles of each party to the contract.[66] Finally, because they foster confidence that the outcomes of the contractual relationship will be equitable, psychological contracts direct and motivate total quality performance toward fulfilling the terms of the agreement in return for equitable remuneration.[67]

Psychological contracts develop through communications at critical total quality HR junctures.[68] One juncture is the selection process, where employees and employers make implicit and explicit promises to fulfill certain reciprocal obligations to one another. By the time an employee accepts a job offer, he or she has established a psychological contract with that organization.[69]

Over the course of the employment relationship, parties engage in reciprocal exchanges in accordance with each party's psychological contract. Each party may vary in the degree to which it fulfills the terms of the contract.[70] A party may fully comply with the contract, go beyond the terms of the contract and honor the spirit rather than the letter of the contract, or violate or breach some of the terms of the agreement. Maintenance of the employment relationship requires that each party engage in actions that fulfill or exceed the obligations it has promised the other. Fulfillment of the psychological contract may be a standard or referent against which an employee judges the employment relationship;[71] total quality employees attempt to fulfill their part of the contract and look to the organization to fulfill its contractual obligations. Over time, as parties contribute to the relationship and engage in reciprocal exchange in accordance with the contract, mutual trust and loyalty between the two parties grows,[72] lending stability and predictability to the employment relationship.[73] Although fulfillment of the psychological contract enhances or maintains the employment relationship, violation of the contract can damage or destroy it.[74]

Psychological contract violation *refers to one party's perception that the other party has failed to comply with some of the terms of their contract.*[75] Like psychological contracts themselves, psychological contract violation is perceptual in nature. Psychological contract violation may produce unique and intense attitudinal, behavioral, and emotional reactions for the parties involved.[76] These reactions emanate from two sources. First, the violated party experiences a form of injustice that comes from a violation of the "balance principle," whereby one judges the fairness of an action by comparing it against other similar actions in similar situations.[77] When the employer violates the employee's psychological contract, the employee perceives that he or she has fulfilled his or her side of the bargain but the employer has failed to fulfill its side of the deal. The employee experiences reactions similar to those which follow unmet expectations or perceptions of inequity.

Second, the violated party experiences a form of injustice that comes from a violation of the "correctness standard," whereby one judges an action on the basis of consistency, accuracy, and compatibility with morals and values.[78] The violated employee receives treatment that is inconsistent with standards of law, good faith dealing, contracts, and general standards of right and wrong expected of the ethical work culture at the level of the House of Total Quality. Psychological contracts involve elements of trust, a sense of relationship, and a belief in the existence of a promise of future benefits. An employee paid less than market rates might feel inequitably treated, but one who was promised a raise for hard work and fails to get it after working hard is likely to feel wronged and betrayed. When promises and considerations have been exchanged in the context of a relationship, violation goes far beyond the sense of inequity or unmet expectations of specific rewards or benefits. It also includes more general beliefs about respect for people, codes of conduct, and other patterns of behavior associated with relationships involving trust.[79]

Violations of the psychological contract in today's workplace have become more the norm than the exception.[80] Contemporary employment relationships are in transition. As cost reduction trends in the form of restructuring, downsizing, and rightsizing respond to global competition, organizations are economically pressured to make rapid changes, accommodations to unforeseen circumstances, and HR outsourcing decisions.[81] These organizational changes often alter the employee–employer relationship. Thus, it is becoming increasingly necessary for organizations to manage, renegotiate, and, in some cases, violate the previous employment agreements they have established with their employees.[82] As Robinson and Rousseau found in 1994, 55% of employees believed their employment contract had been broken by their employer in the previous two years.[83] HR practitioners are often the individuals who operationalize these cost reduction policies, and to do so without voicing the adverse HR impact or proposing appropriate alternatives to help the company compete for the future is to abdicate a key responsibility of a total quality HR professional.

Psychological contract violations have been shown to have at least three adverse effects: *lowered trust, reduced individual performance,* and *reduced OCB.*[84] First, **trust** *is an expectancy held by an individual or a group that the word, promise, or verbal or written statement of another individual or group can be relied upon.*[85] Trust underlies every psychological contract. For a psychological contract to exist, there must at least be a belief that contributions will be reciprocated and that the actions of one party are bound to those of the other. Trust is often tied to past exchange, developing from repeated cycles of reciprocity.[86] In the context of the employment relationship, the longer the employee and employer engage in repeated exchange over time, the more each party believes that such actions will continue in the future. Hence, the more the parties trust each other.[87] The exchange process can also lower one's trust in another. When one party fails to fulfill promised obligations, the other party may lower the trust it places in the reneging party. Trust is measured and accumulated in the absence of violation, and once trust is lost as a result of contract violation, it is not easily restored.[88]

Trust is central to long-term total quality organizational success.[89] It influences organizational members' attitudes and feelings about their organizations and their jobs[90] as well as their willingness to cooperate.[91] Katz identified several distinct forms of employee contributions: performing prescribed roles as part of one's job, engaging in innovative and spontaneous behaviors which are not specified by job requirements but which facilitate organizational effectiveness, and joining and remaining in the organization. While all of these contributions are important to the organization as a whole, psychological contract violation undermines each of these types of employee contributions.[92]

Second, violation of the psychological contract usually decreases employees' regular role performance. When the violation occurs, employees perceive inequity in that they believe that they have fulfilled their side of the employment role agreement while their employer has not. Employees perceiving inequity are motivated to restore the balance of contributions and inducements in the employment relationship and usually do so by reducing their subsequent performance. Psychological contract violation also influences performance through a decline in trust. Once trust is lost through a perceived violation in the contract, the violated party may question whether future contributions to the relationship will be reciprocated.[93] In other words, violation may decrease employees' expectations that their extra effort and performance will lead to desired outcomes. This in turn reduces employees' motivation to perform.

Third, total quality organizations could not survive unless employees were willing to engage in OCB, the extra-role employee behavior that promotes organizational effectiveness.[94] Violation of the psychological contract will directly reduce OCB. When violation occurs, employees will experience inequity because although they have fulfilled their promised obligations to the organization, their employer has not reciprocated. Equity is a necessary condition for OCB.[95] Research studies have found strong relationships between OCB and perceptions of justice.[96] Just as employees seek to restore inequity by reducing their level of intra-role job performance, employees also seek to restore inequity by reducing their extra-role behavior (OCB). Psychological contract violation also impacts OCB by diminishing trust. OCB is dependent, in part, on subordinates' trust in their supervisors.[97] When followers trust and respect their leader, they are motivated to do more than they are expected to do.[98] Generalizing this proposition to organizations, employees who respect and trust their employer will be more likely to engage in citizenship behaviors. Psychological contract violation destroys trust and, with it, motivation for OCB.

Violation also impacts employees' intentions to remain with their employer. Employees hold global beliefs about the extent to which the organization values and cares about their well-being.[99] These beliefs are based on how employees feel they are treated by the organization. When employees believe their employer has reneged on an employment agreement, they will perceive that their employer is unconcerned about their well-being and does not value their contributions. When this happens, employees may not form or may lose their affective attachment to, or identification with, the organization. These employees will be more inclined to leave the employment relationship.

In order to maintain self-respect and protect themselves from disrespectful treatment in today's workplace, many employees have adopted a careerist mindset and a cynical attitude.[100] Careerists perceive their current employer as an instrumental stepping-stone up the interorganizational career ladder and are likely to adopt a more "transactional" (rather than "transformational") employment relationship with their employer.[101] This relationship is not intended to be long term, and what is exchanged has a short-term focus—the immediate rewards of pay, training, and credentials to obtain a better job in another organization. However, as job mobility decreases due to oversupply of domestic and foreign labor, frustration leads to cynical attitudes, which in time may lead to high levels of organizational cynicism (correlated with ethical work culture stage 2—Machiavellianism).[102]

Psychological contract violations have a different impact upon employees whose career motives differ. Careerists, who place less value on the current employment relationship itself, experience less loss from psychological contract violation than do those low on careerism. In contrast, those low on the careerist scale have a more "relational" orientation.[103] Individual career planning and community commitment, therefore, are important dimensions of total quality HR performance assessment planning. Balancing the intrinsic value of the work community with the instrumental value of career mobility is an important responsibility for the total quality HR professional.

Given the real costs associated with psychological contract violation, total quality HR practitioners need to identify potential antecedents of perceived violation. Perceived psychological contract violation can emanate from two sources.[104] First, a violation may arise from a discrepancy between the two parties' perceptions of what was originally promised as part of the employment agreement. The parties may disagree about *whether* a particular promise was made, or they may disagree about *what* was promised. Thus, for example, the employer may inadvertently violate the employee's psychological contract because the employer is trying to fulfill an agreement that is different from that of the employee. Second, a violation may occur because of intentional or unintentional reneging on the part of the employer or employee. Total quality HR professionals need to proactively clarify, monitor, and strategically intervene, if necessary, to maintain a psychological contract that meets both individual and organizational needs.

In addition, total quality HR practitioners must adjust 1980s quality programs in the wake of 1990s downsizing to ensure that balanced, sustainable employment relationships can endure tough times.[105] In some instances, this means that individuals need to assume more responsibility for their own future employability (e.g., personal learning programs, professional networking, and gaining broad project experience). However, even careerists must receive clear indications of desirable total quality performance standards from total quality HR practitioners (i.e., even those who are "moving on" should perform up to quality standards). In other instances, total quality HR practitioners must take steps strategically and tactically to ensure that if the company expects OCB from individuals operating at the ethical level of the House of Total Quality, top management and company policies also demonstrate a reciprocal commitment to a more holistic concern for the total quality employee. Procter & Gamble's Work/Life Plan, which supports employees who must manage family caretaking responsibilities along with high work performance standards, is a good case in point. Too often, companies raise individual performance standards to the ethical work culture level of the House of Total Quality and then develop company policies that treat people with disrespect at the level of the House of Manipulation. If companies want to equip themselves with a committed, versatile, creative, continually learning, sustainable work community that repeatedly generates high performance, they must act to attract, deserve, and keep that high-performance work force.[106] One such way is to plan and implement alternative total quality approaches to downsizing in tough times that respect both individual and organizational needs in line with today's total quality psychological contract. Alternative total quality approaches to downsizing based on time required for implementation and percentage payroll (or headcount) reduction needed for global competitive effectiveness are depicted in Table 5.2.

While facilitating the transition of employees who will be laid off as a result of a corporate downsizing, the total quality HR professional must not forget the organizational change survivors. Downsizing survivors normally

Table 5.2 Alternative Total Quality Approaches to Downsizing Based on Time Required for Implementation and Percentage Payroll Reduction Needed

% reduction	Less than 1 year	1–3 years	3 years
15%+	• Deep, across-the-board terminations based on performance records	• Spin off business units; series of early retirement or buy-out records	• Close down business unit and redeploy/retrain employees at lower wages
6–14%	• Widespread early retirement or buy-out program	• Mobilizing the troops; selective terminations; retrain, redeploy	• Managed attrition; spin off staff departments
	• Bring subcontracted work back in-house; pay reduction, job sharing, move to lower paying jobs when possible	• Retrain; transition services provided to find jobs outside the company; loan staff	• Retrain and redeploy
1–5%	• Selective terminations based on performance records	• Managed attrition; convert staff to consultants	• Managed attrition (and carefully selected options already cited)
	• Targeted early retirement or buy-out program	• Market staff services outside the company	
	• Retrain and redeploy at lower wages		

Source: Tomasko, Robert M. (1990). *Downsizing: Reshaping the Corporation for the Future.* New York: AMACOM, p. 200. Modified by the authors.

experience a range of feelings, including fear, frustration, guilt, and unfairness.[107] The outcome is that most downsized U.S. organizations are trying to compete globally with risk-averse, relatively unproductive, and anxious employees.

To counter this situation, total quality HR practitioners need to develop the intervention skills that will heal the wounds of the survivors and revitalize their performance commitment.[108] This means that HR professionals need to be able to facilitate emotional release (i.e., acknowledge the legitimacy of grieving); they must be able to break organizational co-dependency habits and assist employees in assuming responsibility for adjusting to change. The glue that should bond the total quality learning community is the commitment to do good work that adds value to clients and customers (i.e., discharge personal mission). In a total quality environment, personal mission is much more aligned with service (e.g., meeting or exceeding customers' real needs) than with self-protection (e.g., keeping one's job).[109]

Total quality HR practitioners who actively support *all* employees in a downsizing effort by attending to their needs for emotional healing, retraining, and redeployment demonstrate commitment to total quality principles at the level of the House of Total Quality. They are preparing for quantum quality.[110]

TOTAL QUALITY HUMAN RESOURCE PERFORMANCE MANAGEMENT

Quantum quality *is a term used to describe achieving breakthroughs in customer delight through increased personal motivation and commitment to quality.*[111] Employees come to define quality not only through lack of statistical process variation but also in moral–emotional terms, such as pride in craftsmanship and satisfaction in delighting customers. The four dimensions of quantum quality that require total quality HR practitioner attention, support, and respect include *learning, integrity, creativity,* and *sustainability.*[112]

First, respecting individual self-managed **learning** contributes to performance improvement and creates the learning community so necessary for collective adaptation to changing survival pressures.[113] As recently as the 1960s, almost one-half of all workers in the industrialized countries were involved in making (or helping to make) things. In 1991, for the first time ever, companies spent more money on computing and communications gear than the combined monies spent on industrial, mining, farm, and construction equipment. Already an estimated two-thirds of U.S. employees work in the service sector, where knowledge is the most important "product." By the year 2000, however, no developed country will have more than one-sixth or one-eighth of its work force in the traditional roles of making and moving goods.[114] The Industrial Age has given way to the Information Age. This calls for learning different kinds of work, preparing different kinds of workers, and ultimately building different kinds of organizations (i.e., continually improving organizations that support workers who engage in self-managed learning activities and design meaningful work to satisfy multiple customers).[115]

As work, workers, and organizations change, HR practitioners will be asked to take on new roles. HR practitioners have often functioned as trainers who were working against time to ensure that the work force had the requisite skills. They are not being asked to drop this challenge, but they are being asked, in addition, to help the work force face an unknown future that is changing at unbelievable rates in an unpredictable fashion. HR practitioners increasingly recognize that people learn all the time on the job but that this learning is not necessarily sound or shared. HR practitioners can extend their impact in almost exponential fashion by working with all employees to make *self-managed learning* more effective and by creating ways for people *to share what they learn*. At the same time, they can work with managers to create and sustain the level of ethical work culture that supports continuous learning in the House of Total Quality. They can help build the infrastructure of a learning system by, for instance, *ensuring that individuals have budgets for self-managed learning* and that the organization has policies that *reward knowledge acquisition and the teaching of others*.

Second, respecting personal and organizational **integrity** requires that total quality HR practitioners institutionalize ethical work culture policies and practices that help individuals become better persons (i.e., reinforcing OCB, rewarding continual self and process improvement, and designing work so that employees feel that they are not only putting in time but also leaving a legacy of positive work contributions for future generations). It means managing human resources as if personal standards of integrity (e.g., honest, trustworthy, respectful, and sincere human interactions) are important and those standards also apply to organizational ethical integrity.[116] Quantum quality means that the workplace is a place where persons and organizations develop and improve their moral characters; people become ennobled rather than exploited and organizations become energized instead of extinct. Managing for integrity entails assessing and developing the ethical work culture to identify moral lapses and supportively encourage renewed commitment to quality work performance.

Third, respecting personal **creativity** means not only providing ample resources for R&D innovations but insisting that individual employees creatively analyze their daily work to eliminate irrationality, waste, and inconsistency.[117] A model of daily work queries to continually stimulate the creative imagination of workers with regard to goals and means in order to continually improve daily work processes is provided in Figure 5.9. Total quality HR practitioners train both for current work competence and future work improvement; commitment to creatively developing mastery at work becomes a total quality employee obligation.[118]

Fourth, respecting **sustainability** means considering the personal stage of readiness of employees to absorb and sustain new work changes. If total quality employers want long-term high performance to be sustained, they

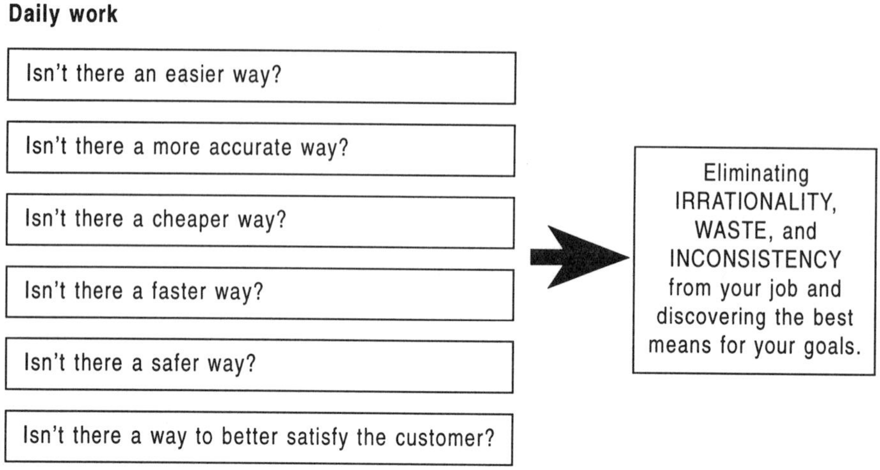

Daily work

Isn't there an easier way?

Isn't there a more accurate way?

Isn't there a cheaper way?

Isn't there a faster way?

Isn't there a safer way?

Isn't there a way to better satisfy the customer?

Eliminating IRRATIONALITY, WASTE, and INCONSISTENCY from your job and discovering the best means for your goals.

Figure 5.9 Daily Work Queries for Personal Performance Improvement.

cannot treat their employees as inert, recalcitrant commodities to be replaced if any proposed work changes are resisted. Introducing total quality work performance changes in a way that respects the personal stages of readiness to creatively absorb new work changes builds a sustainable work community. A model of the personal stages and expressions of work performance change concerns is provided in Table 5.3. HR interventions that manage work changes by addressing appropriate personal concerns of workers are more likely to secure endorsement of work changes and build a sustainable work community. This means that a routine total quality HR practice should be to survey employee attitudes toward current and future work changes and avoid forced change on workers, which ignores their concerns.

Building a sustainable work community is one of the most important tasks facing workers and leaders today.[119] Empowered workers in a productive work unit recognize when they have lost that sense of community and quickly expend the necessary effort to rapidly regain it.[120] Within the supportive environment of the sustainable work community, people can learn as much from their failures as their successes, and they will come to respect the needs of other communities. Great companies respect their customers and employees at all levels. "Out of showing respect for others, an organization itself becomes respected. It rises in stature as a role model, and makes a positive impact on the world."[121]

Table 5.3 Building Community By Respecting Personal Stages and
Expressions of Total Quality Work Performance Change Concerns

Personal change	Stages of total quality performance concern	Typical personal expressions of change concern
6	Refocusing	I endorse total quality and have some ideas about how to improve and sustain total quality performance.
5	Collaboration	I accept the value of total quality performance expectations, but am concerned about how to relate them to what other managers and co-workers are doing.
4	Consequences	I am concerned about the effects total quality performance expectations will have on my employees.
3	Management	I am concerned about the amount of time I spend doing paperwork and attending meetings.
2	Personal impact	I am concerned about how extensively total quality performance expectations will affect me.
1	Information	I would like to know more about substantive aspects of the total quality performance expectations without making any commitment.
0	Awareness	I am not aware of, nor do I want to be bothered with, any work changes brought about by total quality performance expectations.

Source: Mink, Oscar G., Esterhuysen, Pieter W., Mink, Barbara P, and Owen, Kevin Q. (1993). *Change at Work.* San Francisco: Jossey-Bass, p. 119. Modified by the authors.

REVIEW QUESTIONS

5.1. Identify five characteristics of people who respect themselves and others and their five parallel implications in a total quality work culture.

5.2. Define work performance and elaborate on the four categories of factors that influence it.

5.3. Elaborate on personal leadership style and the individual empowerment cycle.

5.4. Elaborate in detail on the four performance management tools that facilitate and document personal performance improvement.

5.5. Elaborate in detail on the model of individual motivation and performance as it applies to total quality management of human resources.

5.6. Define psychological contract, elaborate on the three adverse effects of psychological contract violation, and describe the alternative total quality approaches to downsizing.

5.7. Define quantum quality and elaborate on its four dimensions as they impact human resource practitioners in a total quality environment.

DISCUSSION QUESTIONS

5.1. Discuss seven steps you would take as a total quality manager of human resources to enhance the individual self-respect of employees and employee respect for others.

5.2. Discuss the respective roles of personal autonomy, respect preferences, and individual empowerment cycles on work performances.

5.3. Use two of the personal performance management tools for one week to analyze your work (study) habits, and discuss the results with your instructor/trainer and a significant other.

5.4. Discuss the theories and roles of intrinsic motivation and equity of rewards in relation to their impacts on work performance and work satisfaction.

5.5. Discuss the role of the total quality human resource practitioner in managing the terms of the total quality psychological contract so that both individual and organizational needs are respected.

5.6. Describe the extent to which you have experienced quantum quality at work. In what four ways would regular implementation of the four dimensions of quantum quality improve work performance?

ENDNOTES

1. Roberts, Harry V. and Sergesketter, Bernard F. (1993). *Quality Is Personal: A Foundation for Total Quality Management.* New York: Free Press, pp. 1–27; Schultz, Louis (1991). *Personal Management: A System for Individual Performance Improvement.* Minneapolis: Process Management International, pp. 2–7.

2. Voehl, Frank W. (1992). *Total Quality: Principles and Processes within Organizations.* Coral Springs, Fla.: Strategy Associates, p. 5.

3. Roberts, Harry V. and Sergesketter, Bernard F. (1993). *Quality Is Personal: A Foundation for Total Quality Management.* New York: Free Press, pp. 15–16.

4. The authors have selected concepts in column one of Table 5.1 from the following works and have created the rest of the material in the figure: Brockner, J. (1988). *Self-Esteem at Work.* Lexington, Mass.: Lexington Books, p. 144; Weiss, H.M., and Knight, P.A. (1980). "The Utility of Humility: Self-Esteem, Information Search, and Problem Solving Efficiency." *Organizational Behavior and Human Performance.* Vol. 25, No. 3, pp. 216–223; Martin, Mike (1995). *Everyday Morality: An Introduction to Applied Ethics.* Belmont, Calif.: Wadsworth, pp. 99–112

5. Fernandez, John (1991). *Managing a Diverse Workforce.* New York: Free Press, pp. 15–90; Fernandez, J. and Barr, M. (1993). *The Diversity Advantage.* Lexington, Mass.: Heath and Company, pp. 10–70; Simons, G.F., Vazquez, C., and Harris, P.R. (1993). *Transcultural Leadership: Empowering the Diverse Workforce.* Houston: Gulf, pp. 6–49.

6. Sheaffer, Robert (1988). *Resentment against Achievement: Understanding the Assault upon Ability.* Buffalo, N.Y.: Prometheus Books, pp. 138–173; Murphy, Kevin R. (1993). *Honesty in the Workplace.* Belmont, Calif.: Brooks/Cole Publishing, pp. 1–30.

7. Campbell, J.P. (1990). "Modeling the Performance Prediction Problem in Industrial and Organizational Psychology." In M.D. Dunnette and L.M. Hough, Eds. *Handbook of Industrial and Organizational Psychology.* 2nd edition, Vol. 1, Palo Alto, Calif.: Consulting Psychologists' Press, pp. 687–732.

8. Bushe, G.R. (1988). "Cultural Contradictions of Statistical Process Control in American Manufacturing Organizations." *Journal of Management.* Vol. 14, No. 1, pp. 19–31; Wagner, J.A. III (1995). "Studies of Individualism–Collectivism: Effects on Cooperation in Groups." *Academy of Management Journal.* Vol. 38, No. 1, pp. 152–172.

9. Moorman, R.H. and Blakely, G.L. (1993). *Individualism–Collectivism as an Individual Difference Predictor of Organizational Citizenship Behavior.* Paper presented at the Annual Meeting of the Academy of Management, Atlanta; Van Dyne, L., Graham, J.W., and Dienesch, R.M. (1994). "Organizational Citizenship Behavior: Construct Redefinition, Measurement and Validation." *Academy of Management Journal.* Vol. 37, No. 4, pp. 765–802.

10. Scholtes, P.R. (1988). *The Team Handbook: How to Use Teams to Improve Quality.* Madison, Wisc.: Joiner Associates; Sashkin, M. and Kiser, K.L. (1993). *Total Quality Management.* San Francisco: Berett-Koehler, pp. 15–20.

11. Waldman, David A. (1994). "The Contributions of Total Quality Management to a Theory of Work Performance." *Academy of Management Review.* Vol. 19, No. 3, p. 516; Dobbins, G.H., Cardy, R.L., and Carson, K.P. (1991). "Examining Fundamental Assumptions: A Contrast of Person and Sys-

tem Approaches to Human Resource Management." *Research in Personnel and Human Resource Management.*" Vol. 3, pp. 1–38; Dobbins, G.H., Cardy, R.L., and Carson, K.P. (1993). "Total Quality Management and Work Characteristics: Behavior and Personality Measures." Paper presented at the Annual Meeting of the Academy of Management, Atlanta. This portion of the chapter relies heavily on Waldman's work.

12. Dobbins, G.H., Cardy, R.L., and Carson, K.P. (1991). "Examining Fundamental Assumptions: A Contrast of Person and System Approaches to Human Resource Management." *Research in Personnel and Human Resource Management.*" Vol. 3, p. 11.

13. Deming, W.E. (1986). *Out of the Crisis.* Cambridge, Mass.: Massachusetts Institute of Technology, pp. 95–105; Juran, J.M. (1989). *Juran on Leadership for Quality: An Executive Handbook.* Wilson, Conn.: Juran Institute, pp. 55–60.

14. Campbell, J.P. (1990). "Modeling the Performance Prediction Problem in Industrial and Organizational Psychology." In M.D. Dunnette and L.M. Hough, Eds. *Handbook of Industrial and Organizational Psychology.* 2nd ed., Vol. 1, Palo Alto, Calif.: Consulting Psychologists' Press, pp. 701–703; Blumberg, M. and Pringle, C.C. (1982). "The Missing Opportunity in Organizational Research: Some Implications for a Theory of Work Performance." *Academy of Management Review.* Vol. 7, No. 4, pp. 560–569.

15. Fossum, J.A., Arvey, R.D., Paradise, C.A., and Robbins, N.E. (1986). "Modeling the Skills Obsolescence Process: A Psychological/Economic Integration." *Academy of Management Review.* Vol. 11, No. 2, pp. 362–374; Williams, E.S. and Bunker, D.R. (1993). "Sorting Outcomes: A Revision of the JCM." Paper presented at the Annual Meeting of the Academy of Management, Atlanta; Waldman, David A. (1994). "The Contributions of Total Quality Management to a Theory of Work Performance." *Academy of Management Review.* Vol. 19, No. 3, pp. 519–523; Conger, J.A. and Kanungo, R.N. (1988). "The Empowerment Process: Integrating Theory and Practice." *Academy of Management Review.* Vol. 13, No. 3, pp. 471–482.

16. Hambrick, D.C. and Finkelstein, S. (1987). "Managerial Discretion: A Bridge Between Polar Views of Organizational Outcomes." *Research in Organizational Behavior.* Vol. 9, No. 4, pp. 369–406; Hambrick, D.C. and Mason, P.A. (1984). "Upper Echelons: The Organization as a Reflection of Its Top Managers." *Academy of Management Review.* Vol. 9, No. 3, pp. 193–206; Ashforth, B.E. (1990). "The Organizationally Induced Helplessness Syndrome: A Preliminary Model." *Canadian Journal of Administrative Science.* Vol. 7, No. 2, pp. 30–36.

17. Hambrick, D.C. and Finkelstein, S. (1987). "Managerial Discretion: A Bridge Between Polar Views of Organizational Outcomes." *Research in Organizational Behavior.* Vol. 9, No. 4, pp. 401–403.

18. Ashforth, B.E. (1989). "The Experience of Powerlessness in Organizations." *Organizational Behavior and Human Decision Processes.* Vol. 43, pp. 207–242; Ashforth, B.E. (1990). "The Organizationally Induced Helpless-

ness Syndrome: A Preliminary Model." *Canadian Journal of Administrative Science.* Vol. 7, No. 2, pp. 30–36.

19. Adler, P.S. (1993). "Time-and-Motion Regained." *Harvard Business Review.* Vol. 71, No. 1, pp. 97–108.

20. Waldman, David A. (1994). "The Contributions of Total Quality Management to a Theory of Work Performance." *Academy of Management Review.* Vol. 19, No. 3, p. 529.

21. Steel, R.P. and Mento, A.S. (1986). "Impact of Situational Constraints on Subjective and Objective Criteria of Managerial Job Performance." *Organizational Behavior and Human Decision Processes.* Vol. 37, No. 3, pp. 254–265; Bowen, D.E., Ledford, G.E., and Nathan, B.R. (1991). "Hiring for the Organization, Not the Job." *Academy of Management Executive.* Vol. 5, No. 4, pp. 40–42; Sashkin, M. and Kiser, K.J. (1993). *Total Quality Management.* San Francisco: Berett-Koehler, pp. 140–150; Chatman, J.A. (1989). "Improving Interactional Organizational Research: A Model of Person–Organization Fit." *Academy of Management Review.* Vol. 14, pp. 333–349.

22. Thomas, K.W. and Velthouse, B.A. (1990). "Cognitive Elements of Empowerment: An Interpretive Model of Intrinsic Task Motivation." *Academy of Management Review.* Vol. 15, No. 4, pp. 666–681; McWhirter, E.H. (1991). "Empowerment in Counseling." *Journal of Counseling and Development.* Vol. 69, No. 2, pp. 222–227.

23. Greenberger, D.B. and Strasser, S. (1986). "Development and Application of a Model of Personal Control in Organizations." *Academy of Management Review.* Vol. 11, No. 4, p. 165.

24. Greenberger, D.B., Strasser, S., Cummings, L.L., and Dunham, R.B. (1989). "The Impact of Personal Control on Performance and Satisfaction." *Organizational Behavior and Human Decision Processes.* Vol. 43, No. 2, pp. 29–51.

25. Hackman, J.R. and Oldham, G.R. (1976). "Motivation through the Design of Work: Test of a Theory." *Organizational Behavior and Human Performance.* Vol. 16, No. 3, pp. 250–279.

26. Bandura, A. (1977). "Self-Efficacy: Toward a Unifying Theory of Behavior Change." *Psychological Review.* Vol. 84, No. 1, pp. 191–215.

27. Herzberg, F., Mausner, B., and Snyderman, B.B. (1959). *The Motivation to Work.* 2nd edition, New York: John Wiley & Sons; Thomas, K.W. and Velthouse, B.A. (1990). "Cognitive Elements of Empowerment: An Interpretive Model of Intrinsic Task Motivation." *Academy of Management Review.* Vol. 15, No. 4, pp. 666–681.

28. Greenberger, D.B. and Strasser, S. (1991). "The Role of Situational and Dispositional Factors in the Enhancement of Personal Control in Organizations." *Research in Organizational Behavior.* Vol. 13, No. 2, pp. 111–145; Hackman, J.R. and Oldham, G.R. (1976). "Motivation through the Design of Work: Test of a Theory." *Organizational Behavior and Human Performance.* Vol. 16, No. 3, pp. 250–279; Bandura, A. (1977). "Self-Efficacy: Toward a Unifying Theory of Behavior Change." *Psychological Review.* Vol. 84, No. 1, pp. 191–215; Herzberg, F., Mausner, B., and Snyderman,

B.B. (1959). *The Motivation to Work.* 2nd edition, New York: John Wiley & Sons, pp. 42–60.

29. Eisenberger, R., Fasolo, P., and Davis-LaMastro, V. (1990). "Perceived Organizational Support and Employee Diligence, Commitment, and Innovation." *Journal of Applied Psychology.* Vol. 75, No. 5, pp. 51–59; Mathieu, J.E. and Zajac, D.M. (1990). "A Review and Meta-Analysis of the Antecedents, Correlates, and Consequences of Organizational Commitment." *Psychological Bulletin.* Vol. 108, No. 2, pp. 171–194; Meyer, J.P. and Allen, N.J. (1991). "A Three-Component Conceptualization of Organizational Commitment." *Human Resource Management Review.* Vol. 1, No. 1, pp. 61–69; Mowday, R.T., Porter, L.W., and Steers, R.M. (1982). *Employee–Organization Linkages: The Psychology of Commitment, Absenteeism, and Turnover.* New York: Academic Press, pp. 15–46; Conner, D.R. and Patterson, R. (1981). *Building Commitment to Organizational Change.* Atlanta: OD Resources, pp. 20–65.

30. Beck, John D. and Yeager, Neil M. (1994). *The Leader's Window.* New York: John Wiley & Sons, pp. 30–32.

31. Haas, Howard (1992). *The Leader Within: An Empowering Path of Self-Discovery.* New York: Harper Collins, pp. 55–70; Manz, Charles P., Muto, Maria, and Sims, Henry P. Jr. (1990). "Super Leadership Creates New Perspectives for Managers." *Journal for Quality and Participation.* Vol. 7, No. 3, pp. 12–15; Manz, Charles P. and Sims, Henry P. Jr. (1989). *Superleadership: Leading Others to Lead Themselves.* New York: Simon and Shuster, pp. 5–50.

32. Bennis, Warren and Goldsmith, Joan (1994). *Learning to Lead: A Workbook on Becoming a Leader.* Reading, Mass.: Addison-Wesley, pp. 7–8.

33. Beck, John D. and Yeager, Neil M. (1994). *The Leader's Window.* New York: John Wiley & Sons, p. 234.

34. Cameron, Kim (1994). "An Empirical Investigation of Quality Cultures, Practices and Outcomes." Paper presented at the Annual Meeting of the Academy of Management, Dallas.

35. Cameron, Kim (1994). "An Empirical Investigation of Quality Cultures, Practices and Outcomes." Paper presented at the Annual Meeting of the Academy of Management, Dallas, p. 5.

36. Schultz, Louis (1991). *Personal Management: A System for Individual Performance Improvement.* Minneapolis: Process Management International, pp. 8–22; Roberts, Harry V. and Sergesketter, Bernard F. (1993). *Quality Is Personal: A Foundation for Total Quality Management.* New York: Free Press, pp. 15–44.

37. Schultz, Louis (1991). *Personal Management: A System for Individual Performance Improvement.* Minneapolis: Process Management International, p. 18.

38. Schultz, Louis (1991). *Personal Management: A System for Individual Performance Improvement.* Minneapolis: Process Management International, p. 19.

39. Schultz, Louis (1991). *Personal Management: A System for Individual Performance Improvement.* Minneapolis: Process Management International, p. 20.
40. Wagner, John A. III and Hollenbeck, John R. (1992). *The Management of Organizational Behavior.* Englewood Cliffs, N.J.: Prentice-Hall, p. 200. This subsection of the chapter relies heavily upon material from this text.
41. Maslow, A. (1970). *Motivation and Personality.* 2nd edition, New York: Harper and Row; Alderfer, C.P. (1972). *Existence, Relatedness and Growth: Human Needs in Organizational Settings.* New York: Free Press; Murray, H.A. (1938). *Explorations in Personality.* New York: Oxford University Press; McClelland, D.C. (1963). *The Achieving Society.* Princeton, N.J.: Van Nostrand.
42. Wanous, J.P. and Zwang, A. (1977). "A Cross-Sectional Test of Need Hierarchy Theory." *Organizational Behavior and Human Performance.* Vol 18, No. 3, pp. 78–97.
43. Watson, J.B. and Raynor, R. (1920). "Conditioned Emotional Reactions." *Journal of Experimental Psychology.* Vol 20, No. 1, pp. 1–14; Skinner, B.F. (1971). *Beyond Freedom and Dignity.* New York: Blantaze; Bandura, A. and Walters, R.H. (1963). *Social Learning and Personality Development.* New York: Holt, Rinehart and Winston.
44. Bandura, A. (1976). "Self-Reinforcement: Theoretical and Methodological Considerations." *Behaviorism.* Vol. 4, No. 3, pp. 135–155.
45. Wagner, John A. III and Hollenbeck, John R. (1992). *The Management of Organizational Behavior.* Englewood Cliffs, N.J.: Prentice-Hall, p. 214.
46. Petrick, Joseph A. and Pullins, Ellen B. (1992). "Organizational Ethics Development and the Expanding Role of the Human Resource Professional." *The Healthcare Supervisor.* Vol. 2, No. 2, pp. 52–61.
47. Vroom, V.H. (1964). *Work and Motivation.* New York: John Wiley, pp. 55–71; Porter, L.W. and Lawler, E.E. (1968). *Managerial Attitudes and Performance.* Homewood, Ill.: Irwin, pp. 107–139.
48. Bandura, A. (1982). "Self-Efficacy Mechanism in Human Behavior." *American Psychologist.* Vol. 37, No. 7, pp. 122–147.
49. Waldman, D.A. (1993). "A Theoretical Consideration of Leadership and Total Quality Management." *Leadership Quarterly.* Vol. 4, No. 2, pp. 65–79.
50. Kanfer, R. and Ackerman, P.L. (1989). "Motivation and Cognitive Abilities: An Integrative/Aptitude Treatment Interaction Approach to Skill Acquisition." *Journal of Applied Psychology.* Vol. 74, No. 3, pp. 657–690; Hunter, J.E. (1986). "Cognitive Ability, Cognitive Attitudes, Job Knowledge, and Job Performance." *Journal of Vocational Behavior.* Vol. 29, No. 3, pp. 340–362.
51. Van Dyne, L., Graham, J.W., and Dienesch, R.M. (1994). "Organizational Citizenship Behavior: Construct Redefinition, Measurement and Validation." *Academy of Management Journal.* Vol. 37, No. 4, pp. 770–774.
52. Wagner, John A. III and Hollenbeck, John R. (1992). *The Management of Organizational Behavior.* Englewood Cliffs, N.J.: Prentice-Hall, p. 219.

53. Locke, E.A. (1968). "Toward a Theory of Task Motivation and Incentives." *Organizational Behavior and Human Performance.* Vol. 3, No. 3, pp. 140–147; Waldman, David A. (1994). "The Contributions of Total Quality Management to a Theory of Work Performance." *Academy of Management Review.* Vol. 19, No. 3, pp. 510–516; Davenport, T. (1993). *Process Innovation.* Boston: Harvard University Press, pp. 48–59.

54. Greenberg, J. (1982). "Approaching Equity and Avoiding Inequity in Groups and Organizations." In J. Greenberg and R.L. Cohen, Eds. *Equity and Justice in Social Behavior.* New York: Academic Press, pp. 389–435; Solomon, Robert C. (1990). *A Passion For Justice.* Reading, Mass.: Addison-Wesley, pp. 54–62, 102–241.

55. Adams, J.S. (1963). "Toward an Understanding of Inequity." *Journal of Abnormal and Social Psychology.* Vol. 67, No. 5, pp. 422–436; Greenberg, J. and McCarty, C.L. (1990). "Comparable Work: A Matter of Justice." In G. Ferris and K. Rowland, Eds. *Research in Personnel and Human Resource Management.* Vol. 8. Greenwich, Conn.: JAI Press, pp. 265–301; Sheppard, B.H., Lewicki, R., and Minton, John W. (1992). *Organizational Justice.* New York: Lexington Books, pp. 9–43, Solomon, Robert C. (1990). *A Passion For Justice.* Reading, Mass.: Addison-Wesley, pp. 242–298.

56. Sheppard, B.H., Lewicki, R., and Minton, John W. (1992). *Organizational Justice.* New York: Lexington Books, pp. 67–102.

57. Sheppard, B.H., Lewicki, R., and Minton, John W. (1992). *Organizational Justice.* New York: Lexington Books, pp. 102–103; Folger, R. and Konovsky, M.A. (1989). "Effects of Procedural and Distributive Justice on Reactions to Pay Raise Decisions." *Academy of Management Journal.* Vol. 32, No. 4, pp. 115–130; Solomon, Robert C. (1990). *A Passion For Justice.* Reading, Mass.: Addison-Wesley, pp. 102–152.

58. Schein, E.H., (1980). *Organizational Psychology.* Englewood Cliffs, N.J.: Prentice-Hall, pp. 19–29; Rousseau, D. and McLean Parks, J. (1993). "The Contracts of Individuals and Organizations." In L.L. Cummings and B.M. Staw, Eds. *Research in Organizational Behavior.* Vol. 15, Greenwich, Conn.: JAI Press, pp. 1–47; Solomon, Robert C. (1990). *A Passion For Justice.* Reading, Mass.: Addison-Wesley, pp. 149–152. According to Solomon, and the authors concur, any psychological or social contracts originate from and are founded upon a shared sense of justice and caring.

59. Rousseau, D. (1989). "Psychological and Implied Contracts in Organizations." *Employee Responsibilities and Rights Journal.* Vol. 2, No. 1, pp. 121–139.

60. Rousseau, D. (1989). "Psychological and Implied Contracts in Organizations." *Employee Responsibilities and Rights Journal.* Vol. 2, No. 1, pp. 132–134.

61. Rousseau, D. (1990). "New Hire Perceptions of Their Own and Their Employers' Obligations: A Study of Psychological Contracts." *Journal of Organizational Behavior.* Vol. 11, No. 4, pp. 389–400.

62. Schein, E.H., (1980). *Organizational Psychology.* Englewood Cliffs, N.J.:

Prentice-Hall, pp. 115–121; Dunahee, M. and Wangler, L., (1974). "The Psychological Contract: A Conceptual Structure of Management/Employee Relations." *Personnel Journal.* Vol. 10, No. 3, pp. 518–548.

63. Robinson, S., Kraatz, M., and Rousseau, D. (1994). "Changing Obligations and the Psychological Contract: A Longitudinal Study." *Academy of Management Journal.* Vol. 37, No. 5, pp. 137–152; Robinson, S. and Rousseau, D. (1994). "Violating the Psychological Contract: Not the Exception but the Norm." *Journal of Organizational Behavior.* Vol 15, No. 6, pp. 245–259.

64. Rousseau, D. (1989). "Psychological and Implied Contracts in Organizations." *Employee Responsibilities and Rights Journal.* Vol. 2, No. 1, pp. 136–138; Argyris, C. (1960). *Understanding Organizational Behavior.* Homewood, Ill.: Dorsey, pp. 82–87.

65. Rousseau, D. and McLean Parks, J. (1993). "The Contracts of Individuals and Organizations." In L.L. Cummings and B.M. Staw, Eds. *Research in Organizational Behavior.* Vol. 15, Greenwich, Conn.: JAI Press, pp. 25–28.

66. McLean Parks, J.M. (1992). "The Role of Incomplete Contracts and Their Governance in Delinquency, In-Role, and Extra-Role Behaviors." Presented at the Society for Industrial and Organizational Psychology Meeting, Montreal.

67. Ouchi, W. (1980). "Markets, Bureaucracies, and Clans." *Administrative Science Quarterly.* Vol. 25, pp. 129–141; Sheppard, B.H., Lewicki, R., and Minton, John W. (1992). *Organizational Justice.* New York: Lexington Books, pp. 98–101.

68. Rousseau, D. and McLean Parks, J. (1993). "The Contracts of Individuals and Organizations." In L.L. Cummings and B.M. Staw, Eds. *Research in Organizational Behavior.* Vol. 15, Greenwich, Conn.: JAI Press, pp. 16–18.

69. Dunahee, M. and Wangler, L., (1974). "The Psychological Contract: A Conceptual Structure of Management/Employee Relations." *Personnel Journal.* Vol. 10, No. 3, pp. 518–548; Robinson, S., Kraatz, M., and Rousseau, D. (1994). "Changing Obligations and the Psychological Contract: A Longitudinal Study." *Academy of Management Journal.* Vol. 37, No. 5, pp. 137–152.

70. McLean Parks, J.M. (1992). "The Role of Incomplete Contracts and Their Governance in Delinquency, In-Role, and Extra-Role Behaviors." Presented at the Society for Industrial and Organizational Psychology Meeting, Montreal, pp. 7–9.

71. Shore, L.M. and Tetrick, L.E. (1994). "The Psychological Contract as an Explanatory Framework in the Employment Relationship." In C.L. Cooper and D.M. Rousseau, Eds. *Trends in Organizational Behavior.* Vol. 1, New York: John Wiley & Sons, pp. 91–109.

72. Argyris, C. (1960). *Understanding Organizational Behavior.* Homewood, Ill.: Dorsey; Levinson, H. (1962). *Men, Management and Mental Health.* Cambridge, Mass.: Harvard University Press, pp. 52–59; Rousseau, D. (1989). "Psychological and Implied Contracts in Organizations." *Employee Responsibilities and Rights Journal.* Vol. 2, No. 1, pp. 14–19.

73. Rousseau, D. and McLean Parks, J. (1993). "The Contracts of Individuals and Organizations." In L.L. Cummings and B.M. Staw, Eds. *Research in Organizational Behavior*. Vol. 15, Greenwich, Conn.: JAI Press, pp. 29–34.

74. Robinson, S. and Rousseau, D. (1994). "Violating the Psychological Contract: Not the Exception but the Norm." *Journal of Organizational Behavior*. Vol 15, No. 6, pp. 146–148; Rousseau, D. (1989). "Psychological and Implied Contracts in Organizations." *Employee Responsibilities and Rights Journal*. Vol. 2, No. 1, pp. 130–131.

75. Rousseau, D. (1989). "Psychological and Implied Contracts in Organizations." *Employee Responsibilities and Rights Journal*. Vol. 2, No. 1, pp. 132–136.

76. Rousseau, D. (1989). "Psychological and Implied Contracts in Organizations." *Employee Responsibilities and Rights Journal*. Vol. 2, No. 1, p. 134; Rousseau, D. and McLean Parks, J. (1993). "The Contracts of Individuals and Organizations." In L.L. Cummings and B.M. Staw, Eds. *Research in Organizational Behavior*. Vol. 15, Greenwich, Conn.: JAI Press, pp. 11–15.

77. Sheppard, B.H., Lewicki, R., and Minton, John W. (1992). *Organizational Justice*. New York: Lexington Books, pp. 9–22.

78. Sheppard, B.H., Lewicki, R., and Minton, John W. (1992). *Organizational Justice*. New York: Lexington Books, pp. 23–44.

79. Rousseau, D. (1989). "Psychological and Implied Contracts in Organizations." *Employee Responsibilities and Rights Journal*. Vol. 2, No. 1, p. 137.

80. Robinson, S. and Rousseau, D. (1994). "Violating the Psychological Contract: Not the Exception but the Norm." *Journal of Organizational Behavior*. Vol 15, No. 6, pp. 245–248.

81. Quinn, James Brian (1992). *Intelligent Enterprise*. New York: Free Press, pp. 71–100.

82. Hirsch, P. (1991). "Undoing the Managerial Revolution? Needed Research on the Decline of Middle Management and Internal Labor Markets." Working Paper No. 72. Evanston, Ill.: Northwestern University; Tichy, N. (1983). *Managing Strategic Change*. New York: Wiley, pp. 60–69.

83. Robinson, S. and Rousseau, D. (1994). "Violating the Psychological Contract: Not the Exception but the Norm." *Journal of Organizational Behavior*. Vol 15, No. 6, pp. 252–255.

84. Zucker, L. (1986). "Production of Trust: Institutional Sources of Economic Structure, 1840–1920." In L.L. Cummings and B.M. Staw, Eds. *Research in Organizational Behavior*. Vol. 8, Greenwich, Conn.: JAI Press, pp. 53–111; Rousseau, D. (1989). "Psychological and Implied Contracts in Organizations." *Employee Responsibilities and Rights Journal*. Vol. 2, No. 1, pp. 134–138; Moorman, R.H. (1991). "The Relationship between Organizational Justice and Organizational Citizenship Behaviors: Do Fairness Perceptions Influence Employee Citizenship?" *Journal of Applied Psychology*. Vol. 76, No. 4, pp. 845–855.

85. Rotter, J.B. (1967). "A New Scale for the Measurement of Interpersonal Trust." *Journal of Personality*. Vol 35, No. 7, p. 651.

86. Haas, D. (1981). "Trust and Symbolic Knowledge." *Social Psychology Quarterly*. Vol. 44, No. 3, pp. 3–13; Osgood, C. (1966). *Perspective of Foreign Policy*. Palo Alto, Calif.: Pacific Books; Zand, D.E. (1972). "Trust and Managerial Problem Solving." *Administrative Science Quarterly*. Vol. 17, No. 6, pp. 229–239; Zucker, L. (1986). "Production of Trust: Institutional Sources of Economic Structure, 1840–1920." In L.L. Cummings and B.M. Staw, Eds. *Research in Organizational Behavior*. Vol. 8. Greenwich, Conn.: JAI Press, pp. 87–92.

87. Axelrod, R. (1984). *The Evolution of Cooperation*. New York: Basic Books, pp. 10–25; Gulate, Ranjay (1995). "Does Familiarity Breed Trust? The Implications of Repeated Ties for Contractual Choice in Alliances." *Academy of Management Journal*. Vol. 38, No. 1, pp. 85–112.

88. McLean Parks, J.M. (1992). "The Role of Incomplete Contracts and Their Governance in Delinquency, In-Role, and Extra-Role Behaviors." Presented at the Society for Industrial and Organizational Psychology Meeting, Montreal, pp. 4–6.

89. Kegan, D.L. (1971). "Organizational Adaptation: Description, Issues and Some Research Results." *Academy of Management Journal*. Vol. 14, No. 2, pp. 453–464.

90. Driscoll, J.W. (1978). "Trust and Participation in Organizational Decision Making as Predictors of Satisfaction." *Academy of Management Journal*. Vol. 21, No. 4, pp. 44–56.

91. Deutsch, M. (1973). *The Resolution of Conflict*. New Haven, Conn.: Yale University Press, pp. 44–64; McAllister, D.J. (1995). "Affect- and Cognition-Based Trust as Foundations for Interpersonal Cooperation in Organizations." *Academy of Management Journal*. Vol. 38, No. 1, pp. 24–59.

92. Katz, D. (1964). "The Motivational Basis of Organizational Behavior." *Behavioral Science*. Vol. 9, No. 3, pp. 131–146.

93. Rousseau, D. (1989). "Psychological and Implied Contracts in Organizations." *Employee Responsibilities and Rights Journal*. Vol. 2, No. 1, pp. 124–125.

94. Van Dyne, L., Graham, J.W., and Dienesch, R.M. (1994). "Organizational Citizenship Behavior: Construct Redefinition, Measurement and Validation." *Academy of Management Journal*. Vol. 37, No. 4, pp. 771–783.

95. Organ, D.W. (1990). "The Motivational Basis of Organizational Behavior." In L.L. Cummings and B.M. Staw, Eds. *Research in Organizational Behavior*. Vol 12, Greenwich, Conn.: JAI Press, pp. 43–72.

96. Moorman, R.H. (1991). "The Relationship between Organizational Justice and Organizational Citizenship Behaviors: Do Fairness Perceptions Influence Employee Citizenship?" *Journal of Applied Psychology*. Vol. 76, No. 4, pp. 849–852; Organ, D.W. and Konovsky, M. (1989). "Cognitive versus Affective Determinants of Organizational Behavior." *Journal of Applied Psychology*. Vol. 74, No. 4, pp. 157–164.

97. Bateman, T.S. and Organ, D.W. (1983). "Job Satisfaction and the Good Soldier: The Relationship between Affect and Employee Citizenship."

Academy of Management Journal. Vol. 26, No. 5, pp. 587–595; Yukl, Gary A. (1994). *Leadership in Organizations.* 3rd ed., Englewood Cliffs, N.J.: Prentice-Hall, pp. 359–373.

98. Yukl, Gary A. (1994). *Leadership in Organizations.* 3rd ed., Englewood Cliffs, N.J.: Prentice-Hall, pp. 354–360; Yukl, G.A. (1989). "Managerial Leadership: A Review of Theory and Research." *Yearly Review of Management.* Vol. 15, No. 7, pp. 251–289.

99. Eisenberger, R., Huntington, R., Hutchison, S., and Sowa, D. (1986). "Perceived Organizational Support." *Journal of Applied Psychology.* Vol. 71, No. 3, pp. 500–507.

100. Rousseau, D. (1990). "New Hire Perceptions of Their Own and Their Employer's Obligations: A Study of Psychological Contracts." *Journal of Organizational Behavior.* Vol. 11, No. 4, pp. 389–400.

101. Dean, James W. Jr. and Goodman, Paul S. (1994). "Toward a Theory of Total Quality Integration." Paper presented at the Annual Meeting of the Academy of Management, Dallas, pp. 16–17.

102. Bennett, Amanda (1990). *The Death of the Organizational Man.* New York: William Morrow, pp. 252–257; Whitney, John O. (1994). *The Trust Factor: Liberating Profits and Restoring Corporate Vitality.* New York: McGraw-Hill, pp. 15–30.

103. Robinson, S. and Rousseau, D. (1994). "Violating the Psychological Contract: Not the Exception but the Norm." *Journal of Organizational Behavior.* Vol 15, No. 6, p. 249.

104. Robinson, S.L. (1994). "The Impact of Psychological Contract Violation on Employment Relationships." Paper presented at the Annual Meeting of the Academy of Management, Dallas, p. 22.

105. Niven, Daniel (1993). "When Times Get Tough, What Happens to TQM?" *Harvard Business Review.* Vol. 27, No. 3, pp. 20–23.

106. Petrick, Joseph A. and Quinn, John F. (1995). *Management Ethics and Organization Integrity.* Thousand Oaks, Calif.: Sage, pp. 25–36.

107. Noer, D.M. (1993). *Healing the Wounds: Overcoming the Trauma of Lay-offs and Revitalizing Downsized Organizations.* San Francisco: Jossey-Bass, pp. 59–66.

108. Noer, D.M. (1993). *Healing the Wounds: Overcoming the Trauma of Lay-offs and Revitalizing Downsized Organizations.* San Francisco: Jossey-Bass, pp. 8–12.

109. Noer, D.M. (1993). *Healing the Wounds: Overcoming the Trauma of Lay-offs and Revitalizing Downsized Organizations.* San Francisco: Jossey-Bass, pp. 96–104; Drath, W.H. and Palus, C.J. (1994). *Leadership as Meaning Making in Communities of Practice.* Greensboro, N.C.: Center for Creative Leadership, pp. 25–40.

110. Miller, William C. (1994). "Quantum Quality: The Innovative Resolution." *Quality Digest.* Vol. 3, No. 4, pp. 53–57.

111. Miller, William C. (1994). "Quantum Quality: The Innovative Resolution." *Quality Digest.* Vol. 3, No. 4, p. 56.

112. Miller, William C. (1994). "Quantum Quality: The Innovative Resolution." *Quality Digest.* Vol. 3, No. 4, p. 57.

113. Senge, Peter M. (1990). *The Fifth Discipline: The Art and Practice of the Learning Organization.* New York: Doubleday, pp. 139–173; Watkins, Karen E. and Marsick, Victoria J. (1993). *Sculpting the Learning Organization.* San Francisco: Jossey-Bass, pp. 3–23; Howard, Robert, Ed. (1993). *The Learning Imperative: Managing People for Continuous Innovation.* Boston: Harvard Business School, pp. 41–57.

114. Pritchett, Price (1994). *The Employee Handbook of New Work Habits for a Radically Changing World.* Dallas: Pritchett, pp. 1–5.

115. Watkins, Karen E. and Marsick, Victoria J. (1993). *Sculpting the Learning Organization.* San Francisco: Jossey-Bass, pp. 262–278.

116. Petrick, Joseph A. and Quinn, John F. (1995). *Management Ethics and Organization Integrity.* Thousand Oaks, Calif.: Sage, pp. 10–17; Paine, Lynn S. (1994). "Managing for Organizational Integrity." *Harvard Business Review.* Vol. 28, No. 3, pp. 106–113.

117. Roberts, Harry V. and Sergesketter, Bernard F. (1993). *Quality Is Personal: A Foundation for Total Quality Management.* New York: Free Press, pp. 5–19.

118. Senge, Peter M. (1990). *The Fifth Discipline: The Art and Practice of the Learning Organization.* New York: Doubleday, pp. 150–173; Stewart, Thomas A. (1994). "Your Company's Most Valuable Asset: Intellectual Capital." *Fortune.* Vol. 130, No. 7, pp. 68–74.

119. Conger, Jay A. (1992). *Learning to Lead: The Art of Transforming Managers into Leaders.* San Francisco: Jossey-Bass, pp. 15–61.

120. Senge, Peter M. (1990). *The Fifth Discipline: The Art and Practice of the Learning Organization.* New York: Doubleday, pp. 233–270; Daly, Markate, Ed. (1994). *Communitarianism: A New Public Ethics.* Belmont, Calif.: Wadsworth, pp. 3–345; Etzioni, Amitai (1993). *The Spirit of Community.* New York: Simon and Schuster, pp. 1–207; Etzioni, Amitai (1988). *The Moral Dimension: Toward a New Economics.* New York: Free Press, pp. 10–95; Glendon, Mary Ann (1991). *Rights Talk: The Impoverishment of Political Discourse.* New York: Free Press, pp. 5–85.

121. Collins, James and Lazier, William (1992). *Beyond Entrepreneurship.* Englewood Cliffs, N.J.: Prentice-Hall, p. 55.

EXERCISES

PRACTITIONER ASSESSMENT INSTRUMENT 5A: PERSONALITY DIVERSITY PROFILE

DIRECTIONS

This questionnaire consists of 26 statements. There are no right or wrong answers. The best answers are your true opinions. For each statement, indicate which of the three alternatives, *a*, *b*, or *c*, is most true or most important to you by circling *a*, *b*, or *c* in the MOST column. Then choose the least true or least important of the three alternatives and circle its letter in the LEAST column. For every statement, be sure you circle one alternative in each column. If *a* is circled under MOST, then either *b* or *c* should be circled under LEAST. Do not skip any questions and do not debate too long over any one statement. Your first reaction is desired.

	MOST	LEAST
	1 2 3	4 5 6
1. When I enter new situations, I let my actions be guided by: a. my own sense of what I want to do. b. the direction of those who are responsible. c. discussion with others.	b c b	b c a
2. When faced with a decision, I consider: a. precedent and traditions. b. the opinions of those affected. c. my own judgment	a b c	a b c
3. People see me as: a. a team player. b. a free spirit. c. a dependable person.	c a b	c a b
4. I feel most satisfied when: a. I am working on personal goals. b. I do things according to standards. c. I contribute to a project.	b c a	b c a
5. I try to avoid: a. not being myself. b. disappointing those in authority. c. arguments with my friends.	b c a	b c a

	MOST			LEAST		
	1	2	3	4	5	6

6. In my opinion, people need:
      a. guidelines and rules for conduct.
      b. warm and supportive human relationships.
      c. freedom to grow.

   MOST: a b c   LEAST: a b c

7. Over time, I have learned:
      a. no person is an island.
      b. old paths are true paths.
      c. you only pass this way once.

   MOST: b a c   LEAST: b a c

8. I want to be treated:
      a. as a unique person.
      b. as an equal.
      c. with respect.

   MOST: c b a   LEAST: c b a

9. I avoid:
      a. not meeting my responsibilities.
      b. compromising my personality.
      c. the loss of good friends.

   MOST: a c b   LEAST: a c b

10. What the world needs is:
       a. more people who think independently.
       b. more understanding among diverse people.
       c. more people who respect and abide by the law.

    MOST: c b a   LEAST: c b a

11. I am most happy when:
       a. I am free to choose what I want to do.
       b. there are clear guidelines and rewards for
          performance.
       c. I share good times with others.

    MOST: b c a   LEAST: b c a

12. I am most responsible to _____ for my actions:
       a. family and friends.
       b. higher authorities.
       c. myself.

    MOST: b a c   LEAST: b a c

13. In order to be a financial success, one should:
       a. relax; money is not important.
       b. work in cooperation with others.
       c. work harder than others.

    MOST: c b a   LEAST: c b a

14. I believe:
       a. there is a time and place for everything.
       b. promises to friends are debts to keep.
       c. he who travels fastest travels alone.

    MOST: a b c   LEAST: a b c

15. I want the value of my work to be known:
       a. soon after completion.
       b. with the passage of time.
       c. while I am doing it.

    MOST: b a c   LEAST: b a c

	MOST			LEAST		
	1	2	3	4	5	6

16. A group member should support:
    a. the decisions of the majority.
    b. only those policies with which one personally agrees.
    c. those who are in charge.

MOST: c a b **LEAST:** c a b

17. I believe feelings and emotions:
    a. should be shared with discretion.
    b. should be shared openly.
    c. should be kept to oneself.

MOST: c b a **LEAST:** c b a

18. The people I enjoy working with are:
    a. free thinking.
    b. well organized.
    c. friendly.

MOST: b c a **LEAST:** b c a

19. I value:
    a. teamwork.
    b. independent thinking.
    c. order and organization.

MOST: c a b **LEAST:** c a b

20. I believe in the saying:
    a. all work and no play makes Jack a dull boy.
    b. united we stand, divided we fall.
    c. there are no gains without pains.

MOST: c b a **LEAST:** c b a

21. My work day goes best when I:
    a. have freedom of operation.
    b. know what is expected of me.
    c. experience fellowship with good colleagues.

MOST: b c a **LEAST:** b c a

22. If I suddenly received a large sum of money, I would:
    a. use most of it now for the things I want.
    b. invest most of it for the future.
    c. spend half of it now and save the rest.

MOST: b c a **LEAST:** b c a

23. I grow best by:
    a. following established truths.
    b. interacting with others.
    c. learning from personal experience.

MOST: a b c **LEAST:** a b c

24. It is important that I:
    a. plan a year or two ahead.
    b. live my life to the fullest now.
    c. think about life in a long-range way.

MOST: c a b **LEAST:** c a b

	MOST	LEAST
	1 2 3	4 5 6

25. I am known for: c b a | c b a
    a. making my own decisions.
    b. sharing with others.
    c. upholding traditional values.

26. I work best: a b c | a b c
    a. with structure and organization.
    b. as a member of a team.
    c. as an independent agent.

SCORING

Step 1: There are three columns of answers (1 to 3) under the "MOST" heading and three (4 to 6) under the "LEAST" heading. Add the total responses circled in column 1 for all questions. Do the same for columns 2 to 6. There should be a total of 26 answers in the "MOST" section and 26 answers in the "LEAST" section.

Step 2: Place the total number of responses from column 1 on the line marked "T" below in the MOST category, the total number of responses from column 2 on the line marked "P" below in the MOST category, and the total number of responses from column 3 on the line marked "I" below in the MOST category. Follow the same procedure for columns 4 to 6 in the LEAST category.

Step 3: Determine your final scores for T, P, and I by using the following formula: Score = 26 + MOST – LEAST. For example, if your T MOST was 20 and your T LEAST was 12, your T score would be 26 + 20 – 12 = 34. Complete the following:

$$\textbf{T Score} = 26 + \underline{\hspace{2cm}} - \underline{\hspace{2cm}} = \underline{\hspace{2cm}}$$
$$\text{T MOST} \qquad \text{T LEAST}$$

$$\textbf{P Score} = 26 + \underline{\hspace{2cm}} - \underline{\hspace{2cm}} = \underline{\hspace{2cm}}$$
$$\text{T MOST} \qquad \text{T LEAST}$$

$$\textbf{I Score} = 26 + \underline{\hspace{2cm}} - \underline{\hspace{2cm}} = \underline{\hspace{2cm}}$$
$$\text{T MOST} \qquad \text{T LEAST}$$

INTERPRETATION

The letters T, P, and I represent three different personality profiles: T = traditional, P = participative, and I = individualistic. If your highest score is T, you are *traditional*. If your highest score is P, you are *participative*. If your highest score is I, you are *individualistic*. If you are within one point of the same score for all three, you have built-in versatility for dealing with different types of people. If your two high scores are T and I, this means there are two opposite forces in your world pulling you in two different directions. One force is saying, "Be traditional," and the other is saying, "Be individualistic." Although this can present internal gridlock problems, it can also be good if it allows you to better understand others and reap the benefits of both styles in appropriate situations. Most people have characteristics of all three profiles, but tend to develop a preference for one or two over the other(s).

Traditional world cultures tend to be formal and structured, such as old England, Germany, and Hungary. Many non-Western cultures, including Japan, China, and India, are traditional in nature. Participative world cultures are melting-pot societies, such as the United States—20 % traditional, 60% participative, and 20% individualistic. Individualistic world cultures include the French, Italian, and Greek.

An interpretive comparison chart of personality diversity profiles is provided in Table 5A.1. Action implications of the table to enhance respect for people and build community at work are indicated following the table.

Table 5A.1   Personality Diversity Interpretation Grid

Behavior/value	Traditional	Participative	Individualist
Form of control	Rules, laws, and policies	Interpersonal commitments	What I think is right or needed
Basis of action	Direction from authorities	Discussion and agreement with others	Direction from within
Perception of responsibility	Superordinate powers	Colleagues and self	Self
Goals desired	Compliance	Consensus and smooth human relations	Individual freedom
Basis for growth	Following the established order	Human interaction	Introspection and personal experience
Position in relation to others	Member of hierarchy	Peer group member	Separate person
Material goods	Competition	Collaboration	Taken for granted
Identification and loyalty	Organization	Group	Individual
Time perspective	Future	Near future	Present

ACTION GUIDELINES FOR MANAGING DIFFERENT PERSONALITY TYPES

1. Action guidelines for managing traditionals effectively: Provide work rules and job descriptions with duties spelled out in priority order. Provide an organization chart showing reporting relationships; respect the chain of command. Respect traditions and established ways; appeal to historical precedent. Avoid changes when possible; if impossible, introduce changes slowly. Accentuate reason over emotion when handling problems. Mind your manners and language; be courteous. Establish a career plan with benchmarks for progress, rewards expected, and time frames. Provide tangible rewards for good performance, preferably money. Recognize good work with signs of status, such as diplomas, uniforms, medals, and titles. Reinforce company loyalty through service pins, award banquets, and personal appreciation. Communicate the mission, goals, and objectives of the organization, and provide an action plan. Keep work areas organized, clean, and safe. Finally, be clear and logical when giving orders.

2. Action guidelines for managing participatives effectively: Include participatives in the decision-making process; use participative management. Provide opportunity for off-the-job social interaction—company picnics, recreation programs, annual meetings. Emphasize employee teamwork on the job through task forces, committee projects, quality circles, and other group involvement activities. Have regular, well-run staff meetings; provide ample opportunity for sharing ideas. Ask for opinions, listen to what is said, and then demonstrate responsiveness. Get to know the person—family makeup, off-the-job interests, and personal goals. Appeal to both logic and feelings when dealing with problems; emphasize joint approach and talk with, not at, the person. Use communication vehicles such as bulletin boards, newsletters, telephone hotlines, and the open-door policy to exchange information. Allow people skills to shine in public relations, teaching, and mediation projects. Provide growth opportunities through in-service training and staff development programs. Finally, keep human relations smooth; consider personal feelings.

3. Action guidelines for managing individualists effectively: Recognize independence and personal freedom; don't supervise too closely. Provide immediate reward for good performance; don't delay gratification. Talk in terms of present; deemphasize past and future. Provide opportunity for personal growth through self-discovery. Keep things stimulating; keep things fun. Focus on meaningful personal experiences, satisfying interpersonal relationships, and important social causes. Provide individual job assignments and assign work by projects when possible. Accentuate feelings over logic when handling problems. Reward good performance with personal time off and personal fulfillment activities. Keep things casual; minimize formality. Avoid rigid controls; allow for questions and creativity. Finally, treat the individualist as a separate individual, not as a member of a group or organization.

Source: Manning, George, Curtis, Kent, and McMillan, Steve (1995). *The Human Side of Work: Building Community in the Workplace.* Cincinnati: South-Western Publishing, pp. 42–46.

PRACTITIONER ASSESSMENT INSTRUMENT 5B: INTERPERSONAL SELF-DISCLOSURE STYLE

DIRECTIONS

Below is a 5-point scale to be used in assessing yourself and other co-workers on interpersonal self-disclosure styles and the use of 24 behaviors important for respectful and trust-building human relations. Read each behavior and determine how much it is like yourself and the other person(s) you are rating. Select a numerical value from the scale and enter the number in the appropriate space to the right.

Scale value	Meaning
5	Extremely characteristic; always does this
4	Quite characteristic; usually does this
3	Somewhat characteristic; occasionally does this
2	Quite uncharacteristic; seldom does this
1	Extremely uncharacteristic; never does this

		HUMAN RELATIONS BEHAVIORS	Self	Co-worker(s)
(T)	1.	States opinions in an uncensored manner	_____	_____
(R)	2.	Invites ideas from others; does not dominate discussion	_____	_____
(T)	3.	Admits to confusion or lack of knowledge when uncertain	_____	_____
(R)	4.	Shows interest in what others have to say through body posture and facial expressions	_____	_____
(T)	5.	Expresses self openly and candidly	_____	_____
(R)	6.	Gives support to others who are struggling to express themselves	_____	_____
(T)	7.	Admits to being wrong, rather than attempting to cover up or place blame	_____	_____
(R)	8.	Keeps private conversations private; does not reveal confidences	_____	_____
(T)	9.	Tells others what they need to know, even if it is unpleasant	_____	_____
(R)	10.	Listens to others without being defensive	_____	_____
(T)	11.	Is honest with his or her feelings	_____	_____
(R)	12.	Shows respect for the feelings of others	_____	_____

HUMAN RELATIONS BEHAVIORS	Self	Co-worker(s)

(T) 13. Shares concerns, hopes, and goals with others _____ _____

(R) 14. Does not act as if others are wasting their time _____ _____

(T) 15. Shares thoughts, no matter how "far out" they may seem _____ _____

(R) 16. Does not fake attention or merely pretend to listen _____ _____

(T) 17. Speaks truthfully; refuses to lie _____ _____

(R) 18. Does not act hurt, angry, or mistreated when others disagree _____ _____

(T) 19. Is sincere; does not pretend _____ _____

(R) 20. Values suggestions from others _____ _____

(T) 21. Uses language and terms others can understand _____ _____

(R) 22. Tries to prevent interruptions, such as telephone calls and people walking in during important discussions _____ _____

(T) 23. Tells others when they are wrong or need to change _____ _____

(R) 24. Encourages others to express themselves _____ _____

SCORING

Step 1:   Total the scores you gave yourself for the odd-numbered questions (all questions with (T) in front of them). This total represents your evaluation of your willingness to express yourself. Record the score on the TRUST axis in Figure 5B.1. Next, total the scores you gave yourself for the even-numbered questions (all questions with (R) in front of them). This is your willingness to listen to others. Record this score on the RESPECT axis. Then find the point where the two scores intersect and shade in the enclosed area.

Step 2:   You are now ready to analyze the scores you gave your co-worker. Total the scores you gave your co-worker for all odd-numbered questions (all questions with (T) in front of them). Record this score on the TRUST axis in Figure 5B.2. Next, total the scores you gave your co-worker for the even-numbered questions (all questions with (R) in front of them). Record this score on the RESPECT axis. Then find the point where these two scores intersect and shade in the enclosed area.

Step 3:   Exchange evaluations with your co-worker.

Step 4:   Compare your self-evaluation and your co-worker's evaluation of you with the four interpersonal self-disclosure style types in Figure 5B.3. Which style do you think you are most like? Which does your co-worker think you are most like? Does your co-worker see you as you see yourself?

Step 5: Go back to the questionnaire and ask your co-worker what specific things you could do to raise your low scores. Also give recommendations to your co-worker to raise low scores.

Step 6: Discuss the importance of self-expression (showing trust) and listening (showing respect) as they relate to your work relationship.

GRAPHIC PROFILES

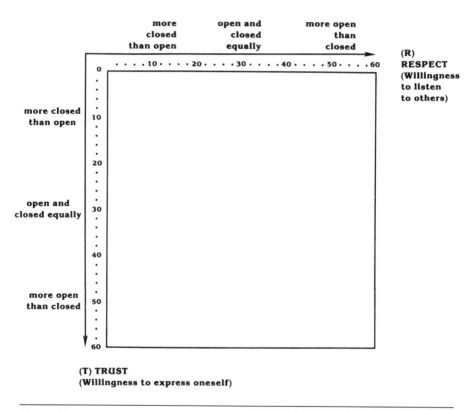

Figure 5B.1 Personal Profile.

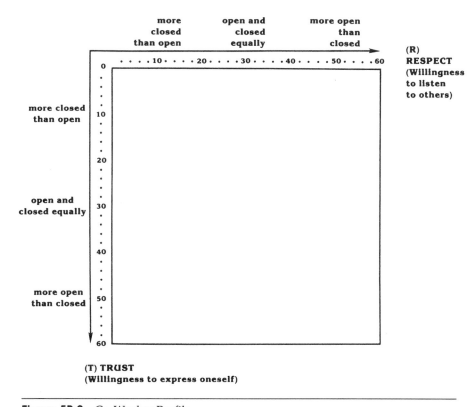

Figure 5B.2 Co-Worker Profile.

INTERPRETATION

The scores in this instrument are designed to produce four standard profiles: the Turtle profile, the Owl profile, the Bull-in-the-China-Shop profile, and the Picture Window profile. As indicated in Figure 5B.3, each category exhibits different degrees of respect and trust. These graphic profiles are translated into written descriptions in Table 5B.1. The four profiles differ in three important respects: (1) skills used in listening and expressing, (2) effects on the individual, and (3) effects on the relationship. The optimal interpersonal self-disclosure profile is the Picture Window because it enlarges the areas known to self and others, thereby allowing more of the performance potential of an individual to be recognized and invested in the organization.

Source: Luft, Joseph. (1970). *Group Process: An Introduction to Group Dynamics.* 2nd ed., Palo Alto, Calif.: National Press; Manning, G., Curtis, K., and McMillan, S. (1995). *The Human Side of Work: Building Community in the Workplace.* Cincinnati: South-Western Publishing, pp. 85-89.

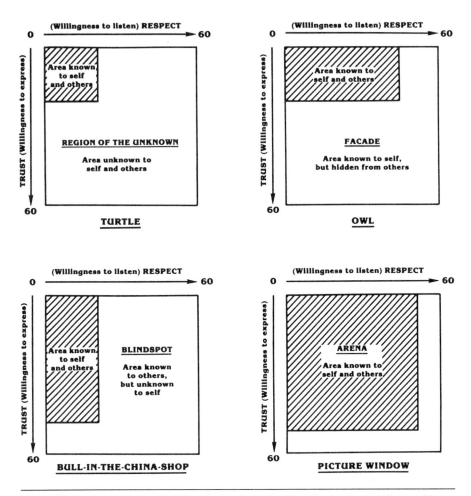

Figure 5B.3   Interpersonal Self-Disclosure Style Profiles: Turtle, Owl, Bull-in-a-China-Shop, and Picture Window.

Table 5B.1 Summary of Interpersonal Self-Disclosure Styles

	Turtle	Own	Bull-in-a China Shop	Picture Window
Features of the relationship	The "region of the unknown" dominates	The "facade" dominates	The "blind spot" dominates	The "arena" dominates
Skills used: Listening	Minimal	Often used	Rarely used	Often used
Expressing	Minimal	Rarely used	Often used	Often used
Effects on the individual	Distrust: overconcern with self-protection; detachment	Self-censure: relationships important but guarded; lack of spontaneity	Need to assert ego; unaware of impact on others and their responses	Trust and respect for others
Effects on the relationship	Misunderstanding; aversion to risk taking; untapped creativity; impersonal relationships; low satisfaction	Suspicion; avoidance of conflict; reduced problem solving	Resentment; reduced quality; lack of cooperation	Consensus out of confrontation; creative problem solving; emotional support; stimulating and satisfying relationships

PRACTITIONER ASSESSMENT INSTRUMENT 5C: ETHICAL WORK CULTURE ASSESSMENT

PURPOSE
The purpose of this self-assessment instrument is to determine the perceived level of moral development within the organization as a whole and the work unit in particular. Demographic variables may be added before or after the instrument to determine perceptual differences, for instance between individuals in managerial and nonmanagerial roles.

DIRECTIONS
Think about what it takes for you and people like yourself (e.g., your co-workers, people in similar positions) to "fit in" and meet expectations in your organization and in your particular work unit (e.g., department, team, or work group). Select the number correlated with each response option below that best describes the current interpersonal behavioral styles of your organization and work unit. Respond in terms of your perceptions of *"how things are now"* rather than *"how you would like them to be"* in both your organization and your work unit. Place the number that correlates with each option in the appropriate blank spaces below under the columns labeled "Organization" and "Work Unit:"

> 1 = Not at all
> 2 = To a slight extent
> 3 = To a moderate extent
> 4 = To a great extent
> 5 = To a very great extent

SURVEY INSTRUMENT
Most people at work...

	Organization	Work Unit
1. Turn the job into a contest	_____	_____
2. Play "politics" to gain influence	_____	_____
3. Do things to avoid the disapproval of others	_____	_____
4. Focus on pleasing those in positions of authority	_____	_____
5. Involve others in decisions affecting them	_____	_____
6. Trust that conflicts at work will be resolved fairly	_____	_____
7. Appear hard, tough, and intimidating	_____	_____
8. Oppose things indirectly	_____	_____
9. Wait for others to act first	_____	_____
10. Never challenge superiors	_____	_____
11. Resolve conflicts by majority vote	_____	_____
12. Help others to think for themselves	_____	_____
13. Compete rather than cooperate	_____	_____

Most people at work...	Organization	Work Unit
14. Try to avoid appearing as a loser	_____	_____
15. Conform to the "way things are"	_____	_____
16. Treat rules as more important than ideas	_____	_____
17. Encourage and help others to participate in decision making at work	_____	_____
18. Demonstrate sincere caring for others at work	_____	_____
19. Maintain an image of superiority	_____	_____
20. Focus on building and maintaining a power base	_____	_____
21. Make "popular" rather than necessary decisions	_____	_____
22. Accord highest priority to respecting the "chain of command"	_____	_____
23. Think in terms of what would be supported by the majority of people	_____	_____
24. Try to "do the right thing" rather than "take the easy way out"	_____	_____

SCORING

	Organization	Work Unit
A. Add response numbers from questions 1, 7, 13, and 19	_____	_____
B. Add response numbers from questions 2, 8, 14, and 20	_____	_____
C. *House of Manipulation Score* (total of A and B scores)	_____	_____
D. Add response numbers from questions 3, 9, 15, and 21	_____	_____
E. Add response numbers from questions 4, 10, 16, and 22	_____	_____
F. *House of Compliance Score* (total of D and E scores)	_____	_____
G. Add response numbers from questions 5, 11, 17, and 23	_____	_____
H. Add response numbers from questions 6, 12, 18, and 24	_____	_____
I. *House of Total Quality Score* (total of G and H scores)	_____	_____

INTERPRETATION

Step 1: The highest total score among scoring steps C, F, and I indicates the level of moral development perceived by the respondent in both the organization and work unit. If C is the highest total score, the ethical work culture of the

House of Manipulation predominates; if F is the highest score, the ethical work culture of the House of Compliance prevails; and if I is the highest total score, the ethical work culture of the House of Total Quality prevails. Any level score ties are to be interpreted as indicating the lower (or lowest) work environment level of moral development.

The Organizational House is _____

The Work Unit House is _____

Step 2: Once the work environment level has been determined (House of Manipulation, House of Compliance, or House of Total Quality), the higher of the two scores that led to the level totals indicates the specific ethical work culture stage. Again, any stage score ties are to be interpreted as indicating the lower stage of moral development.

Work Environment Level Scores		Ethical Work Culture Stage	
If A is the higher total within the House of Manipulation	=	Social Darwinism	(Stage 1)
If B is the higher total within the House of Manipulation	=	Machiavellianism	(Stage 2)
If D is the higher total within the House of Compliance	=	Popular Conformity	(Stage 3)
If E is the higher total within the House of Compliance	=	Allegiance to Authority	(Stage 4)
If G is the higher total within the House of Total Quality	=	Democratic Participation	(Stage 5)
If H is the higher total within the House of Total Quality	=	Organizational Integrity	(Stage 6)

Organizational Ethical Stage is _____

Work Unit Ethical Stage is _____

Step 3: Note any difference between organizational and work unit scores since these disparities are points of both potential ethical conflict and opportunities for ethical work culture alignment and improvement. Persons caught between conflicting ethical work cultures for long periods of time experience "fight or flight" symptoms that inevitably impair optimal quality performance. Proactive management of ethical work culture development indicates human resource respect for people and commitment to building community at work.

Source: Petrick, Joseph A. and Quinn, John F. (1994). *Abbreviated Variation Four of Ethical Work Culture Assessment Instrument.* Cincinnati: Organizational Ethics Associates

CHAPTER 6

IMPLEMENTING TOTAL QUALITY HUMAN RESOURCE MANAGEMENT

In one sense, Chapters 3 to 6 provided the general strategic implementation guidelines for total quality human resource management (HRM). The focus of this chapter is on three areas: (1) an integrative operational model for directing the transformational steps needed to systematically implement total quality HRM, (2) a current case study of successfully managing human resources by total quality principles, and (3) a brief overview of the international total quality human resource (HR) practices that already exist in three major regions of the globe.

Implementing total quality HRM is easier said than done.[1] Implementation failure has been identified as one of three reasons why total quality initiatives appear to languish:[2]

1. **Programmatic overexpectation:** Unrealistic expectations for success
2. **Conceptual failure:** The theories about causation and the relationships underlying the policies and programs are inaccurate or incomplete

3. **Implementation failure:** The failure to carry out the policy or program as designed

There is very little one can do to avoid failures due to programmatic overexpectations (e.g., "we thought the situation would be turned around in six months") except to warn potential customers to be careful (if it sounds too good to believe, it probably is) or warn advocates to avoid excess (do not promise what you cannot deliver).

Regarding the second cause of total quality failure, stories abound about how only the symptoms, not the causes, of the problem were addressed or "people did not understand the need to coordinate all parts of the total quality program to form an integrated system response." The need to identify the real causes and provide comprehensive, integrated resolutions (not relying solely on one method of implementation) is crucial for total quality implementation success.

With regard to the third cause of total quality failure, stories exist about "the gap between total quality rhetoric and total quality implementation action in HR departments and top management teams," or "the President told us we were now 'empowered' to make decisions, but we were so 'lean' we no longer had the necessary resources or budget to complete our tasks," or "the President didn't provide the leadership or even attend the training sessions for the quality improvement program." The leadership actions, resources, and monitoring activities to consistently carry out total quality policies and programs for HRM are necessary ingredients to ensure implementation success in good times as well as tough times.[3]

There are at least six distinct theoretical models for implementing total quality:

1. **Total quality element approach:** Uses elements of quality improvement programs rather than full implementation of a total quality system, such as quality circles, statistical process control, and quality function deployment used in isolation.

2. **Guru approach:** Uses the writings of Deming, Juran, and Crosby for analysis and implementation. Deming's fourteen-point model is an example.

3. **Japanese model approach:** Uses the writings of such Japanese writers as Kaoru Ishikawa and the educational guidelines of the Union of Japanese Scientists and Engineers.

4. **Industrial company model approach:** Leaders from one organization visit an organization using total quality, identify its system, and integrate this information with their own or European Quality Award ideas to

create a customized approach. Visiting winners of the Deming Prize, the Baldrige Award, or the European Quality Award is an example.

5. **Hoshin planning approach:** Focuses on successful planning, deployment, and execution and monthly diagnosis; developed by the Japanese firm Bridgestone and used successfully by Hewlett-Packard.

6. **Prize/award criteria approach:** Uses the criteria for the Deming Prize, the Baldrige Award, and/or the European Quality Award to identify areas for improvement and follow criteria guidelines for system change.[4]

The most useful total quality implementation plan would be an integrated blend of all approaches mentioned above.

TOTAL QUALITY INTEGRATED IMPLEMENTATION PLAN FOR MANAGING HUMAN RESOURCES

An integrated plan for implementing total quality HRM must meet a number of criteria to incorporate the material in this text and be operationally useful at the same time:

1. It must identify activities, indicators, and timelines related to adopting total quality HR improvement efforts at distinct phases in the total quality HR implementation process.

2. It must recognize the need for completing institutional assessment efforts (speaking with facts) and ethical work culture diagnoses at critical phases in the development process.

3. It must identify four levels at which total quality HR improvement efforts may be initiated: **strategy implementation** (Chapter 2), **process implementation** (Chapter 3), **project implementation** (Chapter 4), and **individual performance implementation** (Chapter 5).

4. It must recognize the need for continual evaluation and control of the HR area and its quality improvement efforts, with the evaluation and control based on facts.

The total quality integrated implementation plan in Table 6.1 meets the above criteria and presents a flow of seven operational steps for systematic implementation: (1) goal setting implementation, (2) assessment implementation, (3) strategy implementation, (4) process implementation, (5) project implementation, (6) individual performance implementation, and (7) evaluation and control implementation.[5] This integrated approach to implementation is necessary if the situational feasibility of every organization is to be considered. In some organizations, beginning at the initial, organization-wide stages (e.g., goal setting, assessment, strategy, and evaluation and control implementation) may not always be politically advisable. In such situations, intervention at other levels (e.g., process, project, or individual performance implementation) may be the most appropriate approach for initiating total quality improvement in managing human resources. The ideal situation is to systematically incorporate all seven steps into the total quality implementation of HRM.

The total quality integrated implementation plan consists of actions required to achieve each implementation stage. Each action, in turn, specifies **what** should be done, **who** should be doing it, **why** this particular action is

Table 6.1   Total Quality Integrated Implementation Plan

No.	Action	What	Who
1.0 GOAL SETTING IMPLEMENTATION			
1.1	Commit to transformation	Explore strategic issues, opportunities, and competitive status; identify business imperatives for change; commit to quality focus	President (head of sponsoring unit) and Executive Management Group
1.2	Develop organization change strategy and plan	Develop mission, vision, guiding principles, and goals for QC	President and the QC (or EIT)
1.3	Communications plan	Plan to communicate the organization change process	President and QC (or EIT)
1.4	Education plan	Develop plan to introduce the quality principles and strategies	President and QC (or EIT), EWCT, and PIT
1.5	Introduce quality improvement	Implement and communicate education plans to set the stage for change and introduce all members to quality improvement principles and techniques	President and QC (or EIT), EWCT, and PIT

necessary, **how** the action should be carried out, **when** it should be done, and what **indicators** are required to ensure that it has been completed. While still an operational framework model upon which a specific plan applicable to HRM must be designed and developed, this summary provides an extensive guide for initiating a thorough and, hopefully, more effective and productive total quality transformation plan for total quality HRM.

The implementation action plan in Table 6.1 provides conceptual and operational integration for firms that want to apply total quality principles to HRM. In addition to this integrated conceptual model, it is important to recognize many organizations moving in this direction, including the Michigan Consolidated Gas Company (MichCon).[6]

Table 6.1 Total Quality Integrated Implementation Plan

No.	Why	How	When	Indicators
1.0 GOAL SETTING IMPLEMENTATION				
1.1	To ensure top-level commitment to the effort	Off-site strategy formulation and goal setting sessions; tentative formation of Quality Council (QC) or Executive Improvement Team (EIT)	Month 1	Executive Management Group minutes
1.2	To develop the framework for the quality improvement effort	Tap internal organization development expertise, internal quality champions, and external consulting support	Months 1 and 2	QC (or EIT) minutes, written documentation
1.3	To ensure systematic and consistent communication about the change effort	Appoint a Process Improvement Team (PIT) and Ethical Work Culture Team (EWCT) to report to the QC (or EIT) for system design and development	Month 1 and continuously throughout the effort	Written materials, QC (or EIT), PIT, and EWCT minutes
1.4	To initiate the transformation process with all members of the organization	Publication of the plan, newsletters, employee meetings, seminars, workshops	Month 2	QC (or EIT), PIT, and EWCT minutes, written documentation
1.5	To initiate the transformation process with all members of the organization	Official documents, newsletters, employee meetings, seminars, and workshops	Month 2	QC (or EIT), PIT, and EWCT minutes

Table 6.1 Total Quality Integrated Implementation Plan (continued)

No.	Action	What	Who
2.0 ASSESSMENT IMPLEMENTATION			
2.1	Develop assessment plan	Develop a plan to assess the organization and its leadership in terms of quality improvement principles and issues	President and QC (or (EIT), EWCT, and PIT
2.2	Conduct assessment	Conduct the assessment with customers (internal and external) and suppliers; analyze the results	PIT and EWCT
2.3	Prepare and circulate report	Prepare assessment report; circulate to the President, QC (or EIT), and key individuals	PIT and EWCT
2.4	Develop gap analysis	Identify gaps between current reality and "desired state"; identify opportunity areas for quality improvement	President and QC (or EIT), PIT, and EWCT
3.0 STRATEGY IMPLEMENTATION			
3.1	Begin planning the transformation	Develop basic plans for the quality improvement effort at the strategic level	President and Executive Management Group
3.2.1	Determine the charter and composition of the Steering Team: QC (or EIT)	Appoint QC (or EIT) from key positions in the organization (executive management, operations groups, unions, professional staff, other employee groups)	President and Executive Management Group
3.2.2	Select a BPI champion	Identify one person who will be visible and accountable to lead the effort	President in collaboration with Executive Management Group and QC (or EIT)

Table 6.1 Total Quality Integrated Implementation Plan (continued)

No.	Why	How	When	Indicators
2.0 ASSESSMENT IMPLEMENTATION				
2.1	To obtain data to assess the current state of "quality" and "ethics" in the organization	Review existing literature for assessment, gather benchmarking data and internal data, seek consultants	Month 2	Assessment instruments
2.2	To collect data on quality and ethical work culture in the organization	Surveys, preview of documents, existing databases	Month 2	Completed data files
2.3	To share data, obtain feedback, and involve members	Formal meetings, written reports, newsletters	Month 3	Assessment report, other related documents, record of the meetings
2.4	To select target areas for quality improvement efforts	Analysis of report(s), discussions with key members	Month 3	List of target opportunities
3.0 STRATEGY IMPLEMENTATION				
3.1	To ensure top-level commitment to the effort	Form QC (or EIT)	Month 1	Minutes of Executive Management Group
3.2.1	To provide ongoing leadership in establishing and maintaining total quality effort	Establish QC (or EIT), plus its parameters and outcome expectations	Month 1	Minutes of Executive Management Group and the QC (or EIT)
3.2.2	To dedicate one person at a senior level, to ensure all foundations are properly laid for the transition to quality, and to build commitment and remove barriers to implementation	Select a formal leader with broad-based credibility, total quality competency, clout, and reputation for integrity	Month 1	Minutes of Executive Management Group and the QC (or EIT)

Table 6.1 Total Quality Integrated Implementation Plan (continued)

No.	Action	What	Who
3.2.3	Form the PIT and EWCT	Create the PIT and EWCT	QC (or EIT)
3.3	Top-level education and training	Train the QC (or EIT), PIT, and EWCT	Qualified individuals, which may include outside consultants initially
3.4	Establish and/ or clarify mission, vision, guiding principles, and goals	Conduct meetings (workshops) focused on the organization's vision, mission, guiding principles, and overarching goals	QC (or EIT), PIT, and EWCT
3.5	Select and train functional department improvement team (DIT)	Select and train DIT	Coordinated by PIT and EWCT in consultation with the QC (or EIT); done by appropriate persons (may be outside consultants)
3.6	DIT works on improving own process	DIT focuses on internal process improvement efforts	DIT, PIT, and EWCT

Table 6.1 Total Quality Integrated Implementation Plan (continued)

No.	Why	How	When	Indicators
3.2.3	To have a multilevel cross-functional team responsible for development and monitoring the total quality plan; to encourage everyone to contribute to the quality improvement effort	Select formal and informal leaders from critical divisions and departments; establish parameters and outcome expectations for the team	Month 2	Minutes of the QC (or EIT), PIT, and EWCT
3.3	To increase the understanding of quality and ethical work culture improvement principles and build commitment to the change process	Intensive workshops (a location away from work would be very beneficial); combine initial training with follow-through sessions	Months 1 and 2, with follow-through session continuous during the project	Training designed and delivered; written initial vision, mission, guiding principles, and goals
3.4	To ensure collective ownership and commitment to the mission, vision, guiding principles, and overarching goals	Discussion of assessment report and development of material related to the mission, vision, principles, and goals "Challenge process" to enable all employees to provide input and shape the future context	Months 1 and 2	QC (or EIT), PIT, and EWCT minutes; draft statement of vision, mission, guiding principles, and goals
3.5	To increase understanding of and commitment to quality improvement efforts among key persons in the major functional areas	Select, appoint, and train DIT	Months 3 and 4	PIT and EWCT minutes; training designed and delivered to DIT
3.6	To provide team members with the opportunity to analyze and improve internal processes	Process and problem analysis	Months 5 and 6	PIT, EWCT, and DIT minutes

Table 6.1 Total Quality Integrated Implementation Plan (continued)

No.	Action	What	Who
3.7	Select and train local area Task Teams (TTs)	Select and train TTs	Coordinated by the PIT, in cooperation with the EWCT, DIT; training done by appropriate persons
3.8	Identify emergent opportunities	Identify opportunities for quality improvement efforts based on process and problem analysis	TTs, DITs, PITs, and EWCTs
3.9	Integrate quality and ethical work culture into planning	Integrate quality and organizational ethics improvement principles and techniques into organization planning	Led by the QC (or EIT), in cooperation with the other teams that have been formed

4.0 PROCESS IMPLEMENTATION

No.	Action	What	Who
4.1	Identify initial process improvement projects	Identification of the core processes	QC (or EIT), PIT, and EWCT
4.2	Select and train DIT and TTs	Select and train DITs and TTs	QC (or EIT), PIT, and EWCT
4.3	Solve process improvement problems	Identify and solve process improvement problems with PIT, DIT, and EWCT	Cross-functional process improvement with PIT, DIT, and EWCT
4.4	Prioritize organizational process improvement issues	Identify issues and priorities of the organization	PITs, DITs, TTs, and EWCT

Table 6.1 Total Quality Integrated Implementation Plan (continued)

No.	Why	How	When	Indicators
3.7	To have local area TTs address issues related to major core process	Select persons directly involved in the processes to be addressed and train TTs	Months 6 and 7	Minutes of QC (or EIT), PIT, EWCT, and DIT
3.8	To assist the QC (or EIT) in identifying opportunities for quality improvement efforts	Analysis of all materials produced by the assessment and process management activities	Months 6 and 7	Reports to DITs, PITs, EWCTs, and QC (or EIT)
3.9	To institutionalize quality and ethical work culture improvement principles and techniques into ongoing planning of activities of the organization	Train all team members in quality and organizational ethics improvement principles and techniques, development of policies and procedures	Month 6 and continuously throughout the effort	Training designed and delivered to all team members; written policies and procedures

4.0 PROCESS IMPLEMENTATION

No.	Why	How	When	Indicators
4.1	To assure that all key processes are working in harmony to maximize organizational effectiveness	Systematic effort by the QC (or EIT), PIT, or EWCT to identify core processes of the organization	Months 3 and 4	List of core processes of the organization
4.2	To enhance the understanding of and commitment to quality and ethics improvement principles and techniques	Selected reading materials on quality improvement principles and techniques, workshops on improvement principles and techniques	Months 4 and 5	Training designed and delivered to DITs and TTs
4.3	To ensure that the major processes of the organization are effective, efficient, and meet customer needs and expectations	Systematic efforts using PIT, DIT, and EWCT and appropriate quality tools and techniques	Months 5 and 6	Process improvement problems identified and addressed by PIT, DIT, and EWCT
4.4	To have an accepted set of issues that need to be addressed by the organization	PITs, DITs, TTs, EWCT	Months 6 and 7	Reports on activities and results of PITs, DITs, TTs, and EWCT

Table 6.1 Total Quality Integrated Implementation Plan (continued)

No.	Action	What	Who
4.5	Gain organizational endorsement of process improvement efforts	Process management improvement efforts recommended and approved	PITs, DITs, TTs, EWCT, QC (or EIT)

5.0 PROJECT IMPLEMENTATION

No.	Action	What	Who
5.1	Identify initial project management projects	Identify the initial projects based on the list of core processes of the organization (step 4.1)	DITs and TTs in cooperation with PIT, EWCT, and QC (or EIT)
5.2	Plan the project management activities	Initiate the overall plan for each of the selected projects	DITs and TTs
5.3	Organize the project management activities	Coordinate the organizational framework of each project; conduct training on shared responsibilities (cross-training)	DITs and TTs
5.4	Implement the project management activities	Begin each project based on the developed plan and organizational framework	DITs and TTs
5.5	Control the project management activities	Utilize the control strategies developed in the overall plan of each project	DITs and TTs

Table 6.1 Total Quality Integrated Implementation Plan (continued)

No.	Why	How	When	Indicators
4.5	To ensure selection of appropriate processes, authorization, commitment, and support	DITs and TTs recommend priorities and target processes; they are reviewed and approved by PITs, EWCT, and QC (or EIT)	Months 7 and 8	Approved reports on process improvement priorities and target processes

5.0 PROJECT IMPLEMENTATION

No.	Why	How	When	Indicators
5.1	To ensure that projects are based on the core processes and to select problems with a high chance of success as the initial projects	Each DIT and TT identifies the problem processes they would like to initially address	Months 8 and 9	Approved list of initial projects
5.2	To identify all the necessary steps, required resources, and areas of collaboration with other teams for each project	Each DIT and TT develops the overall plan and strategy for the selected projects	Months 8 and 9	Fully developed plan for each selected project; DIT and TT minutes
5.3	To organize all the necessary steps, required resources, and areas of collaboration with other teams for each project	Each team collaboratively organizes its project, with the help of a lead person as the facilitator; conduct workshops on cross-training	Months 8 and 9	Fully developed and understood organizational framework for each project
5.4	To initiate the selected team-centered quality improvement projects	"Just do it"; get started with the projects, applying PDCA and the appropriate quality tools and techniques	Months 9 and 10	Visible indication of projects beginning, initial progress reports from DITs and TTs
5.5	To assure the progress of each project, based on planned control systems	Utilize the appropriate quality evaluation and feedback tools and techniques	Months 9 and 10	Scheduled progress reports from DITs and TTs

Table 6.1 Total Quality Integrated Implementation Plan (continued)

No.	Action	What	Who
5.6	Complete the projects	Complete each project within the designated objective, specified time, and budget	DITs and TTs
6.0 INDIVIDUAL PERFORMANCE IMPLEMENTATION			
6.1	Undertake personal performance assessment and development	Provide assessment and training for personal performance improvement	Each person in the organization on a voluntary basis, and preferably in teams to facilitate co-development
6.2	Align personal performance with organizational priorities	Provide education in developing personal vision, mission, objectives, and plans	Each person in the organization on a voluntary basis, and preferably in teams to facilitate co-development
6.3	Personalize customer–supplier orientation	Sensitivity to meeting, even anticipating, needs of customers/ constituents; establish long-term relations with suppliers	Each person in the organization within the framework of the teams and in cooperation with the PIT, EWCT, and QC (or EIT)
6.4	Develop personal skills matrix	Development of personal skills matrix and database	Each person in the organization within the framework of DIT and TT

Table 6.1 Total Quality Integrated Implementation Plan (continued)

No.	Why	How	When	Indicators
5.6	To demonstrate the success of team-centered project management	Successful implementation of steps 4.5, 5.1–5.5, and 6.4	Months 10 and 11	Scheduled progress and end-of-project reports from DITs and TTs

6.0 INDIVIDUAL PERFORMANCE IMPLEMENTATION

No.	Why	How	When	Indicators
6.1	To develop the organization's most important resource, its people, for the benefit of the people and the company	Provide courses and seminars on total quality skills, personal improvement, and team building	Begin in month 4 (see step 4.2) and continue throughout the effort	Positive evaluation of the courses/seminars; measurable impact on personal effectiveness
6.2	To demonstrate the organization's commitment to personal empowerment and self-direction; to align team development with personal development	Provide courses and seminars in developing personal and team vision, mission, and objectives/plans; use appropriate quality tools	Begin in month 4 (see step 4.2) and continue throughout the effort	Positive evaluation of the courses/seminars; measurable impact on personal effectiveness
6.3	To actualize the 2 basic purposes of the project: implement the basic mission of the organization and totally serve the customers/constituents	Provide courses and seminars on customer service; team-based projects addressing customer service process (steps 4.1–4.5 and 5.1–5.6)	Begin in month 6 (see step 4.4) and continue throughout the effort	Successful completion of and measurable impacts on customer service and supplier orientation projects
6.4	To provide a personal skills matrix for each person, identifying present and future skills; facilitate the cross-training of each team and its members	Establish a personal skills matrix database for each person; coordinate with a team-centered database	Begin in month 6 (see step 3.7) and continue throughout the effort	Personal skills matrix database of each person established, coordinated with a team-centered database

Table 6.1 Total Quality Integrated Implementation Plan (continued)

No.	Action	What	Who
7.0 EVALUATION AND CONTROL IMPLEMENTATION			
7.1	Conduct process and project evaluation	Evaluation criteria and procedures built into *all* quality improvement efforts; quality improvement efforts reviewed and evaluated	DITs and TTs responsible for improvement effort, with reports reviewed by PIT, EWCT, and QC (or EIT)
7.2	Benchmark best practices	Identification of best practices and performances on target processes and projects	DITs and TTs responsible for improvement effort, with reports reviewed by PIT, EWCT, and QC (or EIT)
7.3	Provide training, remediation, and enhancement opportunities	Develop and deliver additional training for persons identified in steps 4.1 and 4.2 or on topics identified through the benchmarking process (step 7.2)	DIT and EWCT, in cooperation with the DITs and TTs
7.4	Measure overall quality and ethical work culture programs	Develop and conduct efforts to monitor and evaluate the overall impact of the quality and ethical work culture improvement efforts	QC (or EIT), PIT, and EWCT in cooperation with DITs and TTs

Table 6.1 Total Quality Integrated Implementation Plan (continued)

No.	Why	How	When	Indicators
7.0 EVALUATION AND CONTROL IMPLEMENTATION				
7.1	To learn whether the improvements occurred in terms of effectiveness, efficiency, and meeting the needs of the customers; to maintain orientation to continuous improvement	Application of total quality tools such as control charts and other more formal evaluation techniques	Begin with initiation of the project (steps 4.1–4.5 and 5.1–5.6) and continue throughout the effort	Evaluation criteria and procedures identified for each project; periodic project reports
7.2	To maintain continuous improvement orientation; to obtain data on best practices	Review of data concerning the performance of outside quality leaders in each process area (field, related fields, similar functions)	Begin with initiation of the effort and continue throughout	Benchmarking data, internal reviews comparing process/project performance with outside quality leaders
7.3	To maintain the relevance of the established education and training program; to enhance the knowledge, skills, and attitudes of everyone	Formal training programs, newsletters with an educational focus, written material (job aids, manuals, performance guidelines)	Begin with initiation of the effort and continue throughout	Additional training completed and evaluated; written materials published
7.4	To obtain data on the impact of the quality and ethics improvement efforts; to ensure a fact-driven organizational environment	Use of quality audit, ethical work culture audit, and HR audit to evaluate and control; identification of successes and failures; corrective measures taken when warranted	Begin with initiation of the effort and continue throughout	Completed quality audits, ethical work culture audits, and HR audits with identification of goal fulfillment and shortfalls; corrective recommendations

THE MICHCON CASE: A SNAPSHOT OF SUCCESSFUL TOTAL QUALITY HUMAN RESOURCE MANAGEMENT

Michigan Consolidated Gas Company (MichCon),[7] headquartered in Detroit, embarked on the road to total quality in 1989. With one million customers and over a billion dollars in annual revenues, MichCon was the fifth largest natural gas utility in the United States. The long-term effort was initiated when the senior officers asked a provocative question for a regulated utility: "With the natural gas distribution business becoming more competitive, how can we ensure that customers will come to us by choice?"

To create an environment at MichCon in which every employee would be focused and enabled to act on the customer's behalf, a dramatic cultural shift was required. MichCon's history had been characterized by a mindset of heavy regulation (virtual monopoly) and "captive" customers (called "ratepayers") who, due to regulatory protection, had no ability to choose service among competing natural gas providers. The challenge of change was further complicated by the sense of security—bordering on complacency—that frequently comes with success. When MichCon began this journey, it had just completed six of the most successful years in its 150 year history, as reflected by traditional financial measures. This recent success made it difficult for some to feel any sense of urgency in addressing new challenges.

Senior leadership at MichCon recognized that employee participation and empowerment would be keys to the transformation required. Even the very name of the transition effort, developed by a group of frontline employees with the help of the Corporate Communications Department, acknowledged the crucial role all employees would play in transforming the company: "The Power of You...Build the Future." Rather than launching the change as many companies do—with a corporate vision developed by the executive team and imposed on the organization—MichCon created a *deployment challenge process* that offered every employee the opportunity to challenge "draft" thinking by the executive team and help shape the long-term corporate vision and the principles that would guide day-to-day operations and decision making along the journey. Five months and 262 meetings later, the executive team had some 6000 pages of suggested changes, additions, and revisions to blend together in a final statement of vision and guiding principles or values.

Thanks to this involvement process, employees began to develop a heightened sense of personal ownership for the new company direction, an ownership that would be essential in fulfilling MichCon's vision to become "a premier organization, and the best natural gas company."[8] In their statement of guiding principles, employees acknowledged the important roles that personal responsibility, mutual support, innovation, honesty, and integrity would play in meeting and exceeding customer expectations and providing for service, safety, and quality of life.

The revised vision and values statement was finalized, made into a "life-size" document with 3300 signature spaces, and "ceremoniously unveiled at one of the company's smallest field offices, illustrating that even the smallest of stations would need to change."[9] As the model made its way around the state, to all company locations, each employee was invited to review and actually sign it, if they could commit to being guided by this document.

Subsequent stages of the change strategy—the identification of quality service as the business imperative for change and the formation of quality councils, business process analysis teams, and quality improvement teams—were highlighted in the earlier version of this case study. Additional components of the change strategy focused primarily on results measurement, employee satisfaction, personal development, leader certification, job evaluation, and organization design. These efforts—plus experiments in peer discipline, peer safety review, and peer hiring—are highlighted here in this updated version to emphasize the HRM impacts of total quality approaches.

Measurement of Results

As a key component in its transition to a total quality environment, MichCon developed a corporate measurement system that integrated a series of strategic and operational measures with the corporate business objectives, guiding principles, and, ultimately, the corporate vision. This linkage provided a clear "big picture" view of how key measures throughout the operation supported the broader strategic corporate direction.

As a result of MichCon's experience in developing and implementing this approach to corporate measurement, four lessons emerged that are worthy of note for executives and HR practitioners. First, each business objective should be assigned an "owner" who should form a cross-functional team to support that objective. Second, the objective owner and the team should create a strategy outcome statement for each business objective to ensure widespread understanding and identify the strategic indicators that would reflect the relative "health" of that objective. Third, the team should subsequently identify the most significant business processes that are related to the achievement of that business objective, as well as the gaps and opportunities that could lead to improved performance. Fourth, improvement plans should then be developed to fill in those gaps or capitalize on those opportunities.

This process is demonstrated in Figure 6.1 using MichCon's key business objective of customer satisfaction. The figure shows the business objective—achieving and maintaining 100% customer satisfaction—and its linkage to MichCon's corporate vision and guiding principles:

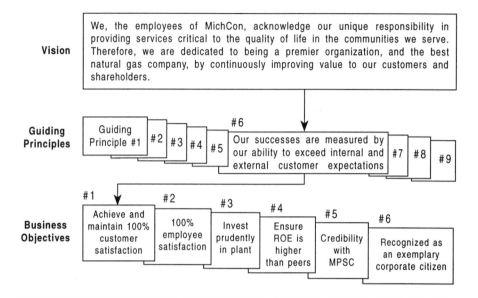

Figure 6.1 Linkage of MichCon Vision, Guiding Principles, and Business Objectives.

Being truly customer-focused, according to MichCon President and CEO Steve Ewing, will be the natural outcome of finding good answers to four basic questions:

- Who is the customer?
- What do we do for them?
- How well do we do it?
- How do we know?

MichCon's strategy statement for this business objective consists of three important components:

1. Develop programs and handle internal interfaces to meet customers' needs and eliminate unnecessary customer contacts

2. In every customer interaction, increase each of the following service satisfaction dimensions: accessibility, courtesy, responsiveness, sense of power, control over the encounter, and favorability toward the company

3. Establish a line of site for each employee's responsibility for satisfying customers

The strategic indicators targeted for regular, executive monitoring include:

1. Percent customer satisfaction overall
2. Percent bills to actual meter reads
3. Percent calls handled
4. Percent category 1 leak responses in less than 30 minutes
5. Percent new services installed on time
6. Number of telephone/business office contacts (000s)

Gaps and opportunities for improvement were identified in five areas: people, systems, inflexible organization objectives/processes/structures, customers, and external publics. These gaps or opportunities and the improvement plans formed to address them focused on such things as availability and accuracy of information, proactive methods for identifying customer needs and problems, the extent of employees' ability to solve the customers' problems, and meaningful communication with customers, employees, and other constituencies (e.g., regulators, legislators).

Finally, strategic indicators are elaborated in Table 6.2 by identifying four elements of measure and those additional indicators to be monitored within the operations.

Performance against each indicator is tracked against specific targets: current month vs. plan, year-to-date vs. plan, year-end forecast vs. plan, and next year-end forecast vs. plan.

As a result of his experience in supporting the development and implementation of this corporate measurement system, MichCon's Director of Corporate Measurement offers this additional advice:

1. Each indicator should be tied directly to a business objective. Each key indicator must support a business objective and support the larger strategic direction. Companies can (and do) measure many things; they need to ensure they measure those things that will enhance the achievement of their desired future.

2. Measures need to be outcome-based, from the view of the customer, not process-based from the view of the employee. An example of this distinction at MichCon would be the number of outages (customers without service) rather than the number of engineering drawings completed on time (which support the provision of service to customers). The amount of "behind-the-scenes" activity matters little if the customer is still without gas.

3. Measures need to be interdependent and balanced. It is appropriate to define measures broadly in terms of customer satisfaction, cost, accuracy,

Table 6.2 Elements of Measure and Key Indicators Used at MichCon

Elements of measure	Key indicators
Customer satisfaction	Percent customer satisfaction
	Percent favorable comments
	Number of customer contacts (000s)
	Percent customer satisfaction—accessibility
	Percent customer satisfaction—encounter control
	Percent customer satisfaction—favorability
	Percent customer satisfaction—pleasantness
	Percent customer satisfaction—power
	Percent customer satisfaction—responsiveness
Cost	Cost per customer—customer service
Accuracy	Percent bills—actual reads
	Percent nonadjusted bills
	Percent service calls without repeat
Timeliness	Percent business office wait less than 15 minutes
	Percent calls handled
	Percent calls waiting less than 5 minutes
	Percent category 1 leak response less than 30 minutes
	Percent category 2 leak response less than 45 minutes
	Percent commitments met
	Percent new services installed on time

and timeliness, but the ultimate objective is not customer satisfaction at any cost, nor is it lowest cost at the expense of customer satisfaction. *All* targets must be met simultaneously (e.g., achieving increasing levels of customer satisfaction *while* decreasing cost).

4. Measures must be clearly defined so people understand them. It may be tempting to define measures only in terms of what employees "control" in their day-to-day work. Defining measures in terms of outcomes from the viewpoint of the customer, however, may challenge the organization to be proactive outside of its normal range of influence. The number of outages, for example, can be defined as any outage for any reason that affects the customer (including outages caused by other contractors hitting gas transmission lines as they dig to provide other utility service). Regardless of the causal source, the customer is dealing with the reality of the outage and the customer's satisfaction level will be affected by the severity of the outage and the repair responsiveness of the company. A proactive stance to problem prevention would replace the more traditional "there's nothing we can do" attitude. One example of this prevention approach would be to improve the effectiveness of "Miss Dig" programs, which facilitate inter-utility cooperation to miss existing utility lines when digging to install new services.

5. Measures need to be easy to monitor. Increased use of estimates and samples sufficiently large to accurately reflect performance needs to become an acceptable practice. Measures can be broken into subsets (e.g., large, medium, small projects) and assigned weights to put appropriate emphasis on the priority of certain results. Investing time and money in measuring to precision at some point will yield diminishing returns. Measures need only be sufficiently rigorous to support well-grounded, fact-based decision making and problem solving.

6. Each indicator should have an owner who is responsible for the outcomes. Someone has to be responsible for knowing where the company is with respect to each measure, knowing what is being done to improve it, and recognizing and rewarding where targets are exceeded. Ultimately, these outcome measures need to be tied directly to compensation.

100% Employee Satisfaction

MichCon recognized "100% Customer Satisfaction" as critical to the short-term and long-term viability of its business. But MichCon also recognized that customers could never be served at a "premier" level without the commitment and competence of another key stakeholder group—employees. Thus, "100% Employee Satisfaction" became another compelling business objective at MichCon.

A cross-functional, multi-level planning team was created to address this business objective, and the team identified the following key themes or contributors to employee satisfaction at MichCon:

- Employees have work that is meaningful, clearly linked and aligned to the corporate agenda, and that offers challenge and growth.

- Employees have open access to opportunities and resources to learn and grow.

- Employees work with "quality" co-workers and leaders and know that all employees are ready, willing, and able to contribute to their fullest.

- The corporation holds all employees truly accountable, expectations are clear, and both rewards and consequences flow from measuring one's contribution.

- The environment feels fair and equitable and preserves employee self-esteem.

- A sense of security comes from knowing what to expect, being armed with a full set of data, feeling confident in one's skills, and the contribution one can make. That security is liberating in that it comes *not* from knowing the corporation will offer guarantees and protection, but from knowing that options and choices exist and that one is free to take a chance.

Given these satisfaction themes, the planning team challenged and confirmed the strategy statement originally proposed by the business objective owners. This strategy outlined the key initiatives believed to be needed in order to achieve 100% employee satisfaction.

- Create an environment that supports the value of individuals and their contribution, characterized by:

  - A line of sight to business objectives for each employee

  - Openness and ongoing conversation (coaching, feedback)

  - Accountability for results and continuous improvements

  - Reward and recognition systems linked to behavior and results

- Develop leaders who employ MichCon's participative, value-based leadership model.

- Identify current and future business needs and link them to the selection and development of all employees.

Seven planned improvement areas were targeted to implement this strategy, each complementing the others in reinforcing a new mindset and urgency in creating a challenging, rewarding environment. The improvement areas were (1) a work force planning process, (2) an enhanced selection process, (3) leader certification, (4) compensation tied to corporate performance, (5) corporate alignment, (6) new payroll/personnel system, and (7) new policies, processes, services, and messages. Four major initiatives within these improvement areas—Personal Development System, Leader Certification Process, Job Evaluation System, and Human Resources Organization Redesign—are highlighted below, to exemplify MichCon's systematic transition to an empowered work force.

Personal Development System

A Strategic Development Plan and Personal Development System were created at MichCon as a multi-year effort to empower employees with the skills, knowledge, and attitudes necessary to achieve the corporate vision, operate within the values/guiding principles, and accomplish the business focus of quality service. Traditional expectations for employees at MichCon had included basing action on education (supervisors and others will teach employees what they need to know), developing job-specific skills, setting job-specific goals, taking direction from management, knowing and following the rules, and self-discipline. In contrast, "The Power of You...Build the Future" brought a new set of expectations for employees.

Employee action, rather than being driven by education and direction by others, would be employee initiated, based on a clearly articulated corporate belief system. Employees, rather than developing only job-specific skills, would be expected to develop a more empowered "state of being" from which multiple jobs could be performed, thus increasing impact and flexibility. Instead of focusing only on job-specific goals set by others, employees would develop their own broader foundation of personal vision/purpose and align that with the corporate vision/purpose. Employees would become *initiators* of direction through meaningful involvement instead of just implementers of direction from management. Instead of just following rules, employees would be expected to change the rules and make sound judgments from personal experience and continuous learning. The old value of self-discipline must be enhanced by a new value of self-worth.

System-wide training set the broad context for future expectations and was based on the themes of choice, commitment, and personal responsibility.

Leadership Choice

A four-day residential program entitled "Leadership Choice" was offered to all people in formal leadership roles, including union officers, plus some frontline employees considered to be strong informal leaders. Seventy-five percent of the design took place outdoors, with a series of increasingly challenging team problem-solving initiatives.

The major learning themes of "Leadership Choice" included self-awareness as the core of leadership (i.e., leadership is more about who leaders are than what they do or how they do it), personal responsibility for results created (versus being merely "victims" of the actions of others), the importance of personal choice amidst perceived risk (i.e., becoming more aware of the choices each person makes, what they perceive as risk, and expanding their "comfort zone" to enable better choices on behalf of themselves and the organization), what it takes to create high performance in a team, and the essential role that coaching and feedback play in personal and team development.

Participation was voluntary; interested participants "nominated" themselves by filling out a lengthy application form. The application was designed to stimulate reflection about personal leadership development needs and objectives, heighten commitment, and begin the learning process well in advance of the session. This self-nomination form was supplemented with two supporting nominations from two colleagues chosen by the aspiring participants (supervisors, co-workers, and customers were frequently chosen). This supporting nomination process enabled others to provide the participant with feedback in advance of the session, identifying that individual's perceived strengths and developmental needs.

The design addressed three perspectives: self as a team member, the role of a team leader, and the team as part of a system of interdependent teams. Teams of 8 to 12 people—representing diverse combinations of gender, race, department, job level, and geography—went through the program together, thus providing by design an opportunity to increase understanding and break down stereotypes and barriers between and among various groups.

Discovery!

"Discovery!" was a three-day, highly interactive program designed to carry the context to all frontline employees. The foundation for this program was created by a group of employees representing all areas of the company; they had been asked to come together and identify the key cultural shifts which must occur if MichCon was to be successful in achieving its vision of becoming a premier organization and the best natural gas company. These employees identified seven key shifts that would be required to move into the future:

From	To
"Going through the motions" (just doin' my job)	Caring for the Customer
"I just work here"	"I own it; it's mine"
[Being a Helpless] Victim	[Assuming] Responsibility [for choices]
Blaming and Complaining	Problem solving
Competition (win/lose)	Partnership (win/win)
"Power of You" = Power of *Me*	"Power of You" = Power of *Us*
Feeling Discounted	Feeling Valued, Worthwhile

The learning themes for "Discovery!" were built around the following shifts: the importance of taking personal responsibility for results, the superior role of partnership with others (versus internal competition) to maximize beneficial outcomes and the effective use of resources, the importance of really caring for customers (and showing it in all aspects of work), the value

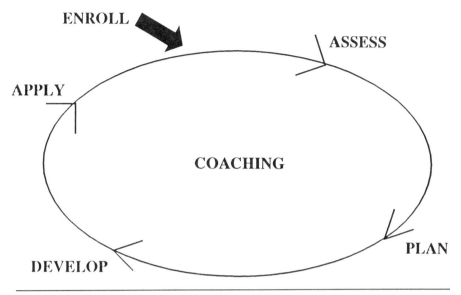

Figure 6.2 MichCon Personal Development System.

of personal growth in an environment of continuous improvement, and the creation of shared meaning around what it takes to be a premier company.

Personal Development System Stages

"Leadership Choice" and "Discovery!" provided the foundation for development and enrollment in the Personal Development System (PDS). PDS, which consists of five stages with coaching as the central support mechanism, is depicted in Figure 6.2.

Stage One: Enroll

The purpose of Orientation I is to discuss the broader context of change at MichCon, inform employees about "Discovery!" and encourage people to enroll. In an interactive discussion format, employees are asked to reflect on the company's competitive environment, the definition of a "premier" organization and employee, the changes that are evident since "The Power of You...Build the Future" began, and how these changes will help the company and its people become premier. The session further describes the purpose and format for "Discovery!" and invites employee participation.

Orientation II, following participation in "Discovery!", describes the tools and resources available in the PDS and how they will support the culture of continuous improvement.

Stage Two: Assess

Stage Two encourages gathering of feedback by employees through a number of sources, e.g., supervisors, direct reports, co-workers, customers. Feedback at MichCon may be gathered through informal discussions and surveys, aptitude tests, Assessment Center exercises that simulate on-the-job tasks with observations by trained raters, and performance appraisals. In addition to these options, PDS offers several instruments to assist employees in the assessment process.

A 360-Degree Feedback Instrument assesses each employee's current level of proficiency in competency areas considered crucial to MichCon's vision. Employee development time and dollars will focus in the next few years on the five competencies considered to be the highest priorities to develop: analysis/decision making, communication, interpersonal skills, quality service, and teamwork. This assessment tool is intended to be a learning resource, to establish a baseline and subsequently measure progress over time.

A Leadership Profile questionnaire is used for gathering feedback on how well individuals model the "desired state" definitions of quality service, results, leadership, recognition, team, communication, and strategy. The profile solicits both quantitative and qualitative feedback from direct and indirect reports.

A Coaching Inventory ranks the importance and skill level of major components of coaching, creating a supportive environment, influencing development, and accomplishing desired results.

Stage Three: Plan

A Personal Development Plan is filled out by all employees, with the support of a coach. Six items are addressed: (1) development areas (What do I need to develop?), (2) development activities (What will I do?), (3) support (Who will help me?), (4) progress and review (When and how will I check my progress?), (5) application (How will my development impact my job?), and (6) measures (How do I measure my progress?).

Employees are encouraged to outline specific activities, tasks, assignments, or learning experiences that are needed for improvement in their current position and/or for a potential future position. Both short-term (one year or less) and long-term (two to five years) development goals should be included in the plan.

Stage Four: Develop

Development is person-specific and should acknowledge and reflect the individual's preferred learning style(s). While employees may take advantage of MichCon-provided workshops and seminars, they are also encouraged to incorporate other developmental experiences into their plan.

Nonclassroom learning opportunities may include new on-the-job assignments; rotational assignments; task forces or special projects; a mentor relationship with a more experienced employee; self-directed instruction with the aid of workbooks, audiotapes, study guides, and videotapes; manufacturers' course for use and maintenance of technical equipment; college-level course work; professional trade conferences and network groups; and participation in civic and community service groups.

Step Five: Apply

The focus of any developmental activity is application to the workplace and the continuous improvement of results. Ongoing personal development is an expectation for every employee and accountability for that development is built into the performance management system. Development progress is measured quantitatively, where possible, and qualitatively through self-assessment and feedback from colleagues.

Central Support: Coaching

The environment characterized by "The Power of You...Build the Future" is one in which employees throughout the organization take personal responsibility for results. As employees grown in their capacity to be self-directed and accountable for decision making, the role of formal leaders must shift from "command and control" to "coaching and development." Thus, coaching becomes the central support mechanism to facilitate the PDS.

At MichCon, a "coach" is defined as someone in the employee's workplace who provides support through materials, tools, and resources needed to do the job; helps create a work environment in which learning, continuous improvement, and quality service are the primary goals; can help the employee evaluate and improve performance by providing feedback and suggestions; works to develop relationships built on trust, open communication, and respect for each person's value; can assist in difficult situations which require higher level of skills in planning and problem solving; and can coordinate and get additional help when needed.

Although the immediate supervisor is normally thought to be the best person to serve as a coach, the selection of a coach is up to the employee. At any rate, the supervisor must endorse the employee's development plan.

After developing his or her plan, an employee meets with the coach/ supervisor to gain agreement and support. Using their development plan as an outline for the meeting, they review the developmental areas to work on, the specific developmental activities identified, and other issues, including how the plan will work, time frames, and expected benefits. The coach/ supervisor then plays an ongoing role of guidance and support throughout the improvement process.

Leader Certification Process

To build on MichCon's tradition of developing and selecting its leaders from within, a leadership certification process was recommended as a way to consistently identify those employees who demonstrate those leadership dimensions necessary for effective leadership at MichCon. To "Build the Future" might well require different leadership responsibilities and capabilities than had been present in the past. Therefore, past leadership tenure or experience would not ensure future leadership opportunity. Thus, a leadership certification process would enable MichCon to go beyond its existing pool of leaders ("Who holds leadership positions now?") and define its future leadership needs ("What leadership will be needed in the future and who can best fulfill those needs?")

To benchmark best practices in leadership certification, MichCon looked to Federal Express and its Leadership Evaluation and Awareness Process (LEAP), a qualification process for permanent employees interested in assuming leadership positions.[10]

A mid-year employee satisfaction survey at MichCon identified a number of improvement areas that future leaders needed to address: actively demonstrating respect for employees and treating them as assets to the organization; nurturing and developing employee perceptions of greater co-worker interdependence and reliability; ensuring fair and equitable treatment of employees by supervisors; and challenging employees, promoting their understanding of how they can make MichCon a premier company.

The leadership certification process at MichCon represents a series of "gates" through which current and potential leaders must pass to be considered for a leadership position. It is a certification process, not a selection process, and is limited only to the leadership aspects of the job (not technical competencies which might be required.) The process includes awareness of leadership requirements, including education, development, and training; assessment of leadership abilities, through profiles, core competencies, and performance results; and endorsements of leader candidates by customers, clients, and peers.

Specific implementation steps include definition of the new role of the leader at MichCon (including levels, skills), development of the certification process (including specific instruments, measures/thresholds required), implementation of the certification process (including candidate feedback), and managing the results (e.g., future development, retraining, job design, or redeployment through inplacement or outplacement, whichever might be required).

Job Evaluation System

For more than a decade, MichCon's job evaluation system consisted of the following: a point system which had generated 40 salary grades, internal and external equity comparisons, and centralized decision making. There were some 800 job titles for 2100 employees, and dissatisfaction was evident with both grades and the grading system.

With the advent of "The Power of You...Build the Future," job demands and the work environment were changing substantially. An evolution was occurring in what MichCon *valued* in jobs and performance: skills versus tasks, results versus effort, the individual versus the job, and contribution versus level. Other new expectations also had significant implications for the nature of jobs: a desire for decision making at the lowest level possible in the organization, a growing emphasis on teamwork and collaboration versus individual effort, and a desire for flexibility and breadth of contribution.

In an effort to address these changing needs, a 37-member task force—the Job Evaluation Team (JET)—convened in July 1992. The JET mission became the following: "We, the Job Evaluation Team, are committed to develop an alternative to the current job evaluation system which recognizes the dynamic nature of jobs. The system will encourage and value the acquisition and application of skills and behaviors supporting corporate vision and values."

The team worked into 1993, scanning internal needs, external trends, alternative systems, and case examples from other companies to come up with a creative new concept design. The team also laid out a number of design criteria for the new system. First, it must be aligned with the organization's vision and values, desired states, and corporate objectives. Second, it must be efficient, clear, and easily understood. Third, it must emphasize management's role for responsible decision making. Fourth, it must balance and recognize dual career opportunities, individual and team contributions, and the employees, their skills, *and* job accountabilities. Fifth, it must be able to retain and attract the highest caliber employees. Finally, it must be legally defensible and not discriminate against employees.

The JET concept was finally approved by executives in February 1993 and represented a radical shift from the old job evaluation system at MichCon. In short, JET would be an external market-based, skills-driven system with no grades.

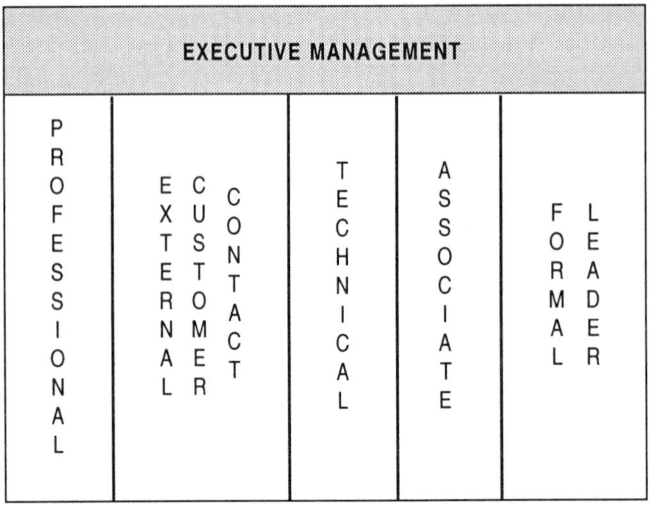

Figure 6.3 MichCon Job Groupings Under JET.

The overall corporate framework included six primary job groupings and is reflected in Figure 6.3.

Each job grouping would be further subdivided into detailed "tracks," indicating the various job competencies and how they would correspond to salary ranges and each other. A hypothetical example of a detailed track for the professional job grouping is shown in Figure 6.4.

The JET concept is intended to methodically link job documentation with market pay surveys, internal paylines, required competencies, and pay change opportunities.

Job Documentation

Under JET, ownership of job documentation at MichCon will transfer from the compensation department to the organization. The number of job descriptions and titles will be reduced as job descriptions are collapsed into job families and assigned paylines.

Market Surveys

Market surveys will collect the most relevant and current market data possible in order to develop paylines that have broad, comprehensive, and credible coverage of the organization.

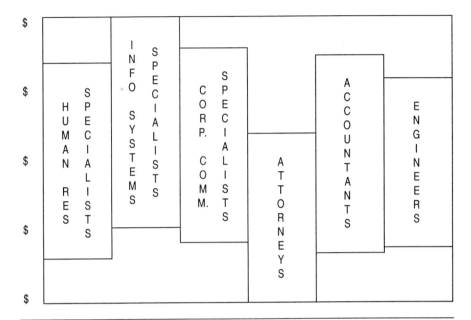

Figure 6.4 Detailed Professional Track Example from MichCon.

Paylines

Market and job family data will be integrated to develop paylines and employees will be placed within those paylines, based on current salaries. Three reference "yardsticks" will be established within each payline, indicating competency levels expected at various salary levels (entry, fully functioning, and advanced).

Competencies

Specific competencies and skills needed or required will be developed for each job family and market yardstick. Therefore, once the JET concept is fully in place, an employee's current salary should accurately reflect that the competencies required at that pay level are, in fact, possessed and demonstrated by that employee.

Pay Change Opportunities

Part of the system's development must include documentation of how pay can change. Employees need to understand their place in the new system and the opportunities and challenges that are present in shifting to a market-driven system. Opportunities for pay changes through market adjustments, competency adjustments, or job changes (within paylines or to new paylines) must all be spelled out. Credible methodologies for skills assessments must also be present so employees can compare their competency levels with some confidence to benchmarks/yardsticks for their payline, as well as understand competencies that must be mastered to move up within each payline.

The final stage of transformation to market-based job evaluation will involve the redesign of merit reward systems. Incentives tied to corporate and team performance will provide a "line of sight" from each employee's work to corporate results and align performance rewards with shareholder and customer interests.

Human Resources Organization Redesign

A critical phase in MichCon's transformation to total quality concerned the very design of the organization itself. This part of the effort has been termed Corporate Alignment and involves the realignment of organizational structure around core business processes versus traditional functional departments, placing new emphasis on customer-driven outcomes, process ownership, and cross-functional teamwork.

Continuing in the spirit of "The Power of You...Build the Future," this realignment has been approached via a "search conference" model, tapping the knowledge and experience present at all levels of the company to create an appropriate new organizational design.[11] Three search conferences were held in 1994 involving some 700 MichCon employees and numerous customers and suppliers in a systematic review of past and present achievements and shortcomings, future challenges and opportunities, and organization design options.

The Human Resources Activity recognized early on its own imperative to change in order to contribute to this corporate realignment process, as indicated by the following excerpt from an internal memorandum: "MichCon demands a superior, cost-effective, client-focused Human Resources. The data we have collected indicate that we are far from this goal." In an effort to better equip itself to support the organization, Human Resources initiated its own search process beginning in late 1993, prior to the corporation's overall effort.

The HR search process was created to accomplish several objectives: to forecast and clarify Human Resources' role in helping MichCon change, to prepare Human Resources to support the MichCon of the future, to create common understanding of what the organization considers value-added, and to determine the core competencies required for Human Resources. All Human Resources Activity members, closely aligned stakeholders, and client representatives were involved in the process.

A number of key learnings came out of the HR search conference, concerning both the future direction of Human Resources and search conference methodology.

Future Direction for Human Resources

The HR search conference questionnaires resulted in the following feedback: "We must be client focused"…"We cannot continue to be fragmented, separate, not focused and Us-oriented versus Client-oriented"…"Many of us continue to discount our clients' input."

The Human Resources Quality Council (HRQC) noted, in a follow-up to the HR search conference, that client focus was a common theme: "Virtually every group spoke about doing work that clients actively wanted. One group suggested allocating budget dollars to operating units to purchase HR services and that we would not do what was not purchased. Another group spoke about a contracting approach to HR and service recipients, getting to essentially the same end point."[12]

Client desires identified during the conference included a number of important themes that would guide future Human Resources strategy and planning at MichCon:

- Provide clear, concise communication based on fact

- Know and understand the client's business

- Identify critical issues and focus on them (versus trying to do everything)

- Eliminate divisional/specialized structure within Human Resources (everyone in Human Resources should be able to address multiple tasks/issues)

- Let clients do those things they can so Human Resources can focus on "big picture" and provide essential services

- Involve clients in program design

- Be less theoretical, more practical

- Partner local training attempts with HR trainers

- Be more accessible (versus invisible behind the maze of voice mail)

- Reduce costs

- Review current programs (e.g., sick leave) to verify they meet employee/organizational needs

- Remove barriers to dealing with performance issues

- Expect this list to grow!

As a result of small group work to create a vision of future Human Resources Activity at MichCon, several common themes emerged, in addition to customer focus, including cost effectiveness, strategic business partnering, and a move toward a generalist HR role.

In responding to the common theme of cost effectiveness, several groups proposed an entrepreneurial approach for Human Resources (e.g., selling HR services to non-MichCon organizations and competing with non-MichCon HR service providers for MichCon business). Regardless of the specific approach, the underlying need for Human Resources is to provide high-quality service at a price lower than other service providers. To support this direction, HR professionals must become more adept at measuring results, in order to validate high-value service.

Numerous groups noted that strategic business partnering will require a superior knowledge of client operations by HR professionals. In many group visions, HR representatives were seen as employees of operating departments rather than a centralized HR department.

There was also common acknowledgment of the need to address the role of HR specialists and generalists in service delivery. Every group depicted a role for generalists who would serve as liaisons between operating departments and sophisticated HR specialists providing technical services. This team approach would maximize client service by linking generalists who are well-grounded in both HR disciplines and business issues, with specialized technical expertise as needed.

The HR search process sent a message to everyone. Before HR professionals could meet the needs of their clients and assist in the realignment of the company, they had to first understand their own expectations and perceived limitations, realign their own thought processes in some nontraditional ways, and find ways to get beyond "We don't do that" attitudes and "turfism" and become a supportive part of the total quality process in managing human resources.

Search Conference Methodology

A number of specific recommendations emerged with respect to the design and facilitation of search conferences. This information proved useful in enhancing the corporate search conference process and may be useful to others considering this methodology:

- Make expectations clear prior to and at the start of the conference; then check progress against those objectives. Specific objectives and outcomes *must* be established for people to feel that their time was well spent.

- Recognize that participation by leadership is key; lack of attendance or participation may be viewed with skepticism and interpreted as lack of commitment.

- Make sure clients know up front what their role will be and how it will impact the conference. Make good, productive use of clients' time and incorporate their input as early as possible in the design.

- Allow adequate time in the design for client feedback; this is one of the richest opportunities for interaction and heightened understanding of needs, so do not short-change it.

- Ensure that data/information from clients is summarized, recorded, and reviewed with clients after the conference, along with a strategy for response (including specific action steps and measures to ensure client needs are being addressed).

- Make sure there is adequate representation from all stakeholder groups (e.g., employee groups, home and district offices). Also, where historical conflicts have existed between departments or areas, consciously ensure that the design supports the building of bridges between those areas (instead of exacerbating old wounds).

- Make sure, in a multi-level conference such as this (with multiple levels of "bosses" in the room), the design enables everyone to "have a say," not just those who are naturally vocal or who are "simply trying to impress."

- Assign pre-work readings and questions to help prepare people for the conference; pre-work should help enrich discussion/interaction time in the session. Make effective use of pre-work assignments during the session, so people recognize a payoff for the time invested.

- Resist spending too much time and emphasis on past/present discussions which may paralyze the group's thinking and hinder breakthrough ideas. This data, if it is to be gathered, must have some apparent usefulness for the group.

- Provide typing support with lap-top computers to gather and record information during the session for rapid turnaround of data.

- Be careful that specific design approaches match the "culture" of the audience. In this case, an exercise calling for artistic representations using nontraditional materials (pipe cleaners, glitter, glue, plastic beads) provided avenues for creativity, but also provoked resistance (e.g., "elementary school materials for the group presentation only emphasize a lack of respect for professional adults," and "Why do we deliberately set up exercises that focus on aesthetics (whose picture is prettiest) rather than on content and quality or clarity of thought?"...It is important to set a business tone for the conference).

- Provide an evaluation opportunity at the end of each conference to enable learning and continuous improvement.

- Recognize that the search conference process is a new and evolving methodology. Listen to the participants; if the design does not work, change it. Do not assume that it is not working because the participants don't get it. If they don't, it is a design problem. Respect the audience—do not assume they "just don't understand" or "are in pain."

The "reinvention" of the Human Resources Activity as MichCon's corporate realignment enfolds is sure to be a challenging, stimulating, and sometimes painful process.

While these corporate-wide efforts focused on new systems for personal development, leader certification, job evaluation, and organization design, other pilot experiments were underway in operational areas to reshape peer relationships among employees and to foster new employee responsibility in areas previously reserved for management. Three noteworthy experiments in sharing HR power are highlighted below: peer discipline, peer safety, and peer hiring.

Peer Discipline

In an attempt to be responsive to employee concerns about the fairness of disciplinary actions for minor work rule violations, an operations manager, labor relations manager, and union vice president in MichCon's distribution area met to brainstorm new and improved ways to handle disciplinary action. This "organizing committee" got the endorsement of the distribution director and the legal department to try a pilot program at one station on peer dispute review.

The pilot involved creating a new Disciplinary Review Committee (DRC), consisting of employees who would review cases of peers accused of minor work rule violations. This "council of peers" would be made available to employees on a voluntary basis as an alternative to the traditional disciplinary approach through the management hierarchy. The ruling of the review committee would be considered final (not to be appealed by the supervisor);

employees, however, would still have the option to file a grievance following this peer review if dissatisfied with the outcome. It was hoped that a credible disciplinary process involving peers would, in the long run, increase the sense of fairness in handling discipline problems and reduce the number of grievances overall.

One station requested that it be given the opportunity to pilot the effort. The organizing committee thought certain types of people should be invited to join the review team—people who were outspoken but not belligerent and people who would stand up for their beliefs and not fold easily to the pressure of peers or management. Six names were identified, five for the committee and one alternate. A supervisor was added to the team to demonstrate that it was a company committee and create a sense of everyone being "in it together." The alternate was considered important if another committee member felt it necessary to opt out of a given situation or if the supervisor on the review committee was also the supervisor disciplining an employee whose case was before the group (e.g., conflict of interest).

The pilot organizers met with the six potential committee members, explained the concept, asked for input and invited them to participate. Initial reactions varied greatly, including:

- "I'm all for it."

- "Good idea, but I'm quiet...could I really judge people?"

- "I'm not sure this is the best thing...I'm not sure it will work."

- "What's my role as union steward? Represent the employee? Serve on the committee? Whether the employee's right or wrong, shouldn't I always advocate for the employee?"

People were not asked for their answer at this initial time of invitation, but to think about it for a couple of weeks. When they reconvened in two weeks, all six agreed to serve.

To better equip the team in its work, three days of initial training/ team building were held. During this session, team members learned about each other's personality preferences and strengths/weaknesses, built a basis for trust and open communication, created a team charter which articulated their vision for this effort and the guidelines by which they would operate, and agreed upon criteria by which to evaluate their effectiveness as a team. The operational guidelines they developed are a testimonial to the ability and willingness of employees to take personal responsibility for doing *the right thing*, for both the employee and the company:

We, the Disciplinary Review Committee,
will be governed by the following guidelines:

Trust: Having confidence in our ability to act with integrity.

Fairness: To be just and honest as we strive to determine the facts.

Contact with Understanding: Willingness to learn from [another] point of view or interpretation.

Openness: Willing to discuss matters in a frank and candid manner.

Will Not Prejudge: We will look at the *facts* and not the person (without personal bias or prejudice).

Empathy: To be able to identify with [someone else's] situation.

Respect: To show honor for and highly value each individual.

In the first 9 months of the pilot program, the DRC heard 16 cases out of a total of 21. In six cases, the level of discipline recommended by the supervisor was upheld. In four cases, the employee was counseled by the review committee, but no discipline was issued. In the remaining six cases, no discipline was issued.

The original pilot organizers, the DRC and the department director all agreed that the pilot had been effective in a number of ways: employees seemed to be satisfied with the opportunity to "state their case" and be heard, the committee took proactive steps to eliminate possible problems in the future by addressing concerns brought to their attention through the review process, team members grew in self-confidence and pride in playing a more responsible role with their peers, and employees moved from an adversarial interaction with management regarding discipline issues to a shared sense of responsibility to each other and the company. The pilot was expanded to four other stations in 1994, and the original pilot team played a key role in preparing new DRC members by sharing key learnings from their own experience.

Peer Safety

Another opportunity to bring "The Power of You" to life with frontline employees involved the area of safety. MichCon's approach to safety had been fairly traditional prior to the advent of "The Power of You." A safety manager would conduct safety inspections in the field and provide feedback reports to employees' supervisors and managers. Some managers would put pressure on supervisors to "write employees up" or impose disciplinary sanctions for safety violations, using the safety inspections as a means to threaten or trigger discipline. Not surprisingly, this approach was perceived by employees as another example of management harassment.

With the atmosphere created by "The Power of You," managers and employees began to ask how they could apply the principles inherent in the vision and values statement to the important area of safety. With some initial support from the safety department manager and the union vice president, a pilot project was initiated in one operational area to create a peer safety review team made up of twelve frontline employees.

Working in pairs, employees on the Peer Safety Team would conduct surprise safety inspections at every station every month (going to stations other than their own work site), give immediate feedback to employees for unsafe conditions or practices, work with employees to determine ways of improving safety, and document the number and nature of incidents occurring, *without employee names*. Documenting the occurrence of unsafe practices without identifying individuals would encourage individuals, the department, and the organization to become more conscious about safety issues and to solve and prevent safety problems without fear of punishment or retribution.

A number of roadblocks became evident immediately, not the least of which was the "baggage" employees carried from past relationships with management. Many people did not believe management was serious. Some employees were afraid that station managers would not support the peer safety teams and would undermine their effectiveness by questioning "who's going to do your work?" and only grudgingly allow them to participate while making snide remarks that could be picked up by peers.

Encouraged by the support of the union and department management, employees finally believed this was a serious effort. Employees took responsibility to select the team members (all union employees), basing their decisions on what they believed to be the most crucial criteria of credibility— that team members would be credible, respected by their peers, on the basis of their own work and safety record; in other words, they truly practiced what they were about to preach.

The team was formed and participated in a one-day training/team building session designed to (1) understand and agree upon their role, (2) define their procedures, and (3) understand more about interpersonal communication styles and what elements trigger negativity and resistance or reinforce acceptance and cooperation. Equipped with these new tools and insights, the team began conducting safety inspections.

One major insight came from the safety department manager, who had to let go of his former power and authority to enable the team to be effective in its role. Team members were clear that they would not participate on the team unless this manager was "out of the process" from the beginning. All shared one concern: their credibility was on the line with respect to confidentiality. If any word got out about individual safety violations, that person would be embarrassed and the team members would be perceived as "company snitches." The real needs for team accountability were clear and shared by both management and employees:

1. *Never* walk away from an unsafe situation

2. Take responsibility to make individuals aware of how their actions are contributing to unsafe conditions

3. Work with employees to correct the current situation and identify opportunities for problem prevention

4. Anonymously document both the unsafe practices observed and the corrective action taken so the larger organization could learn from these experiences and apply that learning to other stations or situations beyond the scope of the pilot project

To his credit, the safety department manager recognized that he had to "let go"; in doing so, there were twelve people out in the field promoting safety instead of just him. He saw his job evolving to support this team and shifted his own thinking from doing inspections to doing whatever he could to make the team successful. In this new role, he worked with the public affairs department to facilitate communication of the team's efforts throughout the company so it could become a model for others. He also became an advocate for the team with management, working behind the scenes in a supportive role and challenging management in other areas to respond to resource needs to solve safety problems (e.g., more timely repair of trucks and equipment modifications for safety reasons).

Initial results have been dramatic. In the first year following implementation of the Peer Safety Team, the department experienced a 30% reduction in injuries overall, and an all-time low in OSHA-recordable injuries. The pilot program's success has resulted in an expansion of the effort to several other locations. The longer term safety goal has been set at zero injuries by January 1998.

Peer Hiring

"The Power of You" began to change the approach to employee recruitment and selection at MichCon as well. Management had traditionally hired all employees working through the employment department. In the spirit of

"The Power of You," the question was asked: "How could employees play a responsible role in hiring fellow workers?" Thanks to the progressive thinking of a key operations director who was willing to experiment with new ways of doing business, a pilot effort was started that involved union employees in the hiring process.

The effort began in year one with union employees only conducting interviews; management still selected those candidates to be interviewed and kept a close watch on the entire process. For the subsequent two years, however, employees took full responsibility for reviewing resumes, selecting candidates for interviews, conducting interviews, and making the actual hiring decisions.

The membership pool for the employee hiring team was created through a self-nomination process; it seemed important that members serving in this capacity be motivated to do so. Selection from this pool was made on the basis of the quality of work demonstrated by the employees and the type of involvement they had already exhibited in the spirit of "The Power of You"; in other words, this additional responsibility became a reward or recognition for those who had taken the initiative to become involved and contribute.

The operations director and HR department served in supporting roles to the employees; while technically they retained the authority to approve a hiring decision, in no instance was a selection made by the employee hiring team ever reversed. The role of the employment specialist in the HR department became one of coaching and challenging: coaching with regard to the scope of issues to be addressed in responsible hiring and challenging the team's thinking to ensure that important compliance and diversity issues were addressed appropriately. One desired outcome of this process was to broaden the appreciation among employees for what it takes to make good hiring decisions.

Training in recruitment and selection was provided to team members for one day and included such topics as recruitment and selection, job analysis, and effective interviewing techniques. Actual interview questions were developed in this training by employees, with the support of recruitment specialists. The HR professionals never sat in on interviews; they reviewed documentation to ensure legal compliance and participated in consensus meetings where hiring decisions were made, to challenge thinking and add new perspectives.

The process has not been without its challenges. There was some concern that the tendency for people to hire others just like them might prove to be a block to hiring the kind of gender and ethnic diversity needed for the future. In some cases, nonpeers were built into the interview process to ensure that a broader perspective of job requirements and candidate capabilities was represented (e.g., separate interview teams consisting of union employees, nonunion employees, peer employees, and department management). These separate teams then came to consensus with each other about recommended candidates.

By the end of 1993, some 30 employees had been hired through this employee-directed process. Although this effort started out as a pilot in one department, early success was so promising that most operational departments now engage in some form of employee team interviewing.

Summary

MichCon has made significant progress since 1989, when it initiated its transformation to becoming a premier organization and the best natural gas company. In setting its sights at the highest level possible, MichCon has embarked on a journey that will carry it into the next millennium.

The most powerful testimonials possible for the impact and value of making quality personal at MichCon come from frontline employees who have worked together to achieve breakthroughs in quality results. In 1993, representatives of employee teams who had received MichCon's first Quality Achievement Awards convened to discuss how employees can build and support the quality effort at the "grass roots" level.

Employees shared insights gained from their own quality improvement team experiences—factors that had contributed to their success—and compiled an education piece that was subsequently shared with other employees through staff meetings, presentations, and networking.

Total Quality Human Resource Lessons for the Entire Organization

Employees felt they had the freedom to make decisions and try new things/take risks (do whatever it takes, within reason). Employees perceived they had real support, which reduced their fear of failure. Thus, managers were credited with giving power to workers, and workers boldly took that power to responsibly create change.

The dedication of group members, their personal commitment to a common goal, and their ability to adapt to constant changes were seen as crucial. The total group became involved, with no "fence sitters." The groups created and lived by their own ground rules—listening to each other, respecting everyone's opinion (no titles), and communicating openly and honestly without fear of repercussions.

Teams were effective at researching and analyzing problems, seeking feedback, planning and following through. Effective problem solving was not enough, however; effective teamwork was also key. Teams learned to address a problem and come to agreement through patience and learned not to take disagreements personally. They also learned the importance of recognizing and celebrating organizational results and individual contributions.

Total Quality Human Resource Lessons for Frontline Employees

In learning from their experiences, the teams had some important advice to offer other quality improvement teams or efforts. The advice itself is not new, but it may serve as a "common sense" reminder to those who know the power of employee involvement and support it on a regular basis. The source—a collection of frontline employees who rose to a new challenge together and, through no small amount of effort, achieved breakthrough results in a changing environment—gives this advice special weight. The recommendations of frontline employees at MichCon are presented in their own words as a gift to frontline employees everywhere who want to succeed at quality at the "grass roots" level:

- Think about what you *can* do, not what you cannot.
- Be objective.
- Be willing to give feedback. Be straightforward and honest.
- Establish ground rules as a team and live by them.
- Be a good coach!
- Ensure that the overall philosophy is shared and participants support the vision and values.
- Get commitment!
- Recognize that people may select not to participate.
- Keep others informed (co-workers, other departments, team members, management, etc.).
- Allow people to live with the consequences of their behavior.
- Respect others' decisions. Don't force it.
- Make it easy to participate.
- Make achievements visible (i.e., goal boards).
- Thank people, and appreciate people. Remind them that their contributions are invaluable.
- Treat our co-workers (internal customers) as external customers.

- Share positive experiences! Take time to enjoy what you did.

- Start small and build.

- Be willing to listen to others and adjust your thinking.

- Avoid having different levels have different power. There are no big "I's and little "you's" (everyone is equal).

- Share the "big picture" with employees (company goals).

- Set a good example for others.

- Provide personal recognition that doesn't happen every day.

- Just do it—don't wait for someone else to do it.

- Constant communication is essential (e.g., talk about what's going on in section meetings, solve problems).

- Stop blaming others. Let people know why decisions are made.

- Foster pride in the work and in others. Support others in developing positive self-esteem.

- Reach out and include others...*invite* others to participate.

- Recognize that we are all in this together (management and employees).

- Talk about fear and see how actions can actually work.

- Avoid making excuses. Admit mistakes and work them through.

Total Quality Human Resource Lessons for Senior Management

Another set of lessons emerged for senior management, given the role they had played throughout the early years of the effort:

1. The need for leaders to "walk the talk" is paramount. In the midst of such continuous and substantive change, leadership behaviors become intensely magnified.

2. Officer time commitment is extensive and should not be underestimated.

3. Some 20% of the employee population will be ready and willing to step out and make change. Senior leaders need to utilize and support that 20% right from the start.

4. The path of change is not smooth; therefore, consistency and persistence are essential to ensure long-term success of a quality transformation of this magnitude.

As the MichCon experience documents, the challenges of creating a premier organization characterized by quality service and total quality human resources are not inconsequential. Business news stories provide dramatic reminders almost daily that no one can take his or her livelihood for granted anymore and traditional ground rules no longer apply. New answers must be created by effectively developing and tapping *all* available resources, most importantly people. MichCon's investment in applying total quality principles in managing human resources has reaped impressive returns.

Having provided a conceptually integrated total quality implementation action plan and an empirical case study of MichCon as a domestic success story, it is time to turn to information about the global implementation of total quality HR practices.

INTERNATIONAL IMPLEMENTATION OF TOTAL QUALITY HUMAN RESOURCE PRACTICES

In 1989 the American Quality Foundation and Ernst and Young undertook a massive international study of quality practices on three continents.[13] The study analyzed 580 organizations in Japan, the United States, Canada, and Germany and focused on more than 900 separate management practices from those organizations. Eighty-four percent of the firms responded to the last comprehensive questionnaire, which provided a measure of the use of quality management practices in general, as well as quality developments in different parts of the world.

The firms selected for the study came from four industries: automotive, banking, computer, and health care. The firms were selected from these industries regardless of their commitment to the principles of the quality revolution. The study indicates the degree of implementation of total quality in these industries in each country.

From the more than 900 quality practices, ten core practices were identified as distinguishing firms that implemented total quality from those that had not.[14] The ten practices are categorized as those related to strategic planning, customer expectations, core technology, evaluating performance, and teams and participation.[15] These practices address many of the key elements of the House of Total Quality. They point toward the use of customer information to guide strategic decisions and develop new products, process improvement efforts using simplification and cycle time analysis to guide internal quality efforts, and the interaction of employees in teams or other participatory involvement.

1. Strategic Planning: *Customer satisfaction (CS) is used as a primary criterion in the strategic planning process.* Using CS information in the strategic planning process shows the depth of the quality commitment in the organization. With the pervasive use of CS data, all parts of the organization will adjust to, sustain, and/or improve the level of the customer's satisfaction.

- **Japan:** About 42% of the firms currently use quality information in the strategic planning process. About 80% of the Japanese firms intend to use quality information in the next three years.

- **North America:** Canadian firms lead the world in considering CS information as primary in strategic planning. About 80% of the Canadian firms forecast using CS as a primary indicator over the next three years. About 70% of the U.S. firms thought they would use CS as a primary criterion in the future. About 17% of the U.S. firms relegate CS to secondary importance.

- **Germany:** Only about 22% presently consider CS to be of primary importance in the strategic planning process. About 27% of the firms put CS in a secondary role, while 51% consider it to be of major importance.

- **Summary:** CS is not as important a measure in Germany as it is in the other countries. Japan leads, with about 95% of the firms considering CS as a major or primary measure in the planning process. The U.S. and Canada still have a significant percentage of firms that do not use CS in their planning process. All organizations are increasing their use of CS information as a primary criterion. Germany still lags significantly behind in its use of CS information.

2. Strategic Planning: *Importance of competitor comparisons in the strategic planning process.* Competitor comparisons (CC), benchmarking exercises, and reverse engineering products are some ways organizations obtain competitor information. Comparing the organizations against information from competitors illustrates strengths and weaknesses of the present organization. Maturity in this area indicates an organization that is confident about the competitive quality of its product or service.

- **Japan:** More than 90% of the Japanese firms use CC in the strategic planning process.

- **North America:** Canadian firms use CC less than do U.S. firms (67% to 82%) in a primary or major way. About 31% of the Canadian firms feel such comparisons are secondary in importance.

- **Germany:** Less than 5% of the German firms use CC as a component in strategic planning. About 56% of the firms consider it of major importance, while 39% relegate it to secondary importance.

- **Summary:** The Japanese place greater importance than do other countries on CC. The Germans give it less importance, with a large percentage considering it to be of secondary importance (39%). About 31% of the Canadian firms also consider CC to be of secondary importance.

3. Customer Expectations: *Departments develop new products or services based on customer expectations.* If an organization is going to sustain quality leadership, the design unit has to be very effective. Success in this criterion depends on a commitment to the customer, a well-developed information system, and the depth of the product or service design system.

- **Japan:** About 90% of the firms usually or always use customer expectations to develop new products.

- **North America:** In both countries, less than 70% of the firms usually or always use customer expectations in product development. About 30% of the firms do not use expectations at all.

- **Germany:** About 83% of the German firms always or usually use customer expectations for new product development.

- **Summary:** German and Japanese firms lead the North American firms in usually or always using customer expectations in developing new products. About 30% of the North American firms use customer expectations occasionally or less, compared to about 20% of the German and 10% of the Japanese firms.

4. Customer Expectations: *Importance of technology in meeting customer expectations.* The use of technology can enable an organization to meet customer expectations. Technology enhances problem solving, decision making, and service capabilities of the frontline worker in numerous ways. Technology enables superior service or manufacturing because it empowers people to rapidly respond to customer inquiries.

- **Japan:** About 98% of the Japanese firms value technology as of prime or major importance in meeting customer expectations. The intensity of the use of technology to meet customer expectations will increase in the next three years.

- **North America:** About 80% of the firms in North America place primary or major emphasis on technology in meeting customer expectations. A surprising 20% relegate technology to secondary importance. Over the next three years, both countries will increase their intensity dramatically.

- **Germany:** About 93% of the German firms place primary or major emphasis on the use of technology. Only 7% relegate technology to secondary importance. Over the next three years, the German firms intend to use technology more intensely as a primary strategy.

- **Summary:** Both Japan and Germany place significantly more importance on the use of technology than do the North American firms. About 23% of the U.S. firms relegate technology to secondary or no value. More Japanese firms use technology as a primary support of their quality efforts.

5. Core Technology: *The use of process simplification (PS) to improve business processes.* Process simplification is the focus on continually understanding smaller subprocesses of key business processes, as indicated in Chapter 4. The overall philosophy is the basic approach of both the functional and the quality network structures. Continual improvement is based on the logic of PS.

- **Japan:** About 82% usually or always use PS.

- **North America:** Significantly more Canadian firms than U.S. firms use PS (72% to 47%). About 54% of the American firms use PS occasionally or less, indicating a lack of emphasis on improving operations.

- **Germany:** Only 34% of the German firms usually or always use PS. About 66% use it occasionally or less.

- **Summary:** Using PS as a measure of the maturity of the quality commitment in the operations area puts the Japanese and Canadians in the lead. The Americans and Germans place less value on the process. In the American case, there is a tendency to rely on innovation to improve the company's quality. German firms tend to emphasize heavy engineering design at the beginning of PS with minor adjustments at the end of PS. The Japanese work at improving the process constantly.

6. Cycle Time Technology: *The use of process cycle time (PCT) analysis to improve business processes.* In the changing external world, a firm's rapid cycle time gives it a competitive advantage. When customer expectations are turned into requirements, then into specifications, and finally into a product/service in a rapid sequence, this cycle time technology is perceived as superior and deserving of customer allegiance.

- **Japan:** About 84% of the Japanese firms usually or always use cycle time to improve business processes.

- **North America:** About 84% of Canadian firms usually or always use cycle time. About 60% of the U.S. firms use cycle time.

- **Germany:** Less than 47% of the German firms usually or always use PCT. About 53% use cycle time occasionally or less.

- **Summary:** Japanese and Canadian firms use cycle time significantly more than firms in other countries. Over half the German firms only use PCT occasionally or seldom. About 40% of the U.S. firms use PCT occasionally or less.

7. Evaluating Performance: *Executive compensation depends on performance-compensation-quality criteria.* Executive compensation has traditionally been based on increasing profits. Bonuses, stock options, and profit pools are some of the traditional approaches, particularly in North America. Relating incentives to quality is an important change in for-profit enterprises.

- **Japan:** About 20% of Japanese executives' salaries are dependent on the firm's quality performance. This soon will increase to about 30%.

- **North America:** The number of firms that apply incentives to quality criteria has doubled in the last couple of years. This trend is expected to double again in the next three years as well. Canada will go to about 40% and the U.S. to about 50% of executives with quality incentives. This is greater than any of the other countries.

- **Germany:** The Germans just began to look at quality items for their incentives, increasing to about 10% currently. Other companies are planning to convert to quality incentives, which will raise Germany's total to about 30% in three years.

- **Summary:** Germany lags behind the other countries in providing quality incentives for top management. The Japanese adaptation to quality incentives is moderate. They are not adopting quality incentives as readily as the North Americans. It is clear, though, that providing quality incentives is increasing in world executive suites.

8. Evaluating Performance: *Quality information used to evaluate business performance.* The commitment to use quality information has to be supported by the appropriate information system. How frequently quality information makes it to the desk of the decision makers is a measure of the commitment of a firm to quality.

- **Japan:** About 90% of the Japanese firms use quality information at least quarterly to evaluate performance.

- **North America:** About 70% of the U.S. firms use quality information at least quarterly. An interesting statistic is that about 18% of firms use it less than annually or not at all. Canadian firms showed some of the same tendencies as U.S. firms.

- **Germany:** About 70% of the German firms use quality information at least quarterly. About 25% use quality information yearly for evaluation.

- **Summary:** About 15% of the North American firms do not use quality information to evaluate business performance. This is an indication of how far the quality revolution has to go in North America in terms of using data collection in decision making. About the same number of German and North American firms use quality information quarterly or better. Japan's organizations are most likely to use quality information to evaluate performance during the year.

9. Teams and Participation: *Percentage of employees in quality-related teams (QRTs).* The team network is a key component of the quality effort, as indicated in Chapters 3 and 4. Teams are formed to deal with unit problem solving (functional teams) or with cross-functional processes (process management teams). This question determines the percentage of firms that have one of three levels of employees involved on a team.

- **Japan:** About 36% of the Japanese firms have more than 25% of their employees in QRTs. They intend to increase this percentage only slightly, to about 39%, in the next three years.

- **North America:** U.S. firms have about 49% of their employees in QRTs, about 10% more than the Canadians. The Canadians and Americans expect to increase their QRTs significantly, to 77% and 70%, respectively.

- **Germany:** Only 20% of the German firms have more than 25% of their employees in QRTs. The intent is to double this to about 42% in the next three years.

- **Summary:** The U.S. and Canadian firms use QRTs more than do other countries and intend to increase the intensity of the use of QRTs. The Germans use QRTs less than the others, and the Japanese have only moderate usage. The heavy union/government socialism in Germany has an impact on this criterion.

10. Teams and Participation: *Percentage of employees participating in meetings about quality (QM).* Meetings are another component of the quality leadership firm. Meetings to problem solve, communicate, coordinate, and control quality-related efforts are an important form of employee involvement. Such firms depend on a high-intensity communication structure to sustain their success. A willing commitment to QMs is a major indicator of the maturity of a new organization.

- **Japan:** About 65% of the firms have over 25% of their employees participate in QMs.

- **North America:** About 40% of the North American firms use QMs, in which over 25% of employees participate.

- **Germany:** About 32% of the firms have more than 25% of their employees participating in QMs.

- **Summary:** About 39% of Japan's firms have more than 75% of their employees involved in regular QMs. About 68% of German firms have 25% or less of their employees in QMs.

The preceding ten international total quality practices impact HR policies and indicate the range of relative global quality implementation. It is clear that Japanese organizations use total quality practices more intensively than do firms in other major global trading regions. *North American firms exhibit the widest range of implementation variation, with heavy reliance on executive incentive programs rather than internal system improvements to stimulate total quality initiatives.* German firms have implemented the fewest total quality practices, in part because their fastidious concentration on internal operational detail detracts from their concern for either the competition or customers.[16] Nevertheless, the extent of total quality implementation indicates that it is a pervasive world phenomenon that has or will impact the global competitiveness and HR policies of any firm.

Two major motivators are among the many incentives to implement total quality systems and practices: winning a significant quality prize/award and meeting international quality certification standards. A comparison profile of both the quality prize/awards (Deming Prize: Japan; Baldrige Award: United States; and European Quality Award: Europe) and the leading quality certification standard (ISO 9000 certification) is provided in Table 6.3. Firms that win the quality prize/awards and meet global quality process certification are, with rare exceptions, leaders in their respective industries. The best total quality firms do not approach award winning and certification as ends in and of themselves, but as valuable and sometimes necessary vehicles for institutionalizing continuous improvement and competitive advantage.

The respective emphases of the Deming Prize, which focuses on statistical control, problem solving, and continual incremental improvement, and the Baldrige and European Quality Awards, which focus on organizational-level systems and leadership development, are partly due to cultural differences and partly due to historical changes in the quality movement. The technical approach of the Deming Prize in Japan is due to the prize being structured and administered by academic scientists and engineers (Deming and the Union of Japanese Scientists and Engineers). The less technical organizational management approach of the Baldrige and European Quality

Table 6.3 Comparison of International Quality Prize/Awards and Certification Standards

	Deming Prize	Baldrige Award	European Quality Award	ISO 9000 Certification
Year created	1951	1987	1992	1987
Basic form	Long-term prize	Annual contest for award	Long-term award	Certification
Primary geographic applicability	Japan	United States	Europe	World
Winners	Few	Few	Very few	Many
Emphasis	Statistical control; problem solving; continual incremental improvement	Customer leadership; support organization; measurement; benchmarking	Organizational enablers and results; leadership, processes, and results	Equal minimal global quality standards; documentation of system control, operating processes, and support activities
Cost	High	Medium-high	Medium-high	Low-medium

Awards is due to their formulation and determination by groups of businesspeople concerned about quality from the managerial leadership perspective. The early historical advances in technical quality control procedures catapulted many Japanese firms into world-class leaders in manufacturing in the 1970s and accelerated the comeback of selected U.S. firms in the 1980s. However, the organizational management approach to the quality movement has incorporated the broader strategic implications of change management, the impact of information technology, the leadership influence on HR performance, and the service/nonprofit sectors, in addition to the manufacturing sector, in its widespread use in the 1990s in the United States and Europe. The total quality HRM criteria in all the prize/awards are useful tactical guides for continuous improvement of HR performance.

ISO 9000 is a set of certification standards designed to promote international trade by creating a level playing field for producers worldwide to compete equally.[17] The intent is to certify individual firms, making it easy for an organization to purchase goods and services from around the world and be assured of their minimal uniform quality. While the ISO 9000 series of standards was developed in Europe, it is gaining global applicability.[18] The certification series consists of five standards: ISO 9000 provides concepts and definitions; ISO 9001, 9002, and 9003 cover specific aspects of a quality assurance program; and ISO 9004 focuses on creating and sustaining a quality management system, including specific HR training and development issues, leadership issues, and performance recognition issues.

By meeting ISO 9004 standards regarding managing human resources according to total quality principles and policies and by remaining competitive for major quality prize/awards, organizations gain world-class performance from their human resources. It is this external global challenge, as much as the internal, intrinsic merit of managing human resources by total quality principles, that is propelling firms to examine the total quality integrated implementation plan in Table 6.1, emulate the success of MichCon, and begin applying total quality approaches to managing human resources at all levels in every country in the world.

REVIEW QUESTIONS

6.1. Describe the six distinct theoretical models for implementing total quality.

6.2. Relying upon Table 6.1, describe goal-setting implementation.

6.3. Relying upon Table 6.1, describe strategy implementation.

6.4. Relying upon Table 6.1, describe project implementation.

6.5. From the MichCon case, describe in detail the following implementation actions: measurement of results and the personal development system.

6.6. From the MichCon case, describe in detail the peer hiring and peer discipline implementation actions.

6.7. Compare and contrast the total quality implementation practices of Japan, North America, and Germany with regard to strategic planning and customer expectations.

6.8. Compare and contrast the total quality implementation practices of Japan, North America, and Germany with regard to core technology, performance evaluation, and teams and participation.

6.9. Provide a detailed comparison of the major total quality award/prizes and the major global certification standards that often guide implementation efforts.

DISCUSSION QUESTIONS

6.1. Discuss the advantages and disadvantages of selecting *only one* theoretical model for implementing total quality and using it consistently and exclusively in an organization.

6.2. Relying upon Table 6.1, conceptually apply the first three total quality operational steps to either your current workplace or school and determine what kinds of changes would have to be made in order to fully implement those total quality steps.

6.3. Relying upon Table 6.1, conceptually apply the last four total quality operational steps to either your current workplace or school and determine what kinds of changes would have to be made in order to fully implement those total quality steps.

6.4. From the MichCon case, apply each of the "grass roots" quality recommendations of frontline employees to your current or a selected past workplace and describe the difference each application would make or would have made in the quality of work and the quality of work life.

6.5. How would you begin to institute the personal development system and peer hiring and peer discipline policies in your current workplace or school?

6.6. From your analyses of the comparative global implementation of total quality practices, what five areas should the United States focus on in the near future to reduce or eliminate major total quality implementation gaps in relation to Japanese practices?

6.7. Conduct research to determine ten ways in which total quality award/ prize winners in Japan, North America, and Europe are more competitive than nonwinners in their respective industries. What lessons do they offer to total quality human resource practitioners in all firms, domestically and globally?

ENDNOTES

1. Reger, R.K., Gustafson, L.T., De Marie, S.M., and Mullane, J.V. (1994). "Reframing the Organization: Why Implementing Total Quality Is Easier Said Than Done." *Academy of Management Review.* Vol. 19, No. 3, pp. 565–584.

2. Lewis, Ralph G. and Smith, Douglas H. (1994). *Total Quality in Higher Education.* Delray Beach, Fla.: St. Lucie Press, pp. 233–234. This section of the chapter relies heavily on their work.

3. Niven, Daniel (1993). "When Times Get Tough, What Happens to TQM?" *Harvard Business Review.* Vol. 27, No. 3, pp. 21–24.

4. Lewis, Ralph G. and Smith, Douglas H. (1994). *Total Quality in Higher Education.* Delray Beach, Fla.: St. Lucie Press, p. 235.

5. Lewis, Ralph G. and Smith, Douglas H. (1994). *Total Quality in Higher Education.* Delray Beach, Fla.: St. Lucie Press, pp. 240–251.

6. Spechler, Jay W. (1993). *Managing Quality in America's Most Admired Companies.* San Francisco: Berrett-Koehler, pp. 359–363.

7. The authors wish to thank MichCon President and CEO Stephen Ewing for his generosity in providing access to corporate documents and members of his organization, both of which enabled the preparation of this updated case study. An earlier version of this case study appeared in Spechler, Jay W. (1993). *Managing Quality in America's Most Admired Companies.* San Francisco: Berrett-Koehler, pp. 359–363. This updated study was written from the personal consulting experience of one of the authors with the cooperation of individuals who played key roles in the transformation strategy at MichCon: the Directors of Organizational Development, Quality Service, Corporate Measurement Distribution, Corporate Communication, Labor Relations, Employment, and Compensation. The updated case reflects the first three years of effort and the foundation of the change strategy as it impacted HRM policies and practices. While some total quality strategies are highlighted here, practitioners may benefit from the other details contained in the original case study.

8. The entire text of MichCon's vision and values statement is printed here with the company's permission:

"We, the employees of MichCon, acknowledge our unique responsibility in providing services critical to the quality of life in the communities we serve.

Therefore, we are dedicated to being a premier organization, and the best natural gas company, by continuously improving value to our customers and shareholders.

Our actions are guided by the following *principles*:

We respect diversity and the value of each individual.

We take personal responsibility for our actions, and pride in making a difference.

We work together as a team committed to open, candid communication and mutual support.

Our safety and the safety of our customers and the general public will not be compromised.

Our successes are measured by our ability to exceed internal and external customer expectations.

We act with honesty and integrity.

We protect the environment and improve the quality of live where we work and live.

We are committed to being innovative and creative in our jobs."

9. Spechler, Jay, W. (1993). *Managing Quality in America's Most Admired Companies*. San Francisco: Berrett-Koehler, p. 360.
10. Federal Express (1992). *Leadership Evaluation and Awareness Process Guide*.
11. Weisbord, Marvin R. (1987). *Productive Workplaces: Organizing and Managing for Dignity, Meaning and Community*. San Francisco: Jossey-Bass, pp. 284–295.
12. MichCon Human Resources Quality Council (December 20, 1993). "Internal Memorandum to HR Employees."
13. Ernst and Young (1991). *International Quality Study*. Cleveland: Ernst and Young.
14. Ernst and Young (1991). *Top-Line Findings*. Cleveland: Ernst and Young.
15. Vroman, H. William and Luchsinger, V.P. (1994). *Managing Organizational Quality*. Burr Ridge, Ill.: Irwin, pp. 287–296. This section of the chapter relies heavily on this work.
16. Tillier, Alan (1993). *Doing Business in Today's Western Europe*. Lincolnwood, Ill.: NTC Books, pp. 207–208.

17. Voehl, Frank, Ashton, Peter, and Ashton, David (1994). *ISO 9000: An Implementation Guide for Small to Mid-Sized Businesses*. Delray Beach, Fla.: St. Lucie Press, pp. 12–34; Kalinsky, I.S. (1993). "The Total Quality System: Going Beyond ISO 9000." *Quality Progress*. Vol. 3, No. 5, pp. 50–54; Jackson, S.L. (1992). "What You Should Know about ISO 9000." *Training*. Vol. 15, No. 4, pp. 48–50.
18. Timbers, M.J. (1992). "ISO 9000 and Europe's Attempts to Mandate Quality." *Journal of European Business*. Vol. 4, No. 4, pp. 22–24.

MINICASES

For extended treatment of organizational case studies on the use of total quality in managing human resources, consult the following: Bowles, J. and Hammond J. (1991). *Beyond Quality: How 50 Winning Companies Use Continuous Improvement.* New York: G.P. Putnam's Sons; Lefevre, H. (1990). *Government Quality and Productivity—Success Stories.* Milwaukee: ASQC Quality Press; Spechler, J.W. (1988). *When America Does It Right: Case Studies in Service Quality.* Norcross, Ga.: Industrial Engineering and Management Press; Hiam, A. (1992). *Closing the Quality Gap: Lessons from America's Leading Companies.* Englewood Cliffs, N.J.: Prentice-Hall; Waterman, Robert H. Jr. (1994). *What America Does Right: Learning from Companies that Put People First.* New York: W.W. Norton.

The following four minicases, discussion questions, and action steps are adapted from various sources and organized around the four pillars of the House of Total Quality to demonstrate concrete success in using total quality to manage human resources.

MINICASE 1: THE FIRST PILLAR
XEROX CORPORATION:
CUSTOMER SATISFACTION PRIORITY
AND STRATEGIC QUALITY LEADERSHIP

Xerox Corporation is a global firm, headquartered in Stanford, Connecticut, that develops, manufactures, markets, services, and finances a wide array of copiers, scanners, printers, and document-processing software.[1] It has earned a reputation for technological innovation and quality products and provides a good example of customer satisfaction, the first pillar of the House of Total Quality.

David Kearns, former chairman and CEO of Xerox, provides an excellent example of quality leadership and placing priority on customer satisfaction, the first pillar of the House of Total Quality. Xerox's problems in the early 1980s were legion and typical of American manufacturers facing serious foreign competition for the first time. Xerox discovered that Japanese companies were able to sell copiers in the United States for roughly what it cost Xerox to build them. Its former lion's share of the copier market had dwindled to only 8%. Xerox was hardly complacent; productivity was increasing by as much as 7 or 8% every year, but Kearns calculated that gains closer to 18% a year were needed to catch Xerox's competitors.

About this time, Kearns contacted Philip Crosby and David Nadler and invited them to address Xerox's management. Kearns' pleas for change initially were resisted by a management team who said they were already doing everything they could, but he persisted.

In 1983, the top management team at Xerox designed a new approach to quality that was dubbed "Leadership through Quality." The primary principle of the new strategic plan was that *quality would be defined as customer satisfaction, not meeting internal standards.* If customers were not satisfied, quality had not been attained. A second principle was to focus on processes rather than just outcomes. In the past, poor outcomes were an occasion to blame someone and to hammer into them the importance of doing better. This was replaced with an approach that focused on examining the process that had created the outcome and improving it.

In order to operate according to these principles, a number of specific human resource (HR) practices were undertaken. Xerox is perhaps best known for its extensive use of *benchmarking*—a process of comparing your operations to the best practices of other companies. The company's approach is to benchmark against the best, in whatever industry it is found. Xerox has benchmarked its billing processes against American Express and its distribution process against L.L. Bean.

To demonstrate their commitment to these principles and the role of HR training and development, Kearns and his management team were the first to undergo the newly devised *quality training.* They then became the teachers for the next level of management, and HR training, reviewed and continually improved, flowed throughout the organization in this manner. In a move that represented a major departure from tradition, *each senior manager was made responsible for taking calls from customers one day a month.* Xerox managers still interrupt their meetings to take such calls.

Although Kearns' efforts were crucial to this process, he believes that leadership must (and in this case did) come from other sources as well, including the Amalgamated Clothing and Textile Workers, the union representing Xerox's production employees:

We've also learned that it's important to have union leaders as deeply committed to the quality process as management. A strong and enlightened union leadership shared management's vision and understood that changes had to be made if there was to be a future for all Xerox employees. We shared each other's trust.[2]

Xerox's competitive resurgence was dramatic. Market share, revenues, and profits all have recovered substantially. In 1989, Xerox became one of the first winners of both the American and Canadian National Quality Award. Kearns believes that "Xerox is probably the first American company in an industry targeted by the Japanese to regain market share without the aid of tariffs or government help."[3] Despite the recovery and the awards, however, Kearns has reiterated his commitment to Xerox's third principle of continuous improvement:

We take great satisfaction in winning these awards, but the fact is that we're far from finished with our drive to improve. We have learned that the pursuit of quality is a race with no finish line. We see an upward and never ending spiral of increased competition and heightened customer expectations.[4]

David Kearns was succeeded as Xerox's chairman in 1991 by Paul Allaire. Kearns is now guest faculty at the Harvard University Graduate School of Education, where is specializes in the use of quality to improve educational systems.

Discussion Questions/Action Step

1. Kearns began a practice of having senior managers personally take phone calls from customers with problems and go through quality training. What messages did that send to the organization about customer satisfaction as a priority and the role of human resources in its strategic initiations?

2. What roles in shaping, introducing, maintaining. and reviewing Xerox total quality initiatives did human resources have? Identify eight other ways, using your text, that human resource strategy planning and management could have and should have made a difference.

3. Should service orientation testing be a part of all employee recruitment processes if customer satisfaction is to be accorded strategic priority? Is it a part of your current employer's staffing processes? Do you expect it to be in the future?

4. **Action step:** Call the president of an organization of which you are a customer and report a quality or service problem you are experiencing. Will the president take the call? Will the president or someone else return your call? (If you get to talk to someone, congratulate them on their responsiveness and be as constructive as possible in describing your problem.)

MINICASE 2: THE SECOND PILLAR
MOTOROLA CORPORATION:
CONTINUOUS IMPROVEMENT AND
QUALITY PROCESS DEVELOPMENT

Motorola is a 63-year-old company that employs nearly 130,000 workers at 53 major facilities worldwide, with headquarters in Shaumberg, Illinois (outside of Chicago), and provides a good example of exemplary continuous improvement, the second pillar of the House of Total Quality.[5] Motorola manufactures mobile and portable cellular phones (number one maker worldwide), semiconductors (number three maker worldwide), multifunction computer systems, two-way land-mobile radios (number one maker worldwide), cellular infrastructure equipment (number two worldwide), radio products, pagers, cordless phones, positioning and navigation systems, LAN systems, and data communications equipment.

During a 1986 team benchmarking trip to Japan, Motorola executives visited various (noncompeting) electronics firms and discovered that they were operating at a defect rate that was as much as a *thousand times lower* than Motorola's! (The defect rate is computed by dividing the number of defects per unit of product by the number of opportunities for defects to occur. Each additional component or process adds another opportunity for failure). This rationale for assessing quality led to the development of the now-famous and widely used Six Sigma defect-free process standard. Each sigma represents one standard deviation from the norm; Six Sigma represents an almost complete inclusion of any sample. In practical terms, this means only 3.4 deviations (errors) in a million opportunities—99.9997% perfect! Most companies are content to operate at a four sigma level, tolerating a 99.4% rate.

To achieve its goal, Motorola changed its HR and business processes. First, it invested heavily in quality staffing and training. Motorola tightened its selection processes by creating its Quality for Hire program to identify future production workers with the requisite core, problem-solving, and interpersonal team skills, as well as the commitment to continuous learning required of a world-class, high-performance workplace. Part of the recruitment process that identifies prospective employee work habits and predisposition to work in teams is a 45-minute video consisting of 15 hypothetical scenarios that might occur in a Motorola workplace. Prospective employees watch each hypothetical work scenario and then answer multiple choice questions which attempt to uncover an individual's natural work habits on the job. Grading is based upon what a Motorola performance management team expects in terms of preferred performance in the workplace. After the on-site half-day testing is concluded, prospective employees are interviewed by *future peer teammates* to obtain optimal organizational fit and to empower current employees in the staffing process. Second, following selection, all employees worldwide are expected to participate in 40 hours of training, according to Bill Wiggenhorn, Director of Motorola University. The training target is that a minimum of 2% of employees' annual time be spent in formal training classes, on-the-job training, and application training assistance. At the heart of the training is a course titled "Utilizing the Six Steps to Six Sigma."

In addition to HR processes, Motorola also focused on the measurement and reduction of cycle time (the time from new product conception to actual end-user purchase). Through using a variety of quality tools, including detailed flowcharting, designs for improved manufacturability were reengineered to eliminate sources of recurring defects and reduce cycle time. The combined impact of the Six Sigma defect level standard and cycle time improvement was reduced waste, overhead, and production costs and increased responsiveness to customer orders, R&D innovative productivity, and product performance.

Motorola's process of continuous improvement has also had ancillary benefits on improved monthly meetings with suppliers and heightened expectations of suppliers. Since suppliers were benefiting from Motorola's success, Motorola could not improve in the future without every supplier also improving; therefore, every supplier that wanted to do business with Motorola in the future would have to apply for the Baldrige Award. This expansion of continuous improvement processes into what the Japanese refer to as the "cross-unit" is sustaining Motorola's competitive position (e.g., partnering with educational institutions that supply prospective employees to guarantee the reliability of core work skills).

Discussion Questions/Action Step

1. In what ways do you think that Motorola's combination of business quality process changes and human resource quality process changes were interdependent, necessary, and mutually reinforcing?

2. What are the advantages and disadvantages of Motorola's Quality for Hire employee selection process? Could it be used to enhance community relations? Would you like to be hired this way? Why or why not?

3. Elaborate on the ancillary benefits of emphasizing Six Sigma, cycle reduction, and quality human resource processes for Motorola. Imagine three other benefits that could accrue to Motorola.

4. **Action step:** Tour a plant/office in your locale and determine if business and human resource quality process improvements are measured and integrated. Ask about specific quality process improvements that have reduced cycle time, improved human resource selection and training results, and reduced defects (errors).

MINICASE 3: THE THIRD PILLAR FEDERAL EXPRESS CORPORATION: SPEAKING WITH FACTS AND QUALITY PROJECT TEAMWORK

Memphis-based Federal Express has the world's largest fleet of air cargo delivery planes and is a leader in the U.S. overnight package delivery market.[6] It provides a good example of an organization that "speaks with facts" and develops project team commitment, the essence of the third pillar of the House of Total Quality.

A basic business and HR quality belief established by CEO Fred Smith, and held throughout Federal Express, is that "customer satisfaction begins with employee satisfaction." The assumption is that employees who feel empowered and well treated will treat customers in a courteous, confident, and competent manner. This kind of service will result in customer satisfaction, and profits will be a natural result. These profits, in turn, will return to the employees (as well as to the stakeholders) in the form of job security, various kinds of rewards, recognition, and opportunities for advancement.

To implement its total quality HR approach, three elements are continually employed at Federal Express: the Survey Feedback Action (SFA) Program, the Guaranteed Fair Treatment (GFT) Procedure, and the Quality Action Team (QAT) Program. First, the SFA Program is an annual employee survey of the leadership effectiveness at Federal Express, and it gives people an opportunity to express attitudes about the company, management, pay and benefits, and service. What is different about the SFA Program is the focus of the first ten statements that comprise the leadership index that determines annual managerial bonuses. Those ten statements do not evaluate how closely managers supervise their people, nor do they assess how well

1. I feel free to tell my manager what I think.
2. My manager lets me know what's expected of me.
3. Favoritism is not a problem in my work group.
4. My manager helps us find ways to do our jobs better.
5. My manager is willing to listen to my concerns.
6. My manager asks for my ideas about things affecting our work.
7. My manager lets me know when I've done a good job.
8. My manager treats me with respect and dignity.
9. My manager keeps me informed about things I need to know.
10. My manager lets me do my job without interfering.
11. My manager's boss gives us the support we need.
12. Upper management (directors and above) lets us know what the company is trying to accomplish.
13. Upper management (directors and above) pays attention to ideas and suggestions from people at my level.
14. I have confidence in the fairness of management.
15. I can be sure of a job as long as I do good work.
16. I am proud to work for Federal Express.
17. Working for Federal Express will probably lead to the kind of future I want.
18. I think Federal Express does a good job for our customers.
19. All things considered, working for Federal Express is a good deal for me.
20. I am paid fairly for the kind of work I do.
21. Our benefit programs seem to meet most of my needs.
22. Most people in my work group cooperate with each other to get the job done.
23. There is cooperation between my work group and other groups in Federal Express.
24. In my work environment, we generally use safe work practices.
25. Rules and procedures do not interfere with how well I am able to do my job.
26. I am able to get the supplies or other resources I need to do my job.
27. I have enough freedom to do my job well.
28. My work group is involved in activities to improve service to our group's customers.
29. The concerns identified in my work group during last year's SFA feedback session have been satisfactorily addressed.

Figure 1 Questions for Federal Express Survey Feedback Action (SFA) Program.

they manage their budgets. Instead, the leadership index reveals how well managers support their people and how well they empower them, *as perceived by each manager's customers*—the people who report to him or her. A list of the SFA questions is provided in Figure 1.

While individual responses are kept confidential, overall results are passed on to all managers, who must then meet with their work groups to develop an action plan for resolving any problems that surface. To ensure that this part of the SFA process really works over time, Statement 29 states: "The concerns identified by my work group in last year's survey feedback have been satisfactorily addressed."

Second, the GFT Procedure is designed to maintain a truly fair environment, in which anyone who has a grievance or concern about his or her job or who feels that he or she has been mistreated (for whatever reason) can have these concerns addressed through the management chain. Every week the chief HR officer, two rotating senior vice-presidents, and the CEO meet to review the three-step internal process to the final stage, the appeals board. The GFT Procedure is one way to implement part of an ethical work culture that institutionalizes organizational justice as a key component of any total quality progress.

Third, the QAT Program, which currently involves 1000 teams all over the world, was cited by Baldrige examiners as a model for involving people at all corporate levels. Cross-divisional root cause teams, each led by a vice president, focus on each one of the twelve major process/project improvement indices. Divisional and work group QATs solve hundreds of little problems and come up with solutions that improve service, save money, and correct strategy. Policy deployment based on QAT feedback has literally saved Federal Express millions of dollars.

Finally, the end result of this total quality HR investment is a heightened group commitment to process/project improvement as demonstrated in the Service Quality Indicator (SQI) in Table 1. The SQI is a twelve-item index of customer satisfaction that is quantified (speaking with facts) and provides directive outcome measures for all Federal Express employees. It was devised in the following manner. Federal Express teams considered how much irritation and inconvenience each error would create for the customer and assigned a weight of failure points. In Table 1, for example, a lost package counts for 10, a wrong day late counts for 5, and a right day late counts for 1. The total score from twelve such errors provides a daily SQI, which is communicated to every Federal Express facility via the FedEx TV network. Surveys show that as the SQI goes down, customer satisfaction goes up. To accelerate the improvement process, an action team headed by a senior executive has been assigned to study each of the failure points to determine how they can be reduced or eliminated. The first year the SQI was instituted, Federal Express averaged 152,000 daily points. By 1991, the monthly rate was 99,959, and Federal Express continued to set new daily, weekly, and monthly records on its way to 15,000 annual SQI points.

In essence, the Baldrige-Award-winning ways of Federal Express are in

Table 1 Federal Express Service Quality Indicators

Indicator(s)	Weight
Abandoned calls	1
Complaints reopened	5
Damaged packages	10
International	1
Invoice adjustments requested	1
Lost packages	10
Missed pick-ups	10
Missing proofs of delivery	1
Overgoods (lost and found)	5
Right day late deliveries	1
Traces	1
Wrong day late deliveries	5

part due to its progressive HR quality practices and the process/project improvements that result from that commitment to total quality.

Discussion Questions/Action Step

1. Elaborate on the synergies obtained from SFA, GFT, QAT, and SQI as total quality business and human resource activities.

2. What advantages and disadvantages do you see with Federal Express' linking managerial bonuses to favorable SFA outcomes? As an employee/manager, would you like to work in such an organization? Why or why not?

3. In what ways do you see organizational justice, team project involvement, and "speaking with facts" uniquely implemented at Federal Express? What improvements would you recommend? Why?

4. **Action step:** Tour a plant/office in your locale and determine if business and human resource quality project improvements are measured and integrated. Ask about specific quality human resource processes with regard to emphasis on employee feedback, grievance procedures, team project involvement, and quantified customer satisfaction indices.

MINICASE 4: THE FOURTH PILLAR
ENSONIQ:
SMALL BUSINESS AND
QUALITY PERSONAL PERFORMANCE

Ensoniq Corporation, a small U.S. privately held business founded in 1982, manufactures professional-level electronic musical instruments (synthesizers, digital samplers, and electric pianos).[7] Its products have been highly successful and include two of the best-selling keyboards in the world; its personal performance practices provide a good example of pillar four of the House of Total Quality. Approximately 200 people work at the company's single facility in Malvern, Pennsylvania, a suburb northwest of Philadelphia. Because Ensoniq designs all its own products, the work force ranges from engineers to blue-collar manufacturing staff.

Ensoniq began using a total quality approach in 1985, when the need for quality became apparent to Bruce Crockett, president and co-owner, and Roy Thomas, operations manager. Keyboard manufacturing is a worldwide business, and Ensoniq's major competitors include Japanese companies famous for high quality: Yamaha, Casio, Korg, and Roland. Although Ensoniq quickly developed a reputation for innovative features, high-quality sound, and good feel (all critical measures for electronic keyboards), its reputation for manufacturing quality, reliability, and durability was not competitive. Furthermore, Ensoniq's Japanese competitors were much larger and better financed; they could afford to reduce the price of their keyboards if customers balked at the quality/price ratio of a particular model. Ensoniq did not have that option; its survival required that its products be better than its competitors' products on most measures and equal on the others and that those products be delivered at low cost.

Ensoniq staff visited a Harley-Davidson Corporation plant in Pennsylvania and used it as an American quality model. Harley-Davidson was going through a successful transition to quality management and faced world-class competitors from the same nations as Ensoniq. The learning experience at Harley-Davidson provided important insights into manufacturing and supplier relationships as well as the Deming treatment of HR systems and variation.

Ensoniq offers convincing evidence that its quality efforts are paying off. Returns on the company's latest model have dropped by around 50% from previous models. Estimates show Ensoniq gaining 3 to 4 percentage points in market share even in a shrinking market. Productivity (manufacturing work-hours required to produce a finished product) has improved 33%. Costs have dropped in a similar fashion. Employee turnover is below 2.5%

per year. Employee complaints have dropped dramatically, and Ensoniq enjoys a high level of employee cooperation in the quality improvement effort.

Ensoniq offers two lessons in HR quality performance: (1) responsible quality performance appraisal and (2) personal responsibility for absentee discipline. At Ensoniq, performance appraisal is separated from compensation decisions and HR performance appraisal practices are geared to avoid scapegoating and instead to enhance personal responsibility for system performance. Workers, for example, use control charts and other statistical measures of production extensively, so they obtain immediate and direct quantitative feedback from the system. If an employee's output at a workstation falls outside the system for that workstation, the employee or his or her supervisor initiates an investigation into the causes of that deviation. ("Outside the system" typically means that performance measures are more than three standard deviations from the average performance or that a consistent pattern is revealed for seven or more consecutive measurements. Such a pattern may involve all measurements being above or below average, all moving in one direction, or measurements alternating between above and below average.) Discovery of the source of the anomaly leads to corrective action on the system performance. If the employee is responsible, that action might include additional training, counseling, or reassignment, as conditions warrant. If machinery or tools are malfunctioning, they receive maintenance. If supplies are defective, production is halted until good supplies can be obtained. Relatively speaking in a small business, therefore, there is no incentive at Ensoniq to "look good" at the expense of co-workers since everyone who is performing within the workstation performance range is similarly commended.

Second, with regard to personal responsibility for absentee discipline, Ensoniq addresses the issues of consistency and fairness by making workers enforce rules. Except for egregious offenses (e.g., arriving at work drunk, fighting at work, bringing weapons to work) and during an initial 90-day probation period, managers do not dismiss employees. Peers handle all employee discipline, removal, and appeals according to rules established by management.

Since quality production at Ensoniq allows little buffering between work stations, the primary cause of dismissal involves exceeding the attendance boundaries specified in the Personnel Policies Handbook. Ensoniq calls these rules "no fault absence" because they define attendance, absence, and tardiness independently of the reason for absence. An employee accumulates points for various forms of absence, as shown in the following list:

Type of offense	Points
1. Late 1 to 12 minutes	1
2. Late more than 12 minutes with prior notice	1
3. Late more than 12 minutes without prior notice	2
4. Absent up to 8 hours with prior notice	2
5. Absent up to 8 hours without prior notice	3
6. Absent more than 8 consecutive hours	3
7. Absent without calling in or prior notice	4

These points accumulate during a floating 90-day period. The following list shows the sanctions imposed for the accumulation of various point totals. An employee's only recourse is to appeal these sanctions to a committee composed of two peers and the HR manager.

Infraction	Sanction
1. Accumulating 9 to 11 points in a 90-day period	Warning
2. Accumulating 12 or more points in a 90-day period	Discharge
3. Accumulating 3 warnings in a 90-day period	Discharge
4. Being absent for 3 consecutive days without notifying the company	Discharge

Because discipline is based on rules and data, workers perceive it as being consistent. Employee acceptance and the rigor of the peer committee (few win an appeal) attest to perceived fairness. At Ensoniq, employees no longer say, "The manager fired so-and-so"; they say, "So-and-so fired himself (or herself)." And since no excuse is good enough to prevent accumulating points, employees appear less inclined to resort to deception and lying to managers. Personal responsibility for performance is now an accepted norm at Ensoniq.

Discussion Questions/Action Step

1. What prompted Ensoniq to begin the total quality journey, and what beneficial results has it achieved to demonstrate the effectiveness of its quality efforts?

2. Elaborate on the advantages and challenges faced by small businesses that would implement Ensoniq's performance appraisal and absentee discipline policies. Do the same for gaining the commitment of employees to use personal work quality improvement instruments cited in the text.

3. Do you believe that small businesses underutilize the opportunity to learn lessons from larger successful total quality firms? If so, what can be done about it? Can a small firm's size allow for more rapid flexibility and personal accountability for developing total quality work habits than larger organizations?

4. **Action step:** Contact your local small business center (public, private, and/or nonprofit) and offer to provide small business owners/managers information regarding the benefits of total quality management of their human resources and specific total quality human resource practices that would be feasible for them.

ENDNOTES

1. This minicase is based on and adapted from Kearns, David (1990). "Leadership through Quality." *Academy of Management Executive.* Vol. 4, No. 2, pp. 86–89; "A CEO's Odyssey Toward World-Class Manufacturing." *Chief Executive.* September 1990; Fenwick, Alan C. (1991) "Five Easy Lessons." *Quality Progress.* December; Kearns, David and Nadler, David (1991). *Prophets in the Dark: How Xerox Reinvented Itself and Beat Back the Japanese.* New York: Harper Collins; Dean, James W. Jr. and Evans, James R. (1994). *Total Quality.* Minneapolis: West Publishing.

2. Kearns, David (1990). "Leadership through Quality." *Academy of Management Executive.* Vol. 4, No. 2, p. 88.

3. Kearns, David (1990). "Leadership through Quality." *Academy of Management Executive.* Vol. 4, No. 2, p. 89.

4. Kearns, David (1990). "Leadership through Quality." *Academy of Management Executive.* Vol. 4, No. 2, p. 90.

5. This minicase is based on and adapted from Waterman, Robert H. Jr. (1994). *What America Does Right: Learning from Companies that Put People First.* New York: W.W. Norton; Meister, Jeanne C. (1994). *Corporate Quality Universities: Lessons in Building a World-Class Work Force.* Burr Ridge, Ill.: Irwin; Schmidt, W.H. and Finnigan, J.P. (1992). *A Race without a Finish Line: America's Quest for Total Quality.* San Francisco: Jossey-Bass; Shiba, Shoji, Graham, Alan, and Walden, David (1993). *A New American TQM: Four Practical Revolutions in Management.* Cambridge, Mass.: Productivity Press; Slater, Roger (1991). *Integrated Process Management: A Quality Model.* New York: McGraw-Hill.

6. This minicase is based on and adapted from Bounds, Greg, Yorks, Lyle, Adams, Mel, and Ranney, Gipsie (1994). *Beyond Total Quality Management.* New York: McGraw-Hill; Waterman, Robert H. Jr. (1994). *What America Does Right: Learning from Companies that Put People First.* New York: W.W. Norton; Schmidt, W.H. and Finnigan, J.P. (1992). *A Race without a Finish Line: America's*

Quest for Total Quality. San Francisco: Jossey-Bass; Shiba, Shoji, Graham, Alan, and Walden, David (1993). *A New American TQM: Four Practical Revolutions in Management*. Cambridge, Mass.: Productivity Press.

7. This minicase is based on and adapted from Schuler, Randall S. and Harris, Drew L. (1992). *Managing Quality: The Primer for Middle Managers*. Reading, Mass.: Addison-Wesley; Schuler, R.S. and Harris, D.L. (1991). "Deming Quality Improvement: Implications for Human Resource Management as Illustrated in a Small Company." *Human Resource Planning*. Vol. 4, No. 3, pp. 191–208; Reid, P.C. (1990). *Well Made in America: Lessons from Harley Davidson on Being the Best*. New York: McGraw Hill.

INDEX

A

Ability, 246, 249, 250
Accountability, 194, 195
Accounting measures, 66
Ackerman, P.L., 249
Adams, J.S., 249
Adhocracy subculture, 190
Affinity diagram, 21, 150–152
Alderfer, C.P., 247–248
Allegiance to Authority, 29, 30, 138
American Express, 86, 350
Americans with Disabilities Act of 1990, 6
Anderson, John C., 56
Appraisal, 42, 139, 145–147
Arrow diagram, 21, 82, 154, 179
Asaka, Tetsiuchi, 131
Assessment, implementation, 294–295
Attitude adjustment, 204, 205
Attitudinal barriers, 46
Autonomy, 15, 238
Awareness, 204, 205

B

Baldrige Award, see Malcolm Baldrige
    National Quality Award
Bandura, A., 248, 249, 250
Bar graph, 209
Behaviorist approach to HRM, 9, 13
Ben & Jerry's, 148
Benchmarking, 21, 155, 170–173, 181, 182, 184,
    186, 188, 189, 295, 318, 350, see also
    Competitive benchmarking
  international implementation practices,
    336–337
Benefits, 91
"Best-in-class" status, 120
Best-of-breed process, 190
Blinder, Alan S., 148
Block diagram, 22, 213
BPI, see Business process improvement
Breakthrough dominance, 120, 121
Bureaucracy "bashing," 122
Bureaucratic subculture, 190

Business, see also specific topics
  performance (respect for people), 233–246
    management, 242–246
    planning, 237–242
  process (continuous improvement), 119–139
    management, 133–139
    planning, 124–133
  project (speaking with facts), 175–197
    management, 190–197
    planning, 178–190
  strategy (customer satisfaction), 59–86
    management, 81–86
    planning, 62–82
Business process improvement (BPI), 134–139
Business process qualification, 137
Business process reengineering, 134, 135, 138,
    294

C

Canada, implementation of total quality HR
    practices in, 336–341
Capitalism, 32–35
Career development, 150, 151
Careerists, 255
Catchball analysis, 80–81
Cause-and-effect diagram, 22, 83, 179,
    208–209
Change agent, 87, 88
Checklist, 22, 214
Check sheet, 22, 83, 179, 209, 242
Choice, 239
Cigna Reinsurance, 5
Circle graph, 209
Clan subculture, 190
Coaching, 201, 204, 205, 317–318
Cognitive ability, 249
Commitment, 194–195, 204, 205, 297
Communication, 90, 94
Communications plan, 292
Compensation, 91
  international practices, 339
Competence, 239–240
Competition, 120–122
  U.S. HRM and, 2–3

Competitive benchmarking, 21, 155, see also
    Benchmarking
Competitive parity, 120, 121
Computer literacy, 7
Conceptual catchball, 68
Conceptual failure, 289, 290
Conceptual hardball, 68
Consumer, defined, 4
Continuous improvement, 17, 25, 57, 119–173,
    181, 182, 184, 186, 188, 190
  business processes, 119–139
    process management, 133–139
    process planning, 124–133
  defined, 22
  human resource processes, 139–156
    process management, 150–156
    process planning, 142–150
  at Motorola, 352–353
Continuous quality improvement (CQI), 125
Control, 9
Control chart, 22, 83, 179, 212
Cooke, Robert A., 28
Cooperation, 57
Core processes, 298
Core technology, 338
Cost objective, 73
CPM, see Critical path method
CQI, see Continuous quality improvement
Creativity, 258, 259
Critical path method (CPM), 154
Crockett, Bruce, 358
Crosby, Philip, 290, 350
Cross-functional coordinated process objective,
    76
Cross-functional team, 126, 297, 307
Cross-layer team, 126
Cross-organization team, 126
Cross-unit, 125–126, 353
Cullen, J., 28
Cultural barriers, 44
Culture, 235–236, see also Ethical work culture;
    Organizational ethical work culture
  continuous improvement and, 124
  defined, 26
  diversity of, 6
Customer, 3, see also External customer;
    Internal customer
  defined, 4
Customer expectations, international
    implementation practices, 337–338
Customer needs, 299
Customer satisfaction, 17, 25, 59, 59–118
  business strategy
    strategy management, 81–86
    strategy planning, 62–81
  defined, 4, 22
  human resource strategy, 86–102
    strategy management, 96, 98–102
    strategy planning, 88–97

international implementation practices,
    335–337
profile, 114–116
strategy competence profile, 117–118
at Xerox, 349–351
Customer–supplier partnerships, 62, 63, 64
Customer/supplier relations checklist, 22, 214
Cycle time technology, international imple-
    mentation practices, 338–339

D

Daily work queries, 260
Davenport, T., 249
Deal, Terrence, 27, 31
Decider, 62
Defensive patterns, 70–71
Delayered restructured pyramid, 98
Delayering, 122
Delbecq, A.L., 155
Delegating, 201, 204, 205
Delivery objective, 73
Deming, W. Edwards, 18, 19, 146, 290
  Fourteen Points, 23–25
  management method, 56–57
Deming Prize, 101, 131, 132, 133, 291, 341, 342
Democratic Participation, 30, 31, 138
Department improvement team (DIT), 135, 137,
    296, 297, 298, 299, 300, 301, 302, 303, 304
Deployment, 17
  defined, 23
Deployment challenge process, 306
Desire to perform, 247, 250–251
Development, 90, 93–94, 95, 139, 149–150
Diamond-Star Motors, 143
Directing, 201, 204, 205
Disciplinary action, 326
Display graphs, 22, 83, 179, 209–210
Dissatisfier, defined, 4
DIT, see Department improvement team
Diversity of the work force, 6–7, 237
Documentation, 181, 182, 183–184, 185, 187, 189
Downsizing, 4, 122, 256–258

E

Education, 39, 296
Education plan, 292
Educational system, 18, 20, 24, 43–46
Effective process, 183–184
Efficient process, 184–186
Effort, 247, 250–251
EIT, see Executive improvement team
Employee commitment, 4–5, see also
    Commitment
Employee empowerment, 38, 123, see also
    Empowerment
Employee fulfillment, 57
Employee involvement, 38

Employee needs, 4
Empowerment, 38, 123, 176
  assessment, 228–231
  continuum, 202–203
  individual, 241–242
  team, 200–207
End-customer-related measurements, 181, 183, 185, 187, 189
Ensoniq Corporation, 358–360
Enterprise vision, 67–69
Environmental scanning, 60–61, 62–67, 89, 117
Equity, 148, 246, 249–250, 251
Error-free process, 186–188
Ethical integrity/reputation objective, 76
Ethical work culture, 18, 25, 64, 66–67, 134, 137–189, 248, 253, 255, 297, 298, 299
  assessment, 286–288
  expanded human resource roles and, 26–36
Ethical work culture team (EWCT), 134, 135, 200, 292, 293, 294, 296, 297, 298, 299, 300, 301, 302, 304
Ethics, 299
European Quality Award, 133, 290, 291, 341, 342, 343
Evaluation and control, 84–86, 118, 304–305
EWCT, see Ethical work culture team
Ewing, Steve, 308
Excelerator, 21, 156
Exciter/delighter, defined, 4
Executive improvement team (EIT), 134, 137, 138, 292, 293, 294, 295, 296, 297, 298, 299, 300, 302, 303, 304
Expansion, 93, 94, 95
Expectancy, 246, 248–249, 251
Expectancy Theory, 11
External customer, 3–4
External environment, 62–64
Extrinsic reward system, 147
Exxon Valdez, 145

F

Facilitator, 87
FATSUDS, 63
Federal Express Corporation, 123, 318, 354–357
Feedback, 15
Financial capitalism, 33–35
Financial measures, 66
Flexibility, 9
Florida Power and Light, 131–133
Flowchart, 21, 155
Force-field analysis, 212–213
Ford Motor Company, 196
Fourteen Points of Deming, 23–25

G

Gap analysis, 69–71, 249, 307
Gatekeeper, 62

General Electric, 5, 20
Generic strategies, 77–80, 89, 94–95
Germany, implementation of total quality HR practices in, 336–341
Gilligan, Carol, 29
Goal, 72–73, 292, 296, 297, 302, 303
Goal setting, implementation, 292–293
Good citizenship behavior, 92
Government legislation, 13
Grand strategies, 77–80, 89, 93, 94
Greenberg, J., 249
Group, 195
Guidance team, 200
Guiding principles, 292, 296, 297, 302, 303, 307–308
Guru approach, 290

H

Hackman, J. Richard, 14, 15
Hamptom, W.J., 143
Harley-Davidson Corporation, 358
Harrington, H.J., 155
Hawthorne Effect, 10
Hawthorne Works plant, 10
Health, safety, and security, 91, 145
Herman Miller, 148
Herzberg, Frederick, 10
Hewlett-Packard, 214
Hidden persuader, 87, 88
High-performance team, 196
Hiring, 326, 330–332
Histogram, 22, 83, 179, 210
Honda, 20, 143
Hoshin planning, 18, 291
House of Compliance, 29–31, 43, 44, 138
House of Manipulation, 29, 30, 44, 139
House of Quality, 127–130, 153
House of Total Quality, 16–25, 30, 31–36, 44, 127, 248, see also specific topics
  continuous improvement (process dimensions), 119–173
  customer satisfaction (strategy dimensions), 59–118
  respect for people (performance dimensions), 233–288
  speaking with facts (project dimensions), 175–231
HR, see Human resources
HRIS, see Human Resource Information System
HRM, see Human resource management
Human relations approach to HRM, 9, 10–11
Human resource audit, 198
Human Resource Information System (HRIS), 206, 207
Human resource management (HRM), see also Human resources; specific topics
  barriers and responses to total quality, 43–46

defined, 18
grid of organizational approaches to, 9
history of, 7–16
MichCon case study, 306–335
total quality difference and, 36–43
total quality, implementation guidelines,
    289–347
  integrated plan, 291–305
  international practices, 335–343
  MichCon case study, 306–335
traditional definition of, 16
Human resources (HR), see also Human
    resource management; specific topics
organization redesign, 312, 322–332
performance (respect for people), 246–261
  management, 258–261
  planning, 251–258
process (continuous improvement), 139–156
  management, 150–156
  planning, 142–150
project (speaking with facts), 197–215
  management, 208–215
  planning, 200–207
strategy (customer satisfaction), 86–102
  management, 96, 98–102
  planning, 88–97
total quality in managing, 1–58
  barriers and responses to, 43–46
  driving forces reshaping, 2–7
  ethical work culture and, 26–36
  opportunities for, 16–25
Hunter, J.E., 249

I

IBM, 5
Impact, 239, 240
Implementation failure, 290
Implementation guidelines, total quality HRM,
    289–347
  integrated plan, 291–305
  international practices, 335–343
  MichCon case study, 306–335
Inclusivity, 237
Individual empowerment, 241, 242
Individual performance, 144
  business, total quality, 233–246
    management, 242–246
    planning, 237–242
  defined, 233–234
  implementation, 302–303
Individualist personality, 277–279
Industrial company model approach, 290–291
Industrial engineering approach to HRM, 9
Industry environment, 62
Inertia, 70
Influencer, 62
Information revolution, 6–7
Initiator, 62

Innovation objective, 76
Input, 85
Instrumentality, 246, 248, 251
Integrity, 258, 259
Interaction, 249
Internal contractor, 87
Internal customer, 4–5
Internal environment, 64
International implementation of total quality
    HR practices, 335–343
Interpersonal self-disclosure style, 280–285
Interrelationship digraph, 21, 82, 152
Intrinsic reward system, 147–148
Involvement, 38, 90, 94, 204, 205
Involvement continuum, 202–203
Ishikawa, Kaoru, 208, 290
ISO 9000, 101, 133, 341, 342, 343

J

Jaeger, A.M., 27
Japan
  external customer in, 3–4
  financial measures in, 66
  House of Quality in, 130
  HRM in, 3
  implementation of total quality HR practices
      in, 336–341
Japanese model approach, 290
Jiro, Kawakita, 151
Job design, 15, 91
Job evaluation system, 312, 319–322
Juran, J.M., 19, 63, 290
JUSE, see Union of Japanese Scientists and
    Engineers

K

Kaizen, 120, 121
Kanfer, R., 249
Kansai Electric Power Company, 131
Kearns, David, 350, 351
Kennedy, A.A., 27
Kennedy, Allan, 31
Kets de Vries, M.F., 28
Kilmann, R.H., 27
KJ method, 21, 150–152, 179
Knowledge acquisition, 204, 205
Knowledge worker, 4–5
Kohlbert, Lawrence, 29

L

Labor relations, 91, see also Union relations
Labor relations approach to HRM, 9, 12–13
Lawler, Edward, 10, 11
Leader certification process, 312, 318–319
Leader Performance Matrix, 242, 243–244
Leadership, 57, 90
  at Xerox, 349–351

Leadership style, 69, 191, 198, 199, 201, 204–206, 240–242
"Leadership Through Quality," 350
Learning, 57
  self-managed, 258–259
Legal/regulatory compliance approach to HRM, 9, 13
Line graph, 209
Linguistic barriers, 45–46
L.L. Bean, 350
Locke, E.A., 249
Loyalty, 5

M

Machiavellianism, 20, 30, 138, 139, 255
Malcolm Baldrige National Quality Award, 23–25, 38–43, 101, 291, 341, 342, 343, 356
Management system, 18, 20, 24, 43, 45
Manager
  job of, defined, 18
  responsibility of, 42
Managerial capitalism, 33
Market share, 63
Market subculture, 190
Mars, Inc., 148
Maslow, Abraham, 10, 247–248
Matrix data analysis, 21, 82, 154, 179
Matrix diagram, 21, 82, 153, 179
Matsushita, Konosuke, 3
Mayo, Elton, 10
McCarty, C.L., 249
McClelland, D.C., 247
McGregor, Douglas, 10, 11
Meaningfulness, 239
Measurement objective, 76
Michigan Consolidated Gas Company, case study, 306–335
  employee satisfaction, 311–312
  HR organization redesign, 322–332
  job evaluation system, 319–322
  leader certification process, 318–319
  measurement of results, 307–311
  personal development system, 312–318
Miller, D., 28
Milliken, 147
Mission, 71–72, 292, 296, 297, 302, 303
Mitroff, I., 27
Morale, 5
Morale assessment, 226–228
Morale/productivity objective, 75–76
Motivation, 10–11, 246–251
Motorola Corporation, 20, 352–353
Murray, H.A., 247

N

Nadler, David, 350
Networking, 7

Networks/alliances, 98
NGT, see Nominal group technique
Nike, 148
Nominal group technique (NGT), 21, 155–156
Nonworking group, 195
Norris-LaGuardia Act of 1932, 12

O

Objectives, 72–77, 307–308
OCB, see Organizational citizenship behavior
OD, see Organization development, 94, 95
Oldham, Greg R., 14, 15
Olian, J.D., 149
Operational barriers, 46
Organization development (OD), 94, 149–150
Organization structures, 98, 99
Organizational character, 26
Organizational citizenship behavior (OCB), 42–43, 237, 238, 248, 250, 254
Organizational defensive patterns, 70–71
Organizational ethical work culture, 26, 44, 64, 66–67, see also Ethical work culture
Organizational excellence benchmarking, 170–173
Organizational inertia, 70
Organizational Integration Chart, 242–243
Organizational integrity, 26
Organizational personality, 26
Organizational subcultures, 190–191
Ouchi, W.G., 27
Outcome, 84, 85
Output, 84, 85
Ownership, 204, 205, 297

P

Pareto chart, 22, 83, 179, 210–211, 242
Participating, 201, 204, 205
Participation, international practices, 340–341
Participative leadership, 199
Participative management, 31
Participative personality, 277–279
Participative power, 204, 205
Partnership, 62, 63, 64, 126, 144–145
PDCA, see Plan-Do-Check-Act
PDPC, see Process decision program chart
Peer discipline, 326
Peer hiring, 326, 330–332
Peer safety, 326, 328–330
PepsiCo, Inc., 123, 147
Performance, 139, 144–145, 247, 250–251
  implementation, 302–303
Performance appraisal, 42
Performance evaluation, international practices, 339–340
Performance integration, 84
Performance management, 17
  business, total quality, 233–237, 242–246

defined, 22
human resource, total quality, 246–251,
    258–261
Performance measurements, 181–182, 183, 185,
    187, 189
Performance planning, 17
    business, total quality, 233–242
    defined, 22
    human resource, total quality, 246–258
Personal development system, 312–318
Personal performance
    at Ensoniq Corporation, 358–360
    improvement, 302
Personal power, 204, 205
Personal Process Chart, 242, 244–245
Personal Process Planning Charts, 84
Personal skills matrix, 302, 303
Personality diversity profile, 274–280
Person factors, 237, 238
Personnel administration approach to HRM, 9,
    11–12
Person/system interaction factors, 237, 238,
    239
PERT, see Program evaluation review
    technique
Phases of a project, 192–193
PIT, see Process improvement team
Placement, 90
Plan-based HR planning, 89, 93
Plan-Do-Check-Act (PDCA), 178–180, 197, 242,
    301
Policy deployment, 80–81, 356
Popular Conformity, 29, 30, 138
Porter, Lyman, 10, 11
Positional power, 205
Potential team, 196
Power, 204, 205
    redistribution of, 7
Powerlessness, 238
Principled Integrity, 30, 31, 138
Prioritization matrix, 22, 213
Prize/award criteria approach, 291
Problem-solving team, 200
Process, 85
    defined, 81–82, 125
    implementation, 298–301
Process adaptability, 181, 182, 184, 186, 188, 189
Process cycle time, international implementa-
    tion practices, 338–339
Process decision program chart (PDPC), 21, 82,
    154, 179
Process development, at Motorola, 352–353
Process empowerment room, 127
Process improvement, U.S. vs. Japan, 3–4
Process improvement team (PIT), 134, 135, 137,
    181, 200, 29–2294, 296–302, 304
Process integration, 81–82
Process management, 17, 57
    business, total quality, 119–124, 133–139

defined, 21
human resource, total quality, 139–142,
    150–157
Process measurements, 181–182, 183, 185, 187,
    189
Process planning, 17
    business, total quality, 119–133
    defined, 21
    human resource, total quality, 139–150
Process simplification, international implemen-
    tation practices, 338
Procter & Gamble, 5, 256
Product, 85
Productivity, 93, 94, 95
Profitability, U.S. vs. Japan, 3–4
Program evaluation review technique (PERT),
    154
Programmatic overexpectation, 289, 290
Project
    defined, 83, 175
    implementation, 300–303
Project-based HR planning, 89, 92
Project involvement, 83
Project life cycle, 192–193
Project management, 17, 21–22
    business, total quality, 175–178, 190–197
    defined, 21
    human resource, total quality, 197–199,
        208–215
Project planning, 17
    business, total quality, 175–190
    defined, 21
    human resource, total quality, 197–207
Project teamwork, at Federal Express, 354–357
Pseudo-team, 195
Psychological contract, 5, 251–252
    violation of, 252–256
Purchaser, 62
Pyramid, 98, 99

Q

QC, see Quality council
QFD, see Quality function deployment
Quality, 58
Quality audit, 180–190, 305
Quality circles, 31
Quality council (QC), 68–69, 292, 293, 294, 295,
    296, 297, 298, 299, 300, 301, 302, 304, 323
Quality function deployment (QFD), 18, 82,
    127–133, 153
Quality improvement, 292
Quality Journal, 242, 245–246
Quality mapping, 22, 214
Quality objective, 73
Quality Performance Management Journal, 84
Quality training, 149
Quantum quality, 258–261
Questionnaire, 156

R

Radar graph, 209–210
Random system, 39, 42
  factors, 237, 238
Real team, 196
Recognition, 39
Redirection, 93, 94, 95
Reengineering, 121
Regulatory compliance approach to HRM, 9, 13
Regulatory guidelines, 6
Relations diagram, 179
Respect for people, 17, 25, 233–288
  business individual performance, 233–246
    business performance management,
      242–246
    business performance planning, 237–242
  defined, 23
  human resource performance, 246–261
    performance management, 258–261
    performance planning, 251–258
Restructuring, 4, 122
Results alignment, 84
Reward systems, 147–149
Rewards, 139, 147–149
  motivation and, 11
Robinson, S., 253
Role perceptions, 246, 249, 250
Rosenbluth, Hal, 5
Rousseau, D., 253
Run chart, 22, 213
Rungtusanatham, Manus, 56
Rynes, S.L., 149

S

Safety, 326, 328–330
Safety objective, 73–74
Satisfaction, 247, 250–251
Satisfier, defined, 4
Saturn, Inc., 123, 238
Scatter diagram, 22, 83, 179, 211–212
Schroeder, Roger G., 56
Scientific Management, 9
SDCA cycle, 178–180, 197, 242
Selection, 139, 142–143
Self-efficacy, 248–249
Self-managed learning, 258–259
Self-managed team, 200
Service objective, 74
Service orientation, 92
Service quality indicators, 357
Sethia, N.K., 27
Sheppard, B.H., 249
Six Sigma, 352, 353
Skills, 193–194
Skills enhancement, 204, 205
Skinner, B.F., 13, 248
Smith, Fred, 354

SmithKline Beecham Corporation, 86
Social Darwinism, 29, 30, 137–139
Social environment, 62
Social system, 18, 19, 24, 44–45
Speaking with facts, 17, 25
  business projects, 175–197
    project management, 190–197
    project planning, 178–190
  defined, 22
  at Federal Express, 354–357
  human resource projects, 197–215
    project management, 208–215
    project planning, 200–207
Specialization barriers, 44–45
Staffing, 90
Stages of a project, 192–193
Stakeholder capitalism, 33–34
Steering committee, 294
Strategic barriers, 43–44
Strategic Development Plan, 312
Strategic objectives, 72–77
Strategic planning, 17
  international implementation practices,
    335–337
Strategic system approach to HRM, 9, 15–16
Strategy, 77–80
  defined, 60
Strategy evaluation and control, 60–61
Strategy formulation, 60–61, 117
  enterprise vision, 67–69
  gap analysis, 69–71
  mission, 71–72
  objectives, 72–77
  policy deployment, 80–81
  strategies, 7780
Strategy implementation, 60–61, 81–84, 118,
  294–299
Strategy management, 17, 60–61, 118
  defined, 21
  business, total quality, 59–61, 81–86
    evaluation and control, 84–86
    strategy implementation, 81–84
  human resource, total quality, 86–88, 96,
    98–102
Strategy planning, 60–61, 117
  business, total quality
    environmental scanning, 62–67
    strategy formulation, 67–81
  defined, 20
  human resource, total quality, 86–96, 98
Strategy statement, 308
Structural barriers, 45
Structure, defined, 125
Structured survey, 21, 156
Subcultures, 190–191
Sullivan, Lawrence, 130
Supervisory leadership, 199
Supplier partnerships, 62, 63, 64, 181, 182, 183,
  185, 187, 189

Supplier relations, 63, 64
Survey, 21, 156, 295
Sustainability, 258, 259–261
System, 39
  defined, 125
Systematic system, 39
Systematic system factors, 237–238
Szumal, Janet L., 28

T

Tactical strategies, 94
Task identity, 15
Task significance, 15
Task team (TT), 135, 137, 200, 298–304
Taylor, Frederick, 9
Team development, 15
Team empowerment, 200–207
Team empowerment continuum, 200
Team involvement, 94
Team leadership, 198, 199
Team training, 149
Teams, 126, 193, 200
  international practices, 340–341
'Team Taurus," 196
Teamwork, 193
Technical system, 18, 19–20, 24, 46
Technique, defined, 125
Technology, 337–338
Technology revolution, 6–7
Theory X, 11
Theory Y, 11
Thomas, Roy, 358
Tolerance, 236–237
Total customer satisfaction, 58, 59, see also
  Customer satisfaction
Total quality, see also specific topics
  barriers and responses to, 43–46
  changing the role of HR managers and, 36–43
  continuous improvement (process dimensions), 119–173
  customer satisfaction (strategy dimensions), 59–118
  defined, 58
  driving forces reshaping the HR environment, 2–7
  House of Total Quality, 16–25, see also
    House of Total Quality
  HRM and, 36–43, see also Human resources;
    Human resource management
  implementation guidelines, 289–347
    integrated plan, 291–305
    international practices, 335–343
    MichCon case study, 306–335
  nature and scope of, 58
  respect for people (performance dimensions), 233–288
  speaking with facts (project dimensions), 175–231

theoretical model of, 56–57
Total quality continuous improvement, 120,
  see also Continuous improvement
Total quality element approach, 290
Total quality leadership, 204
Total quality management, theoretical model
  of, 56–57
Total quality strategy, defined, 60
Traditional personality, 277–279
Training, 39, 90, 94, 149, 181, 182, 184, 185–186,
  188, 189, 296, 297
Transformational leadership styles, 204
Tree diagram, 21, 82, 153, 179
Trend chart, 21, 156
Trust, 253–254
TT, see Task team

U

Union of Japanese Scientists and Engineers
  (JUSE), 20, 131, 290
Union relations, 12, 144–145
United States, implementation of total quality
  HR practices in, 336–341
U.S. Federal Sentencing Guidelines, 36, 76
User, 62

V

Valence, 246–248, 251
Victor, B., 28
Vision, 292, 296, 297, 302, 303 307–308
Visionary leadership, 57
Voehl, Frank W., 125
Voice of the customer, 128
Volkswagen, 5
Von Glinow, M.A., 27
Vroom, Victor, 10, 11

W

Wagner Act of 1935, 12
Waldman, David A., 249
Western Electric Company, 10
Work culture, 235–236
  diversity of, 6
  ethical, see Ethical work culture
Work empowerment maturity, 201
Work force, diversity and mobility of, 6–7
Working group, 195
Work/organization redesign approach to
  HRM, 9, 14–15
Work performance, 42, 237
Work role, 142
World-class process, 188–190
World-class status, 120, 190

X

Xerox Corporation, 20, 147, 155, 349–351